Bernard Shaw

VOLUME

VII

Bernard Shaw

COLLECTED PLAYS WITH THEIR PREFACES

[VOLUME VII]

Geneva, Cymbeline Refinished
"In Good King Charles's Golden Days"
Buoyant Billions, Farfetched Fables
Shakes versus Shav
and uncollected works including
Passion Play, The Cassone, The Gadfly
and Why She Would Not

INDEX
TO THE ENTIRE EDITION

DODD, MEAD & COMPANY
NEW YORK

EDITORIAL SUPERVISOR
Dan H. Laurence

ISBN 0-396-07131-7
Library of Congress Catalog Card Number: 74-24646
Printed and bound in Great Britain
This edition first published
in the United States of America 1975

Publisher's Note

Bernard Shaw was, throughout his publishing career, an inveterate reviser. His most extensive revision of his plays was undertaken in 1930–32 for the Collected Edition. This text was subsequently reset and issued in 1931–32 as the Standard Edition: it contained corrections but no further textual revision. Shaw, however, did make further alterations in some of the plays and prefaces in the Standard Edition in later years. Accordingly, to ensure a definitive text, we have set type for the Bodley Head edition from the last printing of each volume of plays in the Standard Edition which was authorized for press by Shaw in his lifetime.

Shaw had strong personal opinions about style in printing, many of them highly idiosyncratic, and as he was his own publisher he had no difficulty implementing them. His spellings and contractions were often bizarre (*enterprize* and *wernt*), and sometimes archaic (*shew* for *show*, as in the title of his play *The Shewing-up of Blanco Posnet*). He had equally strong convictions about the superfluous use of punctuation, noting in *The Author* in April 1902:

"The apostrophes in ain't, don't, haven't, etc., look so ugly that the most careful printing cannot make a page of colloquial dialogue as handsome as a page of classical dialogue. Besides, shan't should be sha"n't, if the wretched pedantry of indicating the elision is to be carried out. I have written aint, dont, havnt, shant, shouldnt and wont for twenty years with perfect impunity, using the apostrophe only where its omission would suggest another word: for example, hell for he'll. There is not the faintest reason for persisting in the ugly and silly trick of peppering pages with these uncouth bacilli. I also write thats, whats, lets, for the colloquial forms of that is, what is, let us; and I have not yet been prosecuted."

Throughout this definitive edition we have undertaken to follow Shaw's dictates in all matters of spelling and punctuation. Except for a small number of corrections of obvious misprints, the texts are faithfully reproduced.

One additional technical matter must be noted here. Shaw's aesthetics of typography required that italics be reserved for stage directions. In all editions of Shaw's plays up to and including the Collected Edition emphasis within dialogue passages was obtained by letter-spacing. For technical reasons, however, Shaw's printer (William Maxwell, director of R. & R. Clark, Edinburgh) prevailed upon him to permit the setting of emphasised words in the Standard Edition in a slightly larger type. Shaw virtually eliminated accentuation of words in the plays published after 1934: an occasional stress in the later plays was obtained by use of bold face or uniform capitals. In the present edition the original spaced lettering has been restored. This move, we like to think, would have pleased Shaw.

For permission to reproduce unpublished texts and correspondence in their collections, we are grateful to the Humanities Research Center of the University of Texas at Austin, the British Museum, Mr Bernard F. Burgunder and the Cornell University Library, and the Henry W. and Albert A. Berg Collection, New York Public Library.

CONTENTS

Geneva:
Another Political Extravaganza

WITH

Preface

Author's Note

New Shaw Play and Germany

For the Press

Telescoping "Geneva"

Further Meditations on Shaw's "Geneva"

Composition begun *c.*11 February 1936; completed 29 April 1936, extensively revised prior to publication in 1939. Revised for third printing, 1940, and for French translation, 1946. Additional act and further revisions in Standard Edition (*Geneva, Cymbeline Refinished, & Good King Charles*), 1947. First presented in Polish at the Teatr Polski, Warsaw, on 25 July 1938. First presented in English at the Festival Theatre, Malvern, on 1 August 1938.

Begonia Brown *Eileen Beldon*
The Jew *Donald Eccles*
A Newcomer *Maitland Moss*
The Widow *Phyllis Gill*
A Journalist *Wilson Barrett*
The Bishop *H. R. Hignett*
Commissar Posky *J. O. Twiss*
The Secretary of the League of Nations *Cyril Gardiner*
Sir Orpheus Midlander *Ernest Thesiger*
The Judge *Donald Wolfit*
The Betrothed *Kenneth Villiers*
Bardo Bombardone *Cecil Trouncer*
Ernest Battler *Norman Wooland*
The Deaconess *Marie Ault*
General Flanco de Fortinbras *R. Stuart Lindsell*

Period—The present. Geneva

ACT I *The Office of the International Institute for Intellectual Co-operation. A May morning*

ACT II *Office of the Secretary of the League of Nations. Late afternoon*
ACT III *Lounge of a Fashionable Restaurant overlooking the Lake of Geneva. Afternoon (some time later)*
ACT IV *A Salon in the Old Palace of the Hague. Ten a.m.*

Preface

Contents

When I had lived for 58 years free from the fear that war could come to my doorstep, the thing occurred. And when the war to end war had come to a glorious victory, it occurred again, worse than ever. I have now lived through two "world wars" without missing a meal or a night's sleep in my bed, though they have come near enough to shatter my windows, break in my door, and wreck my grandfather clock, keeping me for nine years of my life subject to a continual apprehension of a direct hit next time blowing me and my household to bits.

I cannot pretend that this troubled me much: people build houses and live on the slopes of Etna and Vesuvius and at the foot of Stromboli as cheerfully as on Primrose Hill. I was too old to be conscribed for military service; and the mathematical probabilities were enormously against a bomb coming my way; for at the worst of the bombardments only from ten to fifteen inhabitants of these islands were killed by air raids every day; and a dozen or so out of fortyfive millions is not very terrifying even when each of us knows that he or she is as likely as not to be one of the dozen. The risk of being run over by a motor bus, which townsmen run daily, is greater.

HOODWINKED HEROISM

It was this improbability which made pre-atomic air raiding futile as a means of intimidating a nation, and enabled the government of the raided nation to prevent the news of the damage reaching beyond its immediate neighborhood. One night early in the resumed war I saw, from a distance of 30 miles, London burning for three hours. Next morning I read in the newspapers that a bomb had fallen on the windowsill of a city office, and been extinguished before it exploded. Returning to London later on I found that half the ancient city had been levelled to the ground, leaving only St. Paul's and a few church towers standing. The wireless news never went beyond "some damage and a few casualties in Southern England" when in fact leading cities and seaports had been extensively wrecked. All threatening news was mentioned only in secret sessions of parliament, hidden under heavy penalties until after the victory. In 1941, after the Dunkirk rout, our position was described by the Prime Minister to the House of Commons in secret session as so desperate that if the enemy had taken advantage of it we should have been helplessly defeated; and it is now the fashion to descant dithyrambically on the steadfast heroism with which the nation faced this terrible emergency. As a matter of fact the nation knew nothing about it. Had we been told, the Germans would have overheard and rushed the threatened invasion they were bluffed into abandoning. Far from realizing our deadly peril, we were exulting in the triumph of our Air Force in "the Battle of Britain" and in an incident in South America in which three British warships drove one German one into the river Plate. Rather than be interned with his crew the German captain put to sea again against hopeless odds; scuttled his ship; and committed suicide. The British newspapers raved about this for weeks as a naval victory greater than Salamis, Lepanto, and Trafalgar rolled into one.

Later on our flight from Tobruk to the border of Egypt did not disturb us at home: it was reported as a trifling setback, whilst trumpery captures of lorries or motor bicycles by British patrols figured as victories. After major engagements German losses were given in figures: Allies' losses were not given at all, the impression left being that the Allies had killed or taken tens of thousands of Axis troops without suffering any casualties worth mentioning. Only by listening to the German broadcasts, similarly cooked, could the real facts and fortunes of the war be estimated. Of course the truth leaked out months later; but it produced only a fresh orgy of bragging about our heroic fortitude in the face of the deadly peril we knew nothing of.

All this was necessary and inevitable. It was dangerous to tell the truth about anything, even about the weather. The signposts on the roads had to be taken down and hidden lest they should help an invader to find his way. It was a crime to give an address with a date, or to scatter a few crumbs for the birds. And it was an act of heroic patriotism to drop a bomb weighing ten thousand pounds on dwellings full of women and children, or on crowded railway trains. Our bombing of foreign cities not only in Germany but in countries which we claimed to be "liberating" became so frightful that at last the word had to be given to two of our best broadcasters of war reports to excuse them on the ground that by shortening the war they were saving the lives of thousands of British soldiers.

Meanwhile nobody noticed how completely war, as an institution, had reduced itself to absurdity. When Germany annexed Poland in 1939, half of it was snatched out of her jaws by Soviet Russia. The British Commonwealth having bound itself to maintain inviolate the frontiers of Poland as they were left after the fighting of 1914–18 with a Polish corridor cut right through Prussia to the Baltic, was committed to declare war on Germany and Russia simultaneously. But the British people and their rulers were in no mood to black out their windows and recommence the Four Years War in defence of this distant and foreign corridor. Being, as usual, unprepared for war, we tried to appease Germany and yet keep the peace with Soviet Russia.

ENGLAND FRIGHTENED AND GREAT

Nations should always be prepared for war, just as people with any property to leave should always have made their wills. But as most of them never do make their wills, and the rest seldom keep them revised and up to date, States, however militarist, are never fully prepared for war. England will do nothing outside her routine until she is thoroughly frightened; but when England is frightened England is capable of anything. Philip II of Spain frightened her. Louis XIV of France frightened her. Napoleon frightened her. Wilhelm II of the German Reich frightened her. But instead of frightening the wits out of her they frightened the wits into her. She woke up and smashed them all. In vain did the Kaiser sing *Deutschland über Alles*, and Hitler claim that his people were the Herrenvolk created by God to rule the earth. The English were equally convinced that when Britain first at Heaven's command arose from out the azure main she was destined to rule the waves, and make the earth her footstool. This is so natural to Englishmen that they are unconscious of it, just as they cannot taste water because it is always in their mouths. Long before England first sang Rule Britannia at Cliveden she had annihilated Philip's Invincible Armada to the music of the winds and waves, and, after being defeated again and again by General Luxemburg, made hay of the French armies at Blenheim, Ramillies, and Malplaquet to the senseless gibberish of Lillibullerobullenalah. She not only took on Hitler singlehanded without a word to the League of Nations nor to anyone else, but outfought him, outbragged him, outbullied him, outwitted him in every trick and turn of warfare, and finally extinguished him and hanged his accomplices.

ENGLAND SECURE AND LAZY

The drawback to England's capacity for doing impossible things when in danger is her incapacity for doing possible things (except repeating what was done last time) in security. The prefabrication in England of harbors for France and planting them there as part of the baggage of the allied invading armies, was a feat which still seems incredible even now that it has actually been achieved; yet during the 20 years armistice England could not bridge the Severn below Gloucester, harness the Pentland tides, nor tap the volcanic fires of the earth's boiling core, much less mechanize the coalmines or even design an alphabet capable of saving billionsworth of British time, ink, and paper, by spelling English speech sounds unequivocally and economically. The moment the Cease Fire is sounded England forgets all the lessons of the war and proves the truth of Dr Inge's old comment on the Anglo-Irish situation as illustrating the difficulty of driving in double harness people who remember nothing with people who forget nothing. Still, as forgetful people who act in the present can master vindictive people who only brood on the past there is much to be said for England's full share of human thoughtlessness. It is sometimes better not to think at all than to think intensely and think wrong.

Statesmen who know no past history are dangerous because contemporary history cannot be ascertained. No epoch is intelligible until it is completed and can be seen in the distance as a whole, like a mountain. The victorious combatants in the battle of Hastings did not know that they were inaugurating feudalism for four centuries, nor the Red Roses on Bosworth Field and the Ironsides at Naseby know that they were exchanging it for Whig plutocracy. Historians and newspaper editors can see revolutions three centuries off but not three years off, much less three hours. Had

Marx and Engels been contemporaries of Shakespear they could not have written the Communist Manifesto, and would probably have taken a hand, as Shakespear did, in the enclosure of common lands as a step forward in civilization.

HISTORY STOPS YESTERDAY: STATECRAFT WORKS BLINDFOLD

This is why history in our schools stops far short of the present moment, and why statesmen, though they can learn the lessons of history from books, must grope their way through daily emergencies within the limits of their ignorance as best they can. If their vision is vulgar and vindictive the guesses they make may be worse than the war. That vision has not widened nor that ability grown of late. But the perils of the situation have increased enormously. Men are what they were; but war has become many times more destructive, not of men, who can be replaced, but of the plant of civilization, the houses and factories, the railways and airways, the orchards and furrowed fields, and the spare subsistence which we call capital, without which civilized mankind would perish. Even the replacement of the slain is threatened because the latest bombs are no respecters of sex; and where there are no women there will soon be no warriors. In some of the air raids, more women were killed than men. The turning point of the war was the siege of Stalingrad, written up by the newspapers more dithyrambically than any siege in history since the siege of Troy. But when the Greeks captured Troy they had the city for their pains as well as the glory. When the Red Army triumphed at Stalingrad they had nothing but festering corpses to bury, heaps of rubble to clear away, and a host of prisoners to feed. Meanwhile the British and American armies were "liberating" French cities, Dutch cities, Belgian cities, Italian cities: that is, they were destroying them exactly as they were destroying German cities, and having to house and feed their surviving inhabitants after wrecking their water mains, electric power stations and railway communications. From the national point of view this was conquest, glory, patriotism, bravery, all claiming to be necessary for security. From the European wider angle it was folly and devilment, savagery and suicide. The ready money collected for it (wars cannot be fought on credit) was called Savings: a barefaced wicked lie. All the belligerents have been bled white, and will find, when they claim their "savings" back from their governments, that their Chancellors of the Exchequer will reply, like the juvenile spendthrift exhorted to pay his debts by Richelieu in Lytton's play, "Willingly, your Eminence: where shall I borrow the money?"; for not a farthing of it (say 12 millions shot away every day for six years) remains; and all of it that achieved its purpose of ruin has imposed on us the added burden of repairing what we have destroyed.

So much for England frightened into fighting. The question now is has war become frightful enough to frighten her out of it? In the last months the bombs launched by young British warriors from airplanes at the risk of their lives grew to such prodigious weight and destructiveness that they wrecked not merely houses but whole streets, and scattered blazing phosphorus and magnesium on such a scale that the victims, chiefly women with children who could not escape by flight as a few of the men did, were stifled by having nothing to breathe but white hot air, and then burnt to cinders and buried under the piles of rubble that had been their houses. We rained these monster bombs on Germany until the destruction of their railways and munition factories made retaliation in kind impossible. Our flame throwing from tanks finished the fugitives.

WE SPLIT THE ATOM

But the resources of decivilization were not exhausted. When we were exulting in our demolition of cities like Cologne and Hamburg we were very considerably frightened by the descent on London of new projectiles, unmanned yet aimed and guided, which demolished not only streets but districts. And when we and our allies "liberated" German-occupied territory (blowing its cities to smithereens largely in the process) we discovered that the manufacture of these new horrors had been planned for on such a scale that but for their capture in time the tables might have been turned on us with a vengeance.

But we had another card up our sleeve: this time a trump so diabolical that when we played it the war, which still lingered in Japan, was brought to an abrupt stop by an Anglo-American contrivance which may conceivably transform the globe into a cloud of flaming gas in which no form of life known to us could survive for a moment. That such explosions have visibly occurred on other stars (called novas) is vouched for by our astronomers, who have seen them with their naked eyes and studied their photographs and spectrographs for years past. When England and the United States of North America got ahead of Germany and Japan with this terrific weapon all their opponents at once surrendered at discretion.

AN AMORAL VICTORY

This time there could be no sustainable pretence of a moral victory, though plenty were made as usual; for nothing yet discovered has cured mankind of lying and boasting. It was what Wellington called Waterloo, a very near thing; for had the Germans not concentrated on the jet propulsion of pilotless aeroplanes instead of on the atomic bomb, they might have contrived it before us and made themselves masters of the situation if not of the world. They may yet cheapen and improve on it. Or they may discover a gas lighter than air, deadly but not destructive. And then where shall we be? Ethical victories endure. Discoveries cannot be guaranteed for five minutes.

Still, though the victory was not a triumph of Christianity it was a triumph of Science. American and British scientists, given *carte blanche* in the matter of expense, had concentrated on a romantic and desperate search for a means of harnessing the mysterious forces that mould and hold atoms into metals, minerals, and finally into such miracles as human geniuses, taking some grains of metal and a few salts purchasable at the nearest oil-shop and fashioning with them the head of Shakespear, to say nothing of my own. It is already known that the energy that makes uranium out of molecules, escapes by slow radiation and both kills and cures living organisms, leaving behind it not radium but lead. If this disintegration could be speeded up to instantaneousness it would make a heat so prodigious that a couple of morsels of uranium dropped from a plane and timed to collide and disintegrate above a city could convert that city and its inhabitants into a heap of flaming gas in a fraction of a second. The experiment was tried on two Japanese cities. Four square miles of them vanished before the experimenters could say Jack Robinson.

There is no getting away from the fact that if another world war be waged with this new weapon there may be an end of our civilization and its massed populations. Even for those philosophers who are of opinion that this would not be any great loss there is a further possibility. An atomic bomb attached to a parachute and exploded in the air would devastate only as many square miles as it was meant to; but if it hung fire and exploded in the earth it might start a continuous process of disintegration in which our planet would become a *nova* to astronomers on Mars, blazing up and dimming out, leaving nothing of it and of us in the sky but a gaseous nebula.

It seems that if "the sport of kings" is to continue it must be fought under Queensberry rules classing atomic bombs with blows below the belt, and barring them. But it was the British refusal to bar aerial bombardment that made the air battles of the world war lawful; and these air battles had already reduced war to economic absurdity before the atomic bomb came into action. War had become logical: enemies were massacred or transported: wayleave was abolished. Thus the victors were left with the terror of their own discovery, and the vanquished with the hope that they may soon discover for themselves how to disintegrate uranium or perhaps some other element with ten times its energy. And two of the great allies, England and America, flatly refuse to share the secret of the new bomb with Russia, the third. Villages in India are still wiped out to "larn" their mostly harmless inhabitants not to snipe at British soldiers. The alarm is general: the cry of all hands, the triumphant even more than the subjugated, is that there must be an end of war. But all the other cries are as warlike as ever. The victorious Allies agree in demanding that Germans and Japanese must be treated as Catholic Ireland was treated by England in the seventeenth century.

Some of them are now consoling themselves with the hope that the atomic bomb has made war impossible. That hope has often been entertained before. Colonel Robinson, in *The Nineteenth Century And After*, has given a list of previous discoveries, dating back to B.C., which have developed the technique of killing from the single combats of the Trojan war, fought man to man, to artillery operations and air raids in which the combatants are hundreds of miles apart on the ground or thousands of feet up in the air dropping bombs and flying away at a speed of ten miles per second, never seeing one another nor the mischief they do. At every development it is complained that war is no longer justifiable as a test of heroic personal qualities, and demonstrated that it has become too ruinous to be tolerated as an institution. War and imperialist diplomacy persist none the less.

CIVILIZATION'S WILL TO LIVE ALWAYS DEFEATED BY DEMOCRACY

Mankind, though pugnacious, yet has an instinct which checks it on the brink of selfdestruction. We are still too close to the time when men had to fight with wild beasts for their lives and with one another for their possessions, and when women had to choose fighters for their mates to protect them from robbery and rapine at their work as mothers, nurses, cooks, and kitchen gardeners. There are still places in the world where after tribal battles the victors eat the vanquished and the women share the feast with the warriors. In others foreign explorers, visitors, and passengers are killed as strangers. The veneer of civilization which distinguishes Europeans from these tribesmen and their wives is dangerously thin. Even English ladies and gentlemen "go Fantee" occasionally. Christmas cards will not prevent them from using atomic bombs if they are again frightened and provoked. But the magnitude of the new peril rouses that other instinct, stronger finally than pugnacity, that the race must not perish. This does not mean that civilization cannot perish. Civilizations have never finally survived: they have perished over and over again because they failed to make themselves worth their cost to the masses whom they enslaved. Even at home they could not master the art of governing millions of people for the common good in spite of people's inveterate objection to be governed at all. Law has been popularly known only as oppression and taxation, and politics as a clamor for less government and more liberty. That citizens get better value for the rates and taxes they pay than for most other items in their expenditure never occurs to them. They will pay a third of their weekly earnings or more to an idle landlord as if that were a law of nature; but a collection from them by the rate collector they resent as sheer robbery: the truth being precisely the reverse. They see nothing extravagant in basing democracy on an assumption that every adult native is either a Marcus Aurelius or a combination of Saint Teresa and Queen Elizabeth Tudor, supremely competent to choose any tinker tailor soldier sailor or any good-looking well dressed female to rule over them. This insane prescription for perfect democracy of course makes democracy impossible and the adventures of

Cromwell, Napoleon, Hitler, and the innumerable conquistadores and upstart presidents of South American history inevitable. There never has been and never will be a government which is both plebiscitary and democratic, because the plebs do not want to be governed, and the plutocrats who humbug them, though they are so far democratic that they must for their own sakes keep their slaves alive and efficient, use their powers to increase their revenues and suppress resistance to their appropriation of all products and services in excess of this minimum. Substitute a plebeian government, and it can only carry on to the same point with the same political machinery, except that the plunder goes to the Trade Unions instead of to the plutocrats. This may be a considerable advance; but when the plebeian government attempts to reorganize production collectively so as to increase the product and bring the highest culture within the reach of all who are capable of it, and make the necessary basic material prosperity general and equal, the dread and hatred of government as such, calling itself Liberty and Democracy, reasserts itself and stops the way. Only when a war makes collective organization compulsory on pain of slaughter, subjugation, and nowadays extinction by bombs, jet propelled or atomic, is any substantial advance made or men of action tolerated as Prime Ministers. The first four years of world war forced us to choose a man of action as leader; but when the armistice came we got rid of him and had a succession of premiers who could be trusted to do nothing revolutionary. Our ideal was "a commonplace type with a stick and a pipe and a half bred black and tan." Even Franklin Roosevelt won his first presidential election more by a photograph of himself in the act of petting a baby than by his political program, which few understood: indeed he only half understood it himself. When Mr Winston Churchill, as a man of action, had to be substituted for the *fainéants* when the war was resumed, his big cigars and the genial romantic oratory in which he glorified the war maintained his popularity until the war was over and he opened the General Election campaign by announcing a domestic policy which was a hundred years out of fashion, and promised nothing to a war weary proletariat eager for a Utopia in which there should be no military controls and a New World inaugurated in which everybody was to be both employed and liberated.

Mr Churchill at once shared the fate of Lloyd George; and the Utopians carried the day triumphantly. But the New World proved the same as the old one, with the same fundamental resistance to change of habits and the same dread of government interference surviving in the adult voter like the child's dread of a policeman.

It may be asked how it is that social changes do actually take place under these circumstances. The reply is that other circumstances create such emergencies, dangers, and hardships, that the very people who dread Government action are the first to run to the Government for a remedy, crying that "something must be done." And so civilization, though dangerously slowed down, forces its way piecemeal in spite of stagnant ignorance and selfishness.

Besides, there are always ancient constitutions and creeds to be reckoned with; and these are not the work of adult suffrage, but inheritances from feudal and ecclesiastical systems which had to provide law and order during the intervals between dominating personalities, when ordinary governments had to mark time by doing what was done last time until the next big boss came along and became a popular idol, worshipped at the polls by 99 per cent majorities.

All the evidence available so far is to the effect that since the dawn of history there has been no change in the natural political capacity of the human species. The comedies of Aristophanes and the Bible are at hand to convince anyone who doubts this. But this does not mean that enlightenment is impossible. Without it our attempts at democracy will wreck our civilization as they have wrecked all the earlier civilizations we know of. The ancient empires were not destroyed by foreign barbarians. They assimilated them easily. They destroyed themselves: their collapse was the work of their own well meaning native barbarians. Yet these barbarians, like our own at present, included a percentage of thinkers who had their imaginations obsessed by Utopias in which perfectly wise governments were to make everybody prosperous and happy. Their old men saw visions and their young men dreamed dreams just as they do now. But they were not all such fools as to believe that their visions and dreams could be realized by Tom, Dick, and Harriet voting for Titus Oates, Lord George Gordon, Horatio Bottomley, Napoleon, or Hitler. My experience as an enlightener, which is considerable, is that what is wrong with the average citizen is not altogether deficient political capacity. It is largely ignorance of facts, creating a vacuum into which all sorts of romantic antiquarian junk and cast-off primitive religion rushes. I have to enlighten sects describing themselves as Conservatives, Socialists, Protestants, Catholics, Communists, Fascists, Fabians, Friends (Quakers), Ritualists, all bearing labels which none of them can define, and which indicate tenets which none of them accept as practical rules of life and many of them repudiate with abhorrence when they are presented without their labels. I was baptized as a member of the then established Protestant Episcopal Church in Ireland. My religious education left me convinced that I was entitled to call myself a Protestant because I believed that Catholics were an inferior species who would all go to hell when they died; and I daresay the Roman Catholic children with whom I was forbidden to play believed that the same eternity of torment awaited me in spite of Pope Pius the Ninth's humane instruction to them to absolve me on the plea of invincible ignorance. We were both taught to worship "a tenth rate tribal deity" of the most vindictive, jealous, and ruthless pugnacity, equally with his Christlike son. Just so today Conservatives know nothing of the Tory creed, but are convinced that the rulers of Russia are bloodstained tyrants, robbers and murderers, and their subjects slaves without rights or liberties. All good Russians believe equally that the capitalist rulers of the Western pluto cracies are ruthless despots out for nothing but exploiting labor in pursuit of surplus value, as Marx called rent, interest, and profit. They group themselves in political parties and clubs in which none of them knows what he or she is talking about. Some of them have Utopian aspirations and have read the prophets and sages, from Moses to Marx, and from Plato to Ruskin and Inge; but a question as to a point of existing law or the function of a County Council strikes them dumb. They are more dangerous than simpletons and illiterates because on the strength of their irrelevant schooling they believe themselves politically educated, and are accepted as authorities on political subjects accordingly.

Now this political ignorance and delusion is curable by simple instruction as to the facts without any increase of political capacity. I am ending as a sage with a very scrappy and partial knowledge of the world. I do not see why I should not have begun with it if I had been told it all to begin with: I was more capable of it then than I am now in my dotage. When I am not writing plays as a more or less inspired artist I write political schoolbooks in which I say nothing of the principles of Socialism or any other Ism (I disposed of all that long ago), and try to open my readers' eyes to the political facts under which they live. I cannot change their minds; but I can increase their knowledge. A little knowledge is a dangerous thing; but we must take that risk because a little is as much as our biggest heads can hold; and a citizen who knows that the earth is round and older than six thousand years is less dangerous than one of equal capacity who believes it is a flat groundfloor between a first floor heaven and a basement hell.

INCOMPETENT GOVERNMENTS ARE THE CRUELLEST

The need for confining authority to the instructed and capable has been demonstrated by terrible lessons daily for years past. As I write, dockfulls of German prisoners of war, male and female, are being tried on charges of hideous cruelties perpetrated by them at concentration camps. The witnesses describe the horrors of life and death in them; and the newspapers class the accused as fiends and monsters. But they also publish photographs of them in which they appear as ordinary human beings who could be paralleled from any crowd or army.

These Germans had to live in the camps with their prisoners. It must have been very uncomfortable and dangerous for them. But they had been placed in authority and management, and had to organize the feeding, lodging, and sanitation of more and more thousands of prisoners and refugees thrust upon them by the central government. And as they were responsible for the custody of their prisoners they had to be armed to the teeth and their prisoners completely disarmed. Only eminent leadership, experience, and organizing talent could deal with such a situation.

Well, they simply lacked these qualities. They were not fiends in human form; but they did not know what to do with the thousands thrown on their care. There was some food; but they could not distribute it except as rations among themselves. They could do nothing with their prisoners but overcrowd them within any four walls that were left standing, lock them in, and leave them almost starving to die of typhus. When further overcrowding became physically impossible they could do nothing with their unwalled prisoners but kill them and burn the corpses they could not bury. And even this they could not organize frankly and competently: they had to make their victims die of illusage instead of by military law. Under such circumstances any miscellaneous collection of irresistibly armed men would be demoralized; and the natural percentage of callous toughs among them would wallow in cruelty and in the exercise of irresponsible authority for its own sake. Man beating is better sport than bear baiting or cock fighting or even child beating, of which some sensational English cases were in the papers at home at the time. Had there been efficient handling of the situation by the authorities (assuming this to have been possible) none of these atrocities would have occurred. They occur in every war when the troops get out of hand.

HITLER

The German government was rotten at the centre as well as at the periphery. The Hohenzollern monarchy in Germany, with an enormous military prestige based on its crushing defeat of the Bonapartist French Army in 1871 (I was fifteen at the time, and remember it quite well) was swept away in 1918 by the French Republic. The rule of the monarch was succeeded by the rule of anybody chosen by everybody, supposed, as usual, to secure the greatest common measure of welfare, which is the object of democracy, but which really means that a political career is open to any adventurer. It happened that in Munich in 1930 there was a young man named Hitler who had served in the Four Years War. Having no special military talent he had achieved no more as a soldier than the Iron Cross and the rank of corporal. He was poor and what we call no class, being a Bohemian with artistic tastes but neither training nor talent enough to succeed as an artist, and was thus hung up between the bourgeoisie for which he had no income and the working class for which he had no craft. But he had a voice and could talk, and soon became a beer cellar orator who could hold his audience. He joined a cellar debating society (like our old Cogers Hall) and thereby brought its numbers up to seven. His speeches soon attracted considerable reinforcements and established him as a leading spirit. Much of what he spouted was true. As a soldier he had learnt that disciplined men can make short work of mobs; that party parliaments on the British model neither could nor would abolish the poverty that was so bitter to him; that the Treaty of Versailles under which Germany, defeated and subjected far beyond the last penny she could spare, could be torn up clause by clause by anyone with a big enough army to intimidate the plunderers; and that Europe was dominated economically by a plutocracy of financiers who had got the whip hand even of the employers. So far he was on solid ground, with unquestionable facts to support him. But he mixed the facts up with fancies such as that all plutocrats are Jews; that the Jews are an accursed race who should be exterminated as such; that the Germans are a chosen race divinely destined to rule the world; and that all she needs to establish her rule is an irresistible army. These delusions were highly flattering to Hans, Fritz, and Gretchen at large as well as to the beer drinkers in the cellar; and when an attempt was made to silence the new Hitlerites by hired gangsters, Hitler organized a bodyguard for himself so effectively that the opposition was soon sprawling in the street.

With this stock in trade Hitler found himself a born leader, and, like Jack Cade, Wat Tyler, Essex under Elizabeth Tudor, Emmet under Dublin Castle, and Louis Napoleon under the Second Republic, imagined he had only to appear in the streets with a flag to be acclaimed and followed by the whole population. He tried the experiment with a general from the Four Years War at his side and such converts to his vogue and eloquence as his beer cellar orations had made. With this nucleus he marched through the streets. A rabble gathered and followed to see the fun, as rabbles always will in cities. In London I have seen thousands of citizens rushing to see why the others were rushing, and to find out why. It looked like a revolutionary *émeute*. On one occasion it was a runaway cow. On another it was Mary Pickford, "World's Sweetheart" of the old silent films, driving to her hotel in a taxi.

For a moment Hitler may have fancied that a success like that of Mussolini's march to Rome (he went by train) was within his grasp. He had the immediate precedent of Kurt Eisner's successful *Putsch* to encourage him. But Eisner was not resisted. When Hitler and his crowd came face to face with the Government troops they did not receive him as the grognards of the Bourbon army received Napoleon on his return from Elba. They opened fire on him. His rabble melted and fled. He and General Ludendorff had to throw themselves flat on the pavement to avoid the bullets. He was imprisoned for eight months for his escapade, not having frightened the Government enough to be considered worth killing as Cade, Tyler, and Essex were killed. In prison, he and his companion-secretary Hess, wrote a book entitled *Mein Kampf* (My Struggle, My Program, My Views or what you please).

Like Louis Napoleon he had now learnt his lesson: namely, that *Putsches* are a last desperate method, not a first one, and that adventurers must come to terms with the captains of finance and industry, the bankers, and the Conservatives who really control the nations wherever the people choose what rulers they please, before he can hope to be accepted by them as a figure head. Hitler had sufficient histrionic magnetism to strike this bargain even to the extent of being made perpetual chancellor of the German Realm with more than royal honors, though his whole stock-in-trade was a brazen voice and a doctrine made up of scraps of Socialism, mortal hatred of the Jews, and complete contempt for pseudo-democratic parliamentary mobocracy.

PSEUDO MESSIAH AND MADMAN

So far he was the creature and tool of the plutocracy. But the plutocracy had made a bad bargain. The moment it made Hitler a figure head, popular idolatry made a prophet and a hero of him, and gave him a real personal power far in excess of that enjoyed by any commercial magnate. He massacred all his political rivals not only with impunity but with full parliamentary approval. Like St Peter on a famous earlier occasion the German people cried "Thou art the Christ", with the same result. Power and worship turned Hitler's head; and the national benefactor who began by abolishing unemployment, tearing up the Treaty of Versailles, and restoring the selfrespect of sixty millions of his fellow countrymen, became the mad Messiah who, as lord of a Chosen Race, was destined to establish the Kingdom of God on earth—a German kingdom of a German God—by military conquest of the rest of mankind. Encouraged by spineless attempts to appease him he attacked Russia, calculating that as a crusader against Soviet Communism he would finally be joined by the whole Capitalist West.

But the Capitalist West was much too shortsighted and jealous to do anything so intelligent. It shook hands with Stalin and stabbed Hitler in the back. He put up a tremendous fight, backed by his fellow adventurers in Italy and Spain; but, being neither a Julius Cæsar nor a Mahomet, he failed to make his initial conquests welcome and permanent by improving the condition of the inhabitants. On the contrary he made his name execrated wherever he conquered. The near West rose up against him, and was joined by the mighty far West of America. After twelve years of killing other people he had to kill himself, and leave his accomplices to be hanged.

The moral for conquerors of empires is that if they substitute savagery for civilization they are doomed. If they substitute civilization for savagery they make good, and establish a legitimate title to the territories they invade. When Mussolini invaded Abyssinia and made it possible for a stranger to travel there without being killed by the native Danakils he was rendering the same service to the world as we had in rendering by the same methods (including poison gas) in the north west provinces of India, and had already completed in Australia, New Zealand, and the Scottish Highlands. It was not for us to throw stones at Musso, and childishly refuse to call his puppet king Emperor. But we did throw stones, and made no protest when his star was eclipsed and he was scandalously lynched in Milan. The Italians had had enough of him; for he, too, was neither a Cæsar nor a Mahomet.

Contemplating the careers of these two poor devils one cannot help asking was their momentary grandeur worth while? I pointed out once that the career of Bourrienne, Napoleon's valet-secretary for a while, was far longer, more fortunate, easier and more comfortable in every commonsense way, than that of Napoleon, who, with an interval of one year, was Emperor for fourteen years. Mussolini kept going for more than twenty. So did Louis Napoleon, backed by popular idolization of his uncle, who had become a national hero, as Hitler will become in Germany presently. Whether these adventurers would have been happier in obscurity hardly matters; for they were kept too busy to bother themselves about happiness; and the extent to which they enjoyed their activities and authority and deification is unknown. They were finally scrapped as failures and nuisances, though they all began by effecting some obvious reforms over which party parliaments had been boggling for centuries. Such successes as they had were reactions from the failures of the futile parliamentary talking shops, which were themselves reactions from the bankruptcies of incompetent monarchs, both mobs and monarchs being products of political idolatry and ignorance. The wider the suffrage, the greater the confusion. "Swings to the Left" followed by "swings to the Right" kept the newspapers and the political windbags amused and hopeful. We are still humbugging ourselves into the belief that the swings to the Left are democratic and those to the Right imperial. They are only swings from failure to failure to secure substantial democracy, which means impartial government for the good of the governed by qualified rulers. Popular anarchism defeats them all.

Upstart dictators and legitimate monarchs have not all been personal failures. From Pisistratus to Porfirio, Ataturk, and Stalin, able despots have made good by doing things better and much more promptly than parliaments. They have kept their heads and known their limitations. Ordinary mortals like Nero, Paul of Russia, our James the Second, Riza Khan in Iran, and some of the small fry of degenerate hereditary tribal chiefs like Theebaw in Burma have gone crazy and become worse nuisances than mad dogs. Lord Acton's dictum that power corrupts gives no idea of the extent to which flattery, deference, power, and apparently unlimited money, can upset and demoralize simpletons who in their proper places are good fellows enough. To them the exercise of authority is not a heavy and responsible job which strains their mental capacity and industry to the utmost, but a delightful sport to be indulged for its own sake, and asserted and reasserted by cruelty and monstrosity.

DEMOCRACY MISUNDERSTOOD

Democracy and equality, without which no State can achieve the maximum of beneficence and stability, are still frightfully misunderstood and confused. Popular logic about them is, like most human logic, mere association of ideas, or, to call it by the new name invented by its monstrous product Pavlov, conditional reflex. Government of the people for the people, which is democracy, is supposed to be achievable through government by the people in the form of adult suffrage, which is finally so destructive of democracy that it ends in a reaction into despot-idolatry. Equality is supposed to mean similarity of political talent, which varies as much as musical or mathematical or military capacity from individual to individual, from William Rufus to Charles II, from Nero to Marcus Aurelius, from Monmouth and Prince Charlie to Alexander and Napoleon. Genuine democracy requires that the people shall choose their rulers, and, if they will, change them at sufficient intervals; but the choice must be limited to the public spirited and politically talented, of whom Nature always provides not only the necessary percentage, but superfluity enough to give the people a choice. Equality, which in practice means intermarriageability, is based on the hard facts that the greatest genius costs no more to feed and clothe and lodge than the narrowest minded duffer, and at a pinch can do with less, and that the most limited craftsman or laborer who can do nothing without direction from a thinker, is, if worth employing at all, as necessary and important socially as the ablest director. Equality between them is either equality of income and of income only or an obvious lie.

Equality of income is practicable enough: any sporting peer with his mind bounded by the race-course can dine on equal terms with an astronomer whose mental domain is the universe. Their children are intermarriageable without misalliance. But when we face the democratic task of forming panels of the persons eligible for choice as qualified rulers we find first that none of our tests are trustworthy or sufficient, and finally that we have no qualified rulers at all, only bosses. The rule of vast commonwealths is beyond the political capacity of mankind at its ablest. Our Solons, Cæsars and Washingtons, Lenins, Stalins and Nightingales, may be better than their best competitors; but they die in their childhood as far as statesmanship is concerned, playing golf and tennis and bridge, smoking tobacco and drinking alcohol as part of their daily diet, hunting, shooting, coursing, reading tales of murder and adultery and police news, wearing fantastic collars and cuffs, with the women on high heels staining their nails, daubing their lips, painting their faces: in short, doing all sorts of things that are child's play and not the exercises or recreations of statesmen and senators. Even when they have read Plato, the Gospels, and Karl Marx, and to that extent know what they have to do, they do not know how to do it, and stick in the old grooves for want of the new political technique which is evolving under pressure of circumstances in Russia. Their attempts at education and schooling end generally in boy farms and concentration camps with flogging blocks, from which the prisoners when they adolesce emerge as trained prejudiced barbarians with a hatred of learning and discipline, and a dense ignorance of what life is to nine tenths of their compatriots.

"GREAT MEN"

Here and there, however, cases of extraordinary faculty shew what mankind is capable of within its existing framework. In mathematics we have not only Newtons and Einsteins, but obscure illiterate "lightning calculators," to whom the answers to arithmetical and chronological problems that would cost me a long process of cyphering (if I could solve them at all) are instantly obvious. In grammar and scripture I am practically never at a loss; but I have never invented a machine, though I am built like engineers who, though they are never at a loss with machinery, are yet so unable to put descriptions of their inventions into words that they have to be helped out by patent agents of no more than common literary ability. Mozart, able in his infancy to do anything he pleased in music, from the simplest sonata to the most elaborate symphony or from the subtlest comic or tragic opera to fugal settings of the Mass, resembled millions of Austrians who could not to save their lives hum a line of *Deutschland über Alles* nor compose a bar of music playable by one finger, much less concerted for 30 different orchestral instruments. In philosophy we spot Descartes and Kant, Swift and Schopenhauer, Butler and Bergson, Richard Wagner and Karl Marx, Blake and Shelley, Ruskin and Morris, with dozens of uncrucified Jesuses and saintly women in every generation, look like vindictive retaliators, pugnacious sportsmen, and devout believers in ancient tribal idols. The geniuses themselves are steeped in vulgar superstitions and prejudices: Bunyan and Newton astound us not only by their specific talents but by their credulity and Bible fetichism. We prate gravely of their achievements and faculties as attainments of mankind, as if every Italian were Michael Angelo and Raphael and Dante and Galileo rolled into one, every German a Goethe, and every Englishman a compound of Shakespear and Eddington. Of this folly we have had more than enough. The apparent freaks of nature called Great Men mark not human attainment but human possibility and hope. They prove that though we in the mass are only child Yahoos it is possible for creatures built exactly like us, bred from our unions and developed from our seeds, to reach the heights of these towering heads. For the moment, however, when we are not violently persecuting them we are like Goldsmith's villagers, wondering how their little heads can carry all they know and ranking them as passing rich on four hundred pounds a year when they are lucky enough to get paid for their work instead of persecuted.

WE CAN AND MUST LIVE LONGER

Considering now that I have lived fourteen years longer than twice as long as Mozart or Mendelssohn, and that within my experience men and women, especially women, are younger at fifty than they were at thirty in the middle of the nineteenth century, it is impossible to resist at least a strong suspicion that the term of human life cannot be fixed at seventy years or indeed fixed at all. If we master the art of living instead of digging our graves with our teeth as we do at present we may conceivably reach a point at which the sole cause of death will be the fatal accident which is statistically inevitable if we live long enough. In short, it is not proved that there is such a thing as natural death: it is life that is natural and infinite.

How long, then, would it take us to mature into competent rulers of great modern States instead of, as at present, trying vainly to govern empires with the capacity of village headmen. In my Methuselah cycle I put it at three hundred years: a century of childhood and adolescence, a century of administration, and a century of oracular senatorism.

But nobody can foresee what periods my imaginary senators will represent. The pace of evolutionary development is not constant: the baby in the womb recapitulates within a few months an evolution which our biologists assure us took millions of years to acquire. The old axiom that Nature never jumps has given way to a doubt whether Nature is not an incorrigible kangaroo. What is certain is that new faculties, however long they may be dreamt of and desired, come at last suddenly and miraculously like the balancing of the bicyclist, the skater, and the acrobat. The development of homo sapiens into a competent political animal may occur in the same way.

THE NEXT DISCOVERY

Meanwhile here we are, with our incompetence armed with atomic bombs. Now power civilizes and develops mankind, though not without having first been abused to the point of wiping out entire civilizations. If the atomic bomb wipes out ours we shall just have to begin again. We may agree on paper not to use it as it is too dangerous and destructive; but tomorrow may see the discovery of that poisonous gas lighter than air and capable before it evaporates through the stratosphere of killing all the inhabitants of a city without damaging its buildings or sewers or water supplies or railways or electric plants. Victory might then win cities if it could repopulate them soon enough, whereas atomic bombing leaves nothing for anyone, victor or vanquished. It is conceivable even that the next great invention may create an overwhelming interest in pacific civilization and wipe out war. You never can tell.

AYOT SAINT LAWRENCE, *1945*

ACT I

A May morning in Geneva, in a meagrely equipped office with secondhand furniture, much the worse for wear, consisting of a dingy writing table with an old typewriter on it in the middle of the room, a revolving chair for the typist, an old press which has not been painted or varnished for many years, and three chairs for visitors against the wall near the door. The stove, an undecorated iron one of the plainest sort, designed rather for central heating in a cellar than for an inhabited apartment, is to the typist's right, the press facing it at the opposite side on the typist's left. The door is beside the press. The window is behind the typist.

A young Englishwoman is seated in the revolving chair. From the state of the table she seems to have been working at the compilation of a card index, as there are cards scattered about, and an open case to put them in, also a pile of foolscap from which she has been copying the card inscriptions. But at present she is not at work. She is smoking and reading an illustrated magazine with her heels on the table. A thermos flask, a cup and saucer, and a packet of cigarettes are beside her on a sliding shelf drawn out from the table. She is a self-satisfied young person, fairly attractive and well aware of it. Her dress, though smartly cut, is factory made; and her speech and manners are London suburban.

Somebody knocks at the door. She hastily takes her heels off the table; jumps up; throws her cigarette into the stove; snatches the things off the sliding shelf and hides them in the press; finally resumes her seat and looks as busy as possible.

THE TYPIST [*calling*] Entrez, s'il vous plaît.

A middle-aged gentleman of distinguished appearance, with a blond beard and moustache, top hatted, frock coated, and gloved, comes in. He contemplates the room and the young woman with evident surprise.

HE. Pardon, mademoiselle: I seek the office of the International Committee for Intellectual Co-operation.

SHE. Yes: thats quite all right. Take a seat, please.

HE [*hesitating*] Thank you; but my business is of great importance: I must see your chief. This is not the head office, is it?

SHE. No: the head office is in Paris. This is all there is here. Not much of a place, is it?

HE. Well, I must confess that after visiting the magnificent palace of the International Labor Office and the new quarters of the Secretariat, I expected to find the Committee for Intellectual Co-operation lodged in some imposingly monumental structure.

SHE. Oh, isnt it scandalous? I wish youd write to the papers about it. Do please sit down.

HE. Thank you. [*He is about to take one of the chairs from the wall*].

SHE. No, not that one: one of its legs isnt safe: it's there only for show. Will you please take the other?

HE. Can the Committee not afford you a new chair?

SHE. It cant afford anything. The intellectual budget is the interest on two million paper francs that one is glad to get threepence for: they used to be tuppence. So here I am in one rotten little room on the third floor of a tumbledown old house full of rats. And as to my salary I should be ashamed to name it. A Church charity would be ashamed to pay it.

HE. I am utterly astounded. [*He takes a sound chair from the wall; places it near the office table; and sits down*]. The intellectual co-operation of sixty nations must be a very extensive business. How can it possibly be conducted in this bare little place?

SHE. Oh, I conduct it all right. It's never in a hurry, you know.

HE. But really—pardon me if I am taking too much of your time—

SHE. Oh, thats quite all right. I'm only too glad to have a bit of chat with somebody. Nobody ever comes in here: people dont seem to know that the Committee exists.

HE. Do you mean that you have nothing to do?

SHE. Oh no. I tell you I have to do all the intellectual co-operation. I have to do it singlehanded too: I havnt even an office boy to help me. And theres no end to the work. If it werent, as I say, that theres no hurry about it, I should never get through it. Just look here at this nice little job theyve given me! A card index of all the universities with the names and addresses of their bursars and their vice chancellors. And there is a correspondence about the protection of professional titles that takes up half my time.

HE. And do they call that intellectual co-operation?

SHE. Well, what else would you call it?

HE. It is mere compilation. How are the intellectual giants who form your committee bringing the enormous dynamic force of their brains, their prestige, their authority, to bear on the destinies of the nations? What are they doing to correct the mistakes of our ignorant politicians?

SHE. Well, we have their names on our notepaper,

you know. What more can they do? You cant expect them to sit in this little hole talking to people. I have never seen one of them.

HE. So they leave it all to you?

SHE. Oh, I wouldnt say all. Theres the head office in Paris, you know, and some offices in other countries. I suppose they do their bit; and anyhow we all do a lot of writing to oneanother. But I must say it's as dull as ditchwater. When I took the job I thought it was going to be interesting, and that I'd see all the great men. I am ambitious, you know: I won a London County Council scholarship. I wanted a job that would draw out my faculties, if you understand me. But theres nothing to do here that any common typist couldnt do. And nobody ever comes near the place. Oh, it is dull.

HE. Shall I give you an interesting job, mademoiselle? One that would get you appreciated and perhaps a little talked about?

SHE. I'll just jump at it—if it is all right.

HE. How all right?

SHE. Morally, you know. No hanky panky. I am respectable; and I mean to keep respectable.

HE. I pledge you my word that my intentions are completely honorable.

SHE. Well, what about the pay? And how long will the job last? The work here may be dull; and the pay is just short of starvation; but I have the appointment for 25 years certain; and I darent give it up for anything chancy. You dont know what it is to be out of a job.

HE. I shall not ask you to give up your post here. On the contrary, it is essential that you should keep it. But I think I can make it more interesting for you. And I should of course make you a suitable present if at any time you found that your emoluments here were insufficient.

SHE. They are. But I mustnt take bribes, you know.

HE. You need not. Any friendly service I may be able to render will be entirely independent of your official work here.

SHE. Look here: I dont half like this. Whats the game?

THE JEW. I must begin by explaining that I am a Jew.

SHE. I dont believe you. You dont look like one.

THE JEW. I am not a primitive Hittite. You cannot draw my nose in profile by simply writing down the number six. My hair is not black, nor do I wear it in excessively oiled ringlets. I have all the marks of a German blond. German is my native language: in fact I am in every sense a German. But I worship in the synagogue; and when I worship I put my hat on, whereas a German takes it off. On this ground they class me as a non-Aryan, which is nonsense, as there is no such thing as an Aryan.

SHE. I'm so glad to hear you say that. The Germans here say that I am an Aryan; but I tell them I am nothing of the kind: I'm an Englishwoman. Not a common Englishwoman, of course: I'm a Camberwell woman; and though the west end may turn up its nose at Camberwell, Camberwell is better than Peckham any day in the week.

THE JEW. No doubt. I have not been there.

SHE. I never could abide Peckham people. They are disliked everywhere. It's instinctive, somehow. Havnt you noticed it?

THE JEW. All peoples are disliked in the lump. The English are disliked: the Germans are disliked: the French are disliked. The Protestants are disliked; and all their hundreds of sects dislike oneanother. So are the Catholics, the Jesuits, the Freemasons. You tell me that the inhabitants of Peckham are disliked: no doubt they deserve it.

SHE. They do.

THE JEW. Some of the greatest men have disliked the human race. But for Noah, its Creator would have drowned it. Can we deny that He had good reasons for disliking it? Can I deny that there are good reasons for disliking Jews? On the contrary, I dislike most of them myself.

SHE. Oh, dont say that. Ive known lots of quite nice Jews. What I say is why pick on the Jews, as if they were any worse than other people?

THE JEW. That is precisely my business here today. I find you most intelligent—most sympathetic.

SHE. Come now! none of that. Whats the game?

THE JEW. I have been assaulted, plundered, and driven from my native soil by its responsible ruler. I, as a ruined individual, can do nothing. But the League of Nations can act through its Committee for Intellectual Co-operation. The Committee can act through the permanent court of International Justice at the Hague, which is also an organ of the League. My business here is to ask the Committee to apply to the court for a warrant against the responsible ruler. I charge him with assault and battery, burglary—

SHE. Burglary! Did they break into your house?

THE JEW. I cannot speak of it. Everything I treasured. Wrecked! Smashed! Defiled! Never will I forgive: never can I forget.

SHE. But why didnt you call the police?

THE JEW. Mademoiselle: the police did it. The Government did it. The Dictator who controls the police is responsible before Europe! before civilization! I look to the League of Nations for redress. It alone can call unrighteous rulers to account. The initiative must be taken by its Committee for Intellectual Co-operation: that is, for the moment, by you, mademoiselle.

SHE. But what can I do? I cant go out and collar your unrighteous ruler.

THE JEW. No, mademoiselle. What you must do is to write to the International Court, calling on it to issue a warrant for the arrest of my oppressor on a charge of attempting to exterminate a section of the human race.

SHE. Well, it seems like taking a lot on myself, doesnt it?

THE JEW. Not at all. You will be acting, not for yourself, but for the intellect of Europe. I assure you it is the correct course.

SHE. But I'm not sure that I know how to write a letter with all those police court things in it.

THE JEW. It is quite simple. But if you will allow me I will draft the letter for you.

SHE. Oh I say, Mister Jew, I dont like this.

THE JEW. Then write the letter yourself. I am sure you will do it perfectly. It will be an opportunity for you to shew the Committee what you are made of.

SHE. Well, look here. I have a particular friend, an American journalist. Would you mind if I shewed him your draft before I send it off?

THE JEW. An American journalist! Excellent, excellent. By all means submit my draft to him and ask him to correct it if necessary. My English is German English, and may leave something to be desired.

SHE. Yes: thatll be splendid. Thank you ever so much.

THE JEW. Not at all. [*Rising*] I will bring the draft in the course of the afternoon. Au revoir, then.

SHE. Au revoir.

They shake hands cordially. Meanwhile the door is

opened by an obstinate-looking middle-aged man of respectable but not aristocratic appearance, speaking English like a shopkeeper from the provinces, or perhaps, by emigration, the dominions.

NEWCOMER. Can I see the boss, miss?

SHE [*with haughty nonchalance in a would-be distinguished accent startlingly unlike her unaffected deference to the gentlemanlike Jew*] I am sorry. Our chiefs are scattered over Europe, very eminent persons, you know. Can I do anything?

NEWCOMER [*looking at the Jewish gentleman*] I'm afraid I'm interrupting.

THE JEW. Not at all: my business is finished. [*Clicking his heels and bowing*] Until the afternoon, mademoiselle. Monsieur— [*He bows to the newcomer, and goes out*].

SHE. You can sit down.

NEWCOMER. I will keep you only a minute, miss. [*He sits and takes out some notes he has made*].

SHE. Be as quick as you can, please. I am busy this morning.

NEWCOMER. Yes: you have the brainwork of the world on your shoulders here. When any of the nations goes off the rails, this is the place to have it put back. Thats so, isnt it?

SHE [*with aplomb*] Undoubtedly.

NEWCOMER. Well, it's like this. In my country weve had an election. We thought it lay between our usual people: the National Party and the Labor Party; but it was won by an upstart kind of chap who called himself a Business Democrat. He got a clear majority over the Nationals and the Labor Party; so it was up to him to form a Government. And what do you suppose the fellow did when he became Prime Minister?

SHE [*bored*] Cant imagine, I'm sure.

NEWCOMER. He said he had been returned to power as a business democrat, and that the business part of it meant that he was not to waste time, but to get the nation's work done as quickly as possible.

SHE. Quite, quite. Nothing to complain of in that, is there?

NEWCOMER. Wait. I'm going to astonish you. He said the country had decided by its democratic vote that it should be governed by him and his party for the next five years, and that no opposition could be tolerated. He said the defeated minority must step down and out instead of staying there to obstruct and delay and annoy him. Of course the Opposition werent going to stand that: they refused to leave the Chamber. So he adjourned the House until next day; and when the Opposition turned up the police wouldnt let them in. Most of them couldnt get as far as the doors, because the Prime Minister had organized a body of young men called the Clean Shirts, to help the police.

SHE. Well?

NEWCOMER. Well!!! Is that all you have to say to me?

SHE. What do you expect me to say? It seems all right to me. It's what any man of business would do. Wouldnt you?

NEWCOMER. Of course I should do it in business; but this is politics.

SHE. Well! arnt politics business?

NEWCOMER. Of course theyre not. Just the opposite. You know that, dont you?

SHE. Oh, quite, quite.

NEWCOMER. What I say is, business methods are business methods; and parliamentary methods are parliamentary methods.

SHE [*brightly*] "And never the twain shall meet," as Kipling puts it.

NEWCOMER. No: I dont hold with Kipling. Too imperialist for me. I'm a democrat.

SHE. But not a business democrat, if I follow you.

NEWCOMER. No, no: not a business democrat. A proper democrat. I'm all for the rights of minorities.

SHE. But I always thought that democracy meant the right of the majority to have its way.

NEWCOMER. Oh no: that would be the end of all liberty. You have nothing to say against liberty, I hope.

SHE. I have nothing to say against anything. I am not here to discuss politics with everyone who walks into my office. What do you want?

NEWCOMER. Well, heres a Prime Minister committing high treason and rebellion and breach of privilege; levying armed forces against the Crown; violating the constitution; setting up a dictatorship and obstructing the lawful ingress of duly elected members to the legislative Chamber. Whats to be done with him?

SHE. Quite simple. I shall apply to the International Court at the Hague for a warrant for his arrest on all those charges. You can look in at the end of the week, when the answer from the Hague will have arrived. You will supply me with the man's name and the particulars—

NEWCOMER [*putting his notes on the table before her*] Here they are, miss. By Gosh, thats a splendid idea.

SHE. Thank you. That is all. Good morning.

NEWCOMER [*rising and going to the door*] Well, you know how to do business here: theres no mistake about that. Good morning, miss.

As he is going out the door opens in his face; and a

widow comes in: a Creole lady of about forty, with the remains of a gorgeous and opulent southern beauty. Her imposing style and dress at once reduce the young lady of the office to nervous abjection.

THE WIDOW. Are you the president of the Intellectual Co-operation Committee of the League of Nations?

NEWCOMER. No, maam. This lady will do all you require [*he goes out*].

THE WIDOW. Am I to take that seriously? My business is important. I came here to place it before a body of persons of European distinction. I am not prepared to discuss it with an irresponsible young woman.

SHE. I am afraid I dont look the part, do I? I am only the staff, so to speak. Still, anything I can do I shall be most happy.

THE WIDOW. But where are your chiefs?

SHE. Ah, there you have me. They live all over the world, as you might say.

THE WIDOW. But do they not come here to attend to their business?

SHE. Well, you see, there is really nothing for them to attend to. It's only intellectual business, you know.

THE WIDOW. But do they not take part in the Assembly of the League?

SHE. Some of them have been, once. Nobody ever goes to the Assembly twice if they can help it.

THE WIDOW. But I must see somebody—somebody of importance.

SHE. Well, I'm sorry. Theres nobody but me. I can do whatever is necessary. Did you by any chance want a warrant from the International Court at the Hague?

THE WIDOW. Yes: that is exactly what I do want. A death warrant.

SHE. A what?!!

THE WIDOW. A death warrant. I will sit down, if you will allow me.

SHE. Oh please—

THE WIDOW [*sitting down*] Do you see that? [*She takes an automatic pistol from her bag, and throws it on the table*].

SHE. Oh, thats not allowed in Geneva. Put it up quick. Somebody might come in.

THE WIDOW [*replacing the pistol in her bag*] This is the most absurd place. In my country everybody carries a gun.

SHE. What country, may I ask?

THE WIDOW. The Republic of the Earthly Paradise.

SHE. My mother has a school prize called The Earthly Paradise. What a coincidence!

THE WIDOW. Then you know that the Earthly Paradise is one of the leading States in the world in culture and purity of race, and that its capital contained more than two thousand white inhabitants before the last revolution. There must be still at least fifteen hundred left.

SHE. But is it a member of the League?

THE WIDOW. Of course it is. And allow me to remind you that by its veto it can put a stop to all action by the League until its affairs are properly attended to.

SHE. Can it? I didnt know that. Of course I shall be only too pleased to apply for a warrant; but I'd rather not call it a death warrant. Death warrant sounds a bit thick, if you understand me. All you need do is to give me a list of the charges you make against—well, against whoever it is.

THE WIDOW. Simply one charge of the wilful murder

of my late husband by the President of the Earthly Paradise.

SHE. Surely if a president kills anyone it's an execution; but if anyone kills a president it's an assassination.

THE WIDOW. And is not that just the state of things the League of Nations is here to put a stop to?

SHE. Oh, dont ask me. All I know about the League is that it pays my salary. Just give me the gentleman's name and who he murdered. Murder stories are thrillingly interesting.

THE WIDOW. You would not think so if you lived in a country where there is at least one murder in every family.

SHE. What an awful place! Is it as barbarous as that?

THE WIDOW. Barbarous! Certainly not. The Earthly Paradise is the most civilized country in the world. Its constitution is absolutely democratic: every president must swear to observe it in every particular. The Church is abolished: no moral authority is recognized except that of the people's will. The president and parliament are elected by adult suffrage every two years. So are all the judges and all the officials, even the road sweepers. All these reforms, which have made The Earthly Paradise the most advanced member of the League of Nations, were introduced by my late husband the sixth president. He observed the constitution strictly. The elections were conducted with absolute integrity. The ballot was secret. The people felt free for the first time in their lives. Immediately after the elections the budget was passed providing for two years. My husband then prorogued the Parliament until the end of that period, and governed the country according to his own ideas whilst the people enjoyed themselves and made money in their own ways without any political disturbances or arguments. He was re-elected three times, and is now known in the Paradise as the father of his country.

SHE. But you said he was murdered, and that the president murdered him. How could that be if he was the president? He couldnt murder himself.

THE WIDOW. Unhappily he had certain weaknesses. He was an affectionate husband: I may even say an uxorious one; but he was very far from being faithful to me. When he abolished the Church he would have abolished marriage also if public opinion would have stood for it. And he was much too indulgent to his enemies. Naturally, whenever he won an election his opponent raised an army and attempted a revolution; for we are a high spirited race and do not submit to the insult of defeat at the polls. But my husband was a military genius. He had no difficulty in putting down these revolutions; but instead of having his opponent shot in the proper and customary way, he pardoned him and challenged him to try again as often as he pleased. I urged him again and again not to trifle with his own safety in this way. Useless: he would not listen to me. At last I found out the reason. He was carrying on an intrigue with his opponent's wife, my best friend. I had to shoot her—shoot her dead—my dearest friend [*she is overcome with emotion*].

SHE. Oh, you shouldnt have done that. That was going a little too far, wasnt it?

THE WIDOW. Public opinion obliged me to do it as a selfrespecting wife and mother. God knows I did not want to do it: I loved her: I would have let her have ten husbands if I had had them to give. But what can you do against the etiquette of your class? My brothers had to fight duels and kill their best friends because it was etiquette.

SHE. But where were the police? Werent you tried for it?

THE WIDOW. Of course I was tried for it; but I pleaded the unwritten law and was acquitted. Unfortunately the scandal destroyed my husband's popularity. He was defeated at the next election by the man he had so foolishly spared. Instead of raising an army to avenge this outrage, my husband, crushed by the loss of his mistress, just moped at home until they came and shot him. They had come to shoot me; and [*with a fresh burst of tears*] I wish to Heaven they had; but I was out at the time; so they thought they might as well shoot my husband as there was nobody else to shoot.

SHE. What a dreadful thing for you!

THE WIDOW. Not at all. It served him right, absolutely. He never spoke to me after I had to kill the woman we both loved more than we loved oneanother. I believe he would have been only too glad if they had shot me; and I dont blame him. What is the use of the League of Nations if it cannot put a stop to such horrors?

SHE. Well, it's not the League's business, is it?

THE WIDOW. Not the League's business! Do you realize, young woman, that if the League does not bring the murderer of my husband to justice my son will be obliged to take up a blood feud and shoot the murderer with his own hands, though they were at the same school and are devoted to oneanother? It is against Nature, against God: if your committee does not stop it I will shoot every member of it, and you too. [*She rises*]. Excuse me. I can bear no more of this: I shall faint unless I get into the fresh air. [*She takes papers and a card from her bag and throws them on the table*]. There are the particulars. This is my card.

Good morning. [*She goes as abruptly as she came in*].

SHE. [*rising*] Good—

But the widow has gone and the young office lady, greatly upset, drops back into her seat with a prolonged Well!!!!!

A smart young American gentleman looks in.

THE GENTLEMAN. Say, baby: who is the old girl in the mantilla? Carmen's grandmother, eh? [*He sits on the table edge, facing her, on her right*].

SHE. A murderess. Her dearest friend. She had to. Horrible. Theyve shot her husband. She says she will shoot me unless the League stops it.

HE. Grand! Fine!

SHE. Is that all you care? Well, look at my morning's work! Persecutions, revolutions, murders, all sorts. The office has been full of people all the morning. We shant have it all to ourselves any more.

HE. No, baby; but I shall have some dough to spend. I have been kicking my heels here for months faking news for my people when there was no news. And here you hand me a mouthful. What a scoop for me, honey! You are a peach. [*He kisses her*].

Someone knocks at the door.

SHE. Shsh! Someone knocking.

They separate hastily, he going to the stove and she composing herself in her chair.

HE. Come in! Entrez! Herein!

A gaitered English bishop enters. He is old, soft, gentle and rather infirm.

THE BISHOP. Excuse me; but does anyone here speak English?

HE [*putting on all the style he is capable of*] My native language, my lord. Also this lady's. [*Exchange of bows*]. Will you take a pew, my lord?

BISHOP [*sitting*] Thank you. Your stairs are somewhat trying to me: I am not so young as I was; and they tell me I must be careful not to overstrain my heart. The journey to Geneva is a terrible one for a man of my years. Nothing but the gravest emergency could have forced me to undertake it.

HE. Is the emergency one in which we can have the honor of assisting you, my lord?

BISHOP. Your advice would be invaluable to me; for I really dont know what to do or where to go here. I am met with indifference—with apathy—when I reveal a state of things that threatens the very existence of civilized society, of religion, of the family, of the purity of womanhood, and even, they tell me, of our commercial prosperity. Are people mad? Dont they know? Dont they care?

HE. My! my! my! [*He takes a chair to the end of the table nearest the stove*] Pray be seated, my lord. What has happened?

BISHOP [*sinking into the chair*] Sir: they are actually preaching Communism in my diocese. Communism!!! My butler, who has been in the palace for forty years, a most devoted and respectable man, tells me that my footman—I am the only bishop in England who can afford to keep a footman now—that my footman is a cell.

HE. A sell? You mean that he has disappointed you?

BISHOP. No: not that sort of cell. C.E. double L. A communist cell. Like a bee in a hive. Planted on me by the Communists to make their dreadful propaganda in my household! And my grandson at Oxford has joined a Communist club. The Union—the Oxford Union—has raised the red flag. It is dreadful. And my granddaughter a nudist! I was graciously allowed to introduce my daughters to good Queen Victoria. If she could see my granddaughter she would call the police. Is it any wonder that I have a weak heart? Shock after shock. My own footman, son of the most respectable parents, and actually an Anglo-Catholic!

HE. I can hardly believe it, my lord. What times we are living in!

SHE [*with her most official air*] Surely this is a case for the International Court at the Hague, my lord.

BISHOP. Yes, yes. An invaluable suggestion. The Court must stop the Bolshies from disseminating their horrible doctrines in England. It is in the treaties.

He is interrupted by the entrance of a very smart Russian gentleman, whom he receives with pleased recognition.

BISHOP [*rising*] Ah, my dear sir, we meet again. [*To the others*] I had the pleasure of making this gentleman's acquaintance last night at my hotel. His interest in the Church of England kept us up talking long after my usual hour for retirement. [*Shaking his hand warmly*] How do you do, my dear friend? how do you do?

RUSSIAN. Quite well, thank you, my lord. Am I interrupting your business?

BISHOP. No no no no: I beg you to remain. You will help: you will sympathize.

RUSSIAN. You are very kind, my lord: I am quite at your service.

BISHOP [*murmuring gratefully as he resumes his seat*] Thank you. Thank you.

RUSSIAN. Let me introduce myself. I am Commissar Posky of the Sovnarkom and Politbureau, Soviet delegate to the League Council.

BISHOP [*aghast, staggering to his feet*] You are a Bolshevik!

COMMISSAR. Assuredly.

The Bishop faints. General concern. The men rush to him.

COMMISSAR. Do not lift him yet. He will recover best as he is.

SHE. I have some iced lemonade in my thermos. Shall I give him some?

BISHOP [*supine*] Where am I? Has anything happened?

HE. You are in the office of the Intellectual Co-operation Committee in Geneva. You have had a slight heart attack.

COMMISSAR. Lie still, comrade. You will be quite yourself presently.

BISHOP [*sitting up*] It is not my heart. [*To the Commissar*] It is moral shock. You presented yourself to me yesterday as a cultivated and humane gentleman, interested in the Church of England. And now it turns out that you are a Bolshie. What right had you to practise such a cruel imposture on me? [*He rises: the Commissar helps him*] No: I can rise without assistance, thank you. [*He attempts to do so, but collapses into the arms of the Commissar*].

COMMISSAR. Steady, comrade.

BISHOP [*regaining his seat with the Commissar's assistance*] Again I must thank you. But I shudder at the touch of your bloodstained hands.

COMMISSAR. My hands are not bloodstained, comrade. I have not imposed on you. You have not quite recovered yet, I think. I am your friend of last night. Dont you recognize me?

BISHOP. A Bolshie! If I had known, sir, I should have repudiated your advances with abhorrence.

HE [*again posting himself at the stove*] Russia is a member of the League, my lord. This gentleman's standing here is the same as that of the British Foreign Secretary.

BISHOP [*intensely*] Never. Never.

SHE [*airily*] And what can we do for you, Mr Posky? I'm sorry I cant offer you a chair. That one isnt safe.

COMMISSAR. Pray dont mention it. My business will take only a moment. As you know, the Soviet Government has gone as far as possible in agreeing not to countenance or subsidize any propaganda of Communism which takes the form of a political conspiracy to overthrow the British National Government.

BISHOP. And in violation of that agreement you have corrupted my footman and changed him from an honest and respectable young Englishman into a Cell.

COMMISSAR. Have we? I know nothing of your footman. If he is intelligent enough to become a Communist, as so many famous Englishmen did long before the Russian revolution, we cannot prevent him. But we do not employ him as our agent nor support him financially in any way.

HE. But what, then, is your difficulty, Comrade Posky?

COMMISSAR. We have just discovered that there is a most dangerous organization at work in Russia, financed from the British Isles, having for its object the overthrow of the Soviet system and the substitution of the Church of England and the British Constitution.

BISHOP. And why not, sir? Why not? Could any object be more desirable, more natural? Would you in your blind hatred of British institutions and of all liberty of thought and speech, make it a crime to advocate a system which is universally admitted to be the the best and freest in the world?

COMMISSAR. We do not think so. And as the obligation to refrain from this sort of propaganda is reciprocal, you are bound by it just as we are.

HE. But what is this seditious organization you have just discovered?

COMMISSAR. It is called the Society for the Propagation of the Gospel in Foreign Parts. It has agents everywhere. They call themselves missionaries.

BISHOP. I cannot bear this: the man is insane. I subscribe to the Society almost beyond my means. It is a body of the highest respectability and piety.

COMMISSAR. You are misinformed: its doctrines are of the most subversive kind. They have penetrated to my own household. My wife is a busy professional woman, and my time is taken up altogether by public work. We are absolutely dependent for our domestic work on our housekeeper Feodorovna Ballyboushka. We were ideally happy with this excellent woman for years. In her youth she was a udarnik, what you call a shock worker.

BISHOP. You are all shock workers in Russia now. You have seen the effect on me?

COMMISSAR. That was in the early days of the revolution, when she was young and ardent. Now she is elderly; and her retirement into domestic service suits her years and her helpful and affectionate temperament. Two months ago an extraordinary change came over her. She refused to do any work that was not immediately necessary, on the ground that the end of the world is at hand. She declared that she was in a condition which she described as "saved," and interrupted my work continually with attempts to save me. She had long fits of crying because she could not bear the thought of my wife spending eternity in hell. She accused the Soviets of being the hornets prophesied in the Book of Revelation. We were about to have her certified as insane—most reluctantly; for we loved our dear Ballyboushka—when we discovered

that she had been hypnotized by this illegal Society. I warned our Secret Police, formerly known to you as the Gay Pay Ooh. They followed up the clue and arrested four missionaries.
BISHOP. And shot them. Christian martyrs! All who fall into the hands of the terrible Gay Pay Ooh are shot at once, without trial, without the ministrations of the Church. But I will have a memorial service said for them. To that extent at last I can defeat your Godless tyranny.
COMMISSAR. You are quite mistaken: they have not been shot. They will be sent back to England: that is all.
BISHOP [*passionately*] What right had you to arrest them? How dare you arrest Englishmen? How dare you persecute religion?
COMMISSAR. They have been very patiently examined by our official psychologists, who report that they can discover nothing that could reasonably be called religion in their minds. They are obsessed with tribal superstitions of the most barbarous kind. They believe in human sacrifices, in what they call the remission of sins by the shedding of blood. No man's life would be safe in Russia if such doctrines were propagated there.
BISHOP. But you dont understand. Oh, what dreadful ignorance!
COMMISSAR. Let us pass on to another point. Our police have found a secret document of your State Church, called the Thirty-nine Articles.
BISHOP. Secret! It is in the Prayer Book!
COMMISSAR. It is not read in church. That fact speaks for itself. Our police have found most of the articles incomprehensible; but there is one, the eighteenth, which declares that all Russians are to be held

accursed. How would you like it if our chief cultural institution, endowed by our government, the Komintern, were to send its agents into England to teach that every Englishman is to be held accursed?

BISHOP. But surely, surely, you would not compare the Komintern to the Church of England!!

COMMISSAR. Comrade Bishop: the Komintern is the State Church in Russia exactly as the Church of England is the State Church in Britain.

The Bishop slides to the floor in another faint.

SHE. Oh! He's gone off again. Shall I get my thermos?

HE. I should break things to him more gently, Mr Posky. People die of shock. He maynt recover next time. In fact, he maynt recover this time.

COMMISSAR. What am I to do? I have said nothing that could possibly shock any educated reasonable person; but this man does not seem to know what sort of world he is living in.

SHE. He's an English bishop, you know.

COMMISSAR. Well? Is he not a rational human being?

SHE. Oh no: nothing as common as that. I tell you he's a bishop.

BISHOP. Where am I? Why am I lying on the floor? What has happened?

HE. You are in the Intellectual Co-operation Bureau in Geneva; and you have just been told that the Russian Komintern is analogous to the Church of England.

BISHOP [*springing to his feet unaided, his eyes blazing*] I still have life enough left in me to deny it. Karl Marx—Antichrist—said that the sweet and ennobling consolations of our faith are opium given to the poor to enable them to endure the hardships of that state of life to which it has pleased God to call them. Does your Komintern teach that blasphemy or does it not?

COMMISSAR. Impossible. There are no poor in Russia.

BISHOP. Oh! [*he drops dead*].

HE [*feeling his pulse*] I am afraid you have shocked him once too often, Comrade. His pulse has stopped. He is dead.

POSKY. Was he ever alive? To me he was incredible.

SHE. I suppose my thermos is of no use now. Shall I ring up a doctor?

HE. I think you had better ring up the police. But I say, Mr Posky, what a scoop!

COMMISSAR. A scoop? I do not understand. What is a scoop?

HE. Read all the European papers tomorrow and youll see.

ACT II

Office of the secretary of the League of Nations. Except for the small writing table at which the secretary is seated there is no office furniture. The walls are covered with engraved prints or enlarged photographs of kings, presidents, and dictators, mostly in military uniforms. Above these bellicose pictures the cornice is decorated with a row of plaster doves in low relief. There is one large picture in oils, representing a lifesize Peace, with tiny figures, also in military uniforms, kneeling round her feet and bowing their heads piously beneath the wreath which she offers them. This picture faces the secretary from the other side of the room as he sits at his table with his back to the window presenting his left profile to anyone entering from the door, which is in the middle of the wall between them. A suite of half a dozen chairs is ranged round the walls, except one, which stands near the writing table for the convenience of people interviewing the secretary.

He is a disillusioned official with a habit of dogged patience acquired in the course of interviews with distinguished statesmen of different nations, all in a condition of invincible ignorance as to the spirit of Geneva and the constitution of the League of Nations, and each with a national axe to grind. On this occasion he is rather exceptionally careworn. One pities him, as he is of a refined type, and, one guesses, began as a Genevan idealist. Age fifty or thereabouts.

There is a telephone on the table which he is at present using.

THE SECRETARY. Yes: send her up instantly. Remind me of her name. What?! . . . Ammonia? Nonsense! that cant be her name. Spell it . . . V E? . . . Oh, *B* E. Do you mean to say that her name is Begonia? Begonia Brown? . . . Farcical.

He replaces the receiver as Begonia enters. She is the Intellectual Co-operation typist. She is in walking dress, cheap, but very smart.

THE SECRETARY. Miss Brown?

BEGONIA [*with her best smile*] Yes.

THE SECRETARY. Sit down.

BEGONIA [*complying*] Kew [*short for Thank you*].

THE SECRETARY [*gravely*] You have heard the news, no doubt?

BEGONIA. Oh yes. Jack Palamedes has won the dancing tournament. I had ten francs on him; and I have won a hundred. Had you anything on?

THE SECRETARY [*still more gravely*] I am afraid you will think me very ignorant, Miss Brown; but I have never heard of Mr Palamedes.

BEGONIA. Fancy that! He's the talk of Geneva, I assure you.

THE SECRETARY. There are other items of news, Miss Brown. Germany has withdrawn from the League.

BEGONIA. And a good riddance, if you ask me. My father lost a lot of money through the war. Otherwise —you wont mind my telling you—youd never have got me slaving at a typewriter here for my living.

THE SECRETARY. No doubt. A further item is that the British Empire has declared war on Russia.

BEGONIA. Well, what could you expect us to do with those awful Bolshies? We should have done it long ago. But thank goodness we're safe in Geneva, you and I.

THE SECRETARY. We are safe enough everywhere, so far. The war is one of sanctions only.

BEGONIA. More shame for us, say I. I should give those Bolshies the bayonet: thats the way to talk to scum of that sort. I cant contain myself when I think of all the murder and slavery of them Soviets— [*correcting herself*] those Soviets.

THE SECRETARY. In consequence Japan has declared war on Russia and is therefore in military alliance with Britain. And the result of that is that Australia, New Zealand and Canada have repudiated the war and formed an anti-Japanese alliance with the United States under the title of the New British Federation. South Africa may join them at any moment.

BEGONIA [*flushing with indignation*] Do you mean that theyve broken up our dear Empire?

THE SECRETARY. They have said nothing about that.

BEGONIA. Oh, then thats quite all right. You know, when I was at school I was chosen five times to recite on Empire Day; and in my very first year, when I was the smallest child there, I presented the bouquet to King George's sister, who came to our prize giving. Say a word against the Empire, and you have finished with Begonia Brown.

THE SECRETARY. Then you went to school, did you?

BEGONIA. Well, of course: what do you take me for? I went to school for seven years and never missed a single day. I got fourteen prizes for regular attendance.

THE SECRETARY. Good God!

BEGONIA. What did you say?

THE SECRETARY. Nothing. I was about to tell you

what has happened in Quetzalcopolis, the chief seaport of the Earthly Paradise.

BEGONIA. I know. In Central America, isnt it?

THE SECRETARY. Yes. The mob there has attacked the British Consulate, and torn down the British flag.

BEGONIA [*rising in a fury*] Insulted the British flag!!!

THE SECRETARY. They have also burnt down three convents and two churches.

BEGONIA. Thats nothing: theyre only Catholic churches. But do you mean to say that they have dared to touch the British flag?

THE SECRETARY. They have. Fortunately it was after hours and the staff had gone home. Otherwise they would assuredly have been massacred.

BEGONIA. Dirty swine! I hope the British fleet will not leave a stone standing or a nigger alive in their beastly seaport. Thatll teach them.

THE SECRETARY. There is only one other trifle of news. The little Dominion of Jacksonsland has declared itself an independent republic.

BEGONIA. It ought to be ashamed of itself. Republics are a low lot. But dont you be anxious about that: the republicans will soon be kicked out. The people may be misled for a while; but they always come back to king and country.

THE SECRETARY. And now, Miss Brown, I must ask you whether you fully realize that all this is your doing?

BEGONIA. Mine!

THE SECRETARY. Yours and nobody else's. In every one of these cases, it was your hand that started the series of political convulsions which may end in the destruction of civilization.

BEGONIA [*flattered*] Really? How?

THE SECRETARY. Those letters that you sent to the Court of International Justice at the Hague—

BEGONIA. Oh, of course. Yes. Fancy that!

THE SECRETARY. But did you not know what you were doing? You conducted the correspondence with very remarkable ability—more, I confess, than I should have given you credit for. Do you mean to tell me that you did not foresee the consequences of your action? That you did not even read the newspapers to see what was happening?

BEGONIA. I dont read political news: it's so dry. However, I seem to be having a big success; and I wont pretend I am not gratified.

THE SECRETARY. Unfortunately the Powers do not consider it a success. They are blaming me for it.

BEGONIA. Oh, if there is any blame I am ready to take it all on myself.

THE SECRETARY. That is very magnanimous of you, Miss Brown.

BEGONIA. Not so magnanimous either: thank you all the same. I tell you I back the Empire; and the Empire will back me. So dont be uneasy.

THE SECRETARY. You are very possibly right. And now may I ask you a personal question? How did you become interested in the League of Nations? How did you get this post of yours, which has placed the world's destiny so unexpectedly in your hands?

BEGONIA. Was I interested in the League? Let me see. You know that there is a Society called the League of Nations Union, dont you?

THE SECRETARY. I do. I shudder whenever I think of it.

BEGONIA. Oh, theres no harm in it. I'd never heard of it until last year, when they opened a branch in Camberwell with a whist drive. A friend gave me a ticket for it. It was opened by the Conservative candidate: an innocent young lad rolling in money. He saw that I was a cut above the other girls there, and picked me for his partner when he had to dance. I told him I'd won a County Council scholarship and was educated and knew shorthand and a bit of French and all that, and that I was looking out for a job. His people fixed me up for Geneva all right. A perfect gentleman I must say: never asked so much as a kiss. I was disappointed.

THE SECRETARY. Disappointed at his not kissing you?

BEGONIA. Oh no: there were plenty of kisses going from better looking chaps. But he was a bit of a sucker; and I thought he had intentions; and of course he would have been a jolly good catch for me. But when his people got wind of it they packed him off for a tour round the Empire, and got me this job here—to keep me out of his way, I suppose. Anyhow here I am, you see.

THE SECRETARY. Were you examined as to your knowledge and understanding of the Covenant of the League, and its constitution?

BEGONIA. No. They didnt need to examine me to find out that I was educated. I had lots of prizes and certificates; and there was my L.C.C. scholarship. You see, I have such a good memory: examinations are no trouble to me. Theres a book in the office about the League. I tried to read it; but it was such dry stuff I went to sleep over it.

THE SECRETARY [*rising*] Well, Miss Brown, I am glad to have made your acquaintance, and delighted to learn that though you have produced a first class political crisis, including what promises to be a world war, and made an amazing change in the constitution of the British Empire all in the course of a single morning's work, you are still in high spirits and in fact rather proud of yourself.

BEGONIA [*she has also risen*] Oh, I am not a bit proud; and I'm quite used to being a success. You know, although I was always at the top of my class at school, I never pretended to be clever. Silly clever, I call it. At first I was frightened of the girls that went in for being clever and having original ideas and all that sort of crankiness. But I beat them easily in the examinations; and they never got anywhere. That gave me confidence. Wherever I go I always find that lots of people think as I do. The best sort of people always do: the real ladies and gentlemen, you know. The others are oddities and outsiders. If you want to know what real English public opinion is, keep your eye on me. I'm not a bit afraid of war: remember that England has never lost a battle, and that it does no harm to remind the foreigners of it when they get out of hand. Good morning. So pleased to have met you.

They shake hands; and he goes to the door and opens it for her. She goes out much pleased with herself.

THE SECRETARY [*ruminating dazedly*] And thats England! [*The telephone rings. He returns to the table to attend to it*]. Yes? . . . Which Foreign Secretary? Every hole and corner in the Empire has its own Foreign Secretary now. Do you mean the British Foreign Secretary, Sir Orpheus Midlander? . . . Well, why didnt you say so? Shew him up at once.

Sir Orpheus comes in. He is a very welldressed gentleman of fifty or thereabouts, genial in manner, quickwitted in conversation, altogether a pleasant and popular personality.

THE SECRETARY. Do sit down. I cant say how I feel about your being dragged here all the way from London in Derby week.

SIR O. [*sitting*] Well, my friend, it's you who have dragged me. And I hope you wont mind my asking you what on earth you think you have been doing? What induced you to do it?

THE SECRETARY. I didnt do it. It was done by the Committee for Intellectual Co-operation.

SIR O. The what??! I never heard of such a body.

THE SECRETARY. Neither did I until this business was sprung on me. Nobody ever heard of it. But I find now that it is part of the League, and that its members are tremendous swells with European reputations. Theyve all published translations from the Greek or discovered new planets or something of that sort.

SIR O. Ah yes: outside politics: I see. But we cant have literary people interfering in foreign affairs. And they must have held meetings before taking such an outrageous step as this. Why were we not told? We'd have squashed them at once.

THE SECRETARY. They are quite innocent: they know no more about it than I did. The whole thing was done by a young woman named Begonia Brown.

SIR O. Begonia Brown! But this is appalling. I shall be personally compromised.

THE SECRETARY. You! How?

SIR O. This woman—it must be the same woman; for there cant be another female with such a name in the world—she's engaged to my nephew.

THE SECRETARY. She told me about it. But I had no idea the man was your nephew. I see how awkward it is for you. Did you ever talk to her about it?

SIR O. I! I never set eyes on her in my life. I remember her ridiculous name: thats all.

THE SECRETARY. Were you in the habit of discussing foreign affairs with your nephew?

SIR O. With Benjy! You might as well discuss Einstein's general theory of relativity with a blue behinded ape. I havnt exchanged twenty words with the boy since I tipped him when he was going from Eton to Oxford.

THE SECRETARY. Then I cant understand it. Her correspondence with the Hague Court has been conducted with remarkable ability and in first-rate style. The woman herself is quite incapable of it. There must be somebody behind her. Can it be your nephew?

SIR O. If, as you say, the work shews political ability and presentable style, you may accept my assurance that Sue's boy has nothing to do with it. Besides, he is at present in Singapore, where the native dancing girls are irresistible.

The telephone rings.

THE SECRETARY. Excuse me. Yes?... Hold on a moment. [*To Sir O.*] The Senior Judge of the Court of International Justice at the Hague is downstairs. Hadnt you better see him?

SIR O. By all means. Most opportune.

THE SECRETARY [*into the telephone*] Send him up.

SIR O. Have you had any correspondence about this business?

THE SECRETARY. Correspondence!!! I havnt read one tenth of it. The Abyssinian war was a holiday job in comparison. Weve never had anything like it before.

The Senior Judge enters. He is a Dutchman, much younger than a British judge: under forty, in fact, but very grave and every inch a judge.

THE SECRETARY. I am desolate at having brought your honor all the way from the Hague. A word from you would have brought me there and saved you the trouble. Have you met the British Foreign Secretary, Sir Orpheus Midlander?

JUDGE. I have not had that pleasure. How do you do, Sir Midlander?

SIR O. How do you do?

They shake hands whilst the Secretary places a chair for the judge in the middle of the room, between his table and Sir Orpheus. They all sit down.

JUDGE. I thought it best to come. The extraordinary feature of this affair is that I have communicated with all the members of the Intellectual Committee; and every one of them denies any knowledge of it. Most of them did not know that they are members.

SIR O. Do you mean to say that it is all a hoax?

JUDGE. It may be that someone was hoaxing the Court. But now that the applications for warrants have been made public, the Court must take them seriously. Otherwise it would cut a ridiculous figure in the eyes of Europe.

SIR O. But surely such a procedure was never contemplated when the Powers joined the League?

JUDGE. I do not think anything was contemplated when the Powers joined the League. They signed the Covenant without reading it, to oblige President Wilson. The United States then refused to sign it to disoblige President Wilson, also without reading it. Since then the Powers have behaved in every respect as if the League did not exist, except when they could use it for their own purposes.

SIR O. [*naïvely*] But how else could they use it?

JUDGE. They could use it to maintain justice and order between the nations.

SIR O. There is nothing we desire more. The British Empire stands for justice and order. But I must tell you that the British Foreign Office would take a very grave view of any attempt on the part of the Court to do anything without consulting us. I need not remind you that without us you have no powers. You have no police to execute your warrants. You cant put the Powers in the dock: you havnt got a dock.

JUDGE. We have a court room at the Hague which can easily be provided with a dock if you consider such a construction necessary, which I do not. We have employees to whom we can assign police duties to any necessary extent.

SIR O. Pooh! You cant be serious. You have no jurisdiction.

JUDGE. You mean that our jurisdiction is undefined. That means that our jurisdiction is what we choose to make it. You are familiar with what you call judge-made law in England. Well, Sir Midlander, the judges of the Court of International Justice are not nonentities. We have waited a long time for a case to set us in motion. You have provided us with four cases; and you may depend on us to make the most of them. They will affirm our existence, which is hardly known yet. They will exercise our power, which is hardly felt yet. All we needed was a *cause célèbre*; and Miss Begonia Brown has found several for us very opportunely.

SIR O. My dear sir: Miss Brown is a nobody.

JUDGE. Unless the highest court can be set in motion by the humblest individual justice is a mockery.

SIR O. Of course I agree with that—in principle. Still, you know, there are people you can take into court and people you cant. Your experience at the bar—

JUDGE [*interrupting him sharply*] I have had no experience at the bar. Please remember that you are not now in England, where judges are only worn-out barristers, most of whom have forgotten any sense of law they may ever have acquired.

SIR O. How very odd! I own I was surprised to find the judicial bench represented by so young a man; and I am afraid I must add that I prefer our British system. We should have had no trouble with a British judge.

JUDGE. Why should you have any trouble with me? I am simply a Judge, first and last. To me it is a continual trouble and scandal that modern statesmen are slipping back, one after another, from the reign of law based on the eternal principle of justice, to the maintenance of governments set up by successful demagogues or victorious soldiers, each of whom has his proscription list of enemies whom he imprisons, exiles, or murders at his pleasure until he is himself overcome by an abler rival and duly proscribed, imprisoned, exiled or assassinated in his turn. Such a state of things is abhorrent to me. I have spent years in trying to devise some judicial procedure by which these law-breakers can be brought to justice. Well, the Intellectual Co-operation Committee—of the existence of which I must confess I was entirely ignorant—has found the procedure; and the Court will back it up to the utmost of its powers.

SIR O. I am afraid you are a bit of an idealist.

JUDGE. Necessarily. Justice is an ideal; and I am a judge. What, may I ask, are you?

SIR O. I! Oh, only a much harassed Foreign Secretary. You see my young friend—if you will allow me to call you so—justice, as you say, is an ideal, and a very fine ideal too; but what I have to deal with is Power; and Power is often a devilishly ugly thing. If any of these demagogue dictators issues a warrant for your arrest or even an order for your execution, you will be arrested and shot the moment you set foot in their country. You may even be kidnapped and carried there: remember Napoleon and the Duc d'Enghien. But if you issue a warrant or pronounce a sentence against one of them Europe will just laugh at you, because you have no power. It will be as futile as a decree of excommunication.

JUDGE. Would you like to be excommunicated?

SIR O. Hardly a serious question, is it?

JUDGE. Very serious.

SIR O. My dear sir, it couldnt happen.

JUDGE. Pardon me: it could.

SIR O. [*obstinately*] Pardon me: it couldnt. Look at the thing practically. To begin with I am not a Roman Catholic. I am a member of the Church of England; and down at my place in the country the Church living is in my gift. Without my subscription the churchwardens could not make both ends meet. The rector has no society except what he gets in my house.

JUDGE. The rector is a freeholder. If you are a notoriously evil liver, he can refuse to admit you to Communion.

SIR O. But I am not a notoriously evil liver. If the rector suggested such a thing I should have him out of his rectory and in a lunatic asylum before the end of the week.

JUDGE. Suppose the rector were prepared to risk that! Suppose the war of 1914 were renewed, and you were responsible for sending the young men of your country to drop bombs on the capital cities of Europe! Suppose your rector, as a Christian priest, took the view that you were in a condition of mortal sin and refused you Communion! Suppose, if you wish, that you had him locked up as a lunatic! Would you like it?

SIR O. Suppose the villagers burnt down his rectory

and ducked him in the horse pond to teach him a little British patriotism! How would he like it?

JUDGE. Martyrdom has its attractions for some natures. But my question was not whether he would like it, but whether you would like it.

SIR O. I should treat it with contempt.

JUDGE. No doubt; but would you like it?

SIR O. Oh, come! Really! Really!

JUDGE. Believe me, Sir Midlander, you would not like it. And if the International Court, moved by the Committee for Intellectual Co-operation, were to deliver an adverse judgment on you, you would not like it. The man whom the Hague condemns will be an uncomfortable man. The State which it finds to be in the wrong will be an uncomfortable State.

SIR O. But you cant enforce anything. You have no sanctions.

JUDGE. What, exactly, do you mean by sanctions, Sir Midlander?

SIR O. I mean what everybody means. Sanctions, you know. That is plain English. Oil, for instance.

JUDGE. Castor oil?

SIR O. No no: motor oil. The stuff you run your aeroplanes on.

JUDGE. Motor oil is a sanction when you withhold it. Castor oil is a sanction when you administer it. Is there any other difference?

SIR O. [*smiling*] Well, that has never occurred to me before; but now you mention it there is certainly an analogy. But in England the castor oil business is just one of those things that are not done. Castor oil is indecent. Motor oil is all right.

JUDGE. Well, you need not fear that the Hague will resort to any other sanction than the sacredness of justice. It will affirm this sacredness and make the necessary applications. It is the business of a judge to see that there is no wrong without a remedy. Your Committee for Intellectual Co-operation has been appealed to by four persons who have suffered grievous wrongs. It has very properly referred them to the International Court. As president of that court it is my business to find a remedy for their wrongs; and I shall do so to the best of my ability even if my decisions should form the beginning of a new code of international law and be quite unprecedented.

SIR O. But, my dear sir, what practical steps do you propose to take? What steps can you take?

JUDGE. I have already taken them. I have fixed a day for the trial of the cases, and summoned the plaintiffs and defendants to attend the court.

THE SECRETARY. But the defendants are the responsible heads of sovereign States. Do you suppose for a moment that they will obey your summons?

JUDGE. We shall see. That, in fact, is the object of my experiment. We shall see. [*He rises*] And now I must ask you to excuse me. Sir Midlander: our interview has been most instructive to me as to the attitude of your country. Mr Secretary: you are very good to have spared me so much of your valuable time. Good afternoon, gentlemen. [*He goes out*].

SIR O. What are we to do with men like that?

THE SECRETARY. What are they going to do with us? That is the question we have to face now.

SIR O. Pooh! They cant do anything, you know, except make speeches and write articles. They are free to do that in England. British liberty is a most useful safety valve.

THE SECRETARY. I was on his honor's side myself once, until my official experience here taught me how hopeless it is to knock supernationalism—

SIR O. Super what? Did you say supernaturalism?

THE SECRETARY. No. Supernationalism.

SIR O. Oh, I see. Internationalism.

THE SECRETARY. No. Internationalism is nonsense. Pushing all the nations into Geneva is like throwing all the fishes into the same pond: they just begin eating oneanother. We need something higher than nationalism: a genuine political and social catholicism. How are you to get that from these patriots, with their national anthems and flags and dreams of war and conquest rubbed into them from their childhood? The organization of nations is the organization of world war. If two men want to fight how do you prevent them? By keeping them apart, not by bringing them together. When the nations kept apart war was an occasional and exceptional thing: now the League hangs over Europe like a perpetual warcloud.

SIR O. Well, dont throw it at my head as if I disagreed with you.

THE SECRETARY. I beg your pardon. I am worried by this crisis. Let us talk business. What are we to do with Begonia Brown?

SIR O. Do with her! Squash her, impudent little slut. She is nobody: she doesnt matter.

The conversation is abruptly broken by the irruption of Begonia herself in a state of ungovernable excitement.

BEGONIA. Have you heard the news? [*Seeing Sir Orpheus*] Oh, I beg your pardon: I didnt know you were engaged.

THE SECRETARY. This is Sir Orpheus Midlander, the British Foreign Secretary, Miss Brown.

BEGONIA. Oh, most pleased to meet you, Sir Orpheus. I know your nephew. We are quite dear friends [*she shakes Sir O.'s hand effusively*]. Have you heard the news? Lord Middlesex is dead.

SIR O. Indeed? Let me see. Middlesex? I dont attach any significance to the news. He must have been a backwoodsman. Remind me about him.

BEGONIA. His son is Lord Newcross.

SIR O. Oh! Then Newcross goes to the Lords to succeed his father. That means a by-election in Camberwell.

BEGONIA. Yes; and the Conservatives want me to stand.

BOTH GENTLEMEN. What!!!

BEGONIA. Dont you think I ought to? I have been a lot in the papers lately. It's six hundred a year for me if I get in. I shall be the patriotic candidate; and the Labor vote will be a split vote; for the Communists are putting up a candidate against the Labor man; and the Liberals are contesting the seat as well. It will be just a walk-over for me.

SIR O. But my nephew is the Government candidate. Has he not told you so?

BEGONIA. Oh, thats quite all right. He has withdrawn and proposed me. He'll pay my election expenses.

SIR O. I thought he was in Singapore.

BEGONIA. So he is. It's all been done by cable. Ive just this minute heard it. You see, dear Billikins is not very bright; and he'd better not be here to muddle everything up. [*She sits*].

SIR O. But will his committee accept you?

BEGONIA. Only too glad to get a candidate that will do them credit. You see, no matter how carefully they coached Bill for the public meetings he made the most awful exhibition of himself. And he knew it, poor lamb, and would never have gone in for it if his mother hadnt made him.

SIR O. And do you think you will be able to make a

better impression at the meetings? You are not a politician, are you?

BEGONIA. The same as anybody else, I suppose. I shall pick up all the politics I need when I get into the House; and I shall get into the House because there are lots of people in Camberwell who think as I do. You bet I shall romp in at the head of the poll. I am quite excited about it. [*To the Secretary*] You were so kind to me just now that I thought you had a right to know before anyone else. [*To Sir O.*] And it's splendid news for the Government, isnt it, Sir Orpheus?

SIR O. Thrilling, Miss Brown.

BEGONIA. Oh, do call me Begonia. We're as good as related, arnt we?

SIR O. I am afraid so.

BEGONIA. I am sure to get in, arnt I?

SIR O. If your three opponents are foolish enough to go to the poll, it's a cert.

BEGONIA. Yes: isnt it? I wonder would you mind lending me my fare to London. I dont like taking money off Billikins. I will pay you when my ship comes home: the six hundred a year, you know.

SIR O. Will a five pound note be any use [*he produces one*]?

BEGONIA [*taking it*] Thanks ever so much: itll just see me through. And now I must toddle off to my little constituency. I have barely time to pack for the night train. Goodbye, Mr Secretary [*They shake hands*]; and [*to Sir O. effusively*] thanks ever so much, and au revoir. [*She goes out*].

THE SECRETARY. What an amazing young woman! You really think she will get in?

SIR O. Of course she will. She has courage, sincerity, good looks, and big publicity as the Geneva heroine. Everything that our voters love.

THE SECRETARY. But she hasnt a political idea in her head.

SIR O. She need not have. The Whips will pilot her through the division lobby until she knows the way. She need not know anything else.

THE SECRETARY. But she is a complete ignoramus. She will give herself away every time she opens her mouth.

SIR O. Not at all. She will say pluckily and sincerely just what she feels and thinks. You heard her say that there are lots of people in Camberwell who feel and think as she does. Well, the House of Commons is exactly like Camberwell in that respect.

THE SECRETARY. But can you contemplate such a state of things without dismay?

SIR O. Of course I can. I contemplated my nephew's candidature without dismay.

THE SECRETARY. The world is mad. Quite mad.

SIR O. Pooh! you need a cup of tea. Nothing wrong with the world: nothing whatever.

THE SECRETARY [*resignedly sitting down and speaking into the telephone*] Tea for two, please.

ACT III

Afternoon in the lounge of a fashionable restaurant overlooking the Lake of Geneva. Three tea tables, with two chairs at each, are in view. There is a writing table against the wall. The Secretary is seated at the centre table, reading a magazine. The American journalist comes in flourishing a cablegram.

THE JOURNALIST. Heard the news, boss?
THE SECRETARY. What news? Anything fresh from the Hague?
THE JOURNALIST. Yes. The International Court has abolished Intellectual Co-operation [*he seats himself at the next table on the Secretary's left*].
THE SECRETARY. What!
THE JOURNALIST. They have had enough of it. The Court also finds the big Powers guilty of flagrant contempt of the League Covenant.
THE SECRETARY. So they are, of course. But the League was doing as well as could be expected until Dame Begonia took a hand in it. By the way, have you heard the latest about her?
THE JOURNALIST. No. She has dropped me completely since she became a Dame of the British Empire.
THE SECRETARY. Well, at a fashion demonstration in the Albert Hall, some blackshirt thought it would be a good joke to pretend to forget her name and call her Mongolia Muggins. Sixteen newspapers quoted this; and Begonia took an action against every one of them.

They settled with her for three hundred apiece. Begonia must have netted at least four thousand.

THE JOURNALIST. And to think I might have married that girl if only I had had the foresight to push myself on her!

THE SECRETARY. Ah! A great opportunity missed: she would have made a most comfortable wife. Pleasant-looking, good-natured, able to see everything within six inches of her nose and nothing beyond. A domestic paragon: a political idiot. In short, an ideal wife.

The widow enters on the arm of Sir Orpheus Midlander. She still carries her handbag, heavy with the weight of her pistol.

SIR O. I assure you, señora, this is the only place in Geneva where you can be perfectly happy after a perfect tea.

THE WIDOW. It is easy for you to be happy. But think of this weight continually hanging on my arm, and reminding me at every moment of my tragic destiny.

SIR O. Oh, you must allow me to carry it for you. I had no idea it was heavy. Do you keep all your money in it?

THE WIDOW. Money! No: it is this [*she takes the weapon from it and throws it on the nearest table on the Secretary's right. The pair seat themselves there*].

SIR O. Good gracious! What do you carry that for? It is against the law in Geneva.

THE WIDOW. There is no longer any law in Geneva. The Hague has abolished the Intellectual Committee, leaving my husband's murder still unexpiated. That throws me back on the blood feud. Properly this is the business of my son. I cabled him to shoot the usurping president at once. But the boy is a shameless dastard.

SIR O. A bastard!

THE WIDOW. No: I wish he were: he has disgraced

me. A dastard, a coward. He has become a Communist, and pretends that the blood feud is a bourgeois tradition, contrary to the teachings of Karl Marx.

SIR O. Well, so much the better. I can hardly believe that Marx taught anything so entirely reasonable and proper as that it is wrong to shoot a president; but if he did I must say I agree with him.

THE WIDOW. But public opinion in the Earthly Paradise would never tolerate such a monstrous violation of natural justice as leaving the murder of a father unavenged. If our relatives could be murdered with impunity we should have people shooting them all over the place. Even cousins five times removed have to be avenged if they have no nearer relative to take on that duty.

SIR O. Dear me! But if your son wont, he wont; and there is an end to it. A very happy end, if I may say so.

THE WIDOW. An end of it! Nothing of the sort. If my son will not shoot the president, I shall have to do it myself. The president has two brothers who will shoot me unless I stay in this ghastly Europe instead of returning to my beloved Earthly Paradise.

SIR O. To me as an Englishman, all this seems ridiculous. You really need not shoot him.

THE WIDOW. You dont know how strong public opinion is in the Earthly Paradise. You couldnt live there if you defied it. And then there is my own sense of right and wrong. You mustnt think I have no conscience.

SIR O. People have such extraordinary consciences when they have not been educated at an English public school! [*To the secretary*] Talking of that, have you read the Prime Minister's speech in the debate on the League last night?

THE SECRETARY [*illhumoredly*] Yes. Half about Harrow as a nursery for statesmen, and the other half about the sacredness of treaties. He might have shewn some consideration for me.

SIR O. But, my dear fellow, in what way could his speech have possibly hurt you? He has made that speech over and over again. You know very well that after a certain age a man has only one speech. And you have never complained before.

THE SECRETARY. Well, he had better get a new speech, and stop talking about the sacredness of treaties. Will you fellows in London never take the trouble to read the Covenant of the League? It entirely abolishes the sacredness of treaties. Article 26 expressly provides for the revision and amendment both of the treaties and the League itself.

SIR O. But how can that be? Surely the League was created to see the Treaty of Versailles carried out. With what other object would we have joined it?

THE SECRETARY [*desperately*] Oh, there is no use talking to you. You all come here to push your own countries without the faintest notion of what the League is for; and I have to sit here listening to foreign ministers explaining to me that their countries are the greatest countries in the world and their people God's chosen race. You are supposed to be international statesmen; but none of you could keep a coffee stall at Limehouse because you would have to be equally civil to sailors of all nations.

SIR O. Nerves, my dear boy, nerves. I sometimes feel like that myself. I tell my wife I am sick of the whole business, and am going to resign; but the mood passes.

The Jew enters, in animated conversation with the quondam newcomer. The rest become discreetly silent, but keep their ears open.

THE JEW. My good sir, what is your grievance compared to mine? Have you been robbed? Have you been battered with clubs? gassed? massacred? Have you been commercially and socially ruined? Have you been imprisoned in concentration camps commanded by hooligans? Have you been driven out of your country to starve in exile?

THE NEWCOMER. No; but if the people vote for it there is no violation of democratic principle in it. Your people voted ten to one for getting rid of the Jews. Hadnt they the right to choose the sort of people they would allow to live in their own country? Look at the British! Will they allow a yellow man into Australia? Look at the Americans! Will they let a Jap into California? See what happened to the British Government in 1906 when it wanted to let Chinese labor into Lancashire!

THE JEW. Your own country! Who made you a present of a piece of God's earth?

THE NEWCOMER. I was born on it, wasnt I?

THE JEW. And was not I born in the country from which I have been cast out?

THE NEWCOMER. You oughtnt to have been born there. You ought to have been born in Jerusalem.

THE JEW. And you, my friend, ought never to have been born at all. You claim a right to shut me out of the world; but you burn with indignation because you yourself have been shut out of your trumpery little parliament.

THE NEWCOMER. Easy! easy! dont lose your temper. I dont want to shut you out of the world: all I say is that you are not in the world on democratic principles; but I ought to be in parliament on democratic principles. If I shoot a Jew, thats murder; and I ought to be hanged for it. But if I vote for a Jew, as I often have, and he is elected and then not let into Parliament, what becomes of democracy?

THE JEW. The question is not what becomes of democracy but what becomes of you? You are not less rich, less happy, less secure, less well or badly governed because you are making speeches outside your Parliament House instead of inside it. But to me the persecution is a matter of life and death.

THE NEWCOMER. It's a bit hard on you, I admit. But it's not a matter of principle.

THE WIDOW [*to the Jew*] Do you know what I would do if I were a president?

THE JEW. No, madam. But it would interest me to hear it.

THE WIDOW. I would shoot every Jew in the country: that is what I would do.

THE JEW. Pray why?

THE WIDOW. Because they crucified my Savior: that is why. I am a religious woman; and when I meet a God murderer I can hardly keep my hands off my gun.

THE JEW. After all, madam, your Savior was a Jew.

THE WIDOW. Oh, what a horrible blasphemy! [*she reaches for her pistol*].

Sir Orpheus seizes her wrist. The Secretary secures her left arm.

THE WIDOW [*struggling*] Let me go. How dare you touch me? If you were Christians you would help me to kill this dirty Jew. Did you hear what he said?

SIR O. Yes, yes, señora: I heard. I assure you he did not mean to blaspheme. Ethnologically, you know, he was right. Only ethnologically, of course.

THE WIDOW. I do not understand that long word. Our Savior and his Virgin Mother were good Catholics, were they not?

SIR O. No doubt, señora, no doubt. We are all good Catholics, I hope, in a sense. You will remember that our Savior was of the house of King David.

THE WIDOW. You will be telling me next that King David was a Jew, I suppose.

SIR O. Well, ethnologically—

THE WIDOW. Eth no fiddlesticks. Give me my gun.

SIR O. I think you had better let me carry it for you, señora. You shall have it when this gentleman has gone.

THE NEWCOMER. Give it to the police. That woman is not safe.

THE WIDOW. I spit upon you.

SIR O. The police would arrest her for carrying arms.

THE WIDOW. Three men and a Jew against one disarmed woman! Cowards.

THE JEW. Fortunate for you, madam, and for me. But for these three gentlemen you would soon be awaiting death at the hands of the public executioner; and I should be a corpse.

THE JOURNALIST. A cadaver. Put it nicely. A cadaver.

THE WIDOW. Do you believe that any jury would find me guilty for ridding the world of a Jew?

THE JEW. One can never be quite certain, madam. If there were women on the jury, or some Jews, your good looks might not save you.

THE WIDOW. Women on juries are an abomination. Only a Jew could mention such a thing to a lady [*she gives up the struggle and resumes her seat*].

The Commissar comes in with Begonia and the Judge, of whom she has evidently made a conquest.

BEGONIA [*to the Secretary*] Good evening, boss. Cheerio, Sir Orpheus. You remember me, señora. You know the judge, boss.

THE SECRETARY. Do me the honor to share my table, your honor.

THE JUDGE. Thank you. May I introduce Commissar Posky. [*He seats himself on the Secretary's left*].

THE SECRETARY. We have met. Pray be seated.

THE JOURNALIST. Take my place, Commissar. I must get on with my work. [*He retires to the writing table, where he sits and sets to work writing his press messages, withdrawing from the conversation, but keeping his ears open*].

THE COMMISSAR [*taking the vacated seat beside the Newcomer*] I thank you.

THE SECRETARY. There is room for you here, Dame Begonia [*indicating chair on his right*].

BEGONIA [*taking it*] There is always room at the top.

THE COMMISSAR. I represent the Soviet.

THE WIDOW [*exploding again*] Another Jew!!!

THE SECRETARY. No, no. You have Jews on the brain.

THE WIDOW. He is a Bolshevist. All Bolshevists are Jews. Do you realize that if I lived under the horrible tyranny of the Soviet I should be shot?

THE JEW. I take that to be a very striking proof of the superior civilization of Russia.

THE COMMISSAR. Why should we shoot her, comrade?

THE JEW. She has just tried to shoot me.

THE COMMISSAR. We do not shoot Jews as such: we civilize them. You see, a Communist State is only possible for highly civilized people, trained to Communism from their childhood. The people we shoot are gangsters and speculators and exploiters and scoundrels of all sorts who are encouraged in other countries in the name of liberty and democracy.

THE NEWCOMER [*starting up*] Not a word against liberty and democracy in my presence! Do you hear?

THE COMMISSAR. And not a word against Communism in mine. Agreed?

THE NEWCOMER [*sits down sulkily*] Oh, all right.

THE COMMISSAR [*continuing*] I find it very difficult to accustom myself to the exaggerated importance you all attach to sex in these western countries. This handsome lady, it seems, has some lover's quarrel with this handsome gentleman.

THE WIDOW. A lover's quarrel!!!

THE COMMISSAR. In the U.S.S.R. that would be a triviality. At the very worst it would end in a divorce. But here she tries to shoot him.

THE WIDOW. You are mad. And divorce is a deadly sin: only Bolsheviks and Protestants would allow such an infamy. They will all go to hell for it. As to my loving this man, I hate, loathe, and abhor him. He would steal my child and cut it in pieces and sprinkle its blood on his threshold. He is a Jew.

THE COMMISSAR. Come to Russia. Jews do not do such things there. No doubt they are capable of anything when they are corrupted by Capitalism.

THE JEW. Lies! lies! Excuses for robbing and murdering us.

THE COMMISSAR. For that, comrade, one excuse is as good as another. I am not a Jew; but the lady may shoot me because I am a Communist.

THE WIDOW. How can I shoot you? They have stolen my gun. Besides, shooting Communists is not a religious duty but a political one; and in my country women do not meddle in politics.

THE COMMISSAR. Then I am safe.

BEGONIA [*recovering from her astonishment at the shooting conversation*] But dont you know, señora, that you mustnt go about shooting people here? It may be all right in your country; but here it isnt done.

THE WIDOW. Where I am is my country. What is right in my country cannot be wrong in yours.

SIR O. Ah, if you were a Foreign Secretary—

THE SECRETARY. If you were the secretary of the League of Nations—

SIR O. You would make the curious discovery that one nation's right is another nation's wrong. There is only one way of reconciling all the nations in a real league, and that is to convert them all to English ideas.

THE COMMISSAR. But all the world is in revolt against English ideas, especially the English themselves. The future is for Russian ideas.

THE NEWCOMER. Where did Russia get her ideas? From England. In Russia Karl Marx would have been sent to Siberia and flogged to death. In England he was kept in the British Museum at the public expense and let write what he liked. England is the country where, as the poet says, "A man may say the thing he wills—"

THE JUDGE. Pardon me: that is an illusion. I have gone into that question; and I can assure you that when the British Government is alarmed there are quite as many prosecutions for sedition, blasphemy and obscenity as in any other country. The British Government has just passed a new law under which any person obnoxious to the Government can be imprisoned for opening his mouth or dipping his pen in the ink.

SIR O. Yes; but whose fault is that? Your Russian propaganda. Freedom of thought and speech is the special glory of Britain; but surely you dont expect us to allow your missionaries to preach Bolshevism, do you?

THE COMMISSAR [*laughing*] I dont expect any government to tolerate any doctrine that threatens its existence or the incomes of its rulers. The only difference is that in Russia we dont pretend to tolerate such doctrines; and in England you do. Why do you give yourselves that unnecessary and dangerous trouble?

THE NEWCOMER. Karl Marx was tolerated in England: he wouldnt have been tolerated in Russia.

THE COMMISSAR. That was a weakness in the British system, not a virtue. If the British Government had known and understood what Marx was doing, and what its effect was going to be on the mind of the world, it would have sent him to prison and destroyed every scrap of his handwriting and every copy of his books. But they did not know where to strike. They persecuted poor men for making profane jokes; they suppressed newspapers in England as well as in Ireland; they dismissed editors who were too independent and outspoken; they burnt the books of novelists who had gone a little too far in dealing with sex; they imprisoned street corner speakers on charges of obstructing traffic; and all the time they were providing Karl Marx with the finest reading room in the world whilst he was writing their death warrants.

SIR O. Those warrants have not yet been executed in England. They never will be. The world may be jolted out of its tracks for a moment by the shock of a war as a railway train may be thrown off the rails; but it soon settles into its old grooves. You are a Bolshevik; but nobody would know it. You have the appearance, the dress, the culture of a gentleman: your clothes might have been made within half a mile of Hanover Square.

THE COMMISSAR. As a matter of fact they were: I buy them in London.

SIR O. [*triumphant*] You see! You have given up all this Marxian nonsense and gone back to the capitalist system. I always said you would.

THE COMMISSAR. If it pleases you to think so, Sir Orpheus, I shall do nothing to disturb your happiness. Will you be so good as to convey to your Government my great regret and that of the Soviet Cabinet that your bishop should have died of his personal contact with Russian ideas. I blame myself for not having been more considerate. But I had never met that kind of man before. The only other British Bishop I had met was nearly seven feet high, an athlete, and a most revolutionary preacher.

SIR O. That is what makes the Church of England so easy to deal with. No types. Just English gentlemen. Not like Catholic priests.

THE WIDOW. Oh, Sir Orpheus! You, of all men, to insult my faith!

SIR O. Not at all, not at all, I assure you. I have the greatest respect for the Catholic faith. But you cannot deny that your priests have a professional air. They are not like other men. Our English clergy are not like that. You would not know that they were clergy at all if it were not for their collars.

THE WIDOW. I call that wicked. A priest should not be like other men.

THE COMMISSAR. Have you ever tried to seduce a priest, madam?

THE WIDOW. Give me my gun. This is monstrous. Have Bolsheviks no decency?

THE NEWCOMER. I knew a priest once who—

THE SECRETARY. No, please. The subject is a dangerous one.

THE COMMISSAR. All subjects are dangerous in Geneva, are they not?

THE JUDGE. Pardon me. It is not the subjects that are dangerous in Geneva, but the people.

THE WIDOW. Jews! Bolsheviks! Gunmen!

THE JEW. What about gunwomen? Gunmolls they are called in America. Pardon my reminding you.

THE WIDOW. You remind me of nothing that I can decently mention.

THE NEWCOMER. Hullo, maam! You know, ladies dont say things like that in my country.

THE WIDOW. They do in mine. What I have said I have said.

THE JUDGE. When the International Court was moved to action by the enterprise of my friend Dame Begonia, it found that the moment the League of Nations does anything on its own initiative and on principle, it produces, not peace, but threats of war or secession or both which oblige it to stop hastily and do nothing until the Great Powers have decided among themselves to make use of it as an instrument of their oldfashioned diplomacy. That is true, Mr Secretary, is it not?

THE SECRETARY. It is too true. Yet it is not altogether true. Those who think the League futile dont know what goes on here. They dont know what Geneva means to us. The Powers think we are nothing but their catspaw. They flout us openly by ignoring the Covenant and making unilateral treaties that should be made by us. They have driven us underground as if we were a criminal conspiracy. But in little ways of which the public knows nothing we sidetrack them. We sabotage them. We shame them. We make things difficult or impossible that used to be easy. You dont know what the atmosphere of Geneva is. When I came here I was a patriot, a Nationalist, regarding my appointment as a win for my own country in the diplomatic game. But the atmosphere of Geneva changed me. I am now an Internationalist. I am the ruthless enemy of every nation, my own included. Let me be frank. I hate the lot of you.

ALL THE OTHERS. Oh!

THE SECRETARY. Yes I do. You the Jew there: I hate you because you are a Jew.

THE JEW. A German Jew.

THE SECRETARY. Worse and worse. Two nationalities are worse than one. This gunwoman here: I hate her because she is heaven knows what mixture of Spaniard and Indian and savage.

THE WIDOW. Men with red blood in them do not hate me.

THE SECRETARY. You, Sir Orpheus, are an amiable and honest man. Well, I never hear you talking politics without wanting to shoot you.

SIR O. Dear me! Fortunately I have the lady's gun in my pocket. But of course I dont believe you.

THE SECRETARY. If you had the Geneva spirit you would believe me. This Russian here: I hate him because his Government has declared for Socialism in a single country.

THE COMMISSAR. You are a Trotskyite then?

THE SECRETARY. Trotsky is nothing to me; but I hate all frontiers; and you have shut yourself into frontiers.

THE COMMISSAR. Only because infinite space is too much for us to manage. Be reasonable.

THE SECRETARY. On this subject I am not reasonable. I am sick of reasonable people: they see all the reasons for being lazy and doing nothing.

THE NEWCOMER. And what price me? Come on. Dont leave me out.

THE SECRETARY. You! You are some sort of half-Americanized colonist. You are a lower middle-class politician. Your pose is that of the rugged individualist, the isolationist, at bottom an Anarchist.

THE NEWCOMER. Anarchist yourself. Anyhow I have more common sense than you: I dont hate all my fellow creatures.

THE SECRETARY. You are all enemies of the human race. You are all armed to the teeth and full of patriotism. Your national heroes are all brigands and pirates. When it comes to the point you are all cut-throats. But Geneva will beat you yet. Not in my time, perhaps. But the Geneva spirit is a fact; and a spirit is a fact that cannot be killed.

ALL THE REST. But—

THE SECRETARY [*shouting them down*] I am not going to argue with you: you are all too damnably stupid.

SIR O. Are you sure you are quite well this afternoon? I have always believed in you and supported you as England's truest friend at Geneva.

THE SECRETARY. You were quite right. I am the truest friend England has here. I am the truest friend of all the Powers if they only knew it. That is the strength of my position here. Each of you thinks I am on his side. If you hint that I am mad or drunk I shall hint that you are going gaga and that it is time for the British Empire to find a younger Foreign Secretary.

SIR O. Gaga!!!

THE SECRETARY. I cannot afford to lose my job here. Do not force me to fight you with your own weapons in defence of my hardearned salary.

THE WIDOW [*to Sir O.*] The best weapon is in your hands. You stole it from me. In my country he would now be dead at your feet with as many holes drilled through him as there are bullets in the clip.

THE SECRETARY. In your country, señora, I might have fired first.

THE WIDOW. What matter! In either case honor would be satisfied.

THE SECRETARY. Honor! The stock excuse for making a corpse.

THE JOURNALIST. A cadaver.

THE WIDOW. Thank you.

THE SECRETARY. A slovenly unhandsome corse. I am quoting Shakespear.

THE WIDOW. Then Shakespear, whoever he may be, is no gentleman.

THE SECRETARY. Judge: you hear what we have to contend with here. Stupidity upon stupidity. Geneva is expected to make a league of nations out of political blockheads.

THE JUDGE. I must rule this point against you. These people are not stupid. Stupid people have nothing to say for themselves: these people have plenty to say for themselves. Take Sir Midlander here for example. If you tell me he is stupid the word has no meaning.

SIR O. Thank you, my dear Judge, thank you. But for Heaven's sake dont call me clever or I shall be defeated at the next election. I have the greatest respect for poetry and the fine arts and all that sort of thing; but please understand that I am not an intellectual. A plain Englishman doing my duty to my country according to my poor lights.

THE JUDGE. Still, doing it with ability enough to have attained Cabinet rank in competition with hundreds of other successful and ambitious competitors.

SIR O. I assure you I am not ambitious. I am not competitive. I happen to be fairly well off; but the money was made by my grandfather. Upon my honor I dont know how I got landed where I am. I am quite an ordinary chap really.

THE JUDGE. Then you have risen by sheer natural ordinary superiority. However, do not be alarmed: all

I claim for the purposes of my argument is that you are not a born fool.

SIR O. Very good of you to say so. Well, I will let it go at that.

THE JUDGE. At the other extreme, take the case of this passionate and attractive lady, whose name I have not the pleasure of knowing.

THE JEW. Try Dolores.

THE WIDOW. I suppose you think you are insulting me. You are simply making a fool of yourself. My name is Dolores.

SIR O. I guessed it, señora. In my undergraduate days I used to quote Oscar Wilde's famous poem.

> "We are fain of thee still, we are fain.
> O sanguine and subtle Dolores
> Our Lady of pain."

THE JOURNALIST. Swinburne, Sir Orpheus.

SIR O. Was it Swinburne? Well, it does not matter: it was one of the literary set.

THE WIDOW. It sounds well; but English is not my native language. I do not understand the first line. "We are fain of thee still: we are fain." What does fain mean?

SIR O. Ah well, never mind, señora, never mind. We are interrupting his honor the Judge. [*To the Judge*] You were about to say—?

THE JUDGE. I was about to point out that whatever is the matter with this lady it is not stupidity. She speaks several languages. Her intelligence is remarkable: she takes a point like lightning. She has in her veins the learning of the Arabs, the courage and enterprise of the Spanish conquistadores, the skyward aspiration of the Aztecs, the selfless devotion to divine purposes of the Jesuit missionaries, and the readiness of them all to face death in what she conceives to be her social duty. If we have been actually obliged to disarm her to prevent her from sacrificing this harmless Jewish gentleman as her ancestors would have sacrificed him to the God Quetzalcoatl on the stepped altars of Mexico, it is not because she is stupid.

THE WIDOW. I hardly follow you, however intelligent you may think me. But I am proud of having Aztec blood in my veins, though I should never dream of insulting Quetzalcoatl by sacrificing a Jew to him.

THE JUDGE. As to the Jewish gentleman himself, I need not dwell on his case as he has been driven out of his native country solely because he is so thoughtful and industrious that his fellow-countrymen are hopelessly beaten by him in the competition for the conduct of business and for official positions. I come to our democratic friend here. I do not know what his business is—

THE NEWCOMER. I'm a retired builder if you want to know.

THE JUDGE. He has had ability enough to conduct a builder's business with such success that he has been able to retire at his present age, which cannot be far above fifty.

THE NEWCOMER. I am no millionaire, mind you. I have just enough to do my bit on the Borough Council, and fight the enemies of democracy.

THE JUDGE. Precisely. That is the spirit of Geneva. What you lack is not mind but knowledge.

THE NEWCOMER. My wife says I'm pigheaded. How is that for a testimonial?

THE JUDGE. A first rate one, sir. Pigs never waver in their convictions, never give in to bribes, arguments, nor persuasions. At all events you are wise enough to be dissatisfied with the existing world order, and as anxious to change it as anybody in Geneva.

THE NEWCOMER. The world's good enough for me. Democracy is what I want. We were all for democracy when only the privileged few had votes. But now that everybody has a vote, women and all, where's democracy? Dictators all over the place! and me, an elected representative, kept out of parliament by the police!

THE JUDGE. I come to our Russian friend. He must be a man of ability, or he could not be a Commissar in a country where nothing but ability counts. He has no fears for the future, whereas we are distracted by the continual dread of war, of bankruptcy, of poverty. But there is no evidence that he is a superman. Twenty years ago he would have been talking as great nonsense as any of you.

THE REST [*except the Russian and Begonia*] Nonsense!

THE JUDGE. Perhaps I should have said folly; for folly is not nonsensical: in fact the more foolish it is, the more logical, the more subtle, the more eloquent, the more brilliant.

SIR O. True. True. I have known men who could hold the House of Commons spellbound for hours; but most unsafe. Mere entertainers.

BEGONIA. My turn now, I suppose. I see you are looking at me. Well, all politics are the same to me: I never could make head or tail of them. But I draw the line at Communism and atheism and nationalization of women and doing away with marriage and the family and everybody stealing everybody's property and having to work like slaves and being shot if you breathe a word against it all.

THE JUDGE. You are intelligent enough, well-meaning enough, to be against such a state of things, Dame Begonia, are you?

BEGONIA. Well, of course I am. Wouldnt anybody?

THE JUDGE. It does you the greatest credit.

THE COMMISSAR. But allow me to remark—

THE JUDGE. Not now, Mr. Posky, or you will spoil my point, which is that Dame Begonia's sympathies and intentions are just the same as yours.

BEGONIA. Oh! I never said so. I hate his opinions.

THE COMMISSAR. I must protest. The lady is a bourgeoise: I am a Communist. How can there be the smallest sympathy between us? She upholds the dictatorship of the capitalist, I the dictatorship of the proletariat.

THE JUDGE. Never mind your opinions: I am dealing with the facts. It is evident that the lady is wrong as to the facts, because the inhabitants of a country conducted as she supposes Russia to be conducted would all be dead in a fortnight. It is evident also that her ignorance of how her own country is conducted is as complete as her ignorance of Russia. None of you seem to have any idea of the sort of world you are living in. Into the void created by this ignorance has been heaped a groundwork of savage superstitions: human sacrifices, vengeance, wars of conquest and religion, falsehoods called history, and a glorification of vulgar erotics and pugnacity called romance which transforms people who are naturally as amiable, as teachable, as companionable as dogs, into the most ferocious and cruel of all the beasts. And this, they say, is human nature! But it is not natural at all: real human nature is in continual conflict with it; for amid all the clamor for more slaughter and the erection of monuments to the great slaughterers the cry for justice, for mercy, for fellowship, for peace, has never been completely silenced: even the worst villainies must pretend to be committed for its sake.

SIR O. Too true: oh, too true. But we must take the world as we find it.

THE JUDGE. Wait a bit. How do you find the world? You find it sophisticated to the verge of suicidal insanity. This makes trouble for you as Foreign Secretary. Why not cut out the sophistication? Why not bring your economics, your religion, your history, your political philosophy up to date? Russia has made a gigantic effort to do this; and now her politicians are only about fifty years behind her philosophers and saints whilst the rest of the civilized world is from five hundred to five thousand behind it. In the west the vested interests in ignorance and superstition are so overwhelming that no teacher can tell his young pupils the truth without finding himself starving in the street. The result is that here we despair of human nature, whereas Russia has hopes that have carried her through the most appalling sufferings to the forefront of civilization. Then why despair of human nature when it costs us so much trouble to corrupt it? Why not stop telling it lies? Are we not as capable of that heroic feat as the Russians?

THE COMMISSAR. Apparently not. There are qualities which are produced on the Russian soil alone. There may be a future for the western world if it accepts the guidance of Moscow; but left to its childish self it will decline and fall like all the old capitalist civilizations.

SIR O. Let me tell you, Mr Posky, that if ever England takes to Communism, which heaven forbid, it will make a first-rate job of it. Downing Street will not take its orders from Moscow. Moscow took all its ideas from England, as this gentleman has told you. My grandfather bought sherry from John Ruskin's father; and very good sherry it was. And John

Ruskin's gospel compared with Karl Marx's was like boiling brandy compared with milk and water.

THE JEW. Yes; but as the British would not listen to Ruskin he produced nothing. The race whose brains will guide the world to the new Jerusalem is the race that produced Karl Marx, who produced Soviet Russia.

THE JUDGE. Race! Nonsense! You are all hopeless mongrels pretending to be thoroughbreds. Why not give up pretending?

SIR O. I am not pretending. I am an Englishman: an Englishman from the heart of England.

THE JUDGE. You mean a British islander from Birmingham, the choicest breed of mongrels in the world. You should be proud of your cross-fertilization.

SIR O. At least I am not a Frenchman nor a negro.

THE JUDGE. At least you are not a Scot, nor an Irishman, nor a man of Kent, nor a man of Devon, nor a Welshman—

SIR O. One of my grandmothers was a Welsh girl. Birmingham is nearer the Welsh border than a Cockney concentration camp like London.

THE JUDGE. In short, you are a mongrel.

THE WIDOW. What is a mongrel? I thought it was a cheap kind of dog.

THE JUDGE. So it is, madam. I applied the word figuratively to a cheap kind of man: that is, to an enormous majority of the human race. It simply indicates mixed ancestry.

THE WIDOW. Ah, that is the secret of the unique distinction of the upper class in the Earthly Paradise. My blood is a blend of all that is noblest in history: the Maya, the Aztec, the Spaniard, the Mexican, the—

THE SECRETARY [*flinging away his pen, with which he*

has been making notes of the discussion]. You see, Judge. If you knock all this nonsense of belonging to superior races out of them, they only begin to brag of being choice blends of mongrel. Talk til you are black in the face: you get no good of them. In China the Manchus have given up binding the women's feet and making them cripples for life; but we still go on binding our heads and making fools of ourselves for life.

THE JUDGE. Yes, but do not forget that as lately as the nineteenth century the world believed that the Chinese could never change. Now they are the most revolutionary of all the revolutionists.

THE JEW [*to the Widow*] May I ask have you any engagement for dinner this evening?

THE WIDOW. What is that to you, pray?

THE JEW. Well, would you care to dine with me?

THE WIDOW. Dine with you! Dine with a Jew!

THE JEW. Only a Jew can appreciate your magnificent type of beauty, señora. These Nordics, as they ridiculously call themselves, adore girls who are dolls and women who are cows. But wherever the Jew dominates the theatre and the picture gallery—and he still dominates them in all the great capitals in spite of persecution—your type of beauty is supreme.

THE WIDOW. It is true. You have taste, you Jews. You have appetites. You are vital, in your oriental fashion. And you have boundless ambition and indefatigable pertinacity: you never stop asking for what you want until you possess it. But let me tell you that if you think you can possess me for the price of a dinner, you know neither your own place nor mine.

THE JEW. I ask nothing but the pleasure of your company, the luxury of admiring your beauty and experiencing your sex appeal, and the distinction of being seen in public with you as my guest.

THE WIDOW. You shall not get them. I will not accept your dinner.

THE JEW. Not even if I allow you to pay for it?

THE WIDOW. Is there any end to your impudence? I have never dined with a Jew in my life.

THE JEW. Then you do not know what a good dinner is. Come! Try dining with a Jew for the first time in your life.

THE WIDOW [*considering it*] It is true that I have nothing else to do this evening. But I must have my gun.

SIR O. [*taking the pistol from his pocket*] Well, as we seem to have got over the Anti-Semite difficulty I have no further excuse for retaining your property. [*He hands her the pistol*].

THE WIDOW [*replacing it in her handbag*] But remember. If you take the smallest liberty—if you hint at the possibility of a more intimate relation, you are a dead man.

THE JEW. You need have no fear. If there are any further advances they must come from yourself.

THE WIDOW. I could never have believed this.

BEGONIA. Geneva is like that. You find yourself dining with all sorts.

SIR O. By the way, Mr. Posky, have you anything particular to do this evening? If not, I should be glad if you would join me at dinner. I want to talk to you about this funny Russian business. You need not dress.

THE COMMISSAR. I will dress if you will allow me. They are rather particular about it now in Moscow.

BEGONIA. Well I never! Fancy a Bolshie dressing!

THE JUDGE. May I suggest, gracious Dame, that you and I dine together?

BEGONIA. Oh, I feel I am imposing on you: I have dined with you three times already. You know, I am a little afraid of you, you are so deep and learned and what I call mental. I may be a Dame of the British Empire and all that; but I am not the least bit mental; and what attraction you can find in my conversation I cant imagine.

THE SECRETARY. Geneva is so full of mental people that it is an inexpressible relief to meet some cheerful person with absolutely no mind at all. The Judge can have his pick of a hundred clever women in Geneva; but what he needs to give his brain a rest is a soft-bosomed goose without a political idea in her pretty head.

BEGONIA. Go on: I am used to it. I know your opinion of me: I am the only perfect idiot in Geneva. But I got a move on the League; and thats more than you ever could do, you old stick-in-the-mud.

THE WIDOW. Take care, señorita! A woman should not wear her brains on her sleeve as men do. She should keep them up it. Men like to be listened to.

BEGONIA. I have listened here until I am nearly dead. Still, when men start talking you can always think of something else. They are so taken up with themselves that they dont notice it.

THE WIDOW. Do not give away the secrets of our sex, child. Be thankful, as I am, that you have made sure of your next dinner.

THE JOURNALIST. What about my dinner?

THE SECRETARY. You had better dine with me. You can tell me the latest news.

THE JUDGE. I can tell you that. The trial of the dictators by the Permanent Court of International Justice has been fixed for this day fortnight.

THE REST. Where?

THE JUDGE. At the Hague, in the old palace.

THE SECRETARY. But the trial will be a farce. The dictators wont come.

THE JUDGE. I think they will. You, Sir Orpheus, will, I presume, be present with a watching brief from the British Foreign Office.

SIR O. I shall certainly be present. Whether officially or not I cannot say.

THE JUDGE. You will all be present, I hope. May I suggest that you telephone at once to secure rooms at the Hague. If you wait until the news becomes public you may find yourselves crowded out.

All except the Judge and the Secretary rise hastily and disappear in the direction of the hotel bureau.

THE SECRETARY. You really think the dictators will walk into the dock for you?

THE JUDGE. We shall see. There will be no dock. I shall ask you to act as Clerk to the Court.

THE SECRETARY. Impossible.

THE JUDGE. It seems so now; but I think you will.

THE SECRETARY. Well, as Midlander is coming I shall certainly be there to hear what he may say. But the dictators? Bombardone? Battler? How can you make them come? You have not a single soldier. Not even a policeman.

THE JUDGE. All the soldiers and police on earth could not move them except by the neck and heels. But if the Hague becomes the centre of the European stage all the soldiers and police in the world will not keep them away from it.

THE SECRETARY [*musing*] Hm! Well—[*he shakes his head and gives it up*].

THE JUDGE [*smiles*] They will come. Where the spotlight is, there will the despots be gathered.

ACT IV

A salon in the old palace of the Hague. On a spacious dais a chair of State, which is in fact an old throne, is at the head of a table furnished with chairs, writing materials, and buttons connected with telephonic apparatus. The table occupies the centre of the dais. On the floor at both sides chairs are arranged in rows for the accommodation of spectators, litigants, witnesses, etc. The tall windows admit abundance of sunlight and shew up all the gilding and grandeur of the immovables. The door is at the side, on the right of the occupant of the chair of state, at present empty. The formal arrangement of the furniture suggests a sitting or hearing or meeting of some kind. A waste paper basket is available.

The Secretary of the League of Nations has a little central table to himself in front of the other. His profile points towards the door. Behind him, in the front row of chairs are the Jew, the Commissar and the Widow. In the opposite front row are Begonia and a cheerful young gentleman, powerfully built, with an uproarious voice which he subdues to conversational pitch with some difficulty. Next to him is the quondam Newcomer. They are all reading newspapers. Begonia and her young man have one excessively illustrated newspaper between them. He has his arm round her waist and is shamelessly enjoying their physical contact. The two are evidently betrothed.

THE JEW. Do you think anything is really going to happen, Mr Secretary?

THE SECRETARY. Possibly not. I am here to be able to report from personal knowledge whether any notice has been taken of the summonses issued by the court.

THE BETROTHED. The judge himself hasnt turned up.

THE SECRETARY [*looking at his watch*] He is not due yet: you have all come too early.

THE BETROTHED. We came early to make sure of getting seats. And theres not a soul in the bally place except ourselves.

Sir Orpheus comes in.

SIR ORPHEUS. What! Nobody but ourselves! Dont they admit the public?

THE SECRETARY. The public is not interested, it seems.

BEGONIA. One free lance journalist looked in; but she went away when she found there was nothing doing.

THE BETROTHED. The doors are open all right. All are affectionately invited.

SIR ORPHEUS [*seating himself next Begonia*] But what a dreadful fiasco for our friend the judge! I warned him that this might happen. I told him to send special invitations to the press, and cards to all the leading people and foreign visitors. And here! not a soul except ourselves! All Europe will laugh at him.

THE SECRETARY. Yes, but if the affair is going to be a fiasco the fewer people there are to witness it the better.

BEGONIA. After all, theres more than half a dozen of us. Quite a distinguished audience I call it. Remember, you are the Foreign Secretary, Nunky. You are an honorable, Billikins. And I'm not exactly a nobody.

THE BETROTHED [*kissing her hand*] My ownest and bestest, you are a Dame of the British Empire. The

Camberwell Times has celebrated your birthday by a poem hailing you as the Lily of Geneva; but on this occasion only, you are not the centre of European interest. The stupendous and colossal joke of the present proceedings is that this court has summoned all the dictators to appear before it and answer charges brought against them by the Toms, Dicks, Harriets, Susans and Elizas of all nations.

THE WIDOW. Pardon me, young señor. I am neither Susan nor Eliza.

THE BETROTHED. Present company excepted, of course, señora. But the point—the staggering paralyzing, jolly bally breath-bereaving point of our assembly today is that the dictators have been summoned and that they wont come. Young Johnny Judge has no more authority over them than his cat.

THE NEWCOMER. But if they wont come, gentlemen, what are we here for?

THE BETROTHED. To see the fun when Johnny Judge comes and finds nothing doing, I suppose.

THE WIDOW. Is he not late? We seem to have been waiting here for ages.

THE SECRETARY [*looking at his watch*] He is due now. It is on the stroke of ten.

The Judge, in his judicial robe, enters. They all rise. He is in high spirits and very genial.

THE JUDGE [*shaking hands with Sir Orpheus*] Good morning, Sir Midlander. [*He passes on to the judicial chair, greeting them as he goes*] Good morning, ladies and gentlemen. Good morning, mademoiselle. Good morning, señora. Good morning. Good morning. [*Takes his seat*] Pray be seated.

They all sit, having bowed speechlessly to his salutations.

THE JUDGE. Any defendants yet, Mr Secretary?

THE SECRETARY. None, your Honor. The parties on your left are all plaintiffs. On your right, Sir Orpheus Midlander has a watching brief for the British Foreign Office. The lady, Dame Begonia Brown, represents the Committee for Intellectual Co-operation. The young gentleman is the public.

THE JUDGE. An impartial spectator, eh?

THE BETROTHED. No, my lord. Very partial to the girl. Engaged, in fact.

THE JUDGE. My best congratulations. May I warn you all that the instruments on the table are microphones and televisors? I have arranged so as to avoid a crowd and make our proceedings as unconstrained and comfortable as possible; but our apparent privacy is quite imaginary.

General consternation. They all sit up as in church.

BEGONIA. But they should have told us this when we came in. Billikins has been sitting with his arm round my waist, whispering all sorts of silly things. Theyll be in The Camberwell Times tomorrow.

THE JUDGE. I'm sorry. You should have been warned. In the International Court no walls can hide you, and no distance deaden your lightest whisper. We are all seen and heard in Rome, in Moscow, in London, wherever the latest type of receiver is installed.

BEGONIA. Heard! You mean overheard.

THE WIDOW. And overlooked. Our very clothes are transparent to the newest rays. It is scandalous.

THE JUDGE. Not at all, señora. The knowledge that we all live in public, and that there are no longer any secret places where evil things can be done and wicked conspiracies discussed, may produce a great improvement in morals.

THE WIDOW. I protest. All things that are private are not evil; but they may be extremely indecent.

BEGONIA. We'd better change the subject, I think.

THE BETROTHED. What about the dictators, my lord? Do you really think any of them will come?

THE JUDGE. They are not under any physical compulsion to come. But every day of their lives they do things they are not physically compelled to do.

SIR ORPHEUS. That is a fact, certainly. But it is hardly a parliamentary fact.

A telephone rings on the Judge's desk. He holds down a button and listens.

THE JUDGE. You will not have to wait any longer, Sir Midlander. [*Into the telephone*] We are waiting for him. Shew him the way. [*He releases the button*]. The very first dictator to arrive is Signor Bombardone.

ALL THE REST. Bombardone!!!

The Dictator enters, dominant, brusque, every inch a man of destiny.

BOMBARDONE. Is this the so-called International Court?

THE JUDGE. It is.

BBDE. My name is Bombardone. [*He mounts the dais; takes the nearest chair with a powerful hand and places it on the Judge's left; then flings himself massively into it*] Do not let my presence embarrass you. Proceed.

THE JUDGE. I have to thank you, Signor Bombardone, for so promptly obeying the summons of the court.

BBDE. I obey nothing. I am here because it is my will to be here. My will is part of the world's will. A large part, as it happens. The world moves towards internationalism. Without this movement to nerve you you would have never have had the audacity to summon me. Your action is therefore a symptom of the movement of civilization. Wherever such a symptom can be detected I have a place: a leading place.

SIR ORPHEUS. But pardon me, Signor: I understand that you are a great nationalist: How can you be at once a nationalist and an internationalist?

BBDE. How can I be anything else? How do you build a house? By first making good sound bricks. You cant build it of mud. The nations are the bricks out of which the future world State must be built. I consolidated my country as a nation: a white nation. I then added a black nation to it and made it an empire. When the empires federate, its leaders will govern the world; and these leaders will have a superleader who will be the ablest man in the world: that is my vision. I leave you to imagine what I think of the mob of bagmen from fifty potty little foreign States that calls itself a League of Nations.

JUDGE. Your country is a member of that League, Signor.

BBDE. My country has to keep an eye on fools. The scripture tells us that it is better to meet a bear in our path than a fool. Fools are dangerous; and the so-called League of Nations is a League of Fools; therefore the wise must join it to watch them. That is why all the effective Powers are in the League, as well as the little toy republics we shall swallow up in due time.

THE ÇI-DEVANT NEWCOMER. Steady on, mister. I dont understand.

BBDE. [*contemptuously to the Judge*] Tell him that this is a court of people who understand, and that the place of those who do not understand is in the ranks of silent and blindly obedient labor.

NEWCOMER. Oh, thats your game, is it? Who are you that I should obey you? What about democracy?

BBDE. I am what I am: you are what you are; and in virtue of these two facts I am where I am and you are where you are. Try to change places with me: you may as well try to change the path of the sun through the heavens.

THE NEWCOMER. You think a lot of yourself, dont you? I ask you again: what about democracy?

An unsmiling middle aged gentleman with slim figure, erect carriage, and resolutely dissatisfied expression, wanders in.

THE DISSATISFIED GENTLEMAN. Is this the sitting of the department of international justice?

BBDE. [*springing up*] Battler, by all thats unexpected!

BATTLER [*equally surprised*] Bombardone, by all thats underhand!

BBDE. You thought you could steal a march on me, eh?

BATTLER. You have ambushed me. Fox!

BBDE. [*sitting down*] Undignified, Ernest. Undignified.

BATTLER. True, Bardo. I apologize. [*He takes a chair from behind Sir Orpheus, and mounts the dais to the right of the Judge, who now has a dictator on each side of him*] By your leave, sir. [*He sits*].

JUDGE. I thank you, Mr Battler, for obeying the summons of the court.

BATTLER. Obedience is hardly the word, sir.

JUDGE. You have obeyed. You are here. Why?

BATTLER. That is just what I have come to find out. Why are you here, Bardo?

BBDE. I am everywhere.

THE BETROTHED [*boisterously*] Ha ha! Ha ha ha! Dam funny, that.

THE JUDGE. I must ask the public not to smile.

NEWCOMER [*who has no sense of humor*] Smile! He was not smiling: he laughed right out. With all respect to your worship we are wasting our time talking nonsense. How can a man be everywhere? The other gentleman says he came here to find out why he came here. It isnt sense. These two gents are balmy.

BBDE. Pardon me. What does balmy mean?

NEWCOMER. Balmy. Off your chumps. If you want it straight, mad.

BBDE. You belong to the lower orders, I see.

NEWCOMER. Who are you calling lower orders? Dont you know that democracy has put an end to all that?

BBDE. On the contrary, my friend, democracy has given a real meaning to it for the first time. Democracy has thrown us both into the same pair of scales. Your pan has gone up: mine has gone down; and nothing will bring down your pan while I am sitting in the other. Democracy has delivered you from the law of priest and king, of landlord and capitalist, only to bring you under the law of personal gravitation. Personal gravitation is a law of nature. You cannot cut its head off.

NEWCOMER. Democracy can cut your head off. British democracy has cut off thicker heads before.

BBDE. Never. Plutocracy has cut off the heads of kings and archbishops to make itself supreme and rob the people without interference from king or priest; but the people always follow their born leader. When there is no leader, no king, no priest, nor any body of law established by dead kings and priests, you have mob law, lynching law, gangster law: in short, American democracy. Thank your stars you have never known democracy in England. I have rescued my country from all that by my leadership. I am a democratic institution.

NEWCOMER. Gosh. You democratic! Youve abolished democracy, you have.

BBDE. Put my leadership to the vote. Take a plebiscite. If I poll less than 95 per cent of the adult nation I will resign. If that is not democracy what is democracy?

NEWCOMER. It isnt British democracy.

BATTLER. British democracy is a lie. I have said it.

NEWCOMER. Oh, dont talk nonsense, you ignorant foreigner. Plebiscites are unEnglish, thoroughly unEnglish.

BEGONIA. Hear hear!

SIR O. May I venture to make an observation?

BATTLER. Who are you?

SIR O. Only a humble Englishman, listening most respectfully to your clever and entertaining conversation. Officially, I am the British Foreign Secretary.

Both Leaders rise and give Fascist salute. Sir Orpheus remains seated, but waves his hand graciously.

BBDE. I must explain to the court that England is no longer of any consequence apart from me. I have dictated her policy for years [*he sits*].

BATTLER. I have snapped my fingers in England's face on every issue that has risen between us. Europe looks to me, not to England. [*He also resumes his seat*].

SIR O. You attract attention, Mr Battler: you certainly do attract attention. And you, Signor Bombardone, are quite welcome to dictate our policy as long as it is favorable to us. But the fact is, we are mostly unconscious of these triumphs of yours in England. I listen to your account of them with perfect complacency and—I hope you will not mind my saying so—with some amusement. But I must warn you that if your triumphs ever lead you to any steps contrary to the interests of the British Empire we shall have to come down rather abruptly from triumphs to facts; and the facts may not work so smoothly as the triumphs.

BATTLER. What could you do, facts or no facts?

SIR O. I dont know.

BATTLER.
BBDE. } You dont know!!!

SIR O. I dont know. Nor do you, Mr Battler. Nor you, signor.

BBDE. Do you mean that I do not know what you could do, or that I do not know what I should do.

SIR O. Both, signor.

BBDE. What have you to say to that, Ernest?

BATTLER. I should know what to do: have no doubt about that.

SIR O. You mean that you would know what to do when you knew what England was going to do?

BATTLER. I know already what you could do. Nothing. I tore up your peace treaty and threw the pieces in your face. You did nothing. I took your last Locarno pact and marched 18,000 soldiers through it. I threw down a frontier and doubled the size and power of my realm in spite of your teeth. What did you do? Nothing.

SIR O. Of course we did nothing. It did not suit us to do anything. A child of six could have foreseen that we should do nothing; so you shook your fist at us and cried "Do anything if you dare." Your countrymen thought you a hero. But as you knew you were quite safe, we were not impressed.

BBDE. You are quite right, Excellency. It was your folly and France's that blew Ernest up the greasy pole of political ambition. Still, he has a flair for power; and he has my example to encourage him. Do not despise Ernest.

BATTLER. I have never concealed my admiration for you, Bardo. But you have a failing that may ruin you unless you learn to keep it in check.

BBDE. And what is that, pray?

BATTLER. Selfconceit. You think yourself the only great man in the world.

BBDE. [*calm*] Can you name a greater?

BATTLER. There are rivals in Russia, Arabia, and Iran.

BBDE. And there is Ernest the Great. Why omit him?

BATTLER. We shall see. History, not I, must award the palm.

JUDGE. Let us omit all personalities, gentlemen. Allow me to recall you to the important point reached by Sir Midlander.

SIR O. What was that, my lord?

JUDGE. When you were challenged as to what your country would do in the event of a conflict of interest, you said frankly you did not know.

SIR O. Well, I dont.

BATTLER. And you call yourself a statesman!

SIR O. I assure you I do not. The word is hardly in use in England. I am a member of the Cabinet, and in my modest amateur way a diplomatist. When you ask me what will happen if British interests are seriously menaced you ask me to ford the stream before we come to it. We never do that in England. But when we come to the stream we ford it or bridge it or dry it up. And when we have done that it is too late to think about it. We have found that we can get on without thinking. You see, thinking is very little use unless you know the facts. And we never do know the political facts until twenty years after. Sometimes a hundred and fifty.

JUDGE. Still, Sir Midlander, you know that such an activity as thought exists.

SIR O. You alarm me, my lord. I am intensely reluctant to lose my grip of the realities of the moment and sit down to think. It is dangerous. It is unEnglish. It leads to theories, to speculative policies, to dreams and visions. If I may say so, I think my position is a more comfortable one than that of the two eminent leaders who are gracing these proceedings by their presence here today. Their remarks are most entertaining: every sentence is an epigram: I, who am only a stupid Englishman, feel quite abashed by my commonplaceness. But if you ask me what their intentions are I must frankly say that I dont know. Where do they stand with us? I dont know. But they know what England intends. They know what to expect from us. We have no speculative plans. We shall simply stick to our beloved British Empire, and undertake any larger cares that Providence may impose on us. Meanwhile we should feel very uneasy if any other Power or combinations of Powers were to place us in a position of military or naval inferiority, especially naval inferiority. I warn you—I beg you—do not frighten us. We are a simple wellmeaning folk, easily frightened. And when we are frightened we are capable of anything, even of things we hardly care to remember afterwards. Do not drive us in that direction. Take us as we are; and let be. Pardon my dull little speech. I must not take more of your time.

BATTLER. Machiavelli!

BBDE. A most astute speech. But it cannot impose on us.

JUDGE. It has imposed on both of you. It is a perfectly honest speech made to you by a perfectly honest gentleman; and you both take it as an outburst of British hypocrisy.

BEGONIA. A piece of damned cheek, I call it. I wont sit here and listen to my country being insulted.

THE BETROTHED. Hear hear! Up, Camberwell!

BATTLER. What does he mean by "Up, Camberwell!"? What is Camberwell?

BEGONIA. Oh! He doesnt know what Camberwell is!

THE SECRETARY. Camberwell, Mr Battler, is a part

of London which is totally indistinguishable from any other part of London, except that it is on the south side of the Thames and not on the north.

BEGONIA. What do you mean—indistinguishable? It maynt be as distangay as Mayfair; but it's better than Peckham anyhow.

BBDE. Excuse my ignorance; but what is Peckham?

BEGONIA. Oh! He doesnt know what Peckham is. These people dont know anything.

THE SECRETARY. Peckham is another part of London, adjacent to Camberwell and equally and entirely indistinguishable from it.

BEGONIA. Dont you believe him, gentlemen. He is saying that just to get a rise out of me. The people in Camberwell are the pick of south London society. The Peckham people are lower middle class: the scum of the earth.

BATTLER. I applaud your local patriotism, young lady; but I press for an answer to my question. What does "Up, Camberwell!" mean?

JUDGE. I think it is the south London equivalent to "Heil, Battler!"

BBDE. Ha ha ha! Ha ha! Good.

BATTLER. Am I being trifled with?

JUDGE. You may depend on me to keep order, Mr Battler. Dame Begonia is making a most valuable contribution to our proceedings. She is shewing us what we really have to deal with. Peace between the Powers of Europe on a basis of irreconcilable hostility between Camberwell and Peckham: that is our problem.

SIR O. Do not deceive yourself, my lord. Fire a shot at England; and Camberwell and Peckham will stand shoulder to shoulder against you.

BATTLER. You hear, Bardo. This Englishman is threatening us.

SIR O. Not at all. I am only telling you what will happen in certain contingencies which we sincerely wish to avoid. I am doing my best to be friendly in manner, as I certainly am in spirit. I respectfully suggest that if an impartial stranger were present his impression would be that you two gentlemen are threatening me: I might almost say bullying me.

BBDE. But we are. We shall not be thought the worse of at home for that. How are we to keep up the self-respect of our people unless we confront the rest of the world with a battle cry? And—will you excuse a personal criticism?

SIR O. Certainly. I shall value it.

BBDE. You are very kind: you almost disarm me. But may I say that your technique is out of date? It would seem amusingly quaint in a museum, say in the rooms devoted to the eighteenth century; but of what use is it for impressing a modern crowd? And your slogans are hopelessly obsolete.

SIR O. I do not quite follow. What, exactly, do you mean by my technique?

BBDE. Your style, your gestures, the modulations of your voice. Public oratory is a fine art. Like other fine arts, it cannot be practised effectively without a laboriously acquired technique.

SIR O. But I am an experienced public speaker. My elocution has never been complained of. Like other public speakers I have taken pains to acquire a distinct articulation; and I have had the best parliamentary models before me all through my public life. I suppose—now that you put it in that way—that this constitutes a technique; but I should be sorry to think that there is anything professional about it.

BATTLER. Yes; but what a technique! I contemplated it at first with amazement, then with a curiosity which obliged me to study it—to find out what it could possibly mean. To me the object of public speaking is to propagate a burning conviction of truth and importance, and thus produce immediate action and enthusiastic faith and obedience. My technique, like that of my forerunner opposite, was invented and perfected with that object. You must admit that it has been wonderfully successful: your parliaments have been swept away by the mere breath of it; and we ourselves exercise a personal authority unattainable by any king, president, or minister. That is simple, natural, reasonable. But what is your technique? What is its object? Apparently its object is to destroy conviction and to paralyze action. Out of the ragbag of stale journalism and Kikkeronian Latin—

SIR O. I protest. I beg. I ask the court to protect me.

THE JUDGE. What is the matter? Protect you from what?

SIR O. From these abominable modern mispronunciations. Kikkeronian is an insult to my old school. I insist on Sisseronian.

THE BETROTHED. Hear hear!

BBDE. Take care, Ernest. This is part of the British technique. Your were talking of something really important. That is dangerous. He switches you off to something of no importance whatever.

SIR O. I did not intend that, I assure you. And I cannot admit that the modern corruption of our old English pronunciation of the classics is a matter of no importance. It is a matter of supreme importance.

JUDGE. We do not question its importance, Sir Midlander; but it is outside the jurisdiction of this court; and we must not allow it to divert us from our proper business. I recall you to a specific charge of a specific crime against a specific section of the community. It is a crime of the most horrible character to drop a bomb upon a crowded city. It is a crime only a shade less diabolical to strew the sea, the common highway of all mankind, with mines that will shatter and sink any ship that stumbles on them in the dark. These abominable crimes are being committed by young men—

SIR O. Under orders, my lord, and from patriotic motives.

JUDGE. No doubt. Suppose a young man picks your pocket, and, on being detected, alleges, first that somebody told him to do it, and second that he wanted your money to pay his income tax—a highly patriotic motive—would you accept that excuse?

SIR O. Ridiculous! Remember, sir, that if our young heroes are the killers, they are also the killed. They risk their own lives.

JUDGE. Let us then add a third plea to our pickpocket's defence. He runs the same risk of having his pocket picked as you. Would you accept that plea also?

SIR O. My lord: I abhor war as much as you do. But, damn it, if a fellow is coming at me to cut my throat, I must cut his if I can. Am I to allow him to kill me and ravish my wife and daughters?

JUDGE. I think that under such circumstances a plea of legitimate defence might be allowed. But what has a tussle with a murderer and a ravisher to do with laying a mine in the high seas to slaughter innocent travellers whose intentions towards yourself, your wife, and your daughters, if they have any intentions, are entirely friendly? What has it to do with dropping a bomb into the bed of a sleeping baby or a woman in childbirth?

SIR O. One feels that. It is terrible. But we cannot help its happening. We must take a practical view. It is like the London traffic. We know that so many children will be run over and killed every week. But we cannot stop the traffic because of that. Motor traffic is a part of civilized life. So is coalmining. So is railway transport. So is flying. The explosions in the mines, the collisions of the trains, the accidents in the shunting yards, the aeroplane crashes, are most dreadful; but we cannot give up flying and coalmining and railway travelling on that account. They are a part of civilized life. War is a part of civilized life. We cannot give it up because of its shocking casualties.

JUDGE. But the mine explosions and railway collisions and aeroplane crashes are not the objects of the industry. They are its accidents. They occur in spite of every possible precaution to prevent them. But war has no other object than to produce these casualties. The business and purpose of a coalminer is to hew the coal out of the earth to keep the home fires burning. But the soldier's business is to burn the homes and kill their inhabitants. That is not a part of civilization: it is a danger to it.

COMMISSAR. Come, Comrade Judge: have you never sentenced a criminal to death? Has the executioner never carried out your sentence? Is not that a very necessary part of civilization?

JUDGE. I sentence persons to death when they have committed some crime which has raised the question whether they are fit to live in human society, but not until that question has been decided against them by a careful trial at which they have every possible legal assistance and protection. This does not justify young men in slaughtering innocent persons at random. It would justify me in sentencing the young men to death if they were brought to trial. What we are here to investigate is why they are not brought to trial.

SIR O. But really, they only obey orders.

THE JUDGE. Why do you say "only"? The slaughter of human beings and the destruction of cities are not acts to be qualified by the word only. Why are the persons who give such atrocious orders not brought to trial?

SIR O. But before what court?

JUDGE. Before this court if necessary. There was a time when I might have answered "Before the judgment seat of God". But since people no longer believe that there is any such judgment seat, must we not create one before we are destroyed by the impunity and glorification of murder?

BBDE. Peace may destroy you more effectually. It is necessary for the cultivation of the human character that a field should be reserved for war. Men decay when they do not fight.

THE WIDOW. And when they fight they die.

BBDE. No no. Only a percentage, to give zest and reality to the conflict.

THE JUDGE. Would you describe a contest of a man against a machine gun, or a woman in childbirth against a cloud of mustard gas, as a fight?

BBDE. It is a peril: a deadly peril. And it is peril that educates us, not mere bayonet fencing and fisticuffs. Nations never do anything until they are in danger.

THE JEW. Is there not plenty of danger in the world without adding the danger of poison gas to it?

BBDE. Yes: there is the danger of getting your feet wet. But it has not the fighting quality that gives war its unique power over the imagination, and through the imagination over the characters and powers of mankind.

THE WIDOW. You have been a soldier. Are you the better for it? Were you not glad when your wounds took you out of the trenches and landed you in a hospital bed?

BBDE. Extremely glad. But that was part of the experience. War is not all glory and all bravery. You find out what a rotten coward you are as well as how brave you are. You learn what it is to be numbed with misery and terror as well as how to laugh at death. Ask my understudy here. He too has been a soldier. He knows.

BATTLER. We all begin as understudies, and end, perhaps, as great actors. The army was a school in which I learnt a good deal, because whoever has my capacity for learning can learn something even in the worst school. The army is the worst school, because fighting is not a whole-time-job, and in the army they pretend that it is. It ends in the discharged soldier being good for nothing until he recovers his civilian sense and the habit of thinking for himself. No, cousin: I am a man of peace; but it must be a voluntary peace, not an intimidated one. Not until I am armed to the teeth and ready to face all the world in arms is my Pacifism worth anything.

SIR O. Admirable! Precisely our British position.

NEWCOMER. I'm British. And what I say is that war is necessary to keep down the population.

BBDE. This man is a fool. War stimulates population. The soldier may go to his death; but he leaves behind him the pregnant woman who will replace him. Women cannot resist the soldier: they despise the coward. Death, the supreme danger, rouses life to its supreme ecstasy of love. When has a warlike race ever lacked children?

THE BETROTHED. Very romantic and all that, old man; but this notion of man on the battlefield and woman in the home wont wash nowadays. Home was a safe place when Waterloo was fought; but today the home is the bomber's favorite mark. The soldier is safe in his trench while the woman is being blown to smithereens by her baby's cot. Kill the women; and where will your population be? Egad, you wont have any population at all.

BATTLER. This man is not a fool. If the object of war is extermination, kill the women: the men do not matter.

BBDE. The object of war is not extermination: it is the preservation of man's noblest attribute, courage. The utmost safety for women, the utmost peril for men: that is the ideal.

THE BETROTHED. I say, signor: do you take any precautions against assassination?

BBDE. I do not encourage it; but it is one of the risks of my position. I live dangerously. It is more intense than living safely.

NEWCOMER. Your worship: these gentlemen are talking nonsense.

JUDGE. All politicians talk nonsense. You mean, I presume, that it is not the sort of nonsense you are accustomed to.

NEWCOMER. No I dont. I am accustomed to hear statesmen talking proper politics. But this about living dangerously is not proper politics: it's nonsense to me. Am I to cross the street without looking to see whether there is a bus coming? Are there to be no red and green lights? Am I to sleep in a smallpox hospital? Am I to cross the river on a tight rope instead of on a bridge? Am I to behave like a fool or a man of sense?

BBDE. You would be a much more wonderful man if you could walk on a tight rope instead of requiring several feet of solid pavement, costing years of labor to construct.

SIR O. Do you seriously propose that we should be ruled by an aristocracy of acrobats?

BBDE. Is it more impossible than your British aristocracy of foxhunters?

SIR O. Signor: acrobats are not foxhunters.

BBDE. And gentlemen are not acrobats. But what a pity!

THE NEWCOMER. Oh, whats the use of talking to you people? Am I dreaming? Am I drunk?

BBDE. No: you are only out of your depth, my friend. And now to business. Strength. Silence. Order. I am here to meet my accusers, if any.

JUDGE. You are accused, it seems, of the murder and destruction of liberty and democracy in Europe.

BBDE. One cannot destroy what never existed. Besides, these things are not my business. My business is government. I give my people good government, as far as their folly and ignorance permit. What more do they need?

THE NEWCOMER. Why am I locked out of the parliament of Jacksonsland, to which I have been lawfully elected: tell me that.

BBDE. Presumably because you want to obstruct its work and discredit its leaders. Half a dozen such obstructionists as you could spin out to two years the work I do in ten minutes. The world can endure you no longer. Your place is in the dustbin.

THE NEWCOMER. I give up. You are too much for me when it comes to talking. But what do I care? I have my principles still. Thats my last word. Now go on and talk yourself silly.

BBDE. It is your turn now, cousin.

BATTLER. Do I stand accused? Of what, pray?

THE JEW [*springing up*] Of murder. Of an attempt to exterminate the flower of the human race.

BATTLER. What do you mean?

THE JEW. I am a Jew.

BATTLER. Then what right have you in my country? I exclude you as the British exclude the Chinese in Australia, as the Americans exclude the Japanese in California.

JEW. Why do the British exclude the Chinese? Because the Chinaman is so industrious, so frugal, so trustworthy, that nobody will employ a white British workman or caretaker if there is a yellow one within reach. Why do you exclude the Jew? Because you cannot compete with his intelligence, his persistence, his foresight, his grasp of finance. It is our talents, our virtues, that you fear, not our vices.

BATTLER. And am I not excluded for my virtues? I may not set foot in England until I declare that I will do no work there and that I will return to my own country in a few weeks. In every country the foreigner is a trespasser. On every coast he is confronted by officers who say you shall not land without your passport, your visa. If you are of a certain race or color you shall not land at all. Sooner than let German soldiers march through Belgium England plunged Europe into war. Every State chooses its population and selects its blood. We say that ours shall be Nordic, not Hittite: that is all.

JEW. A Jew is a human being. Has he not a right of way and settlement everywhere upon the earth?

BATTLER. Nowhere without a passport. That is the law of nations.

JEW. I have been beaten and robbed. Is that the law of nations?

BATTLER. I am sorry. I cannot be everywhere; and all my agents are not angels.

THE JEW [*triumphantly*] Ah! Then you are NOT God

Almighty, as you pretend to be. [*To the Judge*] Your honor: I am satisfied. He has admitted his guilt. [*He flings himself back into his seat*].

BATTLER. Liar. No Jew is ever satisfied. Enough. You have your warning. Keep away; and you will be neither beaten nor robbed. Keep away, I tell you. The world is wide enough for both of us. My country is not.

THE JEW. I leave myself in the hands of the court. For my race there are no frontiers. Let those who set them justify themselves.

BBDE. Mr President: if you allow Ernest to expatiate on the Jewish question we shall get no further before bed-time. He should have waited for a lead from me before meddling with it, and forcing me to banish the Jews lest my people should be swamped by the multitudes he has driven out. I say he should have waited. I must add that I have no use for leaders who do not follow me.

BATTLER. I am no follower of yours. When has a Nordic ever stooped to follow a Latin Southerner?

BBDE. You forget that my country has a north as well as a south, a north beside whose mountains your little provincial Alps are molehills. The snows, the crags, the avalanches, the bitter winds of those mountains make men, Ernest, MEN! The trippers' paradise from which you come breeds operatic tenors. You are too handsome, Ernest: you think yourself a blond beast. Ladies and gentlemen, look at him! Is he a blond beast? The blondest beast I know is the Calabrian bull. I have no desire to figure as a blond beast; but I think I could play the part more plausibly than Ernest if it were my cue to do so. I am everything that you mean by the word Nordic. He is a born Southerner; and the south is the south, whether it be the south of the Arctic circle or the south of the equator.

Race is nothing: it is the number of metres above sealevel that puts steel into men. Our friend here was born at a very moderate elevation. He is an artist to his finger tips; but his favorite play as a boy was not defying avalanches. As to our races, they are so mixed that the whole human race must be descended from Abraham; for everybody who is alive now must be descended from everybody who was alive in Abraham's day. Ernest has his share in Abraham.

BATTLER. This is an intolerable insult. I demand satisfaction. I cannot punch your head because you are at least two stone heavier than I; but I will fight you with any weapon that will give me a fair chance against you.

THE JUDGE. Gentlemen: you are at the Hague, and in a Court of Justice. Duels are out of date. And your lives are too valuable to be risked in that way.

BBDE. True, your Excellency. I admit that Ernest's ancestors are totally unknown. I apologize.

BATTLER. I dont want an apology. I want satisfaction. You shall not rob me of it by apologizing. Are you a coward?

BBDE. We are both cowards, Ernest. Remember 1918. All men are cowards now.

BATTLER [*rising*] I shall go home.

WIDOW [*rising*] You shall not. Here at least we have come to the real business of this court; and you want to run away from it. If a man of you stirs I shall shoot [*Panic*].

BBDE. Hands up, Ernest [*politely holding up his own*].

THE WIDOW. Listen to me. In my country men fight duels every day. If they refuse they become pariahs: no one will visit them or speak to them: their women folk are driven out of society as if they were criminals.

BATTLER. It was so in my country. But I have stopped it.

JUDGE. Yet you want to fight a duel yourself.

BATTLER. Not for etiquette. For satisfaction.

THE WIDOW. Yes: that is what men always want. Well, look at me. I am a murderess [*general consternation*]. My husband wanted satisfaction of another kind. He got it from my dearest friend; and etiquette obliged me to kill her. In my dreams night after night she comes to me and begs me to forgive her; and I have to kill her again. I long to go mad; but I cannot: each time I do this dreadful thing I wake up with my mind clearer and clearer, and the horror of it deeper and more agonizing.

BATTLER [*flinching*] Stop this. I cannot bear it.

BBDE. Who is this woman? What right has she to be here?

WIDOW. My name is Revenge. My name is Jealousy. My name is the unwritten law that is no law. Until you have dealt with me you have done nothing.

JUDGE. You have a specific case. State it.

WIDOW. My husband has been murdered by his successor. My son must murder him if there is to be no redress but the blood feud; and I shall dream and dream and kill and kill. I call on you to condemn him.

BBDE. And condemn you.

WIDOW. I shall condemn myself. Pass your sentence on me; and I shall execute it myself, here in this court if you will.

JUDGE. But do you not understand that the judgments of this court are followed by no executions? They are moral judgments only.

WIDOW. I understand perfectly. You can point the finger of the whole world at the slayer of my husband and say "You are guilty of murder." You can put the same brand on my forehead. That is all you need do, all you can do. Then my dreams will cease and I shall kill myself. As for him, let him bear the brand as best he can.

JUDGE. That is the justice of this court. I thank you, señora, for your comprehension of it.

BATTLER [*distressed by the narrative*] I cannot bear this. Order that woman not to kill herself.

BBDE. No. If she has a Roman soul, who dares forbid her?

JUDGE. My authority does not go so far, Mr Battler.

BATTLER. Your authority goes as far as you dare push it and as far as it is obeyed. What authority have I? What authority has Bardo? What authority has any leader? We command and are obeyed: that is all.

BBDE. That is true, signor judge. Authority is a sort of genius: either you have it or you have not. Either you are obeyed or torn to pieces. But in some souls and on some points there is an authority higher than any other. Of such is the Roman soul; and this is one of the points on which the Roman soul stands firm. The woman's life is in her own hands.

BATTLER. No: I tell you I cannot bear it. Forbid her to kill herself or I will leave the court.

JUDGE. Señora: I forbid you to kill yourself. But I will sentence the slayer of your husband when his offence is proved; and by that act I will deliver you from your dreams.

WIDOW. I thank your Honor [*she sits down*].

JUDGE. Are you satisfied, Mr Battler?

BATTLER. I also thank your Honor. I am satisfied [*he resumes his seat; but his emotion has not yet quite subsided*].

BBDE. No duel then?

BATTLER. Do not torment me. [*Impatiently*] Bardo: you are a damned fool.

BBDE. [*hugely amused*] Ha ha! [*To the Judge*] The incident is closed.

An attractive and very voluble middleaged English lady enters. She is dressed as a deaconess and carries a handbag full of tracts.

DEACONESS. May I address the court? [*She goes on without waiting for a reply*]. I feel strongly that it is my duty to do so. There is a movement in the world which is also a movement in my heart. It is a movement before which all war, all unkindness, all uncharitableness, all sin and suffering will disappear and make Geneva superfluous. I speak from personal experience. I can remember many witnesses whose experience has been like my own. I——

BBDE. [*thundering at her*] Madam: you have not yet received permission to address us.

DEACONESS [*without taking the slightest notice of the interruption*] It is so simple! and the happiness it brings is so wonderful! All you have to do is to open your heart to the Master.

BATTLER. What master? I am The Master.

BBDE. There are others, Ernest.

DEACONESS. If you knew what I was, and what I am, all that you are doing here would seem the idlest trifling.

BATTLER [*shouting*] Who is the Master? Name him.

DEACONESS. Not so loud, please. I am not deaf; but when one is listening to the inner voice it is not easy to catch external noises.

BATTLER. I am not an external noise. I am the leader of my people. I may become leader of many peoples. Who is this Master of whom you speak?

DEACONESS. His beloved name, sir, is Jesus. I am

sure that when you were a child your mother taught you to say "All hail the power of Jesu's name."

THE BETROTHED. "Let angels prostrate fall."

BEGONIA. Now shut up, Billikins. I wont have you laughing at religion.

BBDE. In Ernest's country, madam, they say Heil Battler. He has abolished Jesus.

DEACONESS. How can you say that? Jesus is stronger than ever. Jesus is irresistible. You can perhaps unify your countrymen in love of yourself. But Jesus can unite the whole world in love of Him. He will live when you are dust and ashes. Can you find the way to my heart as Jesus has found it? Can you make better men and women of them as Jesus can? Can——

BATTLER. I have made better men and women of them. I live for nothing else. I found them defeated, humiliated, the doormats of Europe. They now hold up their heads with the proudest; and it is I, Battler, who have raised them to spit in the faces of their oppressors.

DEACONESS. Jesus does not spit in people's faces. If your people are really raised up, really saved, it is Jesus who has done it; and you, sir, are only the instrument.

NEWCOMER [*rising*] A point of order, mister. Is this a court of justice or is it not? Are we to be interrupted by every dotty female who starts preaching at us? I protest.

DEACONESS. It is no use protesting, my friend. When He calls you must follow.

NEWCOMER. Rot. Where are the police?

THE JUDGE. The peculiarity of this court, sir, is that there are no police. The lady is raising a point of general importance: one we must settle before we can come to any fruitful conclusions here. I rule that Jesus is a party in this case.

NEWCOMER. You are as dotty as she is. I say no more. [*He resumes his seat sulkily*].

THE JEW. A party in what capacity, may I ask? I speak as a Jew, if Mr Battler will permit me.

THE JUDGE. In the capacity of a famous prophet who laid down the law in these words, "This commandment I give unto you, that ye love one another." Are you prepared to love one another?

ALL EXCEPT SIR O. [*vociferously*] No.

SIR O. Not indiscriminately.

THE BRITISH CONTINGENT. Hear hear!

SIR O. What about the Unlovables? Judas Iscariot, for instance?

DEACONESS. If he had loved the Master he would not have betrayed Him. What a proof of the truth of my message!

BBDE. Do you love Ernest here?

DEACONESS. Why of course I do, most tenderly.

BATTLER. Woman: do not presume.

BBDE. Ha! ha! ha!

DEACONESS. Why should I not love you? I am your sister in Christ. What is there to offend you in that? Is not this touchiness a great trouble to you? You can easily get rid of it. Bring it to Jesus. It will fall from you like a heavy burden; and your heart will be light, oh, so light! You have never been happy. I can see it in your face.

BBDE. He practises that terrible expression for hours every day before the looking glass; but it is not a bit natural to him. Look at my face: there you have the real thing.

DEACONESS. You have neither of you the light in your eyes of the love of the Master. There is no happiness in these expressions that you maintain so industriously. Do you not find it very tiresome to have to be making faces all day? [*Much laughter in the British section*].

BATTLER. Is this to be allowed? The woman is making fun of us.

DEACONESS. I cannot make fun. But God has ordained that when men are childish enough to fancy that they are gods they become what you call funny. We cannot help laughing at them.

BBDE. Woman: if you had ever had God's work to do you would know that He never does it Himself. We are here to do it for Him. If we neglect it the world falls into the chaos called Liberty and Democracy, in which nothing is done except talk while the people perish. Well, what you call God's work, His hardest work, His political work, cannot be done by everybody: they have neither the time nor the brains nor the divine call for it. God has sent to certain persons this call. They are not chosen by the people: they must choose themselves: that is part of their inspiration. When they have dared to do this, what happens? Out of the Liberal democratic chaos comes form, purpose, order and rapid execution.

NEWCOMER. Yes, the executions come along all right. We know what dictators are.

BBDE. Yes: the triflers and twaddlers are swept away. This trifler and twaddler here can see nothing but his own danger, which raises his twaddle to a squeak of mortal terror. He does not matter. His selfchosen ruler takes him by the scruff of the neck and flings him into some island or camp where he and his like can trifle and twaddle without obstructing God's effectives. Then comes this pious lady to bid me turn to God. There is no need: God has turned to me; and to the best of my ability I shall not fail Him, in spite of all the Democratic Liberal gabblers. I have spoken. Now it is your turn, Ernest, if you have anything left to say.

BATTLER. You have said it all in your oldfashioned way, perhaps more clearly than I could have said it. But this woman's old fairy tales do not explain me, Ernest Battler, born a nobody, and now in command above all kings and kaisers. For my support is no dead Jew, but a mighty movement in the history of the world. Impelled by it I have stretched out my hand and lifted my country from the gutter into which you and your allies were trampling it, and made it once more the terror of Europe, though the danger is in your own guilty souls and not in any malice of mine. And mark you, the vision does not stop at my frontiers, nor at any frontier. Do not mistake me: I am no soldier dreaming of military conquests: I am what I am, and have done what I have done, without winning a single battle. Why is this? Because I have snapped my fingers in the face of all your Jewish beliefs and Roman traditions, your futile treaties and halfhearted threats, and the vulgar abuse you have spat at me from your platforms and newspapers like the frightened geese you are. You must all come my way, because I march with the times, and march as pioneer, not as camp follower. As pioneer I know that the real obstacle to human progress is the sort of mind that has been formed in its infancy by the Jewish Scriptures. That obstacle I must smash through at all costs; and so must you, Bardo, if you mean to be yourself and not the tool of that accursed race.

COMMISSAR. I must intervene. Are we here to discuss the Jewish problem? If so, I have no business here: my country has solved it. And we did not solve it by badinage.

BBDE. Badinage! Are our proceedings to be described as badinage by a Bolshevist?

SECRETARY. You see how hopeless it is for us to get any further. You have only to say the word Jew to Herr Battler or the word Bolshevist to Signor Bombardone, and they cease to be reasonable men. You have only to say Peckham to the representative of the Intellectual Committee of the League of Nations to reveal her as an irreconcilable belligerent. You have—

BEGONIA. Whats that he called me? It sounded awful. What does it mean, Uncle O?

SIR O. I understood the secretary to imply that however large-minded your view of the brotherhood of mankind, you must make an exception in the case of Peckham.

BEGONIA. Okay. No Peckham for me. And mind: on that point I am a representative woman. Sorry I interrupted. Carry on, old man.

SECRETARY. I thank you, Dame Begonia. I must add, with great respect for the British Foreign Secretary, that you have only to say British Empire to discover that in his view the rest of the world exists only as a means of furthering the interests of that geographical expression.

SIR O. Surely the British Empire is something more than a geographical expression. But of course with me the British Empire comes first.

SECRETARY. Precisely. And as a common basis of agreement this lady has proposed the policy of the Sermon on the Mount.

DEACONESS. Love oneanother. It is so simple.

SECRETARY. It turns out that we do not and cannot love oneanother—that the problem before us is how to establish peace among people who heartily dislike oneanother, and have very good reasons for doing so: in short, that the human race does not at present consist exclusively or even largely of likeable persons.

DEACONESS. But I assure you, that does not matter. There is a technique you have not learnt.

SIR O. What! More techniques! Madam: before your arrival, I was accused of having a technique. Can we not keep on the plain track of commonsense?

DEACONESS. But this one is so simple. You have spites. You have hatreds. You have bad tempers. All you have to do is to bring them to Jesus. He will relieve you of them. He will shew you that they are all imaginary. He will fill your hearts with love of Himself; and in that love there is eternal peace. I know so many cases. I know by my own experience.

SECRETARY. You are an amiable lady; and no doubt there are, as you say, other cases—

DEACONESS. Oh, I was not an amiable lady. I was a perfect fiend, jealous, quarrelsome, full of imaginary ailments, as touchy as Mr Battler, as bumptious as Signor Bombardone—

BATTLER. Pardon. What does touchy mean?

BBDE. I am unacquainted with the word bumptious. What am I to understand by it?

DEACONESS. Look within, look within, and you will understand. I brought it all to Jesus; and now I am happy: I am what the gentleman is kind enough to describe as amiable. Oh, why will you not do as I have done? It is so simple.

BBDE. It is made much simpler by the fact that you are protected by an efficient body of policemen with bludgeons in their pockets, madam. You have never had to govern.

DEACONESS. I have had to govern myself, sir. And I am now governed by Jesus.

JUDGE. Allow the lady the last word, Mr Leader. Proceed, Mr Secretary.

SECRETARY. No: I have said enough. You know now

what an impossible job I have here as secretary to the League of Nations. To me it is agony to have to listen to all this talk, knowing as I do that nothing can come of it. Have pity on me. Let us adjourn for lunch.

JUDGE. Oh, it is not lunch time yet, Mr Secretary. We have been here less than an hour.

SECRETARY. It seems to me twenty years.

JUDGE. I am sorry, Mr Secretary. But I am waiting for the arrival of a defendant who has not yet appeared, General Flanco de Fortinbras, who is accused of having slaughtered many thousands of his fellow countrymen on grounds that have never been clearly stated.

BBDE. But he has not yet been elected Leader. He is a mere soldier.

COMMISSAR. Half Europe describes him as your valet.

BBDE. I do not keep valets. But in so far as Flanco is striving to save his country from the horrors of Communism he has my sympathy.

COMMISSAR. Which includes the help of your guns and soldiers.

BBDE. I cannot prevent honest men from joining in a crusade, as volunteers, against scoundrels and assassins.

JUDGE. You also, Mr Battler, sympathize with General Flanco?

BATTLER. I do. He has accepted my definite offer to Europe to rid it of Bolshevism if the western states will co-operate.

JUDGE. And you, Sir Midlander, can of course assure General Flanco of British support?

SIR O. [*rising*] Oh, no, no, no. I am amazed at such a misunderstanding. The British Empire has maintained the strictest neutrality. It has merely recognized General Flanco as a belligerent.

BBDE. Flanco will not come. I have not authorized him to come.

General Flanco de Fortinbras enters at the door. He is a middle aged officer, very smart, and quite conventional.

FLANCO. Pardon. Is this the International Court?

JUDGE. It is.

FLANCO. My name is Flanco de Fortinbras—General Flanco de Fortinbras. I have received a summons.

JUDGE. Quite so, General. We were expecting you. You are very welcome. Pray be seated.

The secretary places a chair between the judge and Bombardone. Flanco crosses to it.

JUDGE [*before Flanco sits down*] You know these gentlemen, I think.

FLANCO [*sitting down carelessly*] No. But I have seen many caricatures of them. No introduction is necessary.

THE JUDGE. You recognize also the British Foreign Secretary, Sir Orpheus Midlander.

Flanco immediately rises; clicks his heels; and salutes Sir Orpheus with a distinguished consideration that contrasts very significantly with his contemptuous indifference to the two leaders. Sir Orpheus, as before, waves a gracious acknowledgment of the salute. Flanco resumes his seat.

FLANCO. I have come here because it seemed the correct thing to do. I am relieved to find that His Excellency the British Foreign Secretary agrees with me.

BBDE. In what capacity are you here, may I ask?

FLANCO. Do I seem out of place between you and your fellow talker opposite? A man of action always is out of place among talkers.

BBDE. Inconceivable nothingness that you are, do you dare to class me as a talker and not a man of action?

FLANCO. Have you done anything?

BBDE. I have created an empire.

FLANCO. You mean that you have policed a place infested by savages. A child could have done it with a modern mechanized army.

BBDE. Your little military successes have gone to your head. Do not forget that they were won with my troops.

FLANCO. Your troops do fairly well under my command. We have yet to see them doing anything under yours.

BBDE. Ernest: our valet has gone stark mad.

FLANCO. Mr Battler may be a useful civilian. I am informed that he is popular with the lower middle class. But the fate of Europe will not be decided by your scraps of Socialism.

JUDGE. May I recall you to the business of the court, gentlemen. General: you are charged with an extraordinary devastation of your own country and an indiscriminate massacre of its inhabitants.

FLANCO. That is my profession. I am a soldier; and my business is to devastate the strongholds of the enemies of my country, and slaughter their inhabitants.

NEWCOMER. Do you call the lawfully constituted democratic government of your country its enemies?

FLANCO. I do, sir. That government is a government of cads. I stand for a great cause; and I have not talked about it, as these two adventurers talk: I have fought for it: fought and won.

JUDGE. And what, may we ask, is the great cause?

FLANCO. I stand simply for government by gentlemen against government by cads. I stand for the religion of gentlemen against the irreligion of cads. For me there are only two classes, gentlemen and cads: only two faiths: Catholics and heretics. The horrible vulgarity called democracy has given political power to the cads and the heretics. I am determined that the world shall not be ruled by cads nor its children brought up as heretics. I maintain that all spare money should be devoted to the breeding of gentlemen. In that I have the great body of public opinion behind me. Take a plebiscite of the whole civilized world; and not a vote will be cast against me. The natural men, the farmers and peasants, will support me to a man, and to a woman. Even the peasants whom you have crowded into your towns and demoralized by street life and trade unionism, will know in their souls that I am the salvation of the world.

BBDE. A Saviour, no less! Eh?

FLANCO. Do not be profane. I am a Catholic officer and gentleman, with the beliefs, traditions, and duties of my class and my faith. I could not sit idly reading and talking whilst the civilization established by that faith and that order was being destroyed by the mob. Nobody else would do anything but read seditious pamphlets and talk, talk, talk. It was necessary to fight, fight, fight to restore order in the world. I undertook that responsibility and here I am. Everybody understands my position: nobody understands the pamphlets, the three volumes of Karl Marx, the theories of idealists, the ranting of the demagogues: in short, the caddishness of the cads. Do I make myself clear?

BBDE. Am I a cad? Is Ernest here a cad?

FLANCO. You had better not force me to be personal.

BBDE. Come! Face the question. Are we cads or gentlemen? Out with it.

FLANCO. You are certainly not gentlemen. You are freaks.

BATTLER. Freaks!

BBDE. What is a freak?

JUDGE. An organism so extraordinary as to defy classification.

BBDE. Good. I accept that.

BATTLER. So do I. I claim it.

JUDGE. Then, as time is getting on, gentlemen, had we not better come to judgment?

BATTLER. Judgment!

BBDE. Judgment!

BATTLER. What do you mean? Do you presume to judge me?

BBDE. Judge me if you dare.

FLANCO. Give judgment against me and you pass out of history as a cad.

BATTLER. You have already passed out of history as a Catholic: that is, nine tenths a Jew.

BBDE. The bee in your bonnet buzzes too much, Ernest. [*To the Judge*] What is the law?

JUDGE. Unfortunately there is no law as between nations. I shall have to create it as I go along, by judicial precedents.

BATTLER. In my country I create the precedents.

BBDE. Well said, Ernest. Same here.

JUDGE. As you are not judges your precedents have no authority outside the operations of your police. You, Mr Battler, are here to answer an accusation made against you by a Jewish gentleman of unlawful arrest and imprisonment, assault, robbery, and denial of his right to live in the country of his birth. What is your defence?

BATTLER. I do not condescend to defend myself.

JEW. You mean that you have no defence. You cannot even find a Jewish lawyer to defend you, because you have driven them all from your country and left it with no better brains than your own. You have employed physical force to suppress intellect. That is the sin against the Holy Ghost. I accuse you of it.

JUDGE. What have you to say to that, Mr Battler?

BATTLER. Nothing. Men such as I am are not to be stopped by academic twaddle about intellect. But I will condescend to tell this fellow from the Ghetto that to every superior race that is faithful to itself a Messiah is sent.

DEACONESS. Oh, how true! If only you would accept him!

JUDGE. I understand you to plead divine inspiration, Mr Battler.

BATTLER. I say that my power is mystical, not rational.

BBDE. Ernest: take care. You are walking on a razor's edge between inspiration and the madness of the beggar on horseback. We two are beggars on horseback. For the credit of leadership let us ride carefully. Leadership, we two know, is mystical. Then let us not pretend to understand it. God may choose his leaders; but he may also drop them with a crash if they get out of hand. Tell yourself that every night before you get into bed, my boy; and you may last a while yet.

Loud applause from the British section.

BATTLER. Physician, cure yourself. You need not prescribe for me.

JUDGE. This is very edifying, gentlemen; and I thank you both in the name of all present. May I ask whether this divine guidance of which you are conscious has any limits? Does it not imply a world State with Mr Battler or Signor Bombardone or the British Foreign Office at its head?

FLANCO. Certainly not in my country. A frontier is a frontier; and there must be no monkeying with it. Let these gentlemen manage their own countries and leave us to manage ours.

JUDGE. Is that your view, Mr Battler?

BATTLER. No. I believe that the most advanced race, if it breeds true, must eventually govern the world.

JUDGE. Do you agree, Sir Midlander?

SIR O. With certain reservations, yes. I do not like the term "advanced race." I greatly mistrust advanced people. In my experience they are very difficult to work with, and often most disreputable in their private lives. They seldom attend divine service. But if you will withdraw the rather unfortunate word "advanced" and substitute the race best fitted by its character—its normal, solid, everyday character—to govern justly and prosperously, then I think I agree.

JUDGE. Precisely. And now may we have your opinion, Signor Leader?

BBDE. In principle I agree. It is easy for me to do so, as my people, being a Mediterranean people, can never be subject to northern barbarians, though it can assimilate and civilize them in unlimited numbers.

JUDGE. Has the Russian gentleman anything to say?

COMMISSAR. Nothing. These gentlemen talk of their countries. But they do not own their countries. Their people do not own the land they starve in. Their countries are owned by a handful of landlords and capitalists who allow them to live in it on condition that they work like bees and keep barely enough of the honey to keep themselves miserably alive. Russia belongs to the Russians. We shall look on whilst you eat each other up. When you have done that, Russia—Holy Russia—will save the soul of the world by teaching it to feed its people instead of robbing them.

FLANCO. Did your landlords ever rob the people as

your bureaucracy now robs them to build cities and factories in the desert and to teach children to be atheists? Your country is full of conspiracies to get the old order back again. You have to shoot the conspirators by the dozen every month.

COMMISSAR. That is not many out of two hundred million people, General. Think of all the rascals you ought to shoot!

JUDGE. Pray, gentlemen, no more recriminations. Let us keep to the point of the superior race and the divine leadership. What is to happen if you disagree as to which of you is the divinely chosen leader and the superior race?

BBDE. My answer is eight million bayonets.

BATTLER. My answer is twelve million bayonets.

JUDGE. And yours, Sir Midlander?

SIR O. This sort of talk is very dangerous. Besides, men do not fight with bayonets nowadays. In fact they do not fight at all in the old sense. Mr Battler can wipe out London, Portsmouth, and all our big provincial cities in a day. We should then be obliged to wipe out Hamburg and all the eastern cities from Munster to Salzburg. Signor Bombardone can wipe out Tunis, Nice, Algiers, Marseilles, Toulouse, Lyons, and every city south of the Loire, and oblige the French, headed by the British fleet, to wipe out Naples, Venice, Florence, Rome, and even Milan by return of post. The process can go on until the European stock of munitions and air pilots is exhausted. But it is a process by which none of us can win, and all of us must lose frightfully. Which of us dare take the responsibility of dropping the first bomb?

BATTLER. Our precautions against attack from the air are perfect.

SIR O. Ours are not, unfortunately. Nobody believes

in them. I certainly do not. You must allow me to doubt the efficiency of yours.

JUDGE. And your precautions, Signor? Are they efficient?

BBDE. They do not exist. Our strength is in our willingness to die.

JUDGE. That seems to complicate murder with suicide. However, am I to take it that you are all provided with the means to effect this destruction, and to retaliate in kind if they are used against you?

SIR O. What else can we do, sir?

JUDGE. I find myself in a difficulty. I have listened to you all and watched you very attentively. You seem to me to be personally harmless human beings, capable of meeting one another and chatting on fairly pleasant terms. There is no reason why you should not be good neighbors. So far, my work of building up a body of international law by judicial precedent would seem to be simple enough. Unfortunately when any question of foreign policy arises you confront me with a black depth of scoundrelism which calls for nothing short of your immediate execution.

The Leaders and the British contingent, except the Newcomer, rise indignantly.

NEWCOMER. Hear hear! Hear hear! Hear hear! SIR O. Scoundrelism! BATTLER. Execution! BOMBARDONE. You are mad.

JUDGE. If you dislike the word execution I am willing to substitute liquidation. The word scoundrelism and its adjectives I cannot withdraw. Your objective is domination: your weapons fire and poison, starvation and ruin, extermination by every means known to science. You have reduced one another to such a condition of terror that no atrocity makes you recoil and say that you will die rather than commit it. You call this patriotism, courage, glory. There are a thousand good things to be done in your countries. They remain undone for hundreds of years; but the fire and the poison are always up to date. If this be not scoundrelism what is scoundrelism? I give you up as hopeless. Man is a failure as a political animal. The creative forces which produce him must produce something better. [*The telephone rings*]. Pardon me a moment. [*Changing countenance and holding up his hand for silence*] I am sorry to have to announce a very grave piece of news. Mr Battler's troops have invaded Ruritania.

General consternation. All rise to their feet except Battler, who preserves an iron calm.

JUDGE. Is this true, Mr Battler?

BATTLER. I am a man of action, not a dreamer. While you have been talking my army has been doing. Bardo: the war for the mastery of the world has begun. It is you and I, and, I presume, our friend Fortinbras, against the effete so-called democracies of which the people of Europe and America are tired.

BBDE. Ernest: you have done this without consulting me. I warned you a year ago, when you were negotiating with a relative of Sir Orpheus here, that I could not afford another war.

FLANCO. Neither can I.

All sit down gradually, greatly relieved, except Battler.

BATTLER [*rising in great agitation*] Bardo: are you going to betray me? Remember the axis. Dare you break it?

BBDE. Damn the axis! Do you suppose I am going to ruin my country to make you emperor of the universe? You should know me better [*He resumes his seat majestically*].

BATTLER. This is the most shameless betrayal in

human history. General Flanco: you owe your victory to my aid. Will you be such a monster of ingratitude as to desert me now?

FLANCO. I owe my victory equally to the aid of Signor Bombardone and to the masterly non-intervention policy of Sir Orpheus Midlander. I cannot prove ungrateful to either of them.

BATTLER. Well, traitors as you are, I can do without you. I can conquer Ruritania single-handed, no thanks to either of you. But where should I be if the British were not afraid to fight. Fortunately for me they do not believe in what they call brute force. [*He sits*].

SIR O. [*rising*] Pardon me. It is true that we abhor brute force, and are willing to make any sacrifice for the sake of peace—or almost any sacrifice. We understood that this was your attitude also. But I had the honor of informing you explicitly—very explicitly, Mr Battler—that Ruritania is, so to speak, our little sister, and that if you laid a finger on her we should—pardon me if in my indignant surprise at your breach of the peace I am unable to adhere to the language of diplomacy—we should be obliged to knock the stuffing out of you. That is our British method of meeting brute force.

BATTLER. What! You will fight?

SIR O. Fight, Mr Battler! We shall wipe you off the face of the earth. [*He resumes his seat*].

BATTLER. Then I am alone: *contra mundum.* Well, I have never failed yet.

FLANCO. Because you have never fought yet.

BATTLER. We shall see. I shall sweep through Ruritania like a hurricane.

COMMISSAR. Do so by all means, Comrade Battler. When you have finished you will settle with me how much of it you may keep.

BATTLER. What! You too! So the encirclement is complete.

SIR ORPHEUS. No! I cannot permit that expression. Outflanked if you like. Hemmed in if you will have it so. I will even go so far as to say surrounded. But encircled, NO.

NEWCOMER. It puts the kybosh on Battlerism anyhow.

The telephone rings again.

ALL EXCEPT THE JUDGE. Hush. Let us hear the news. The news. The news. [*They listen with strained attention*]. Sh-sh-sh-sh-sh-.

JUDGE. What? Say that again: I must take it down: I do not understand. [*Writing as he listens*] "Astronomers report that the orbit of the earth is jumping to its next quantum. Message received at Greenwich from three American observatories. Humanity is doomed." Thank you. Goodbye. Can anyone explain this? Why is humanity doomed?

SECRETARY. It is intelligible enough, and very serious indeed.

JUDGE. It is not intelligible to me. Will you kindly explain?

SECRETARY. The orbit of the earth is the path in which it travels round the sun. As the sun is 93 million miles distant it takes us a year to get round.

JUDGE. We all know that. But the message says that the orbit is jumping to its next quantum. What does quantum mean?

SECRETARY. When orbits change they dont change gradually. They suddenly jump by distances called quantums or quanta. Nobody knows why. If the earth is jumping to a wider orbit it is taking us millions of miles further away from the sun. That will take us into the awful cold of space. The icecaps that we have on the north and south poles will spread over the whole earth. Even the polar bears will be frozen stiff. Not a trace of any sort of life known to us will be possible on this earth.

THE JEW [*rising and hurrying to the door*] Excuse me.

COMMISSAR. No use running away, my friend. The icecap will overtake you wherever you go.

SECRETARY. Let him alone. The shock has made him ill.

THE JEW. No: not that. I must telephone [*he goes out*].

JUDGE [*rising*] Fellow citizens: this is the end. The end of war, of law, of leaders and foreign secretaries, of judges and generals. A moment ago we were important persons: the fate of Europe seemed to depend on us. What are we now? Democracy, Fascism, Communism: how much do they matter? Your totalitarian Catholic Church: does it still seem so very totalitarian?

FLANCO. Do not blaspheme at such a moment, sir. You tell us that nothing matters. Ten minutes ago the judgment of God seemed far off: now we stand at the gates of purgatory. We have to organize absolution for millions of our people; and we have barely priests enough to do it, even if we have no converts to deal with; and we shall have many converts. We Catholics know what to do; and I have no more time to spend trifling here with men who know nothing and believe nothing. [*He moves towards the door. He stops to hear Sir O.*]

SIR O. One moment, I beg of you. This rumor must be contradicted at all costs.

COMMISSAR. How can you contradict a scientific fact?

SIR O. It must be contradicted—officially contradicted. Think of the consequences if it is believed! People will throw off all decency, all prudence. Only the Jews, with the business faculty peculiar to their race, will profit by our despair. Why has our Jewish friend just left us? To telephone, he said. Yes; but to whom is he telephoning? To his stockbroker, gentlemen. He is instructing his stockbroker to sell gilt-edged in any quantity, at any price, knowing that if this story gets about before settling day he will be able to buy it for the price of waste paper and be a millionaire until the icecap overtakes him. It must not be. I will take the necessary steps in England. The Astronomer Royal will deny this story this afternoon. You two gentlemen must see to it at once that it is officially denied in your countries.

COMMISSAR. Suppose your Astronomer Royal refuses to tell a lie. Remember: he is a man of science, not a politician.

SIR O. He is an Englishman, sir, and has some common sense. He will do his duty. Can I depend on the rest of you gentlemen?

BBDE. Can you depend on the icecap? I must go home at once. There will be a rush to the equator. My country stands right in the way of that rush. I must stop it at our frontier at any cost.

COMMISSAR. Why? Will it matter?

BBDE. I will not tolerate disorder. I will not tolerate fear. We shall die decently, stoically, steadfast at our posts, like Romans. Remember: we shall not decay: we shall stand to all eternity in cold storage. When we are discovered by some explorer from another star or another race that can live and breathe at absolute zero, he shall find my people erect at their posts like the Pompeian sentinel. You also, Ernest, must— What! Crying!! For shame, man! The world looks to us for leadership. Shall it find us in tears?

BATTLER. Let me alone. My dog Blonda will be

frozen to death. My doggie! My little doggie! [*He breaks down, sobbing convulsively*].

NEWCOMER. Oh, come, old man. Dont take it so hard. I used to keep dogs myself; but I had to give it up: I couldnt bear the shortness of their lives. Youd have had to lose your little doggie some day.

Battler takes out his handkerchief and controls himself; but the Deaconess bursts into tears.

BEGONIA. Oh for God's sake, dont you start crying. You will set us all off. It's hard enough on us without that.

THE SECRETARY. Yes, maam. Take your trouble to Jesus; and set all the women a good example.

DEACONESS. But in heaven I shall lose my Jesus. There He will be a king; and there will be no more troubles and sorrows and sins to bring to Him. My life has been so happy since I found Him and came to Him a year ago! He made heaven for me on earth; and now that is all over. I cannot bear it. [*Her tears overcome her*].

NEWCOMER. Oh come come! This wont do, you know. All you people seem to think you were going to live for ever. Well, you werent. Our numbers are up; but so they were before, sooner or later. I dont complain: I havnt had such a bad time of it; and I am ready to depart, as the poet says, if it must be. In fact I must depart now and cheer up the missus. [*He rises to go*].

DEACONESS. Oh, sir, do you believe this? May it not be untrue?

NEWCOMER [*gravely*] No: it's true all right enough. If it were a priest's tale or a superstition out of the Bible I shouldnt give a snap of my fingers for it. But Science cannot be wrong. Weve got to face it. Good morning, gents.

The Newcomer goes out; and his departure breaks up the court. The Leaders and the General rise and come forward together.

DEACONESS [*to Flanco*] Oh, General, is Science always right?

FLANCO. Certainly not: it is always wrong. But I await the decision of the Church. Until that is delivered the story has no authority.

SIR O. May I suggest that you use all your influence at Rome to obtain an immediate decision from the Church against this story?

FLANCO. You shock me. The Church cannot be influenced. It knows the truth as God knows it, and will instruct us accordingly. Anyone who questions its decision will be shot. My business is to see to that. After absolution, of course. Good morning. [*He goes out*].

WIDOW. He at least has something to offer to men about to die.

COMMISSAR. Dope.

JUDGE. Why not, if they die comforted?

BATTLER. Men must learn to die undeluded.

BBDE. Flanco is dead; but he does not know it. History would have kicked him out were not History now on its deathbed.

BEGONIA. I must say I thought the general a perfect gentleman. I never wanted to kick him while he was speaking. I wanted to kick you two all the time.

THE BETROTHED. Steady, Gonny, steady! Mustnt be rude, you know.

BEGONIA. Oh, what does it matter now? As we shall all be frozen stiff presently we may as well have the satisfaction of speaking our minds until then.

THE BETROTHED. Take it easy, dear. Have a choc.

BEGONIA. No, thank you.

THE BETROTHED. I say, Uncle O: this is the first time she has ever refused a choc.

SIR O. Our valuations have changed, naturally.

THE BETROTHED. Mine havnt. You know, uncle, I think theres something in your notion of selling out and having a tremendous spree before the icecaps nip us. How does that strike you, Gonny?

BEGONIA. I dont pretend it might not have appealed to me before I represented Intellectual Co-operation. But I am a Dame of the British Empire now; and if I must die I will die like a Dame. [*She goes out*].

SIR O. Go with her, sir. And mind you behave yourself.

THE BETROTHED. Well, it does seem rather a pity. However— [*He shrugs resignedly and goes out*].

SIR O. [*to the Commissar*] Do you, sir, understand what is going to happen? My classical education did not include science.

COMMISSAR. I await instructions. The Marxian dialectic does not include the quantum theory. I must consult Moscow. [*He goes out*].

SIR O. Have these men no minds of their own? One of them must consult Rome: the other must consult Moscow. You two gentlemen fortunately have no one but yourselves to consult. Can I rely on you to do your utmost to stifle this appalling news while I return to London to consult the Cabinet?

BBDE. You can rely on nothing but this. The news has just been broadcast to all the world through the arrangements made for publicity in this court. According to you, the result will be that the people will throw off all decency and repudiate all leadership. I say that the people will want a leader as they have never wanted one before. I have taught them to order their lives: I shall teach them to order their deaths.

The magnitude of the catastrophe is the measure of the leader's greatness.

SIR O. You always have a speech which sounds equal to the occasion. In England that gift would make you Prime Minister. But your very excitable countrymen may run wild.

BBDE. In that case I can do nothing but fall at the head of an attempt to stem the rush. At least one man shall stand for human courage and dignity when the race expires.

SIR O. Yes: that is a very fine attitude and quite a correct one. But have you nothing better to propose than an attitude?

BBDE. Has anyone anything better to propose than an attitude?

SIR O. I suppose not; but I feel strongly that a burst of sincerity would be a great relief.

BBDE. [*to Battler*] Give him his burst of sincerity, Ernest. Cry for your dog again. Good morning, gentlemen. [*He goes to the door*].

BATTLER [*calling after him*] You will have the honor of sharing my little dog's fate. But nobody will weep for you, Bardo.

BBDE. I hope not. I do not deal in tears. [*He strides out*].

BATTLER. What an actor!

SECRETARY. You should be a good judge of that. You have done a good deal in that line yourself.

BATTLER. We all have. But I claim to have done a little good with my acting. I will not have my work undone. We shall not stand in statuesque attitudes in Bardo's manner: we shall work to the last, and set an example to the new race of iceproof men who will follow us.

SIR O. Still, you know, it's no use going on making motor cars that you know will never run.

BATTLER. Yes: when the alternative is to wring our hands in despair or get drunk. We cannot work for ourselves to the last moment; but we can all work for honor. [*He goes out*].

SIR O. Wonderful luck that man has! His dog will get him into all the headlines. [*He goes out*].

JUDGE [*to the Deaconess and the widow*] Ladies: I am afraid there is nothing more to be done here.

DEACONESS [*rising*] None of you understands what this means to me, because none of you has learnt how to live. You are souls in torment, as I was until six months ago. And now I must die when I have only just learnt to live. Excuse me: I cannot bear to speak of it [*she goes out distractedly*].

JUDGE. She, at least, values her life.

SECRETARY. Yes: she belongs to some movement or other.

WIDOW [*taking her pistol from her handbag and rising*] I killed my best friend with this. I kept it to kill myself. It is useless now: God will execute His own judgment on us all. [*She throws it into the waste paper basket*]. But He is merciful; for I shall never dream again. And [*to the Secretary*] I do not belong to any movement.

He bows; and she goes out.

SECRETARY. Can you switch off?

JUDGE [*going to the table and turning a masterswitch*] No one can hear us now. [*Returning*] Can this thing be true?

SECRETARY. No. It is utter nonsense. If the earth made a spring to a wider orbit half a minute would carry us to regions of space where we could not breathe and our blood would freeze in our veins.

JUDGE. Yet we all believed it for the moment.

SECRETARY. You have nothing to do but mention the

quantum theory, and people will take your voice for the voice of Science and believe anything. It broke up this farce of a trial, at all events.

JUDGE. Not a farce, my friend. They came, these fellows. They blustered: they defied us. But they came. They came.

Author's Note

(*Malvern Festival Book*, 1938)

Geneva is a title that speaks for itself. I hope the Malvern pilgrims this year will be reasonable about it. The critics are sure to complain that I have not solved all the burning political problems of the present and future in it, and restored peace to Europe and Asia. They always do. I am flattered by the implied attribution to me of omniscience and omnipotence; but I am also infuriated by the unreasonableness of the demand. I am neither omniscient nor omnipotent; and the utmost I or any other playwright can do is to extract comedy and tragedy from the existing situation and wait and see what will become of it.

Unfortunately, nobody seems to know what the existing situation is. For instance, how many people have heard of the Intellectual Cooperation Committee? It will probably be dismissed by the critics as an overstrained fiction. It is nothing of the sort. The League of Nations had not been long in existence when a Frenchman, perceiving that without intellectual cooperation the League could do nothing but practise the old diplomacy, founded the Committee in Paris. Everyone was delighted; and the most eminent intellects in the world gave their names as intellectual cooperators. The Frenchman gave a million francs to endow the Committee; but as the French franc had dropped to twopence (having been largely borrowed at tenpence) the Committee was stony-broke at the end of a month. It still survived in a little office somewhere (I have invented one in Geneva for it in the play) and even did and does some clerical work in listing universities, learned societies, and the like; but intellectually it sank into profound catalepsy.

When Romain Rolland, with the late Henri Barbusse and their friends, tried from time to time to organize some international movement on the extreme Left and invited me, as they always did, to join them, I asked them why they did not operate through the I.C. Committee of the League, which was sleeping ready to their hands. The suggestion struck them dumb. At last the Committee, which occasionally woke up in the person of Gilbert Murray, asked me to correspond with the League. This very nearly struck me dumb; for what on earth was I to correspond about? Now Gilbert Murray, unlike most fiercely militant Pacifists, has a strong sense of humour and believes in telepathy. He practises it too. And so it came about that I found it growing on me that there was some fun to be got on the stage out of the Committee.

That was how this play began. How it will finish—for in the theatre it only stops; it does not finish—nobody knows. I call your attention, however, to one novelty: instead of making the worst of all dictators, which only drives them out of the League, I have made the best of them, and even given them some measure of fair play. I hope they will like it.

New Shaw Play and Germany

(A letter to the Editor of *The Observer*, London, 21 August 1938)

Sir.—Your Berlin correspondent's interesting account of this matter describes my able and devoted translator, Siegfried Trebitsch, to whom I owed my vogue as a playwright in Germany long before I enjoyed any in these islands, bluntly, as a Jew. Now Herr

Trebitsch is an uncircumcised and baptised Lutheran German who has never as far as I know, set foot in a synagogue in his life, married to a lady of unquestioned Christian authenticity. He may have a Jewish ancestor; but which of us has not; for as Signor Bombardone points out, every person now living must be descended not only from Adam and Eve, but from everyone who was alive in the days of Abraham, including Abraham himself. Christianity has absorbed many millions of Jews since it was founded by a Jew; and it has very completely absorbed Siegfried Trebitsch. The observing circumcised Jew from the Ghetto may still present a problem to Gentile States; but an absorbed Jew presents no problem at all, and must be classed as a citizen of the State under which he was born. It is really misleading to call Herr Trebitsch a Jew in any separate sense.

There will be no difficulty about the appearance of my play entitled "Geneva" in the German language. If the German version is not published in Germany it will be published elsewhere. But there is no need to anticipate any trouble. If the Germans should fancy a resemblance between Herr Hitler and Ernest Battler there is no reason why der Führer should feel otherwise than flattered. The shock if any, will be to his modesty.—Yours, etc.,

G. Bernard Shaw

For the Press

(Press release sent to Roy Limbert on 19 November 1938, prior to the London première of *Geneva* at the Saville Theatre on 22 November. Reproduced from corrected typescript in the Humanities Research Center of the University of Texas at Austin)

I cannot imagine anything more ridiculous than an attempt to work out an equation between the price of theatre seats and the genius of the author of the play or of the performers. It would simply lead to pricing the stalls at a Shakespear or Shaw performance at a hundred guineas. Do any of these foolish people suppose that Henry Irving ever put himself down in his accounts for as high a salary as that commanded by the low comedian Arthur Roberts? Do they consider that my dignity is compromised by the fact that my plays are sometimes performed to audiences who pay nothing at the doors, but drop what they please or can afford into the hat when it is passed round after the fall of the curtain? In the United States I have placed all my published plays at the disposal of the Federal Theatre on condition that the highest price charged for admission is two shillings. Theatregoing in the West End of London is far too dear. When Bancroft made the theatre dependent on the plutocracy by introducing the half guinea stall and crushing the playbill between the upper millstone of the fashionable dinner hour and the nether one of the suburban trains and trams, he knocked serious drama and big acting on the head. It would be more sensible to have different prices on different nights: say all seats a guinea today, all seats a shilling tomorrow, and perhaps all seats half a crown the day after. At the Saville I have not objected to the lower prices: on the contrary I tried to induce them to abolish the half guinea stall. No play is worth half a guinea to our hard-up playgoers; and they are all hard up except the handful of rich people whom I do my best to make uncomfortable. I learnt my business as a playwright in the pit. And the pit then came right up to the orchestra. What do you think of that? Goodmorning.

Telescoping "Geneva"

(*The Times*, London, 22 April 1939)

An ingenious and amusing summary of the first two acts of *Geneva* has been written by Mr. Bernard Shaw to introduce the televised performance of the third act of his play which is to be given on Sunday evening with Mr. Cecil Trouncer and Mr. Walter Hudd as the dictators, Battler and Bombardone, who appear before the International Court of Justice at The Hague to answer charges brought against them by "the Toms, Dicks, Harriets, Susans, and Elizas" of all nations. Sir Orpheus Midlander, the British Secretary of State for Foreign Affairs, will be played by Mr. Ernest Thesiger.

At the beginning of the synopsis Mr. Shaw implicitly admits the need for economy in time in dealing with *Geneva*, and accepts the opinion of the critics that the third act is the one that matters. Following this his summary goes on:—"All that is generally known about the League of Nations is that it holds assemblies in Geneva at which the nations which belong to it confer with one another from time to time. But there is more than this in it. There is a Committee for International Cooperation which is so little known, and so neglected and starved that until Mr. Shaw's play appeared hardly anyone knew of its existence; and even now they believe that it is an invention of Mr. Shaw's. But it is quite real: Mr. Shaw has only transferred its office from Paris to Geneva; and it is at this office that the play opens with nobody in charge of it except a young typist from Camberwell who, as the winner of a County Council scholarship, has a considerable opinion of herself. As nobody ever visits the office or knows of its existence, she is astonished when on one and the same morning she is called upon by five people in succession, each with a grievance which they expect her to remedy as the representative of intellectual cooperation in Europe. She has not the faintest idea of how to set about it until the first visitor, a persecuted Jew, suggests that she apply to the International Court at The Hague for a warrant against his persecutors. The second visitor is a British democrat who has been locked out of a colonial legislature to which he has been elected. The third is the widow of a Central American President who has been shot. She has also been compelled by etiquette to shoot her best friend for having engaged the affection of her husband.

"The fourth is an English Bishop whose grievance is that the Bolshevists have converted his footman to Communism. The fifth is a Russian Commissar who has to complain on behalf of his Government that the Church of England, by number 18 of the 39 Articles, declares that all Russians are accursed. The Bishop drops dead on discovering that he has dined with the Commissar under the impression that he was a Conservative; consequently there are only four plaintiffs left alive.

"The Camberwell typist, at the suggestion of the Jew, and not knowing what else to do, applies to the International Court at The Hague, in the name of her Committee, for summonses against the dictators of Europe. The crisis she creates by this unprecedented step is terrific: and she becomes so popular that she has to be made a Dame of the British Empire to satisfy public feeling. It is expected that the International Court will ignore her application; but an able and resolute young Judge at The Hague insists on taking it seriously; and the summonses to the dictators are duly issued.

"The third act of the play opens in the International Court, with no one present but the four plaintiffs, the secretary of the League of Nations, the Camberwell typist, and an infatuated young gentleman who has become betrothed to her. They are presently joined by Sir Orpheus Midlander, the British Secretary of State for Foreign Affairs. He is the only person in the play whose name is revealed, except the Camberwell lady, whose full style and title is now Dame Begonia Brown. They are all waiting in tense expectation to see what will happen."

Further Meditations on Shaw's "Geneva" by Shaw

(Published from undated typescript [*c.* 1939] in the British Museum: Add. Mss. 50643, ff. 196–199)

I wish I could persuade Englishmen to be logical in their mental operations instead of proceeding recklessly by association of ideas. I cannot admit the most obvious fact of the political situation without being at once accused of harboring a bundle of miscellaneous opinions which happen to be associated with that fact in the minds of my readers. I am repeatedly reminded of an acquaintance of mine, a colonel in the British army, who said to me fifty years ago, when religious controversy was crude and hot, "I happen to know for a fact that the rector's son is the father of his housemaid's child; and after that you may tell me, if you like, that the Bible is true; I dont believe it." All the arguments of Voltaire and Tom Paine would have been thrown away on this officer; but the rector's son made an "infidel" of him at a single entirely irrelevant stroke.

Man is, so far, a failure as a political animal: he can manage neither aggregations of millions of his species nor the powers of destruction that chemistry has put into his hands. His big civilizations have broken down again and again. That is a hard fact which I recognize. But it does not follow that I despair of mankind, that I have fallen at the feet of the dictators, that I am no longer a Socialist but a pessimist, that like Job's wife I call on Mr Rowse and on the Intelligent Woman for whom I wrote a Guide to curse democracy and die. What is democracy? Government in the interest of the whole people and not of a privileged class. What are the ideas associated with the word democracy in the English mind? Adult suffrage, the House of Commons, and the Party System. When I point out the obvious fact that adult suffrage, consummated in England 20 years ago by giving the casting vote to Miss Begonia Brown, is a guarantee of petty snobbery and parochial ignorance in the choice of rulers, and that the party system in Parliament has made the House of Commons quite useless as a check on plutocratic oligarchy and completely effective in paralyzing the government industrially and reducing all democratic leaders to helpless impotence, it is immediately assumed that I have renounced democracy and socialism and am now a Fascist and adore Messrs Mussolini and Hitler, who, not being reduced to impotence by membership of our House of Commons, have both done a lot of things that badly want doing here, but cannot be done because to do them would infringe British liberty to be governed by Begonia. For what is done or not done these two men are responsible and can be brought to account, whereas in England the political responsibility under adult suffrage is everybody's; and what is everybody's responsibility is nobody's responsibility.

A democratic Press is a Press that is open to all reasonable opinions. When I point out that such a Press is impossible in a country where only persons in command of £50,000 can start a magazine and of £250,000 a daily newspaper, I am at once assumed to be opposed to freedom of the Press. When I point out that the English are left without the restraints on individual freedom which continental dictators impose solely because, as my countrymen put it, "It would be waste of time to muzzle a sheep," or, as I put it, waste of time to put chains on people fettered hand, foot and brain by uncertainty as to next week's [*blank in original*], I am supposed to be calling for more and heavy fetters to hang on the free people.

And so on and so forth.

Now the point of all this is that all the mischievous institutions which have produced the poverty, unemployment, class war, and foreign war which threaten us with another collapse of civilization, and which led the late Edward Carpenter, author of Towards Democracy, to describe civilization as a disease for which we had to find a cure, are not results of human cupidity, ferocity, and general depravity. They were all founded with the very best intentions. Private property in land was not established to deprive the cultivator of the fruits of his labor, but to secure it to him. War was not organized to gratify a lust for rapine, pillage, and murder, but to protect society against them. When Shakespear advocated the enclosure of common lands at Welcombe he had not read Karl Marx or Henry George: he was impatient of the frightful extent to which land was being wasted because nobody owned it. The barbarities of our criminal code are meant to prevent crime, not to encourage it. The superstition of blood sacrifice with which our Book of Common Prayer is saturated was meant to propitiate a bloodthirsty God and save the nations from plague, pestilence, and famine; and it is to human nature that we owe the reform of Moloch and the Mexican deities into "Our Father which art in Heaven," and the sacrifices into a symbolic wafer of bread and a sip of cheap wine. When the religion of Europe was founded on the infallibility of Semite scriptures, and Galileo made a statement which knocked that infallibility into a cocked hat, the Church was seeking the salvation of Europe when it gave Galileo his choice between withdrawing his statement and being [*word missing in original*] as a heretic.

It was not until the nineteenth century that a playwright named Ibsen, from Norway, shewed that it is not the villainy of mankind that is destroying us, but those very good intentions and ideals, patriotic, domestic, and religious. It is our good men that we need to get rid of, our bad ones being politically negligible. If Ibsen were alive now he would warn Europe that it was not Mr [Neville] Chamberlain's imagined vices that are to be feared, but his very real virtues, not Herr Hitler's imagined resemblance to King Richard the Third, but his very real resemblance to Saint Louis and Charlemagne.

It is not a change of heart that is needed: our hearts are in the right place. It is a change of head. Scientific education, in short. Teach Shakespear the Ricardian law of rent, and he will see that the remedy for wasted land is not selling it to himself or to the Lucy family. Teach Herr Hitler that the vigor of his nation and ours is due to the fact that we are nations of arrant mongrels, and that if we begin with inbreeding we should end with the brains of Borzoi dogs and a general prevalence of paralysis and hæmophilia, and he will follow my advice and not only invite the Jews back to Germany but make it punishable incest for a Jew to marry anybody but an Aryan. If he could be persuaded to substitute my Intelligent Woman's Guide to Socialism and Capitalism for Mein Kampf we should hear no more indignantly virtuous denunciation of Communism by people who are steeped in it up to the neck and whose civilization would crumble and themselves perish miserably of hunger and violence if it were abolished or even suspended for a week.

Therefore I exhort Mr Rowse to be of good cheer. It is our people who are wrong: it is our education. As Mr Lancelot Hogben words it, we want Scientific Humanism as a basis of all our other isms. It was for lack of that that the old civilization collapsed, and the half a dozen or so of the new ones may collapse too. But the remedy is plain; and we shall round the cape sometime or other without being wrecked.

Finally remember that democracy did great things when it was an ideal. It was its reduction to reality in the idiocy of Begonia Brown that produced the snobocracy of the last twenty years. She and Henry Dubb will not control the destinies of the British Commonwealth for long. If they do there will soon be no British Commonwealth.

Cymbeline Refinished: A Variation on Shakespear's Ending

WITH

Foreword

Composition begun *c.* 3 December 1936; completed December 1936. Published in the *London Mercury*, February 1938. First collected in *Geneva, Cymbeline Refinished, & Good King Charles*, 1947. First presented at the Embassy Theatre, Swiss Cottage, London, on 16 November 1937.

A Captain *Patrick Kinsella*
Philario *Mario Francelli*
Posthumus *Geoffrey Toone*
Iachimo *George Hayes*
Belarius *Earle Grey*
Arviragus *Philip Geddes*
Caius Lucius *Norman Wooland*
Cymbeline *George Woodbridge*
Imogen *Joyce Bland*
Guiderius *Gordon Edwards*
Pisanio *William Devlin*

Period—Britain under the Roman Occupation. First Century B.C.

ACT V *A Rocky Defile. A Wild Evening*

Foreword

The practice of improving Shakespear's plays, more especially in the matter of supplying them with what are called happy endings, is an old established one which has always been accepted without protest by British audiences. When Mr Harley Granville-Barker, following up some desperate experiments by the late William Poel, introduced the startling innovation of performing the plays in the West End of London exactly as Shakespear wrote them, there was indeed some demur; but it was expressed outside the theatre and led to no rioting. And it set on foot a new theory of Shakespearean representation. Up to that time it had been assumed as a matter of course that everyone behind the scenes in a theatre must know much better than Shakespear how plays should be written, exactly as it is believed in the Hollywood studios today that everyone in a film studio knows better than any professional playwright how a play should be filmed. But the pleasure given by Mr Granville-Barker's productions shook that conviction in the theatre; and the superstition that Shakespear's plays as written by him are impossible on the stage, which had produced a happy ending to King Lear, Cibber's Richard III, a love scene in the tomb of the Capulets between Romeo and Juliet before the poison takes effect, and had culminated in the crude literary butcheries successfully imposed on the public and the critics as Shakespear's plays by Henry Irving and Augustin Daly at the end of the last century, is for the moment heavily discredited. It may be asked then why I, who always fought fiercely against that superstition in the days when I was a journalist-critic, should perpetrate a spurious fifth act to Cymbeline, and do it too, not wholly as a literary *jeu d'esprit*, but in response to an actual emergency in the theatre when it was proposed to revive Cymbeline at no less sacred a place than the Shakespear Memorial Theatre at Stratford-upon-Avon.

Cymbeline, though one of the finest of Shakespear's later plays now on the stage, goes to pieces in the last act. In fact I mooted the point myself by thoughtlessly saying that the revival would be all right if I wrote a last act for it. To my surprise this blasphemy was received with acclamation; and as the applause, like the proposal, was not wholly jocular, the fancy began to haunt me, and persisted until I exorcised it by writing the pages which ensue.

I had a second surprise when I began by reading the authentic last act carefully through. I had not done so for many years, and had the common impression about it that it was a cobbled-up affair by several hands, including a vision in prison accompanied by scraps of quite ridiculous doggerel.

For this estimate I found absolutely no justification nor excuse. I must have got it from the last revival of the play at the old Lyceum theatre, when Irving, as Iachimo, a statue of romantic melancholy, stood dumb on the stage for hours (as it seemed) whilst the others toiled through a series of *dénouements* of crushing tedium, in which the characters lost all their vitality and individuality, and had nothing to do but identify themselves by moles on their necks, or explain why they were not dead. The vision and the verses were cut out as a matter of course; and I ignorantly thanked Heaven for it.

When I read the act as aforesaid I found that my notion that it is a cobbled-up *pasticcio* by other hands was an unpardonable stupidity. The act is genuine Shakespear to the last full stop, and late phase Shakespear in point of verbal workmanship.

The doggerel is not doggerel: it is a versified masque, in Shakespear's careless woodnotes wild, complete with Jupiter as *deus ex machina*, eagle and all, introduced, like the Ceres scene in The Tempest, to please King Jamie, or else because an irresistible fashion had set in, just as at all the great continental opera houses a ballet used to be *de rigueur*. Gounod had to introduce one into his Faust, and Wagner into his Tannhäuser, before they could be staged at the Grand Opera in Paris. So, I take it, had Shakespear to stick a masque into Cymbeline. Performed as such, with suitable music and enough pictorial splendor, it is not only entertaining on the stage, but, with the very Shakespearean feature of a comic jailor which precedes it, just the thing to save the last act.

Without it the act is a tedious string of unsurprising *dénouements* sugared with insincere sentimentality after a ludicrous stage battle. With one exception the characters have vanished and left nothing but dolls being moved about like the glass balls in the game of solitaire until they are all got rid of but one. The exception is the hero, or rather the husband of the heroine, Leonatus Posthumus. The late Charles Charrington, who with his wife Janet Achurch broke the ice for Ibsen in England, used to cite Posthumus as Shakespear's anticipation of his Norwegian rival. Certainly, after being theatrically conventional to the extent of ordering his wife to be murdered, he begins to criticize, quite on the lines of Mrs Alving in Ghosts, the slavery to an inhuman ideal of marital fidelity which led him to this villainous extremity. One may say that he is the only character left really alive in the last act; and as I cannot change him for the better I have left most of his part untouched. I make no apology for my attempt to bring the others back to dramatic activity and individuality.

I should like to have retained Cornelius as the exponent of Shakespear's sensible and scientific detestation of vivisection. But as he has nothing to say except that the Queen is dead, and nobody can possibly care a rap whether she is alive or dead, I have left him with her in the box of puppets that are done with.

I have ruthlessly cut out the surprises that no longer surprise anybody. I really could not keep my countenance over the identification of Guiderius by the mole on his neck. That device was killed by Maddison Morton, once a famous farce writer, now forgotten by everyone save Mr Gordon Craig and myself. In Morton's masterpiece, Box and Cox, Box asks Cox whether he has a strawberry mark on his left arm. "No" says Cox. "Then you are my long lost brother" says Box as they fall into one another's arms and end the farce happily. One could wish that Guiderius had anticipated Cox.

Plot has always been the curse of serious drama, and indeed of serious literature of any kind. It is so out-of-place there that Shakespear never could invent one. Unfortunately, instead of taking Nature's hint and discarding plots, he borrowed them all over the place and got into trouble through having to unravel them in the last act, especially in The Two Gentlemen of Verona and Cymbeline. The more childish spectators may find some delight in the revelation that Polydore and Cadwal are Imogen's long lost brothers and Cymbeline's long lost sons; that Iachimo is now an occupant of the penitent form and very unlike his old self; and that Imogen is so dutiful that she accepts her husband's attempt to have her murdered with affectionate docility. I cannot share these infantile joys. Having become interested in Iachimo, in Imogen, and even in the two long lost princes, I wanted to know how their characters would react to the *éclaircissement* which follows the battle. The only way to satify this curiosity was to rewrite the act as Shakespear might have written it if he had been post-Ibsen and post-Shaw instead of post-Marlowe.

In doing so I had to follow the Shakespearean verse pattern to match the 89 lines of Shakespear's text which I retained. This came very easily to me. It happened when I was a child that one of the books I delighted in was an illustrated Shakespear, with a picture and two or three lines of text underneath it on every third or fourth page. Ever since, Shakespearean blank verse has been to me as natural a form of literary expression as the Augustan English to which I was brought up in Dublin, or the latest London fashion in dialogue. It is so easy that if it were possible to kill it it would have been burlesqued to death by Tom Thumb, Chrononhotonthologos, and Bombastes Furioso. But Shakespear will survive any possible extremity of caricature.

I shall not deprecate the most violent discussion as to the propriety of meddling with masterpieces. All I can say is that the temptation to do it, and sometimes the circumstances which demand it, are irresistible. The results are very various. When a mediocre artist tries to improve on a great artist's work the effect is ridiculous or merely contemptible. When the alteration damages the original, as when a bad painter repaints a Velasquez or a Rembrandt, he commits a crime. When the changed work is sold or exhibited as the original, the fraud is indictable. But when it comes to complete forgery, as in the case of Ireland's Vortigern, which was much admired and at last actually performed as a play by Shakespear, the affair passes beyond the sphere of crime and becomes an instructive joke.

But what of the many successful and avowed variations? What about the additions made by Mozart to the score of Handel's Messiah? Elgar, who adored Handel, and had an unbounded contempt for all the lesser meddlers, loved Mozart's variations, and dismissed all purist criticism of them by maintaining that Handel must have extemporized equivalents to them on the organ at his concerts. When Spontini found on his visit to Dresden that Wagner had added trombone parts to his choruses, he appropriated them very gratefully. Volumes of variations on the tunes of other composers were published as such by Mozart and Beethoven, to say nothing of Bach and Handel, who played Old Harry with any air that amused them. Would anyone now remember Diabelli's vulgar waltz but for Beethoven's amazing variations, one of which is also a variation on an air from Don Giovanni?

And now consider the practice of Shakespear himself. Tolstoy declared that the original Lear is superior to Shakespear's rehandling, which he abhorred as immoral. Nobody has ever agreed with him. Will it be contended that Shakespear had no right to refashion Hamlet? If he had spoiled both plays, that would be a reason for reviving them without Shakespear's transfigurations, but not for challenging Shakespear's right to remake them.

Accordingly, I feel no qualm of conscience and have no apology to make for indulging in a variation on the last act of Cymbeline. I stand in the same time relation to Shakespear as Mozart to Handel, or Wagner to

Beethoven. Like Mozart, I have not confined myself to the journeyman's job of writing "additional accompaniments": I have luxuriated in variations. Like Wagner dealing with Gluck's overture to *Iphigenia in Aulis* I have made a new ending for its own sake. Beethoven's Ninth Symphony towers among the classic masterpieces; but if Wagner had been old enough in his Dresden days not only to rescore the first and greatest movement as he did, but to supply the whole work with a more singable ending I should not have discouraged him; for I must agree with Verdi that the present ending, from the change to six-four onward, though intensely Beethovenish, is in performance usually a screaming voice destroying orgy.

I may be asked why all my instances are musical instead of literary. Is it a plot to take the literary critics out of their depth? Well, it may have that good effect; but I am not aiming at it. It is, I suppose, because music has succeeded to the heroic rank taken by literature in the sixteenth century. I cannot pretend to care much about what Nat Lee did in his attempts to impart Restoration gentility to Shakespear, or about Thomas Corneille's bowdlerization of Molière's *Festin de Pierre*, or any of the other literary precedents, though I am a little ashamed of being found in the company of their perpetrators. But I do care a good deal about what Mozart did to Handel, and Wagner to Gluck; and it seems to me that to discuss the artistic morality of my alternative ending without reference to them would be waste of time. Anyhow, what I have done I have done; and at that I must leave it.

I shall not press my version on managers producing Cymbeline if they have the courage and good sense to present the original word-for-word as Shakespear left it, and the means to do justice to the masque. But if they are halfhearted about it, and inclined to compromise by leaving out the masque and the comic jailor and mutilating the rest, as their manner is, I unhesitatingly recommend my version. The audience will not know the difference; and the few critics who have read Cymbeline will be too grateful for my shortening of the last act to complain.

G. B. S.

AYOT SAINT LAWRENCE, *December 1945*

[ACT V]

A rocky defile. A wild evening. Philario, in armor, stands on a tall rock, straining his eyes to see into the distance. In the foreground a Roman captain, sword in hand, his helmet badly battered, rushes in panting. Looking round before he sits down on a rock to recover his breath, he catches sight of Philario.

CAPTAIN. Ho there, signor! You are in danger there.
You can be seen a mile off.
PHILARIO [*hastening down*] Whats your news?
I am sent by Lucius to find out how fares
Our right wing led by General Iachimo.
CAPTAIN. He is outgeneralled. There's no right wing now.
Broken and routed, utterly defeated,
Our eagles taken and the few survivors
In full flight like myself. And you?
PHILARIO. My news
Is even worse. Lucius, I fear, is taken.
Our centre could not stand the rain of arrows.
CAPTAIN. Someone has disciplined these savage archers.
They shoot together and advance in step:
Their horsemen trot in order to the charge
And then let loose th' entire mass full speed.
No single cavaliers but thirty score
As from a catapult four hundred tons
Of horse and man in one enormous shock

Hurled on our shaken legions. Then their chariots
With every axle furnished with a scythe
Do bloody work. They made us skip, I promise you.
Their slingers! [*He points to his helmet*]
—Well: see their work! Two inches further down
I had been blind or dead. The crackbrained Welshmen
Raged like incarnate devils.

PHILARIO. Yes: they thought
We were the Britons. So our prisoners tell us.

CAPTAIN. Where did these bumpkins get their discipline?

PHILARIO. Ay: thats the marvel. Where?

CAPTAIN. Our victors say
Cassivelaunus is alive again.
But thats impossible.

PHILARIO. Not so impossible
As that this witless savage Cymbeline,
Whose brains were ever in his consort's head,
Could thus defeat Roman-trained infantry.

CAPTAIN. 'Tis my belief that old Belarius,
Banned as a traitor, must have been recalled.
That fellow knew his job. These fat civilians
When we're at peace, rob us of our rewards
By falsely charging us with this or that;
But when the trumpet sounds theyre on their knees to us.

PHILARIO. Well, Captain, I must hasten back to Lucius
To blast his hopes of any help from you.
Where, think you, is Iachimo?

CAPTAIN. I know not.
And yet I think he cannot be far off.

PHILARIO. He lives then?

CAPTAIN. Perhaps. When all was lost he fought

Like any legionary, sword in hand.
His last reported word was "Save yourselves:
Bid all make for the rocks; for there
Their horsemen cannot come". I took his counsel;
And here I am.

PHILARIO. You were best come with me.
Failing Iachimo, Lucius will require
Your tale at first hand.

CAPTAIN. Good. But we shall get
No laurel crowns for what we've done today.

Exeunt together. Enter Posthumus dressed like a peasant, but wearing a Roman sword and a soldier's iron cap. He has in his hand a bloodstained handkerchief.

POSTHUMUS. Yea, bloody cloth, I'll keep thee; for I wish'd
Thou shouldst be colour'd thus. You married ones,
If each of you should take this course, how many
Must murder wives much better than themselves
For wrying but a little? O Pisanio!
Every good servant does not all commands:
No bond, but to do just ones. Gods, if you
Should have ta'en vengeance on my faults, I ne'er
Had liv'd to put on this: so had you sav'd
The noble Imogen to repent, and struck
Me (wretch) more worth your vengeance. But, alack,
You snatch some hence for little faults: that's love,
To have them fall no more. You some permit
To second ills with ills, each elder worse,
And make them dread it, to the doers' thrift;
But Imogen is your own: do your best wills,
And make me blest to obey! I am brought hither
Among the Italian gentry, and to fight
Against my lady's kingdom: 'tis enough
That, Britain, I have kill'd thy mistress. Peace!
I'll give no wound to thee. I have disrobed me

Of my Italian weeds, and drest myself
As does a Briton peasant; so I've fought
Against the part I came with; so I'll die
For thee, O Imogen, even for whom my life
Is every breath a death; and thus unknown,
Pitied nor hated, to the face of peril
Myself I'll dedicate. Let me make men know
More valour in me than my habits shew.
Gods, put the strength o' the Leonati in me!
To shame the guise o' the world, I'll begin
The fashion, less without and more within.

He is hurrying off when he is confronted with Iachimo, battle stained, hurrying in the opposite direction. Seeing a British enemy he draws his sword.

POSTHUMUS. Iachimo! Peace, man: 'tis I, Posthumus.

IACHIMO. Peace if you will. The battle's lost and won.
Pass on.

POSTHUMUS. Do you not know me?

IACHIMO. No.

POSTHUMUS. Look closer.
You have some reason to remember me
And I to hate you. Yet we're sworn friends.

IACHIMO. By all the gods, Leonatus!

POSTHUMUS. At your service,
Seducer of my wife.

IACHIMO. No more of that.
Your wife, Posthumus, is a noble creature.
I'll set your mind at rest upon that score.

POSTHUMUS. At rest! Can you then raise her from the grave?
Where she lies dead to expiate our crime?

IACHIMO. Dead! How? Why? When? And expiate! What mean you?

POSTHUMUS. This only: I have had her murdered, I.
And at my best am worser than her worst.

IACHIMO. We are damned for this. [*On guard*] Let's cut each other's throats.

POSTHUMUS [*drawing*] Ay, let us.

They fight furiously. Enter Cymbeline, Belarius, Guiderius, Arviragus, Pisiano, with Lucius and Imogen as Fidele: both of them prisoners guarded by British soldiers.

BELARIUS [*taking command instinctively*] Part them there. Make fast the Roman.

Guiderius pounces on Iachimo and disarms him. Arviragus pulls Posthumus back.

ARVIRAGUS. In the King's presence sheath your sword, you lout.

IACHIMO. In the King's presence I must yield perforce;
But as a person of some quality
By rank a gentleman, I claim to be
Your royal highness's prisoner, not this lad's.

LUCIUS. His claim is valid, sir. His blood is princely.

POSTHUMUS. 'Tis so: he's noble.

CYMBELINE. What art thou?

POSTHUMUS. A murderer.

IMOGEN. His voice! His voice! Oh, let me see his face. [*She rushes to Posthumus and puts her hand on his face*].

POSTHUMUS. Shall's have a play with this? There lies thy part [*he knocks her down with a blow of his fist*].

GUIDERIUS. Accursed churl: take that. [*He strikes Posthumus and brings him down on one knee*].

ARVIRAGUS. You dog, how dare you [*threatening him*].

POSTHUMUS. Soft, soft, young sirs. One at a time, an't please you. [*He springs up and stands on the defensive*].

PISANIO [*interposing*] Hands off my master! He is kin to the king.

POSTHUMUS [*to Cymbeline*] Call off your bulldogs, sir. Why all this coil
About a serving boy?

CYMBELINE. My son-in-law!

PISANIO. Oh, gentlemen, your help. My Lord Posthumus:
You ne'er killed Imogen till now. Help! help!

IMOGEN. Oh, let me die. I heard my husband's voice
Whom I thought dead; and in my ecstasy,
The wildest I shall ever feel again,
He met me with a blow.

POSTHUMUS. Her voice. 'Tis Imogen.
Oh, dearest heart, thou livest. Oh, you gods,
What sacrifice can pay you for this joy?

IMOGEN. You dare pretend you love me.

POSTHUMUS. Sweet, I dare
Anything, everything. Mountains of mortal guilt
That crushed me are now lifted from my breast.
I am in heaven that was but now in hell.
You may betray me twenty times again.

IMOGEN. Again! And pray, when have I e'er betrayed you?

POSTHUMUS. I had the proofs. There stands your paramour.
Shall's have him home? I care not, since thou liv'st.

IMOGEN. My paramour! [*To Iachimo*] Oh, as you are a gentleman,
Give him the lie.

IACHIMO. He knows no better, madam.
We made a wager, he and I, in Italy
That I should spend a night in your bedchamber.

IMOGEN [*to Posthumus*] You made this wager! And I'm married to you!

POSTHUMUS. I did. He won it.

IMOGEN. How? He never came

Within my bedchamber.

IACHIMO. I spent a night there.
It was the most uncomfortable night
I ever passed.

IMOGEN. You must be mad, signor.
Or else the most audacious of all liars
That ever swore away a woman's honor.

IACHIMO. I think, madam, you do forget that chest.

IMOGEN. I forget nothing. At your earnest suit
Your chest was safely houséd in my chamber;
But where were you?

IACHIMO. I? I was in the chest [*Hilarious sensation*].
And on one point I do confess a fault.
I stole your bracelet while you were asleep.

POSTHUMUS. And cheated me out of my diamond ring!

IACHIMO. Both ring and bracelet had some magic in them
That would not let me rest until I laid them
On Mercury's altar. He's the god of thieves.
But I can make amends. I'll pay for both
At your own price, and add one bracelet more
For the other arm.

POSTHUMUS. With ten thousand ducats
Due to me for the wager you have lost.

IMOGEN. And this, you think, signors, makes good to me
All you have done, you and my husband there!

IACHIMO. It remedies what can be remedied.
As for the rest, it cannot be undone.
We are a pitiable pair. For all that
You may go further and fare worse; for men
Will do such things to women.

IMOGEN. You at least

Have grace to know yourself for what you are.
My husband thinks that all is settled now
And this a happy ending!

POSTHUMUS. Well, my dearest,
What could I think? The fellow did describe –
The mole upon your breast.

IMOGEN. And thereupon
You bade your servant kill me.

POSTHUMUS. It seemed natural.

IMOGEN. Strike me again; but do not say such things.

GUIDERIUS. An if you do, by Thor's great hammer stroke
I'll kill you, were you fifty sons-in-law.

BELARIUS. Peace, boy: we're in the presence of the king.

IMOGEN. Oh, Cadwal, Cadwal, you and Polydore,
My newfound brothers, are my truest friends.
Would either of you, were I ten times faithless,
Have sent a slave to kill me?

GUIDERIUS [*shuddering*] All the world
Should die first.

ARVIRAGUS. Whiles we live, Fidele,
Nothing shall harm you.

POSTHUMUS. Child: hear me out.
Have I not told you that my guilty conscience
Had almost driven me mad when heaven opened
And you appeared? But prithee, dearest wife,
How did you come to think that I was dead?

IMOGEN. I cannot speak of it: it is too dreadful.
I saw a headless man drest in your clothes.

GUIDERIUS. Pshaw! That was Cloten: son, he said, to the king.
I cut his head off.

CYMBELINE. Marry, the gods forefend!

I would not thy good deeds should from my lips
Pluck a hard sentence: prithee, valiant youth,
Deny 't again.

GUIDERIUS. I have spoke it, and I did it.

CYMBELINE. He was a prince.

GUIDERIUS. A most incivil one: the wrongs he did me
Were nothing prince-like; for he did provoke me
With language that would make me spurn the sea
If it could so roar to me. I cut off 's head;
And am right glad he is not standing here
To tell this tale of mine.

CYMBELINE. I am sorry for thee:
By thine own tongue thou art condemn'd, and must
Endure our law: thou 'rt dead. Bind the offender,
And take him from our presence.

BELARIUS. Stay, sir king:
This man is better than the man he slew,
As well descended as thyself, and hath
More of thee merited than a band of Clotens
Had ever scar for. [*To the Guard*] Let his arms alone,
They were not born for bondage.

CYMBELINE. Why, old soldier,
Wilt thou undo the worth thou art unpaid for,
By tasting of our wrath? How of descent
As good as we?

GUIDERIUS. In that he spake too far.

CYMBELINE. And thou shalt die for 't.

BELARIUS. We will die all three:
But I will prove that two on 's are as good
As I have given out him.

CYMBELINE. Take him away.
The whole world shall not save him.

BELARIUS. Not so hot.

First pay me for the nursing of thy sons;
And let it be confiscate all so soon
As I've received it.

CYMBELINE. Nursing of my sons!

BELARIUS. I am too blunt and saucy: here's my knee.
Ere I arise I will prefer my sons.
Then spare not the old father. Mighty sir:
These two young gentlemen that call me father,
And think they are my sons, are none of mine.
They are the issue of your loins, my liege,
And blood of your begetting.

CYMBELINE. How? my issue?

BELARIUS. So sure as you your father's. These your princes
(For such and so they are) these twenty years
Have I train'd up: those arts they have as I
Could put into them; my breeding was, sir, as
Your highness knows. Come hither, boys, and pay
Your loves and duties to your royal sire.

GUIDERIUS. We three are fullgrown men and perfect strangers.
Can I change fathers as I'd change my shirt?

CYMBELINE. Unnatural whelp! What doth thy brother say?

ARVIRAGUS. I, royal sir? Well, we have reached an age
When fathers' helps are felt as hindrances.
I am tired of being preached at.

CYMBELINE [*to Belarius*] So, sir, this
Is how you have bred my puppies.

GUIDERIUS. He has bred us
To tell the truth and face it.

BELARIUS. Royal sir:
I know not what to say: not you nor I

Can tell our children's minds. But pardon him.
If he be overbold the fault is mine.

GUIDERIUS. The fault, if fault there be, is in my Maker.
I am of no man's making. I am I:
Take me or leave me.

IACHIMO [*to Lucius*] Mark well, Lucius, mark.
There spake the future king of this rude island.

GUIDERIUS. With you, Sir Thief, to tutor me? No, no:
This kingly business has no charm for me.
When I lived in a cave methought a palace
Must be a glorious place, peopled with men
Renowned as councillors, mighty as soldiers,
As saints a pattern of holy living,
And all at my command were I a prince.
This was my dream. I am awake today.
I am to be, forsooth, another Cloten,
Plagued by the chatter of his train of flatterers,
Compelled to worship priest invented gods,
Not free to wed the woman of my choice,
Being stopped at every turn by some old fool
Crying "You must not", or, still worse, "You must".
Oh no, sir: give me back the dear old cave
And my unflattering four footed friends.
I abdicate, and pass the throne to Polydore.

ARVIRAGUS. Do you, by heavens? Thank you for nothing, brother.

CYMBELINE. I'm glad you're not ambitious. Seated monarchs
Do rarely love their heirs. Wisely, it seems.

ARVIRAGUS. Fear not, great sir: we two have never learnt
To wait for dead men's shoes, much less their crowns.

GUIDERIUS. Enough of this. Fidele: is it true
Thou art a woman, and this man thy husband?
IMOGEN. I am a woman, and this man my husband.
He would have slain me.
POSTHUMUS. Do not harp on that.
CYMBELINE. God's patience, man, take your wife home to bed.
You're man and wife: nothing can alter that.
Are there more plots to unravel? Each one here,
It seems, is someone else. [*To Imogen*] Go change your dress
For one becoming to your sex and rank.
Have you no shame?
IMOGEN. None.
CYMBELINE. How? None!
IMOGEN. All is lost.
Shame, husband, happiness, and faith in Man.
He is not even sorry.
POSTHUMUS. I'm too happy.
IACHIMO. Lady: a word. When you arrived just now
I, as you saw, was hot on killing him.
Let him bear witness that I drew on him
To avenge your death.
IMOGEN. Oh, do not make me laugh.
Laughter dissolves too many just resentments,
Pardons too many sins.
IACHIMO. And saves the world
A many thousand murders. Let me plead for him.
He has his faults; but he must suffer yours.
You are, I swear, a very worthy lady;
But still, not quite an angel.
IMOGEN. No, not quite,
Nor yet a worm. Subtle Italian villain!
I would that chest had smothered you.
IACHIMO. Dear lady

It very nearly did.
IMOGEN. I will not laugh.
I must go home and make the best of it
As other women must.
POSTHUMUS. Thats all I ask. [*He clasps her*].
BELARIUS. The fingers of the powers above do tune
The harmony of this peace.
LUCIUS. Peace be it then.
For by this gentleman's report and mine
I hope imperial Cæsar will reknit
His favour with the radiant Cymbeline,
Which shines here in the west.
CYMBELINE. Laud we the gods,
And let our crooked smokes climb to their nostrils
From our blest altars. Publish we this peace
To all our subjects. Set we forward: let
A Roman and a British ensign wave
Friendly together: so through Lud's town march,
And in the temple of great Jupiter
Our peace we'll ratify; seal it with feasts.
Set on there! Never was a war did cease,
Ere bloody hands were wash'd, with such a peace.
[*Curtain*

THE END

“In Good King Charles’s Golden Days”: A True History That Never Happened

WITH

Preface

"IN GOOD KING CHARLES'S GOLDEN DAYS"

Composition begun *c.* 23 November 1938 (Shaw intended it to be "an educational history film" for Gabriel Pascal); completed prior to 3 May 1939. Published 1939. Revised for Standard Edition (*Geneva, Cymbeline Refinished, & Good King Charles*), 1947. For the latter publication Shaw added quotation marks to the title to indicate that it was a line from an anonymous 18th century song "The Vicar of Bray." First presented at the Festival Theatre, Malvern, on 11 August 1939.

Mrs Basham *Isabel Thornton*
Sally *Phyllis Shand*
Isaac Newton *Cecil Trouncer*
George Fox *Herbert Lomas*
King Charles II ("Mr Rowley") *Ernest Thesiger*
Nell Gwynn *Eileen Beldon*
Barbara Villiers, Duchess of Cleveland *Daphne Heard*
Louise de Kéroualle, Duchess of Portsmouth ("Madam Carwell") *Yvonne Arnaud*
James, Duke of York *Alexander Knox*
Godfrey Kneller *Anthony Bushell*
Queen Catherine of Braganza *Irene Vanbrugh*

Period—Cambridge, 1680

ACT I *The Library in the House of Isaac Newton. Morning*
ACT II *The Boudoir of Catherine of Braganza in Newmarket. Late in the Afternoon on the Same Day*

Preface

Contents

In providing a historical play for the Malvern Festival of 1939 I departed from the established practice sufficiently to require a word of explanation. The "histories" of Shakespear are chronicles dramatized; and my own chief historical plays, Cæsar and Cleopatra and St Joan, are fully documented chronicle plays of this type. Familiarity with them would get a student safely through examination papers on their periods.

STAGE CHAPTERS OF HISTORY

A much commoner theatrical product is the historical romance, mostly fiction with historical names attached to the stock characters of the stage. Many of these plays have introduced their heroines as Nell Gwynn, and Nell's principal lover as Charles II. As Nell was a lively and lovable actress, it was easy to reproduce her by casting a lively and lovable actress for the part; but the stage Charles, though his costume and wig were always unmistakeable, never had any other resemblance to the real Charles, nor to anything else on earth except what he was not: a stage walking gentleman with nothing particular to say for himself.

Now the facts of Charles's reign have been chronicled

so often by modern historians of all parties, from the Whig Macaulay to the Jacobite Hilaire Belloc, that there is no novelty left for the chronicler to put on the stage. As to the romance, it is intolerably stale: the spectacle of a Charles sitting with his arm round Nell Gwynn's waist, or with Moll Davis seated on his knee, with the voluptuous termagant Castlemaine raging in the background, has no interest for me, if it ever had for any grown-up person.

But when we turn from the sordid facts of Charles's reign, and from his Solomonic polygamy, to what might have happened to him but did not, the situation becomes interesting and fresh. For instance, Charles might have met that human prodigy Isaac Newton. And Newton might have met that prodigy of another sort, George Fox, the founder of the morally mighty Society of Friends, vulgarly called the Quakers. Better again, all three might have met. Now anyone who considers a hundred and fiftieth edition of Sweet Nell of Old Drury more attractive than Isaac Newton had better avoid my plays: they are not meant for such. And anyone who is more interested in Lady Castlemaine's hips than in Fox's foundation of the great Cult of Friendship should keep away from theatres and frequent worse places. Still, though the interest of my play lies mainly in the clash of Charles, George, and Isaac, there is some fun in the clash between all three and Nelly, Castlemaine, and the Frenchwoman Louise de Kéroualle, whom we called Madame Carwell. So I bring the three on the stage to relieve the intellectual tension.

NEWTON'S RECTILINEAR UNIVERSE

There is another clash which is important and topical in view of the hold that professional science has gained on popular credulity since the middle of the nineteenth century. I mean the eternal clash between the artist and the physicist. I have therefore invented a collision between Newton and a personage whom I should like to have called Hogarth; for it was Hogarth who said "the line of beauty is a curve," and Newton whose first dogma it was that the universe is in principle rectilinear. He called straight lines right lines; and they were still so called in my school Euclid eighty years ago. But Hogarth could not by any magic be fitted into the year 1680, my chosen date; so I had to fall back on Godfrey Kneller. Kneller had not Hogarth's brains; but I have had to endow him with them to provide Newton with a victorious antagonist. In point of date Kneller just fitted in.

But I must make an exception to this general invitation. If by any chance you are a great mathematician or astronomer you had perhaps better stay away. I have made Newton aware of something wrong with the perihelion of Mercury. Not since Shakespear made Hector of Troy quote Aristotle has the stage perpetrated a more staggering anachronism. But I find the perihelion of Mercury so irresistible as a laugh catcher (like Weston-super-Mare) that I cannot bring myself to sacrifice it. I am actually prepared to defend it as a possibility. Newton was not only a lightning calculator with a monstrous memory: he was also a most ingenious and dexterous maker of apparatus. He made his own telescope; and when he wanted to look at Mercury without being dazzled by the sun he was quite clever enough to produce an artificial eclipse by putting an obturator into the telescope, though nobody else hit on that simple device until long after. My ignorance in these matters is stupendous; but I refuse to believe that Newton's system did not enable him to locate Mercury theoretically at its nearest point to the sun, and then to find out with his telescope that it was apparently somewhere else.

For the flash of prevision in which Newton foresees Einstein's curvilinear universe I make no apology. Newton's first law of motion is pure dogma. So is Hogarth's first law of design. The modern astronomers have proved, so far, that Hogarth was right and Newton wrong. But as the march of science during my long lifetime has played skittles with all the theories in turn I dare not say how the case will stand by the time this play of mine reaches its thousandth performance (if it ever does). Meanwhile let me admit that Newton in my play is a stage astronomer: that is, an astronomer not for an age but for all time. Newton as a man was the queerest of the prodigies; and I have chapter and verse for all his contradictions.

CHARLES'S GOLDEN DAYS

As to Charles, he adolesced as a princely cosmopolitan vagabond of curiously mixed blood, and ended as the first king in England whose kingship was purely symbolic, and who was clever enough to know that the work of the regicides could not be undone, and that he had to reign by his wits and not by the little real power they had left him. Unfortunately the vulgarity of his reputation as a Solomonic polygamist has not only obscured his political ability, but eclipsed the fact that he was the best of husbands. Catherine of Braganza, his wife, has been made to appear a nobody, and Castlemaine, his concubine, almost a great historical figure. When you have seen my play you will not make that mistake, and may therefore congratulate yourself on assisting at an act of historical justice.

Let us therefore drop the popular subject of The Merry Monarch and his women. On the stage, and indeed off it, he is represented as having practically no other interest, and being a disgracefully unfaithful husband. It is inferred that he was politically influenced by women, especially by Louise de Kérouaille, who, as an agent of Louis XIV, kept him under the thumb of that Sun of Monarchs as his secret pensioner. The truth is that Charles, like most English kings, was continually in money difficulties because the English people, having an insuperable dislike of being governed at all, would not pay taxes enough to finance an efficient civil and military public service. In Charles's day especially they objected furiously to a standing army, having had enough of that under Cromwell, and grudged their king even the lifeguards which were the nucleus of such an army. Charles, to carry on, had to raise the necessary money somewhere; and as he could not get it from the Protestant people of England he was clever enough to get it from the Catholic king of France; for, though head of the Church of England, he privately ranked Protestants as an upstart vulgar middle-class sect, and the Catholic Church as the authentic original Church of Christ, and the only possible faith for a gentleman. In achieving this he made use of Louise: there is no evidence that she made use of him. To the Whig historians the transaction makes Charles a Quisling in the service of Louis and a traitor to his own country. This is mere Protestant scurrility: the only shady part of it is that Charles, spending the money in the service of England, gave *le Roi Soleil* no value for it.

The other mistresses could make him do nothing

that his goodnature did not dispose him to do, whether it was building Greenwich Hospital or making dukes of his bastards. As a husband he took his marriage very seriously, and his sex adventures as calls of nature on an entirely different footing. In this he was in the line of evolution, which leads to an increasing separation of the unique and intensely personal and permanent marriage relation from the carnal intercourse described in Shakespear's sonnet. This, being a response to the biological decree that the world must be peopled, may arise irresistibly between persons who could not live together endurably for a week but can produce excellent children. Historians who confuse Charles's feelings for his wife with his appetite for Barbara Villiers do not know chalk from cheese biologically.

THE FUTURE OF WOMEN IN POLITICS

The establishment of representative government in England is assumed to have been completed by the enfranchisement of women in 1928. The enormous hiatus left by their previous disenfranchisement is supposed to have been filled up and finished with. As a matter of fact it has only reduced Votes for Women to absurdity; for the women immediately used their vote to keep women out of Parliament. After seventeen years of it the nation, consisting of men and women in virtually equal numbers, is misrepresented at Westminster by 24 women and 616 men. During the Suffragette revolt of 1913 I gave great offence to the agitators by forecasting this result, and urging that what was needed was not the vote, but a constitutional amendment enacting that all representative bodies shall consist of women and men in equal numbers, whether elected or nominated or co-opted or registered or picked up in the street like a coroner's jury.

THE COUPLED VOTE

In the case of elected bodies the only way of effecting this is by the Coupled Vote. The representative unit must be not a man *or* a woman but a man *and* a woman. Every vote, to be valid, must be for a human pair, with the result that the elected body must consist of men and women in equal numbers. Until this is achieved it is idle to prate about political democracy as existing, or ever having existed, at any known period of English history.

It is to be noted that the half-and-half proportion is valid no matter what the proportion of women to men is in the population. It never varies considerably; but even if it did the natural unit would still be the complete couple and not its better (or worse) half.

The wisdom or expediency of this reform is questioned on various grounds. There are the people who believe that the soul is a masculine organ lacking in women, as certain physical organs are, and is the seat of male political faculty. But, so far, dissection, spectrum analysis, the electronic microscope, have failed to discover in either sex any specific organ or hormone that a biologist can label as the soul. So we christen it The Holy Ghost or The Lord of Hosts and dechristen it as a Life Force or *Élan Vital*. As this is shared by women and men, and, when it quits the individual, produces in both alike the dissolution we call death, democratic representation cannot be said to exist where women are not as fully enfranchised and qualified as men. So far no great harm has been done by their legal disabilities because men and women are so alike that for the purposes of our crude legislation it matters little whether juries and parliaments are packed with men or women; but now that the activities of government have been greatly extended, detailed criticism by women has become indispensable in Cabinets. For instance, the House of Lords is more representative than the House of Commons because its members are there as the sons of their fathers, which is the reason for all of us being in the world; but it would be a much more human body if it were half-and-half sons and daughters.

All this went on with the approval of the women, who formed half the community, and yet were excluded not only from the franchise but from the professions and public services, except the thrones. Up to a point this also did not matter much; for in oligarchies women exercise so much influence privately and irresponsibly that the cleverest of them are for giving all power to the men, knowing that they can get round them without being hampered by the female majority whose world is the kitchen, the nursery, and the drawingroom if such a luxury is within their reach.

But representation on merely plangent Parliamentary bodies is not sufficient. Anybody can complain of a grievance; but its remedy demands constructive political capacity. Now political capacity is rare; but it is not rarer in women than in men. Nature's supply of five per cent or so of born political thinkers and administrators are all urgently needed in modern civilization; and if half of that natural supply is cut off by the exclusion of women from Parliament and Cabinets the social machinery will fall short and perhaps break down for lack of sufficient direction. Competent women, of whom enough are available, have their proper places filled by incompetent men: there is no Cabinet in Europe that would not be vitally improved by having its male tail cut off and female heads substituted.

But how is this to be done? Giving all women the vote makes it impossible because it only doubles the resistance to any change. When it was introduced in England not a single woman was returned at the ensuing General Election, though there were women of proved ability in the field. They were all defeated by male candidates who were comparative noodles and nobodies.

Therefore I suggest and advocate The Coupled Vote, making all votes invalid except those for a bi-sexed couple, and thus ensuring the return of a body in which men and women are present in equal numbers. Until this is done, adult suffrage will remain the least democratic of all political systems. I leave it to our old parliamentary hands to devise a plan by which our electorate can be side-tracked, humbugged, cheated, lied to, or frightened into tolerating such a change. If it has to wait for their enlightenment it will wait too long.

MALVERN, *1939*
AYOT SAINT LAWRENCE, *1945*

ACT I

The library in the house of Isaac Newton in Cambridge in the year 1680. It is a cheerful room overlooking the garden from the first floor through a large window which has an iron balcony outside, with an iron staircase down to the garden level. The division of the window to the left as you look out through it is a glass door leading to these stairs, making the room accessible from the garden. Inside the room the walls are lined with cupboards below and bookshelves above. To the right of the window is a stand-up writing desk. The cupboards are further obstructed by six chairs ranged tidily along them, three to the right of the window and three to the left (as you look out). Between them a table belonging to the set of chairs stands out in the middle with writing materials on it and a prodigious open Bible, made for a church lectern. A comfortable chair for the reader faces away from the window. On the reader's left is a handsome armchair, apparently for the accommodation of distinguished visitors to the philosopher.

Newton's housekeeper, a middle aged woman of very respectable appearance, is standing at the desk working at her accounts.

A serving maid in morning deshabille comes in through the interior door, which is in the side wall to the left of the window (again as you look out through it).

THE MAID. Please, Mrs Basham, a Mr Rowley wants to know when the master will be at home to receive him.

MRS BASHAM. Rowley? I dont know him. This is no hour to call on Mr Newton.

THE MAID. No indeed, maam. And look at me! not dressed to open the door to gentlefolk.

MRS BASHAM. Is he a gentleman? Rowley is not much of a name.

THE MAID. Dressed like a nobleman, maam. Very tall and very dark. And a lot of dogs with him, and a lackey. Not a person you could shut the door in the face of, maam. But very condescending, I must say.

MRS BASHAM. Well, tell him to come back at half past eleven; but I can't promise that Mr Newton will be in. Still, if he likes to come on the chance. And without his dogs, mind. Our Diamond would fight with them.

THE MAID. Yes, maam: I'll tell him [*going*].

MRS BASHAM. Oh, Sally, can you tell me how much is three times seven. You were at school, werent you?

SALLY. Yes, maam; but they taught the boys to read, write, and cipher. Us girls were only taught to sew.

MRS BASHAM. Well, never mind. I will ask Mr Newton. He'll know, if anybody will. Or stop. Ask Jack the fish hawker. He's paunching the rabbit in the kitchen.

SALLY. Yes, maam. [*She goes*].

MRS BASHAM. Three sixpences make one and sixpence and three eightpences make two shillings: they always do. But three sevenpences! I give it up.

Sally returns.

SALLY. Please, maam, another gentleman wants Mr Newton.

MRS BASHAM. Another nobleman?

SALLY. No, maam. He wears leather clothes. Quite out of the common.

MRS BASHAM. Did he give his name?

SALLY. George Fox, he said, maam.

MRS BASHAM. Why, thats the Quaker, the Man in Leather Breeches. He's been in prison. How dare he come here wanting to see Mr Newton? Go and tell him that Mr Newton is not at home to the like of him.

SALLY. Oh, he's not a person I could talk to like that, maam. I dursnt.

MRS BASHAM. Are you frightened of a man that would call a church a steeple house and walk into it without taking off his hat? Go this instant and tell him you will raise the street against him if he doesnt go away. Do you hear. Go and do as I tell you.

SALLY. I'd be afraid he'd raise the street against us. I will do my best to get rid of him without offence. [*She goes*].

MRS BASHAM [*calling after her*] And mind you ask Jack how much three times seven is.

SALLY [*outside*] Yes'm.

Newton, aged 38, comes in from the garden, hatless, deep in calculation, his fists clenched, tapping his knuckles together to tick off the stages of the equation. He stumbles over the mat.

MRS BASHAM. Oh, do look where youre going, Mr Newton. Someday youll walk into the river and drown yourself. I thought you were out at the university.

NEWTON. Now dont scold, Mrs Basham, dont scold. I forgot to go out. I thought of a way of making a calculation that has been puzzling me.

MRS BASHAM. And you have been sitting out there forgetting everything else since breakfast. However, since you have one of your calculating fits on I wonder would you mind doing a little sum for me to check the washing bill. How much is three times seven?

NEWTON. Three times seven? Oh, that is quite easy.

MRS BASHAM. I suppose it is to you, sir; but it beats me. At school I got as far as addition and subtraction; but I never could do multiplication or division.

NEWTON. Why, neither could I: I was too lazy. But they are quite unnecessary: addition and subtraction are quite sufficient. You add the logarithms of the numbers; and the antilogarithm of the sum of the two is the answer. Let me see: three times seven? The logarithm of three must be decimal four seven seven or thereabouts. The logarithm of seven is, say, decimal eight four five. That makes one decimal three two two, doesnt it? What's the antilogarithm of one decimal three two two? Well, it must be less than twentytwo and more than twenty. You will be safe if you put it down as—

Sally returns.

SALLY. Please, maam, Jack says it's twentyone.

NEWTON. Extraordinary! Here was I blundering over this simple problem for a whole minute; and this uneducated fish hawker solves it in a flash! He is a better mathematician than I.

MRS BASHAM. This is our new maid from Woolsthorp, Mr Newton. You havnt seen her before.

NEWTON. Havnt I? I didnt notice it. [*To Sally*] Youre from Woolsthorp, are you? So am I. How old are you?

SALLY. Twentyfour, sir.

NEWTON. Twentyfour years. Eight thousand seven hundred and sixty days. Two hundred and ten thousand two hundred and forty hours. Twelve million six hundred and fourteen thousand, four hundred minutes. Seven hundred and fiftysix million eight hundred and sixtyfour thousand seconds. A long long life.

MRS BASHAM. Come now, Mr Newton: you will turn the child's head with your figures. What can one do in a second?

NEWTON. You can do, quite deliberately and intentionally, seven distinct actions in a second. How do you count seconds? Hackertybackertyone, hackertybackertytwo, hackertybackertythree and so on. You pronounce seven syllables in every second. Think of it! This young woman has had time to perform more than five thousand millions of considered and intentional actions in her lifetime. How many of them can you remember, Sally?

SALLY. Oh sir, the only one I can remember was on my sixth birthday. My father gave me sixpence: a penny for every year.

NEWTON. Six from twentyfour is eighteen. He owes you one and sixpence. Remind me to give you one and sevenpence on your next birthday if you are a good girl. Now be off.

SALLY. Oh, thank you, sir. [*She goes out*].

NEWTON. My father, who died before I was born, was a wild, extravagant, weak man: so they tell me. I inherit his wildness, his extravagance, his weakness, in the shape of a craze for figures of which I am most heartily ashamed. There are so many more important things to be worked at: the transmutations of matter, the elixir of life, the magic of light and color, above all, the secret meaning of the Scriptures. And when I should be concentrating my mind on these I find myself wandering off into idle games of speculation about numbers in infinite series, and dividing curves into indivisibly short triangle bases. How silly! What a waste of time, priceless time!

MRS BASHAM. There is a Mr Rowley going to call on you at half past eleven.

NEWTON. Can I never be left alone? Who is Mr Rowley? What is Mr Rowley?

MRS BASHAM. Dressed like a nobleman. Very tall. Very dark. Keeps a lackey. Has a pack of dogs with him.

NEWTON. Oho! So that is who he is! They told me he wanted to see my telescope. Well, Mrs Basham, he is a person whose visit will be counted a great honor to us. But I must warn you that just as I have my terrible weakness for figures Mr Rowley has a very similar weakness for women; so you must keep Sally out of his way.

MRS BASHAM. Indeed! If he tries any of his tricks on Sally I shall see that he marries her.

NEWTON. He is married already. [*He sits at the table*].

MRS BASHAM. Oh! That sort of man! The beast!

NEWTON. Shshsh! Not a word against him, on your life. He is privileged.

MRS BASHAM. He is a beast all the same!

NEWTON [*opening the Bible*] One of the beasts in the Book of Revelation, perhaps. But not a common beast.

MRS BASHAM. Fox the Quaker, in his leather breeches had the impudence to call.

NEWTON [*interested*] George Fox? If he calls again I will see him. Those two men ought to meet.

MRS BASHAM. Those two men indeed! The honor of meeting you ought to be enough for them, I should think.

NEWTON. The honor of meeting me! Dont talk nonsense. They are great men in their very different ranks. I am nobody.

MRS BASHAM. You are the greatest man alive, sir. Mr Halley told me so.

NEWTON. It was very wrong of Mr Halley to tell you anything of the sort. You must not mind what he says.

He is always pestering me to publish my methods of calculation and to abandon my serious studies. Numbers! Numbers! Numbers! Sines, cosines, hypotenuses, fluxions, curves small enough to count as straight lines, distances between two points that are in the same place! Are these philosophy? Can they make a man great?

He is interrupted by Sally, who throws open the door and announces visitors.

SALLY. Mr Rowley and Mr Fox.

King Charles the Second, aged 50, appears at the door, but makes way for George Fox the Quaker, a big man with bright eyes and a powerful voice in reserve, aged 56. He is decently dressed; but his garments are made of leather.

CHARLES. After you, Mr Fox. The spiritual powers before the temporal.

FOX. You are very civil, sir; and you speak very justly. I thank you [*he passes in*].

Sally, intensely impressed by Mr Rowley, goes out.

FOX. Am I addressing the philosopher Isaac Newton?

NEWTON. You are, sir. [*Rising*] Will your noble friend do me the honor to be seated in my humble dwelling?

Charles bows and takes the armchair with easy grace.

FOX. I must not impose on you by claiming the gentleman as my friend. We met by chance at your door; and his favorite dog was kind enough to take a fancy to me.

CHARLES. She is never mistaken, sir. Her friends are my friends, if so damaged a character as mine can claim any friends.

NEWTON [*taking a chair from the wall and placing it near his table to his left*] Be seated, Mr Fox, pray.

FOX. George Fox at your service, not Mister. But I am very sensible of your civility. [*He sits*].

NEWTON [*resuming his seat at the table*] It seems that it is I who am at your service. In what way can I oblige you?

FOX. As you remind me, I have come here uninvited. My business will keep while you discharge yours with this nobleman—so called.

CHARLES. I also am uninvited, Pastor. I may address you so both truthfully and civilly, may I not?

FOX. You have found the right word. I tended my father's sheep when I was a child. Now I am a pastor of men's souls.

CHARLES. Good. Well, Pastor, I must inform you I have no business here except to waste our host's invaluable time and to improve my own, if he will be good enough to allow me such a liberty. Proceed then with your business; and take no notice of me. Unless, that is, you would prefer me to withdraw.

FOX. I have no business in this world that all men may not hear: the more the better.

CHARLES. I guessed as much; and confess to an unbounded curiosity to hear what George Fox can have to say to Isaac Newton. It is not altogether an impertinent curiosity. My trade, which is a very unusual one, requires that I should know what Tom, Dick and Harry have to say to oneanother. I find you two gentlemen much more interesting and infinitely more important.

MRS BASHAM [*posted behind Newton's chair*] What is your business, Mr Rowley? Mr Newton has much to do this morning. He has no time for idle conversation.

NEWTON. I had forgotten to make this lady known to you, gentlemen. Mrs Basham: my housekeeper, and the faithful guardian of my hours.

CHARLES. Your servant, Mistress Basham.

FOX. God be with you, woman.

NEWTON. Mr Rowley is a gentleman of great consequence, Mrs Basham. He must not be questioned as if he were Jack the fish hawker. His business is his father's business.

CHARLES. No, no. My father's business is abolished in England: he was executed for practising it. But we keep the old signboard up over the door of the old shop. And I stand at the shop door in my father's apron. Mrs Basham may ask me as many questions as she pleases; for I am far less important now in England than Jack the fish hawker.

MRS BASHAM. But how do you live, sir? That is all I meant to ask.

CHARLES. By my wits, Mistress Basham: by my wits. Come, Pastor: enough of me. You are face to face with Isaac Newton. I long to hear what you have to say to him.

FOX. Isaac Newton: I have friends who belong to the new so-called Royal Society which the King has established, to enquire, it seems, into the nature of the universe. They tell me things that my mind cannot reconcile with the word of God as revealed to us in the Holy Scriptures.

NEWTON. What is your warrant for supposing that revelation ceased when King James's printers finished with the Bible?

FOX. I do not suppose so. I am not one of those priestridden churchmen who believe that God went out of business six thousand years ago when he had called the world into existence and written his book about it. We three sitting here together may have a revelation if we open our hearts and minds to it. Yes: even to you, Charles Stuart.

CHARLES: The mind of Charles Stuart is only too open, Pastor.

MRS BASHAM. What did you call the gentleman, Mr Fox?

CHARLES. A slip of the tongue, Mistress Basham. Nowhere in Holy writ, Pastor, will you find any disapproval of Paul when he changed his name from Saul. Need you be more scrupulous than the apostles?

FOX. It is against my sinful nature to disoblige any man; so Mr Rowley you shall be if you so desire. But I owed it to you to let you know that I was not deceived by your new name.

CHARLES. I thank you, Pastor. Your sinful nature makes you the best mannered man in the kingdom. And now, what about the revelations?

FOX. I am troubled. I cannot conceive that God should contradict himself. How must the revelation of today be received if it be contrary to the revelation of yesterday? If what has been revealed to you, Isaac Newton, be true, there is no heaven above us and no hell beneath us. The sun which stood still upon Gibeon and the moon in the Valley of Ajalon had stood still since the creation of the world.

NEWTON. Do not let that trouble you, Pastor. Nothing has ever stood still for an instant since the creation of the world: neither the sun, the moon, the stars, nor the smallest particle of matter, except on two occasions.

CHARLES. Two! I remember only one.

NEWTON. Yes, sir: two. The first was when the sun stood still on Gibeon to give Joshua time to slaughter the Amorites. The second was when the shadow on the dial of Ahaz went ten degrees backward as a sign from God to good King Hezekiah who was dying of a boil until the prophet Isaiah made them put a lump of figs on it.

MRS BASHAM. There is nothing like a poultice of

roasted figs to cure a gumboil. And to think that is because it is in the Holy Bible! I never knew it.
NEWTON. On reflection, the sun has stopped three times; for it must have stopped for an infinitesimal moment when it turned back, and again when it resumed its course.
FOX. I thank God that you are not an unbeliever and would not make me one.
NEWTON. My good friend, there is nothing so wonderful that a philosopher cannot believe it. The philosopher sees a hundred miracles a day where the ignorant and thoughtless see nothing but the daily round, the common task. Joshua was an ignorant soldier. Had he been a philosopher he would have known that to stop the nearest speck of dust would have served his turn as well as to stop the sun and moon; for it could not have stopped without stopping the whole machinery of the heavens. By the way, Mrs Basham, the fact that the sun and moon were visible at the same time may help me to fix the day on which the miracle occurred. [*To the others*] Excuse me, gentlemen: I have written a chronological history of the world; and the dates give me some trouble.
CHARLES. Did not the late Archbishop Ussher fix the dates of everything that ever happened?
NEWTON. Unfortunately he did not allow for the precession of the equinoxes. I had to correct some of his results accordingly.
CHARLES. And, saving the pastor's presence, what the divvle is the precession of the equinoxes?
FOX. I am sinful enough to be glad that you are as ignorant as myself. I suffer greatly from shame at my ignorance.
NEWTON. Shame will not help you, Pastor. I spend my life contemplating the ocean of my ignorance. I

once boasted of having picked up a pebble on the endless beach of that ocean. I should have said a grain of sand.

CHARLES. I can well believe it. No man confronted with the enormity of what he does not know can think much of what he does know. But what is the precession of the equinoxes? If I fire off those words at court the entire peerage will be prostrate before the profundity of my learning.

MRS BASHAM. Oh, tell the gentlemen, Mr Newton; or they will be here all day.

NEWTON. It is quite simple: a child can understand it. The two days in the year on which the day and night are of equal duration are the equinoxes. In each successive sidereal year they occur earlier. You will see at once that this involves a retrograde motion of the equinoctial points along the ecliptic. We call that the precession of the equinoxes.

FOX. I thank you, Isaac Newton. I am as wise as I was before.

MRS BASHAM. You ought to be ashamed of yourself, Mr Newton, injuring the poor gentlemen's brains with such outlandish words. You must remember that everybody is not as learned as you are.

NEWTON. But surely it is plain to everybody—

MRS BASHAM. No: it isnt plain to anybody, Mr Newton.

SALLY [*bursting in*] Mr Rowley: theres a lady in a coach at the door wants to know are you ready to take a drive with her.

CHARLES. Any name?

SALLY. No, sir. She said youd know.

CHARLES. A duchess, would you say?

SALLY. Oh no, sir. Spoke to me quite familiar.

CHARLES. Nelly! Mr Newton: would you like to be

introduced to Mistress Gwynn, the famous Drury Lane actress?

MRS BASHAM [*turning imperatively to Charles*] Oh, I couldnt allow that, Mr Rowley. I am surprised at you mentioning such a person in my presence.

CHARLES. I apologize. I did not know that you disapproved of the playhouse, Mrs Basham.

MRS BASHAM. I do not disapprove of the playhouse, sir. My grandfather, who is still alive and hearty, was befriended in his youth by Mr William Shakespear, a wellknown player and writer of comedies, tragedies, and the like. Mr Shakespear would have died of shame to see a woman on the stage. It is unnatural and wrong. Only the most abandoned females would do such a thing.

CHARLES. Still, the plays are more natural with real women in them, are they not?

MRS BASHAM. Indeed they are not, Mr Rowley. They are not like women at all. They are just like what they are; and they spoil the play for anyone who can remember the old actors in the women's parts. They could make you believe you were listening to real women.

CHARLES. Pastor Fox: have you ever spoken with a female player?

FOX [*shuddering*] I! No, sir: I do not frequent such company.

CHARLES. Why not, Pastor? Is your charity so narrow? Nell is no worse than Mary Magdalen.

MRS BASHAM. I hope Mary Magdalen made a good end and was forgiven; though we are nowhere told so. But I should not have asked her into my house. And at least she was not on the stage. [*She retires behind Newton's chair*].

CHARLES. What do you say, Pastor? Is Nelly not good enough for you?

FOX. Sir: there is nobody who is not good enough for me. Have I not warned our Christian friends who are now captives in Barbary not to forget that the life of God and the power of God are in their heathen masters the Turks and the Moors as well as in themselves? Is it any the less in this player woman than in a Turk or a Moor? I am not afraid of her.

CHARLES. And you, Mr Newton?

NEWTON. Women enter a philosopher's life only to disturb it. They expect too much attention. However, Mistress Gwynn has called to take you away, not to interrupt my work on fluxions. And if you will condescend to go down to her she need not come up to us. [*He rises in dismissal of the King*].

CHARLES [*rising*] I see I must take my leave.

Nelly dashes in. Sally withdraws.

NELLY. Rowley darling: how long more are you going to keep me waiting in the street?

CHARLES. You are known to everyone present, Mistress Gwynn, I think. May I make our host known to you? The eminent philosopher, Mr Newton.

NELLY [*going past Charles to Newton*] I dont know what a philosopher is, Mr Newton; but you look one, every inch. Your servant, sir. [*She curtsies to him*].

NEWTON. Yours, madam. I am ashamed that you should have been kept waiting at the wrong side of my door.

NELLY. It is an honor to be seen at your door, Mr Newton. [*Looking round her*] And who keeps your house so beautifully? I thought philosophers were like Romish priests, not allowed to marry.

NEWTON. Is my house beautifully kept? I have never noticed it. This is Mrs Basham, my housekeeper. [*He sits resignedly*].

NELLY. You never noticed it! You dont deserve such a housekeeper. Your servant, Mrs Basham.

Mrs Basham bows stiffly, trying not to be flattered.

CHARLES. The other gentleman is the famous founder of the sect of Quakers.

FOX. Of Friends, Friend Rowley.

NELLY [*running to Fox*]. I know. I know. The man in the leather breeches.

FOX [*stubbornly seated*] I am also known as George Fox.

NELLY [*clapping him on the shoulder*] What of that? Anybody might be George Fox; but there is only one man in the leather breeches. Your servant, George.

FOX. Yours, Nelly.

NELLY. There! Nelly! [*She goes to the wall for a chair and plants it at Fox's left, quite close*]. If I may add you to the list of my beaus I shall be the proudest woman in London.

FOX. I did not found the order of beaus. I founded that of Friends.

NELLY. Ten times better. Our beaus are our foes: they care for nothing but to steal our honor. Pray for me, Friend Fox: I think you have God by the ear closer than the bishops.

FOX. He is closer to you than you have placed yourself to me. Let no priest come between you.

CHARLES. We must not waste any more of Mr Newton's time, Mistress Gwynn. He is at work on fluxions.

NELLY. On what?

CHARLES. Fluxions I think you said, Mr Newton.

NELLY. What are fluxions?

CHARLES. Mr Newton will tell you. I should be glad to know, myself.

NEWTON. Fluxions, madam, are the rates of change of continuously varying quantities.

NELLY. I must go home and think about that, Mr Philosopher.

NEWTON [*very seriously*] I shall be much indebted to you, madam, if you will communicate to me the result of your reflections. The truth is, I am not quite satisfied that my method—or perhaps I had better say the notation of my method—is the easiest that can be devised. On that account I have never cared to publish it.

NELLY. You really think I could teach you something, Mr Newton? What a compliment! Did you hear that, Rowley darling?

NEWTON. In these very simple matters one may learn from anyone. And you, madam, must have very remarkable mental powers. You repeat long parts from memory in the theatre. I could not do that.

NELLY. Bless me, so I do, Mr Newton. You are the first man I ever met who did not think an actress must be an ignorant ninny—except schoolboys, who think she is a goddess. I declare you are the wisest man in England, and the kindest.

CHARLES. And the busiest, Nelly. Come. He has given us as much of his time as we have any right to ask for.

NELLY. Yes, I know. I am coming. [*She rises and goes to Charles, whose left arm she takes*]. May I come again, Mr Newton?

NEWTON [*rising*] No no no no no, madam, I cannot entertain ladies. They do not fit into my way of life. Mr Rowley: you are well known to be as interested in ladies as I am interested in the Scriptures; and I thank you for bringing this very attractive sample for my diversion—

NELLY [*as if tasting a sweet*] Oh!

NEWTON [*continuing*]—but sufficient unto the day is the evil thereof—

NELLY [*in violent protest*] Oh!!!

NEWTON. —and I beg you will bring no more ladies here until I have time to set aside a day of relaxation for their reception.

NELLY. We must go, Rowley darling. He doesnt want us.

CHARLES. You are fortunate, Mr Newton, in suffering nothing worse than Nell. But I promise you your house shall be a monastery henceforth.

As Charles and Nell turn to the door to go out, the Duchess of Cleveland, 39, formerly Lady Castlemaine, and born Barbara Villiers, bursts into the room and confronts them in a tearing rage.

BARBARA. Ah! I have caught you, have I, with your trull. This is the scientific business which made it impossible for you to see me this morning.

CHARLES. Be silent for a moment, Barbara, whilst I present you to Mr Newton, the eminent philosopher, in whose house you are an uninvited guest.

BARBARA. A pretty house. A pretty philosopher. A house kept for you to meet your women in.

MRS BASHAM [*coming indignantly to the middle of the room*] Oh! Mr Newton: either this female leaves the house this instant or I do.

BARBARA. Do you know, woman, that you are speaking of the Duchess of Cleveland?

MRS BASHAM. I do not care who I am speaking of. If you are the Duchess of Cleveland and this house were what you said it was you would be only too much at home in it. The house being what it is you are out of place in it. You go or I go.

BARBARA. You insolent slut, I will have you taken to the Bridewell and whipped.

CHARLES. You shall not, Barbara. If you do not come down with me to your carriage without another word, I will throw you downstairs.

BARBARA. Do. Kill me; and be happy with that low stage player. You have been unfaithful to me with her a thousand times.

NEWTON. Patience, patience, patience. Mrs Basham: the lady is not in a state of reason: I will prove to you that what she says has no sense and need not distress us. [*To Barbara*] Your Grace alleges that Mr Rowley has been unfaithful to you a thousand times.

BARBARA. A hundred thousand times.

NEWTON. For each unfaithfulness allow a day—or shall I say a night? Now one hundred thousand nights are almost two hundred and seventyfour years. To be precise, 273 years 287 days, allowing 68 days for Leap Year every four years. Now Mr Rowley is not 300 years old: he is only fifty, from which you must deduct at least fifteen years for his childhood.

BARBARA. Fourteen.

NEWTON. Let us say fourteen. Probably your Grace was also precocious. How many years shall we strike off your age for the days of your innocence?

NELL. Five at most.

BARBARA. Be silent, you.

NEWTON. Say twelve. That makes you in effect about twentyeight.

BARBARA. Have I denied it?

NELL. Flatterer!

NEWTON. Twentyeight to Mr Rowley's thirtysix. Your grace has been available since, say, the year 1652, twentyeight years ago. My calculation is therefore correct.

BARBARA. May I ask what you mean by available?

NEWTON. I mean that the number of occasions on which Mr Rowley could possibly be unfaithful to you is ten thousand two hundred and twenty plus seven for leap years. Yet you allege one hundred thousand occasions, and claim to have lived for nearly three centuries. As that is impossible, it is clear that you have been misinformed about Mistress Gwynn.

Nell claps vigorously.

BARBARA [*to Newton*] Are you mocking me, sir?

NEWTON. Figures cannot mock, because they cannot feel. That is their great quality, and their great fault. [*He goes to the door*]. And now may I have the honor of conducting your Grace to your coach—or is it one of those new fangled sedan chairs? Or would your Grace prefer to be thrown down my humble staircase by Mr Rowley? It has twentyfour steps, in two flights.

BARBARA. I will not leave this house until that player woman has gone first. [*She strides past them and plants herself in Newton's chair*].

NELL. After all, dear, it's Mr Newton's house and not ours. He was in the act of putting me out when you burst in. I stayed only because I wanted to see you in one of those tantrums of yours that Rowley so often tells me about. I might copy them on the stage.

BARBARA. He dares talk to you about me!!

NELL. He talks to me about everything, dear, because I let him get in a word occasionally, which is more than you do.

BARBARA [*to Charles*] Will you stand there and let me be insulted by this woman?

CHARLES [*with conviction*] Barbara: I am tired of your tantrums. I made you a duchess: you behave like a streetwalker. I pensioned you and packed you off to Paris; you have no business to be here. Pastor: what have you to say to all this? You are the oldest and wisest person present, are you not?

FOX. Fiftysix. And still a child in wisdom.

BARBARA [*contemptuously, noticing Fox for the first time*] What does this person know about women?

FOX. Only what the woman in myself teaches me.

NELL. Good for leather breeches! What do you think of her, George?

FOX. She prates overmuch about unfaithfulness. The man Rowley cannot be unfaithful to her because he has pledged no faith to her. To his wife only can he be unfaithful.

CHARLES. Wrong, Pastor. You do not know my wife. To her only I can never be unfaithful.

NELL. Yes: you are kind to us; but we are nothing to you. [*Sighing*] I would change places with her.

BARBARA. Will you order this common player to be silent in my presence?

NELL. It is not fair of her to keep mentioning my profession when I cannot decently mention hers.

With a scream of rage the duchess rises to fly at Nell, but is seized by Fox, who drags down her raised fists and throws her back into the chair.

FOX [*sternly*] Woman: behave yourself. In any decent English village you would go to the ducking stool to teach you good manners and gentle speech. You must control yourself—

He is interrupted by the clangor of a church bell, which has a terrible effect on him.

FOX [*in a thundering voice, forgetting all about the duchess*] Ha! I am called: I must go.

He makes for the door but is stopped by Charles, who, releasing Nell, shuts it quickly and posts himself with his back to it.

CHARLES. Stop. You are going to brawl in church. You will be thrown into prison; and I shall not be able to save you.

FOX. The bell, the bell. It strikes upon my life. I am called. Earthly kings cannot stay me. Let me pass.

CHARLES. Stand back, Mr Fox. My person is sacred.

NEWTON. What is the matter?

CHARLES. The church bell: it drives him mad. Someone send and stop it.

The bell stops.

FOX. God has stopped it. [*He falls on his knees and collapses, shivering like a man recovering from a fit*].

Charles and Newton help him to his feet and lead him back to his chair.

FOX [*to Charles*] Another stroke, and I should not have answered for your life.

BARBARA. You must control yourself, preacher. In any decent English village you would be put in the stocks to teach you good manners.

FOX. Woman: I have been put in the stocks; and I shall be put there again. But I will continue to testify against the steeple house and the brazen clangor of its belfries.

MRS BASHAM. Now Mr Fox. You must not say such things here.

FOX. I tell you that from the moment you allow this manmade monster called a Church to enter your mind your inner light is like an extinguished candle; and your soul is plunged in darkness and damned. There is no atheist like the Church atheist. I have converted many a poor atheist who would have been burnt or hanged if God had not sent him into my hands; but I have never converted a churchman: his answer to everything is not his God, but the Church, the Church, the Church. They burn each other, these churchmen: they persecute: they do wickednesses of which no friend of God would be capable.

MRS BASHAM. The Popish Church, not the Protestant one, Mr Fox.

FOX. All, all, all of them. They are all snares of the devil. They stand between Man and his Maker, and take on themselves divine powers when they lack divine attributes. Am I to hold my peace in the face of this iniquity? When the bell rings to announce some pitiful rascal twaddling in his pulpit, or some fellow in a cassock pretending to bind and loose, I hear an Almighty Voice call "George Fox, George Fox: rise up: testify: unmask these impostors: drag them down from their pulpits and their altars; and let it be known that what the world needs to bring it back to God is not Churchmen but Friends, Friends of God, Friends of man, friendliness and sincerity everywhere, superstition and pulpit playacting nowhere."

CHARLES. Pastor: it is not given to every man as it has been to you to make a religion for himself. A ready-made Church is an indispensable convenience for most of us. The inner light must express itself in music, in noble architecture, in eloquence: in a word, in beauty, before it can pass into the minds of common men. I grant you the clergy are mostly dull dogs; but with a little disguise and ritual they will pass as holy men with the ignorant. And there are great mysteries that must be symbolized, because though we feel them we do not know them, Mr Newton having not yet discovered their nature, in spite of all his mathematics. And this reminds me that we are making a most unwarrantable intrusion on our host's valuable time. Mr Newton: on my honor I had no part in bringing upon you this invasion of womanhood. I hasten to take them away, and will wait upon you at some happier moment. Come, ladies: we must leave Mr Newton to his mathematics. [*He is about to go to the door. Barbara rises to accompany him*].

NEWTON [*stopping him*] I must correct that misunderstanding, sir. I would not have you believe that I could be so inhospitable as to drive away my guests merely to indulge in the trifling pursuit of mathematical calculation, which leads finally nowhere. But I have more serious business in hand this morning. I am engaged in a study of the prophecies in the book of Daniel. [*He indicates the Bible*]. It may prove of the greatest importance to the world. I beg you to allow me to proceed with it in the necessary solitude. The ladies have not wasted my time: I have to thank her Grace of Cleveland for some lights on the Book of Revelation suggested to me by her proceedings. But solitude—solitude absolutely free from the pleasant disturbance of ladies' society—is now necessary to me; and I must beg you to withdraw.

Sally, now dressed in her best, throws the door open from without, and proudly announces—

SALLY. Her Grace the Duchess of Portsmouth.

Louise de Kéroualle, a Frenchwoman who at 30 retains her famous babyish beauty, appears on the threshold.

NEWTON [*beside himself*] Another woman! Take her away. Take them all away. [*He flings himself into his chair at the table and buries his face in his hands*].

CHARLES. Louise: it is unlike you to pursue me. We are unwelcome here.

LOUISE [*coming over to him*] Pursue you! But I have never been so surprised in my life as to find you here. And Nelly! And her Grace of Cleveland back from Paris! What are you all doing here? I came to consult Mr Newton, the alchemist. [*Newton straightens up and stares*]. My business with him is private: it is with him, not with you, chéri. I did not know he was holding a reception.

CHARLES. Mr Newton is not an alchemist.

LOUISE. Pardon me: he is.

CHARLES. Mr Newton: are you an alchemist?

NEWTON. My meditations on the ultimate constitution of matter have convinced me that the transmutation of metals, and indeed of all substances, must be possible. It is occurring every day. I understand that you, Mr Rowley, have a private laboratory at Whitehall, in which you are attempting the fixation of mercury.

CHARLES. Without success, Mr Newton. I shall give it up and try for the philosopher's stone instead.

FOX. Would you endanger your souls by dabbling in magic? The scripture says "Thou shalt not suffer a witch to live." Do you think that God is fonder of sorcerers and wizards than of witches? If you count the wrath of God as nothing, and are above the law by your rank, are you not ashamed to believe such old wives' tales as the changing of lead into gold by the philosopher's stone?

NEWTON. Pastor Fox: I thank you for your well-meant warning. Now let me warn you. The man who begins by doubting the possibility of the philosopher's stone soon finds himself beginning to doubt the immortality of the soul. He ends by doubting the existence of the soul. There is no witchcraft about these things. I am as certain of them as I am of the fact that the world was created four thousand and four years before the birth of our Lord.

FOX. And what warrant have you for that? The Holy Bible says nothing of your four thousand and four. It tells us that the world was created "in the beginning": a mighty word. "In the beginning"! Think of it if you have any imagination. And because some fool in a steeplehouse, dressed up like a stage player in robes and mitre, dares to measure the days of the Almighty by his kitchen clock, you take his word before the word of God! Shame on you, Isaac Newton, for making an idol of an archbishop! There is no credulity like the credulity of philosophers.

NEWTON. But the archbishop has counted the years! My own chronology of the world has been founded on his calculation. Do you mean to tell me that all the labor I have bestowed on that book has been wasted?

FOX. Sinfully wasted.

NEWTON. George Fox: you are an infidel. Leave my house.

FOX [*rising*] Your philosophy has led you to the conclusion that George Fox is an infidel. So much the worse for your philosophy! The Lord does not love men that count numbers. Read second Samuel, chapter twentyfour: the book is before you. Good morning; and God bless you and enlighten you. [*He turns to go*].

CHARLES. Stay, Pastor. [*He makes Fox sit down again and goes to Newton, laying a hand on his shoulder*]. Mr Newton: the word infidel is not one to be used hastily between us three. Old Tom Hobbes, my tutor, who was to me what Aristotle was to Alexander the Great, was called an infidel. You yourself, in spite of your interest in the book of Daniel, have been suspected of doubting whether the apple falls from the tree by the act of God or by a purely physical attraction. Even I, the head of the Church, the Defender of the Faith, stand between the Whigs who suspect me of being a Papist and the Tories who suspect me of being an atheist. Now the one thing that is true of all three of us is that if the common people knew our real minds they would hang us and bury us in unconsecrated ground. We must stand together, gentlemen. What does it matter to us whether the world is four thousand years old, or, as I should guess, ten thousand?

NEWTON. The world ten thousand years old! Sir: you are mad.

NELL [*shocked*] Rowley darling: you mustnt say such things.

BARBARA. What business is it of yours, pray? He has always defied God and betrayed women. He does not know the meaning of the word religion. He laughed at it in France. He hated it in Scotland. In England he believes nothing. He loves nothing. He fears nothing except having to go on his travels again, as he calls it. What are ten thousand years to him, or ten million?

FOX. Are ten million years beyond the competence of Almighty God? They are but a moment in His eyes. Four thousand years seem an eternity to a mayfly, or a mouse, or a mitred fool called an archbishop. Are we mayflies? Are we mice? Are we archbishops?

MRS BASHAM. Mr Fox: I have listened to too much blasphemy this morning. But to call an archbishop a mitred fool and compare him to a mouse is beyond endurance. I cannot believe that God will ever pardon you for that. Have you no fear of hell?

FOX. How shall I root out the sin of idolatry from this land? Worship your God, woman, not a dressed-up priest.

MRS BASHAM. The archbishop is not a graven image. And when he is officiating he is not in the likeness of anything in the heavens above or on the earth beneath. I am afraid you do not know your catechism, Mr Fox.

CHARLES [*laughing*] Excellent, Mrs Basham. Pastor: she has gravelled you with the second commandment. And she has put us to shame for quarrelling over a matter of which we know nothing. By the way, where were we when we began to quarrel? I have clean forgotten.

LOUISE. It was my business with Mr Newton, I think. Nellie: will you take our sovereign lord away and leave me to speak with the alchemist in private?

CHARLES. Mr Newton: not for worlds would I deprive you of a *tête-à-tête* with her Grace of Portsmouth. Pastor: you will accompany us. Nellie: you will come with the pastor. But first I must throw the Duchess of Cleveland downstairs [*moving towards her*].

BARBARA [*screaming and making for the door*] Coward! Help! Murder! [*She rushes out*].

CHARLES. Your servant, Mrs Basham.

Mrs Basham curtsies. Charles salutes her and goes out.

NELL [*beckoning to Fox*] Come on, leather breeches.

FOX [*rising and going towards the door*] Well, what you are, God made you. I am bound to be your friend.

NELL [*taking his arm as he passes*] I am proud of your friendship, George.

They go out arm in arm.

Louise, being now the person of highest rank present, follows them as far as the armchair, in which she seats herself with distinguished elegance.

LOUISE [*to Mrs Basham*] Madam: may I have a moment alone with the alchemist?

NEWTON. You certainly may not, your Grace. I will not have Mr Locke and his friends accuse me of having relations with women. If your business cannot be discussed before Mrs Basham it cannot be discussed with me. And you will please not speak of me as "the alchemist" as you might speak of the apothecary or the chimney sweep. I am by profession—if it can be called a profession—a philosopher.

LOUISE. Pardon: I am not habituated to your English manners. It is strange to me that a philosopher should need a chaperon. In France it is I who should need one.

NEWTON. You are quite safe with me and Mrs Basham, madam. What is your business?

LOUISE. I want a love charm.

NEWTON. A what?

LOUISE. A love charm. Something that will make my lover faithful to me if I drop it into his tay. And mind! it must make him love me, and not love everybody. He is far too amorous already of every pretty woman he meets. I make no secret of who he is: all the world knows it. The love charm must not do him any harm; for if we poison the king we shall be executed in the most horrible manner. It must be something that will be good for him.

NEWTON. And peculiar to yourself? Not to Mistress Gwynn?

LOUISE. I do not mind Nellie: she is a dear, and so helpful when there is any trouble or illness. He picked her up out of the gutter; but the good God sometimes drops a jewel there: my nurse, a peasant woman, was worth a thousand duchesses. Yes: he may have Nellie: a change is sometimes good for men.

MRS BASHAM [*fearfully shocked*] Oh! Mr Newton: I must go. I cannot stay and listen to this French lady's talk. [*She goes out with dignity*].

LOUISE. I shall never understand the things that Englishwomen are prudish about. And they are so extraordinarily coarse in other things. May I stay, now that your chaperon has gone?

NEWTON: You will not want to stay when I tell you that I do not deal in love potions. Ask the nearest apothecary for an aphrodisiac.

LOUISE. But I cannot trust a common apothecary: it would be all over the town tomorrow. Nobody will suspect you. I will pay any price you like.

NEWTON. I tell you, madam, I know nothing about

such things. If I wished to make you fall in love with me—which God forbid!—I should not know how to set about it. I should learn to play some musical instrument, or buy a new wig.

LOUISE. But you are an alchemist: you must know.

NEWTON. Then I am not an alchemist. But the changing of Bodies into Light and Light into Bodies is very conformable to the Course of Nature, which seems delighted with Transmutations.

LOUISE. I do not understand. What are transmutations?

NEWTON. Never mind, madam. I have other things to do than to peddle love charms to the King's ladies.

LOUISE [*ironically*] Yes: to entertain the Duchess of Cleveland and Mistress Gwynn, and hire a mad preacher to amuse them! What else have you to do that is more important than my business with you?

NEWTON. Many other things. For instance, to ascertain the exact distance of the sun from the earth.

LOUISE. But what a waste of time! What can it possibly matter whether the sun is twenty miles away or twentyfive?

NEWTON. Twenty or twentyfive!!! The sun is millions and millions of miles from the earth.

LOUISE. Oh! Oh!! Oh!!! You are quite mad, Monsieur Nieuton. At such a distance you could not see it. You could not feel its heat. Well, you cannot see it so plainly here as in France, nor so often; but you can see it quite plainly sometimes. And you can feel its heat. It burns your skin, and freckles you if you are sandyhaired. And then comes a little cloud over it and you shiver with cold. Could that happen if it were a thousand miles away?

NEWTON. It is very very large, madam. It is one million three hundred thousand times heavier than the earth.

LOUISE. My good Monsieur Nieuton: do not be so fanciful. [*Indicating the window*] Look at it. Look at it. It is much smaller than the earth. If I hold up a sou —what you call a ha-pen-ny—before my eye, it covers the sun and blots it out. Let me teach you something, Monsieur Nieuton. A great French philosopher, Blaise Pascal, teached me this. You must never let your imagination run away with you. When you think of grandiose things—hundreds of millions and things like that—you must continually come down to earth to keep sane. You must see: you must feel: you must measure.

NEWTON. That is very true, madam. Above all, you must measure. And when you measure you find that many things are bigger than they look. The sun is one of them.

LOUISE [*rising and going to the table to coax him*] Ah! You are impossible. But you will make me a love potion, will you not?

NEWTON. I will write you a prescription, madam.

He takes a sheet of paper and writes the prescription. Louise watches as he writes.

LOUISE. Aqua? But aqua is only water, monsieur.

NEWTON. Water with a cabalistic sign after it, madam.

LOUISE. Ah, parfaitement. And this long magical word, what is it? Mee-kah-pah-nees. What is that?

NEWTON. Micapanis, madam. A very powerful lifegiving substance.

LOUISE. It sounds wonderful. Is it harmless?

NEWTON. The most harmless substance in the world, madam, and the most precious.

LOUISE. Truly you are a great man, Monsieur Nieuton, in spite of your millions of miles. And this last word here?

NEWTON. Only sugar, to sweeten the micapanis, but with the cabalistic sign after it. Here is your love charm, madam. But it is not a potion: the apothecary will make it into pills for you.

LOUISE [*taking the paper and tucking it into the bosom of her dress*] Good. That is better, much better. It is so much easier to make men take pills than drink potions. And now, one thing more. You must swear to give this prescription to no other woman of the court. It is for me alone.

NEWTON. You have my word of honor, madam.

LOUISE. But a word of honor must be a gentleman's word of honor. You, monsieur, are a bourgeois. You must swear on your Bible.

NEWTON. My word is my word, madam. And the Bible must not be mixed up with the magic of micapanis.

LOUISE. Not black magic, is it? I could not touch that.

NEWTON. Neither black nor white, madam. Shall we say grey? But quite harmless, I assure you.

LOUISE. Good. And now I must make you a little present for your pills. How much shall it be?

NEWTON. Keep your money for the apothecary, madam: he will be amply satisfied with five shillings. I am sufficiently rewarded by the sound scientific advice you have given me from your friend Blaise Pascal. He was anticipated by an Englishman named Bacon, who was, however, no mathematician. You owe me nothing.

LOUISE. Shall I give one of the new golden guineas to the lady I shocked if I meet her on the stairs?

NEWTON. No. She would not take it.

LOUISE. How little you know the world, Monsieur! Nobody refuses a golden guinea.

NEWTON. You can try the experiment, madam. That

would be the advice of your friend Pascal. [*He goes to the door, and opens it for her*].

LOUISE. Perhaps I had better make it two guineas. She will never refuse that.

NEWTON [*at the door, calling*] Sally!

LOUISE [*with a gracious inclination of her head*] Monsieur—

NEWTON. I wish your Grace good morning.

SALLY [*at the door*] Yes, sir?

NEWTON. Shew her Grace the Duchess of Portsmouth to her chair or whatever it is.

LOUISE. Au plaisir de vous revoir, Monsieur le philosophe.

The Duchess goes out, Sally making her a rustic curtsey as she passes, and following her out, leaving Newton alone.

NEWTON [*greatly relieved*] Ouf!

He returns to his place at the table and to his Bible, which, helped by a marker, he opens at the last two chapters of the book of Daniel. He props his head on his elbows.

NEWTON. Twelve hundred and ninety days. And in the very next verse thirteen hundred and thirtyfive days. Five months difference! And the king's daughter of the south: who was she? And the king of the south? And he that cometh against him? And the vile person who obtains the kingdom by flatteries? And Michael? Who was Michael? [*He considers this a moment; then suddenly snatches a sheet of paper and writes furiously*].

SALLY [*throwing open the door, bursting with pride*] His Royal Highness the Duke of York.

The Duke, afterwards James II, comes in precipitately.

JAMES [*imperiously*] Where is his Majesty the King?

NEWTON [*rising in ungovernable wrath*] Sir: I neither know nor care where the King is. This is my house;

and I demand to be left in peace in it. I am engaged in researches of the most sacred importance; and for them I require solitude. Do you hear, sir? solitude!

JAMES. Sir: I am the Duke of York, the King's brother.

NEWTON: I am Isaac Newton, the philosopher. I am also an Englishman; and my house is my castle. At least it was until this morning, when the whole court came here uninvited. Are there not palaces for you and the court to resort to? Go away.

JAMES. I know you. You are a follower of the arch infidel Galileo!

NEWTON. Take care, sir. In my house the great Galileo shall not be called an infidel by any Popish blockhead, prince or no prince. Galileo had more brains in his boots than you have in your whole body.

JAMES. Had he more brains in his boots than the Catholic Church? Than the Pope and all his cardinals, the greatest scholars of his day? Is there more learning in your head than in the libraries of the Vatican?

NEWTON. Popes and cardinals are abolished in the Church of England. Only a fool would set up these superstitious idolaters against the Royal Society, founded by your royal brother for the advancement of British science.

JAMES. A club of damnable heretics. I shall know how to deal with them.

NEWTON [*rising in a fury and facing him menacingly*] Will you leave my house, or shall I throw you out through the window?

JAMES. You throw me out! Come on, you scum of a grammar school.

They rush at one another, and in the scuffle fall on the floor, Newton uppermost. Charles comes in at this moment.

CHARLES. Odsfish, Mr Newton, whats this? A wrestling match?

Newton hastily rolls off James. The two combatants remain sitting on the floor, staring up at Charles.

CHARLES. And what the divvle are you doing here, Jamie? Why arnt you in Holland?

JAMES. I am here where I have been thrown by your friend and protégé, the infidel philosopher Newton.

CHARLES. Get up, man: dont play the fool. Mr Newton: your privilege with me does not run to the length of knocking my brother down. It is a serious matter to lay hands on a royal personage.

NEWTON: Sir: I had no intention of knocking your royal brother down. He fell and dragged me down. My intention was only to throw him out of the window.

CHARLES. He could have left by the door, Mr Newton.

NEWTON. He could; but he would not, in spite of my repeated requests. He stayed here to heap insults on the immortal Galileo, whose shoe latchet he is unworthy to unloose.

He rises and confronts the King with dignity.

CHARLES. Will you get up, Jamie, and not sit on the floor grinning like a Jackanapes. Get up, I tell you.

JAMES [*rising*] You see what comes of frequenting the houses of your inferiors. They forget themselves and take liberties. And you encourage heretics. I do not.

CHARLES. Mr Newton: we are in your house and at your orders. Will you allow my brother and myself to have this room to ourselves awhile?

NEWTON. My house is yours, sir. I am a resolute supporter of the Exclusion Bill because I hope to prove that the Romish Church is the little horn of the fourth beast mentioned by the prophet Daniel. But the great day of wrath is not yet come. Your brother is welcome here as long as you desire it.

Newton goes out. Charles takes the armchair. When he is seated James takes Newton's chair at the table.

JAMES. That fellow is crazy. He called me a Popish blockhead. You see what comes of encouraging these Protestants. If you had a pennorth of spunk in you you would burn the lot.

CHARLES. What I want to know is what you are doing here when you should be in Holland. I am doing what I can to stop this Exclusion Bill and secure the crown for you when I die. I sent you to Holland so that your talent for making yourself unpopular might be exercised there and not here. Your life is in danger in London. You had no business to come back. Why have you done it?

JAMES. Charles: I am a prince.

CHARLES. Oh, do I not know it, God help you!

JAMES. Our father lost his head by compromising with Protestants, Republicans, Levellers and Atheists. What did he gain by it? They beheaded him. I am not going to share his fate by repeating that mistake. I am a Catholic; and I am civil to none but Catholics, however unpopular it may make me. When I am king—as I shall be, in my own right, and not by the leave of any Protestant parliamentary gang—I shall restore the Church and restore the monarchy: yes, the monarchy, Charles; for there has been no real Restoration: you are no king, cleverly as you play with these Whigs and Tories. That is because you have no faith, no principles: you dont believe in anything; and a man who doesnt believe in anything is afraid of everything. Youre a damned coward, Charles. I am not. When I am king I shall reign: these fellows shall find what a king's will is when he reigns by divine right. They will get it straight in the teeth then; and Europe will see them crumble up like moths in a candle flame.

CHARLES. It is a funny thing, Jamie, that you, who are clever enough to see that the monarchy is gone and that I keep the crown by my wits, are foolish enough to believe that you have only to stretch out your clenched fist and take it back again. I sometimes ask myself whether it would not be far kinder of me to push the Exclusion Bill through and save you from the fate of our father. They will have your head off inside of five years unless you jump into the nearest fishing smack and land in France.

JAMES. And leave themselves without a king again! Not they: they had enough of that under old Noll's Major-Generals. Noll knew how to rule: I will say that for him; and I thank him for the lesson. But when he died they had to send for us. When they bully you you give in to them and say that you dont want to go on your travels again. But by God, if they try to bully me I will threaten to go on my travels and leave them without a king. That is the way to bring them down on their marrowbones.

CHARLES. You could not leave them without a king. Protestant kings—Stuart kings—are six a penny in Europe today. The Dutch lad's grandfather-in-law was our grandfather. Your daughter Mary is married to him. The Elector of Hanover has the same hook on to grandfather James. Both of them are rank Protestants and hardened soldiers, caring for nothing but fighting the French. Besides Mary there is her sister Anne, Church of England to the backbone. With the Protestants you do not succeed by divine right: they take their choice and send for you, just as they sent for me.

JAMES. Yes, if you look at it in that way and let them do it. Charles: you havnt the spirit of a king: that is what is the matter with you. As long as they let you have your women, and your dogs, and your pictures, and your music, and your chemical laboratory, you let them do as they like. The merry monarch: thats what you are.

CHARLES. Something new in monarchs, eh?

JAMES. Psha! A merry monarch is no monarch at all.

CHARLES. All the same, I must pack you off to Scotland. I cannot have you here until I prorogue parliament to get rid of the Exclusion Bill. And you will have to find a Protestant husband for Anne: remember that.

JAMES. You pretend you are packing me off to save me from my Catholic unpopularity. The truth is you are jealous of my popularity.

CHARLES. No, Jamie: I can beat you at that game. I am an agreeable sort of fellow: old Newcastle knocked that into me when I was a boy. Living at the Hague on two hundred and forty pounds a year finished my education in that respect. Now you, Jamie, became that very disagreeable character a man of principle. The people, who have all sorts of principles which they havnt gathered out of your basket, will never take to you until you go about shouting No Popery. And you will die rather than do that: wont you?

JAMES. Certainly I shall; and so, I trust, would you. Promise me you will die a Catholic, Charles.

CHARLES. I shall take care not to die in an upstart sect like the Church of England, and perhaps lose my place in Westminster Abbey when you are king. Your principles might oblige you to throw my carcase to the dogs. Meanwhile, however popular you may think yourself, you must go and be popular in Scotland.

JAMES. I am popular everywhere: thats what you dont understand because you are not a fighting man; and I am. In the British Isles, Charles, nothing is more popular than the navy; and nobody is more popular than the admiral who has won a great naval victory. Thats what I have done, and you havnt. And that puts me ahead of you with the British people every time.

CHARLES. No doubt; but the British people do not make kings in England. The crown is in the hands of the damned Whig squirearchy who got rich by robbing the Church, and chopped off father's head, crown and all. They care no more for your naval victory than for a bunch of groundsel. They would not pay for the navy if we called it ship money, and let them know what they are paying for.

JAMES. I shall make them pay. I shall not be their puppet as you are. Do you think I will be in the pay of the king of France, whose bitter bread we had to eat in our childhood, and who left our mother without firewood in the freezing winter? And all this because these rebellious dogs will not disgorge enough of their stolen wealth to cover the cost of governing them! If you will not teach them their lesson they shall learn it from me.

CHARLES. You will have to take your money where you can get it, Jamie, as I do. French money is as good as English. King Louis gets little enough for it: I take care of that.

JAMES. Then you cheat him. How can you stoop?

CHARLES. I must. And I know that I must. To play the king as you would have me I should need old Noll's army; and they took good care I should not have that. They grudge me even the guards.

JAMES. Well, what old Noll could do I can do; and so could you if you had the pluck. I will have an army too.

CHARLES. Of Protestants?

JAMES. The officers will be Catholics. The rank and file will be what they are ordered to be.

CHARLES. Where will you get the money to pay them? Old Noll had the city of London and its money at his back.

JAMES. The army will collect the taxes. How does King Louis do it? He keeps the biggest army in Europe; and he keeps you into the bargain. He hardly knows what a parliament is. He dragoons the Protestants out of France into Spitalfields. I shall dragoon them out of Spitalfields.

CHARLES. Where to?

JAMES. To hell, or to the American plantations, whichever they prefer.

CHARLES. So you are going to be the English Louis, the British Roi Soleil, the sun king. This is a deuced foggy climate for sun kings, Jamie.

JAMES. So you think, Charles. But the British climate has nothing to do with it. What is it that nerves Louis to do all these things? The climate of the Catholic Church. His foot is on the rock of Saint Peter; and that makes him a rock himself.

CHARLES. Your son-in-law Dutch Billy is not afraid of him. And Billy's house is built, not on a rock, not even on the sands, but in the mud of the North Sea. Keep your eye on the Orangeman, Jamie.

JAMES. I shall keep my eye on your Protestant bastard Monmouth. Why do you make a pet of that worthless fellow? Know you not he is longing for your death so that he may have a try for the crown while this rascally Popish plot is setting the people against me?

CHARLES. For my death! What a thought! I grant you he has not the makings of a king in him: I am not blind to his weaknesses. But surely he is not heartless.

JAMES. Psha! there is not a plot in the kingdom to murder either of us that he is not at the bottom of.

CHARLES. He is not deep enough to be at the bottom of anything, Jamie.

JAMES. Then he is at the top. I forgive him for wanting to make an end of me: I am no friend of his. But to plot against you, his father! you, who have petted him and spoilt him and forgiven him treason after treason! for that I shall not forgive him, as he shall find if ever he falls into my hand.

CHARLES. Jamie: this is a dreadful suspicion to put into my mind. I thought the lad had abused my affection until it was exhausted; but it still can hurt. Heaven keep him out of your hand! that is all I can say. Absalom! O Absalom: my son, my son!

JAMES. I am sorry, Charles; but this is what comes of bringing up your bastards as Protestants and making dukes of them.

CHARLES. Let me tell you a secret, Jamie: a king's secret. Peter the fisherman did not know everything. Neither did Martin Luther.

JAMES. Neither do you.

CHARLES. No; but I must do the best I can with what I know, and not with what Peter and Martin knew. Anyhow, the long and the short of it is that you must start for Scotland this very day, and stay there until I send you word that it is safe for you to come back.

JAMES. Safe! What are you afraid of, man? If you darent face these Protestant blackguards, is that any reason why I should run away from them?

CHARLES. You were talking just now about your popularity. Do you know who is the most popular man in England at present?

JAMES. Shaftesbury, I suppose. He is the Protestant hero just as Nelly is the Protestant whoor. I tell you

Shaftesbury will turn his coat as often as you crack your whip. Why dont you crack it?

CHARLES. I am not thinking of Shaftesbury.

JAMES. Then who?

CHARLES. Oates.

JAMES. Titus Oates! A navy chaplain kicked out of the service for the sins of Sodom and Gomorrah! Are you afraid of him?

CHARLES. Yes. At present he is the most popular man in the kingdom. He is lodged in my palace at Whitehall with a pension of four hundred pounds a year.

JAMES. What!!!

CHARLES. And I, who am called a king, cannot get rid of him. This house is Isaac Newton's; and he can order you out and throw you out of the window if you dont go. But my house must harbor the vilest scoundrel in Europe while he parades in lawn sleeves through the street with his No Popery mob at his heels, and murders our best Catholic families with his brazen perjuries and his silly Popish plot that should not impose on a rabbit. No man with eyes in his head could look at the creature for an instant without seeing that he is only half human.

JAMES. Flog him through the town. Flog him to death. They can if they lay on hard enough and long enough. The same mob that now takes him for a saint will crowd to see the spectacle and revel in his roarings.

CHARLES. That will come, Jamie. I am hunting out his record; and your man Jeffries will see to it that the poor divvle shall have no mercy. But just now it is not Oates that we have to kill: the people would say that he was murdered by the Catholics and run madder than ever. They blame the Catholics now for the Great Fire of London and the plague. We must kill the

Popish Plot first. When we have done that, God help Titus Oates! Meanwhile, away with you to Scotland and try your cat-o-ninetails on the Covenanters there.

JAMES. Well, I suppose I must, since England is governed by its mob instead of by its king. But I tell you, Charles, when I am king there shall be no such nonsense. You jeer at me and say that I am the protector of your life, because nobody will kill you to make me king; but I take that as the highest compliment you could pay me. This mob that your Protestant Republicans and Presbyterians and Levellers call the people of England will have to choose between King James the Second and King Titus Oates. And James and the Church—and there is only one real Church of God—will see to it that their choice will be Hobson's choice.

CHARLES. The people of England will have nothing to do with it. The real Levellers today, Jamie, are the lords and the rich squires—Cromwell's sort—and the moneyed men of the city. They will keep the people's noses to the grindstone no matter what happens. And their choice will be not between you and Titus Oates, but between your daughter Mary's Protestant husband and you.

JAMES. He will have to cross the seas to get here. And I, as Lord High Admiral of England, will meet him on the seas and sink him there. He is no great general on land: on water he is nothing. I have never been beaten at sea.

CHARLES. Jamie, Jamie: nothing frightens me so much as your simple stupid pluck, and your faith in Rome. You think you will have the Pope at your back because you are a Catholic. You are wrong: in politics the Pope is always a Whig, because every earthly monarch's court is a rival to the Vatican.

JAMES. Do you suppose that if Orange Billy, the head of the Protestant heresy in Europe, the anti-Pope you might call him, dared to interfere with me, a Catholic king, the Pope could take his part against me in the face of all Europe! How can you talk such nonsense? Do you think Mary would share the crown if he tore it from her father's head? Rochester called you the king that never said a foolish thing and never did a wise one; but it seems to me that you talk silly-clever nonsense all day, though you are too wise: that is, too big a coward, ever to risk a fight with the squirearchy. What are they in France? Lackeys round the throne at Versailles: not one of them dare look King Louis straight in the face. But in France there is a real king.

CHARLES. He has a real army and real generals. And taxes galore. Old Noll went one better than Louis: he was a general himself. And what a general! Preston, Dunbar, Worcester: we could no nothing against him though we had everything on our side, except him. I have been looking for his like ever since we came back. I sometimes wonder whether Jack Churchill has any military stuff in him.

JAMES. What! That henpecked booby! I suppose you know that he got his start in life as your Barbara's kept man?

CHARLES. I know that the poor lad risked breaking his bones by jumping out of Barbara's window when she was seducing him and I came along unexpectedly. I have always liked him for that.

JAMES. It was worth his while. She gave him five thousand pounds for it.

CHARLES. Yes: I had to find the money. I was tremendously flattered when I heard of it. I had no idea that Barbara put so high a price on my belief in her faithfulness, in which, by the way, I did not believe. Poor Barbara was never alone with a pretty fellow for five minutes without finding out how much of a man he was. I threw Churchill in her way purposely to keep her in good humor. What struck me most in the affair was that Jack bought an annuity with the money instead of squandering it as any other man of his age would have done. That was a sign of solid ability. He may be henpecked: what married man is not? But he is no booby.

JAMES. Meanness. Pure meanness. The Churchills never had a penny to bless themselves with. Jack got no more education than my groom.

CHARLES. Latin grammar is not much use on the battlefield, as we found out. Turenne found Jack useful enough in Spain; and Turenne was supposed to be France's greatest general. Your crown may depend on Jack: by the time I die he will be as old a soldier as Oliver was at Dunbar.

JAMES. Never fear. I shall buy him if he's worth it.

CHARLES. Or if you are worth it. Jack is a good judge of a winner.

JAMES. He has his price all the same.

CHARLES. All intelligent men have, Jamie.

JAMES. Psha! Dont waste your witticisms on me: they butter no parsnips. If he can pick a winner he had better pick me.

CHARLES. There are only two horses in the race now: the Protestant and the Catholic. I have to ride both at once.

JAMES. That was what Father tried to do. See what he got by it!

CHARLES. See what I get by it! Not much, perhaps; but I keep my head on my shoulders. It takes a man of brains to do that. Our father unfortunately tried his hand at being also a man of blood, as Noll called him. We Stuarts are no good at that game: Noll beat us at it every time. I hate blood and battles: I have seen too much of them to have any dreams of glory about them. I am, as you say, no king. To be what you call a king I lack military ambition; and I lack cruelty. I have to manage Protestants who are so frightfully cruel that I dare not interfere with Protestant judges who are merciless. The penalty for high treason is so abominable that only a divvle could have invented it, and a nation of divvles crowd to see it done. The only time I risked my crown was when I stopped them after they had butchered ten of the regicides: I could bear no more. They were not satisfied: they dug up the body of old Noll, and butchered it rather than have their horrible sport cut short.

JAMES. Serve the rascals right! A good lesson for them and their like. Dont be such a mollycoddle, Charles. What you need is a bit of my sea training to knock the nonsense out of you.

CHARLES. So you will try your luck as a man of blood, will you?

JAMES. I will do what is necessary. I will fight my enemies if they put me to it. I will take care that those who put me to it shall not die easy deaths.

CHARLES. Well, that will seem very natural to the mob. You will find plenty of willing tools. But I would not light the fires of Smithfield again if I were you. Your pet Jeffries would do it for you and enjoy it; but Protestants do not like being burnt alive.

JAMES. They will have to lump it if they fly in the face of God.

CHARLES. Oh, go to Scotland: go to Jericho. You sicken me. Go.

JAMES. Charles! We must not part like this. You

know you always stand by me as far as you dare. I ought not to talk to you about government and kingcraft: you dont understand these matters and never will; and I do understand them. I have resolved again and again not to mention them to you; for after all we are brothers; and I love you in spite of all the times you have let me down with the Protestants. It is not your fault that you have no head for politics and no knowledge of human nature. You need not be anxious about me. I will leave for Scotland tomorrow. But I have business in London tonight that I will not postpone for fifty thousand Titus Oateses.

CHARLES. Business in London tonight! The one redeeming point in your character, Jamie, is that you are not a man of principle in the matter of women.

JAMES. You are quite wrong there: I am in all things a man of principle and a good Catholic, thank God. But being human I am also a man of sin. I confess it; and I do my penances!

CHARLES. The women themselves are worse penances than any priest dare inflict on you. Try Barbara: a week with her is worse than a month in hell. But I have given up all that now. Nelly is a good little soul who amuses me. Louise manages my French affairs. She has French brains and manners, and is always a lady. But they are now my friends only: affectionate friends, family friends, nothing else. And they alone are faithful to the elderly king. I am fifty, Jamie, fifty: dont forget that. And women got hold of me when I was fourteen, thirtysix years ago. Do you suppose I have learnt nothing about women and what you call love in that time? You still have love affairs: I have none. However, I am not reproaching you: I am congratulating you on being still young and green enough to come all the way from Holland for a night in London.

Mrs Basham returns, much perturbed.

MRS BASHAM. Mr Rowley: I must tell you that I cannot receive any more of your guests. I have not knives nor plates nor glasses enough. I have had to borrow chairs from next door. Your valet, Mr Chiffinch, tells who ever has any business with you this morning to come on here. Mr Godfrey Kneller, the new Dutch painter, with a load of implements connected with his trade, had got in in spite of me: he heard the noise your people were making. There are the two ladies and the player woman, and yourself and your royal brother and Mr Fox and the painter. That makes seven; and Mr Newton makes eight and I make nine. I have nothing to offer them but half a decanter of sherry that was opened last Easter, and the remains of a mouldy cake. I have sent Sally out with orders that will run away with a fortnight's housekeeping money; and that wont be half what theyll expect. I thought they were all going away when they came downstairs; but the French lady wanted to look through Mr Newton's telescope; and the jealous lady wouldnt leave until the French lady left; and the player woman is as curious as a magpie and makes herself as much at home as if she lived here. It has ended in their all staying. And now Mr Newton is explaining everything and shewing off his telescope and never thinking what I am to do with them! How am I to feed them?

CHARLES. Dont feed them, Mrs Basham. Starve them out.

MRS BASHAM. Oh no: I cant do that. What would they think of us? Mr Newton has his position to keep up.

CHARLES. It is the judgment of heaven on you for turning away my pretty spaniels from your door this morning.

MRS BASHAM. There were twelve of them, sir.

CHARLES. You would have found them much better company than nine human beings. But never mind. Sally will tell all the tradesmen that Mr Newton is entertaining me and my brother. They will call themselves Purveyors to his Majesty the King. Credit will be unlimited.

JAMES. Remember that this is Friday: a fast day. All I need is three or four different kinds of fish.

MRS BASHAM. No, sir: in this house you will have to be content with a Protestant dinner. Jack the fish hawker is gone. But he left us a nice piece of cod; and thats all youll get, sir.

CHARLES. Jamie: we must clear out and take the others with us. It seems we cannot visit anyone without ruining them.

JAMES. Pooh! What can a few pounds more or less matter to anybody?

CHARLES. I can remember when they meant a divvle of a lot to me, and to you too. Let us get back to Newmarket.

MRS BASHAM. No, sir: Mr Newton would not like that: he knows his duties as your host. And if you will excuse me saying so, sir: you all look as if a plain wholesome dinner would do you no harm for once in a way. By your leave I will go to look after it. I must turn them all out of the laboratory and send them up here while I lay the table there.

She goes out.

JAMES. "A nice piece of cod!" Among nine people!

CHARLES. "Isnt that a dainty dish to set before a king?" Your fast will be a real fast, Jamie, for the first time in your life.

JAMES. You lie. My penances are all real.

CHARLES. Well, a hunk of bread, a lump of cheese,

and a bottle of ale are enough for me or for any man at this hour.

All the rest come back except Mrs Basham, Barbara, and Newton. Fox comes first.

FOX. I have made eight new friends. But has the Lord sent them to me? Such friends! [*He takes his old seat, much perplexed*].

NELL [*coming in*] Oh, Rowley darling, they want me to recite my big speech from The Indian Emperor. But I cant do that without proper drapery: its classical. [*Going to the Duke*] And what is my Jamie doing here?

LOUISE [*taking a chair from the wall and planting it at Charles's right, familiarly close*] Why not give us a prologue? Your prologues are your best things. [*She sits*].

CHARLES and JAMES. Yes, yes: a prologue.

All are now seated, except Nell.

NELL. But I cant do a prologue unless I am in breeches.

FOX [*rising*] No. Eleanor Gwyn: how much more must I endure from you? I will not listen to a prologue that can be spoken only by a woman in breeches. And I warn you that when I raise my voice to heaven against mummery, whether in playhouse or steeple-house, I can drown and dumb the loudest ribald ranter.

CHARLES. Pastor: Mistress Gwyn is neither a ribald nor a ranter. The plays and prologues in which she is famous are the works of the greatest poet of the age: the poet Laureate, John Dryden.

FOX. If he has given to the playhouse talents that were given to him for the service of God, his guilt is the deeper.

CHARLES. Have you considered, Pastor, that the

playhouse is a place where two or three are gathered together?

NELL. Not when I am playing, Rowley darling. Two or three hundred, more likely.

FOX [*resuming his seat in the deepest perplexity*] Sir: you are upsetting my mind. You have forced me to make friends with this player woman; and now you would persuade me that the playhouse is as divine as my meeting house. I find your company agreeable to me, but very unsettling.

CHARLES. The settled mind stagnates, Pastor. Come! Shall I give you a sample of Mr Dryden at his best?

NELL. Oh yes, Rowley darling: give us your pet speech from Aurengzebe.

LOUISE. Yes yes. He speaks it beautifully. He is almost as good an actor as King Louis; and he has really more of the grand air.

CHARLES. Thank you, Louise. Next time leave out the almost. My part is more difficult than that of Louis.

JAMES. Pray silence for his Majesty the King, who is going to make a fool of himself to please the Quaker.

CHARLES. Forgive Jamie, ladies and gentlemen. He will give you his own favorite recitation presently; but the King comes first. Now listen. [*He rises. They all rise, except Fox*]. No, pray. My audience must be seated. [*They sit down again*].

Charles recites the pessimistic speech from Aurengzebe as follows:

When I consider life, 'tis all a cheat;
Yet, fooled with hope, men favor the deceit;
Trust on, and think tomorrow will repay:
Tomorrow's falser than the former day;
Lies worse; and, while it says we shall be blest
With some new choice, cuts off what we possessed.

Strange cozenage! None would live past years again;
Yet all hope pleasure in what yet remain;
And from the dregs of life think to receive
What the first sprightly running could not give.
I'm tired of waiting for this chemic gold
Which fools us young, and beggars us when old.

Nell and Louise applaud vigorously.

CHARLES. What do you think of that, Pastor? [*He sits*].

FOX. It is the cry of a lost soul from the bottomless blackness of its despair. Never have I heard anything so terrible. This man has never lived. I must seek him out and shew him the light and the truth.

NELL. Tut tut, George! The man in the play is going to be killed. To console himself he cries Sour Grapes: that is all. And now what shall I give you?

JAMES. Something oldfashioned. Give him a bit of Shakespear.

NELL. What! That author the old actors used to talk about. Kynaston played women in his plays. I dont know any. We cannot afford them nowadays. They require several actors of the first quality; and—would you believe it, George?—those laddies will not play now for less than fifteen shillings a week.

FOX [*starting up again*] Fifteen shillings a week to a player when the servants of God can scarce maintain themselves alive by working at mechanical trades! Such wickedness will bring a black judgment on the nation. Charles Stuart: have you no regard for your soul that you suffer such things to be done?

CHARLES. You would not grudge these poor fellows their fifteen shillings if you knew what women cost.

FOX. What manner of world is this that I have come into? Is virtue unknown here, or is it despised? [*He gives it up, and relapses into his seat*].

JAMES. Mr Dryden has an answer for that. [*He recites, seated*].

> How vain is virtue which directs our ways
> Through certain danger to uncertain praise!
> The world is made for the bold impious man
> Who stops at nothing, seizes all he can.
> Justice to merit does weak aid afford;
> She trusts her balance, and ignores her sword.
> Virtue is slow to take whats not her own,
> And, while she long consults, the prize is gone.

FOX. I take no exception to this. I have too good reason to know that it is true. But beware how you let these bold impious fellows extinguish hope in you. Their day is short; but the inner light is eternal.

JAMES. I am safe in the bosom of my Church, Pastor.

LOUISE. Take the gentleman's mind off his inner light, Nell. Give us a speech.

NELL. They dont want a speech from me. Rowley began talking about speeches because he wanted to do one himself. And now His Highness the Duke of York must have his turn.

JAMES. Are we poor devils of princes not to have any of the good things, nor do any of the pleasant things, because we are Royal Highnesses ? Were you not freer and happier when you sold oranges in Drury Lane than you are now as a court lady ?

FOX. Did you sell oranges in Drury Lane ?

NELL. They say I did. The people like to believe I did. They love me for it. I say nothing.

CHARLES. Come! Give us one of Cydara's speeches from The Indian Emperor. It was in that that you burst on the world as the ambitious orange girl.

NELL. A wretched part: I had to stand mum on the stage for hours while the others were spouting. Mr

Dryden does not understand how hard that is. Just listen to this, the longest speech I had.

May I believe my eyes! What do I see?
Is this her hate to him? her love to me?
'Tis in my breast she sheathes her dagger now.
False man: is this thy faith? Is this thy vow?

Then somebody says something.

CHARLES.

What words, dear saint, are these I hear you use?
What faith? what voice? are those which you accuse?

NELL. "Those which you accuse": thats my cue.

More cruel than the tiger o'er his spile
And falser than the weeping crocodile
Can you add vanity to guilt, and take
A pride to hear the conquests which you make?
Go: publish your renown: let it be said
The woman that you love you have betrayed—

Rowley darling: I cannot go on if you keep laughing at me. If only Mr Dryden had given me some really great lines, like the ones he gave to Montezuma. Listen.

Still less and less my boiling spirits flow
And I grow stiff, as cooling metals do.
Farewell, Almira.

FOX. Now do you tell me that living men and women, created by God in His likeness and not in that of gibbering apes, can be bribed to utter such trash, and that others will pay to hear them do it when they will not enter a meeting house for a penny in the plate to hear the words of God Himself? What society is this I am in? I must be dreaming that I am in hell.

NELL. George: you are forgetting yourself. You should have applauded me. I will recite no more for you. [*She takes a chair from the wall and seats herself beside Louise, on her right*].

CHARLES. He does not understand, Nell. Tell him the story of the play, and why Montezuma says such extravagant things.

NELL. But how can I, Rowley darling? I dont know what it is all about: I know only my part and my cue. All I can say is that when Montezuma speaks those lines he drops dead.

FOX. Can you wonder that he does so? I should drop dead myself if I heard such fustian pass my lips.

JAMES. Is it worse than the fustian that passes the lips of the ranters in your conventicles?

FOX. I cannot deny it: the preachers are a greater danger than the players. I had not thought of this before. Again you unsettle my mind. There is one Jeremy Collier who swears he will write such a book on the profaneness and immorality of the stage as will either kill the theatre or shame it into decency; but these lines just uttered by Eleanor Gwyn are not profane and immoral: they are mad and foolish.

LOUISE. All the less harmful, monsieur. They are not meant to be taken seriously; and no one takes them so. But your Huguenot ranters pretend to be inspired; and foolish people are deluded by them. And what sort of world would they make for us if they got the upper hand? Can you name a single pleasure that they would leave us to make life worth living?

FOX. It is not pleasure that makes life worth living. It is life that makes pleasure worth having. And what pleasure is better than the pleasure of holy living?

JAMES. I have been in Geneva, blasphemously called the City of God under that detestable Frenchman

Calvin, who, thank God, has by now spent a century in hell. And I can testify that he left the wretched citizens only one worldly pleasure.

CHARLES. Which one was that?

JAMES. Moneymaking.

CHARLES. Odsfish! that was clever of him. It is a very satisfying pleasure, and one that lasts til death.

LOUISE. It does not satisfy me.

CHARLES. You have never experienced it, Louise. You spend money: you do not make it. You spend ten times as much as Nelly; but you are not ten times as happy. If you made ten times as much as she, you would never tire of it and never ask for anything better.

LOUISE. Charles: if I spent one week making money or even thinking about it instead of throwing it away with both hands all my charm would be gone. I should become that dull thing, a plain woman. My face would be full of brains instead of beauty. And you would send me back to France by the next ship, as you sent Barbara.

CHARLES. What if I did? You will soon be tired of me; for I am an ugly old fellow. But you would never tire of moneymaking.

NELL. Now the Lord be praised, my trade is one in which I can make money without losing my good looks!

LOUISE [*to Charles*] If you believe what you say, why do you not make money yourself instead of running after women?

CHARLES. Because there is a more amusing occupation for me.

LOUISE. I have not seen you practise it, Charles. What is it?

CHARLES. Kingcraft.

JAMES. Of which you have not the faintest conception.

CHARLES. Like Louise, you have not seen me practise it. But I am King of England; and my head is still on my shoulders.

NELL. Rowley darling: you must learn to keep King Charles's head out of your conversation. You talk too much of him.

CHARLES. Why is it that we always talk of my father's head and never of my great grandmother's? She was by all accounts a pretty woman; but the Protestants chopped her head off in spite of Elizabeth. They had Strafford's head off in spite of my father. And then they had his own off. I am not a bit like him; but I have more than a touch in me of my famous grandfather Henry the Fourth of France. And he died with a Protestant's dagger in his heart: the deadliest sort of Protestant: a Catholic Protestant. There are such living paradoxes. They burnt the poor wretch's hand off with the dagger in it, and then tore him to pieces with galloping horses. But Henry lay dead all the same. The Protestants will have you, Jamie, by hook or crook: I foresee that: they are the real men of blood. But they shall not have me. I shall die in my bed, and die King of England in spite of them.

FOX. This is not kingcraft: it is chicanery. Protestantism gives the lie to itself: it overthrows the Roman Church and immediately builds itself another nearer home and makes you the head of it, though it is now plain to me that your cleverness acknowledges no Church at all. You are right there: Churches are snares of the divvle. But why not follow the inner light that has saved you from the Churches? Be neither Catholic nor Protestant, Whig nor Tory: throw your crown into the gutter and be a Friend: then all the rest shall be added to you.

They all laugh at him except Charles.

CHARLES. A crown is not so easy to get rid of as you think, Pastor. Besides, I have had enough of the gutter: I prefer Whitehall.

JAMES [*to Fox*] You would like to have a king for your follower, eh?

FOX. I desire Friends, not followers. I am simple in my tastes. I am not schooled and learned as you two princes are.

CHARLES. Thank your stars for that, Pastor: you have nothing to unlearn.

FOX. That is well said. Too often have I found that a scholar is one whose mind is choked with rubbish that should never have been put there. But how do you come to know this? Things come to my knowledge by the Grace of God; yet the same things have come to you who live a most profane life and have no sign of grace at all.

CHARLES. You and I are mortal men, Pastor. It is not possible for us to differ very greatly. You have to wear leather breeches lest you be mistaken for me.

Barbara storms in with a sheet of drawing paper in her hand.

BARBARA [*thrusting the paper under Charles's nose*] Do you see this?

CHARLES [*scrutinizing it admiringly*] Splendid! Has Mr Kneller done this? Nobody can catch a likeness as he can.

BARBARA. Likeness! You have bribed him to insult me. It makes me look a hundred.

CHARLES. Nonsense, dear. It is you to the life. What do you say, Jamie? [*He hands the drawing to James*].

JAMES. It's you, duchess. He has got you, wrinkle for wrinkle.

BARBARA. You say this to my face! You, who have seen my portrait by Lilly!

NELL. You were younger then, darling.

BARBARA. Who asked you for your opinion, you jealous cat?

CHARLES. Sit down; and dont be silly, Barbara. A woman's face does not begin to be interesting until she is our age.

BARBARA. Our age! You old wreck, do you dare pretend that you are as young as I am?

CHARLES. I am only fifty, Barbara. But we are both getting on.

BARBARA. Oh! [*With a scream of rage she tears the drawing to fragments and stamps on them*].

CHARLES. Ah, that was wicked of you: you have destroyed a fine piece of work. Go back to France. I tell you I am tired of your tantrums.

Barbara, intimidated, but with a defiant final stamp on the drawing, flings away behind James to one of the chairs against the cupboards, and sits there sulking.

Newton comes in from the garden, followed by Godfrey Kneller, a Dutchman of 34, well dressed and arrogant. They are both almost as angry as Barbara.

NEWTON. Mr Kneller: I will dispute with you no more. You do not understand what you are talking about.

KNELLER. Sir: I must tell you in the presence of His Majesty you are a most overweening, a most audacious man. You presume to teach me my profession.

CHARLES. What is the matter, Mr Newton?

NEWTON. Let it pass, Mr Rowley. This painter has one kind of understanding: I have another. There is only one course open to us both; and that is silence. [*Finding his chair occupied by the Duke of York he takes another from beside Barbara and seats himself at the side of the table on the Duke's left*].

CHARLES. Mr Newton is our host, Mr Kneller; and

he is a very eminent philosopher. Will you not paint his picture for me? That can be done in silence.

KNELLER. I will paint his picture if your Majesty so desires. He has an interesting head: I should have drawn it this morning had not Her Grace of Cleveland insisted on my drawing her instead. But how can an interesting head contain no brain: that is the question.

CHARLES. Odsfish, man, he has the greatest brain in England.

KNELLER. Then he is blinded by his monstrous conceit. You shall judge between us, sir. Am I or am I not the greatest draughtsman in Europe?

CHARLES. You are certainly a very skilful draughtsman, Mr Kneller.

KNELLER. Can anyone here draw a line better than I?

CHARLES. Nobody here can draw a line at all, except the Duchess of Cleveland, who draws a line at nothing.

BARBARA. Charles—

CHARLES. Be quiet, Barbara. Do not presume to contradict your King.

KNELLER. If there is a science of lines, do I not understand it better than anyone?

CHARLES. Granted, Mr Kneller. What then?

KNELLER. This man here, this crazy and conceited philosopher, dares to assert in contradiction of me, of ME! that a right line is a straight line, and that everything that moves moves in a straight line unless some almighty force bends it from its path. This, he says, is the first law of motion. He lies.

CHARLES. And what do you say, Mr Kneller?

KNELLER. Sir: I do not say: I know. The right line, the line of beauty, is a curve. My hand will not draw a straight line: I have to stretch a chalked string on my canvas and pluck it. Will you deny that your duchess here is as famous for her beauty as the Psyche of the divine Raphael? Well, there is not a straight line in her body: she is all curves.

BARBARA [*outraged, rising*] Decency, fellow! How dare you?

CHARLES. It is true, Barbara. I can testify to it.

BARBARA. Charles: you are obscene. The impudence! [*She sits*].

KNELLER. The beauty, madam. Clear your mind of filth. There is not a line drawn by the hand of the Almighty, from the rainbow in the skies to the house the snail carries on his back, that is not a curve, and a curve of beauty. Your apple fell in a curve.

NEWTON. I explained that.

KNELLER. You mistake explanations for facts: all you sciencemongers do. The path of the world curves, as you yourself have shewn; and as it whirls on its way it would leave your apple behind if the apple fell in a straight line. Motion in a curve is the law of nature; and the law of nature is the law of God. Go out into your garden and throw a stone straight if you can. Shoot an arrow from a bow, a bullet from a pistol, a cannon ball from the mightiest cannon the King can lend you, and though you had the strength of Hercules, and gunpowder more powerful than the steam which hurls the stones from Etna in eruption, yet cannot you make your arrow or your bullet fly straight to its mark.

NEWTON [*terribly perturbed*] This man does not know what he is saying. Take him away; and leave me in peace.

CHARLES. What he says calls for an answer, Mr Newton.

JAMES. The painter is right. A cannon ball flies across the sea in curves like the arches of a bridge, hop, hop,

hop. But what does it matter whether it flies straight or crooked provided it hits between wind and water?

NEWTON. To you, admiral, it matters nothing. To me it makes the difference between reason and madness.

JAMES. How so?

NEWTON. Sir: if what this man believes be true, then not only is the path of the cannon ball curved, but space is curved; time is curved; the universe is curved.

KNELLER. Of course it is. Why not?

NEWTON. Why not! Only my life's work turned to waste, vanity, folly. This comes of admitting strangers to break into my holy solitude with their diabolical suggestions. But I am rightly rebuked for this vice of mine that led me to believe that I could construct a universe with empty figures. In future I shall do nothing but my proper work of interpreting the scriptures. Leave me to that work and to my solitude. [*Desperately, clutching his temples*] Begone, all of you. You have done mischief enough for one morning.

CHARLES. But, Mr Newton, may we not know what we have done to move you thus? What diabolical suggestions have we made? What mischief have we done?

NEWTON. Sir: you began it, you and this infidel quaker. I have devoted months of my life to the writing of a book—a chronology of the world—which would have cost any other man than Isaac Newton twenty years hard labor.

CHARLES. I have seen that book, and been astounded at the mental power displayed in every page of it.

NEWTON. You may well have been, Mr Rowley. And now what have you and Mr Fox done to that book? Reduced it to a monument of the folly of Archbishop

Ussher, who dated the creation of the world at four thousand and four, B.C., and of my stupidity in assuming that he had proved his case. My book is nonsense from beginning to end. How could I, who have calculated that God deals in millions of miles of infinite space, be such an utter fool as to limit eternity, which has neither beginning nor end, to a few thousand years? But this man Fox, without education, without calculation, without even a schoolboy's algebra, knew this when I, who was born one of the greatest mathematicians in the world, drudged over my silly book for months, and could not see what was staring me in the face.

JAMES. Well, why howl about it? Bring out another edition and confess that your Protestant mathematics are a delusion and a snare, and your Protestant archbishops impostors.

NEWTON. You do not know the worst, sir. I have another book in hand: one which should place me in line with Kepler, Copernicus, and Galileo as a master astronomer, and as the completer of their celestial systems. Can you tell me why the heavenly bodies in their eternal motion do not move in straight lines, but always in ellipses?

CHARLES. I understand that this is an unsolved problem of science. I certainly cannot solve it.

NEWTON. I have solved it by the discovery of a force in nature which I call gravitation. I have accounted for all the celestial movements by it. And now comes this painter, this ignorant dauber who, were it to save his soul—if he has a soul—could not work out the simplest equation, or as much as conceive an infinite series of numbers! this fellow substitutes for my first law of motion—straight line motion—motion in a curve.

JAMES. So bang goes your second volume of Protestant philosophy! Squashed under Barbara's outlines.

BARBARA. I will not have my outlines discussed by men. I am not a heathen goddess: I am a Christian lady. Charles always encourages infidels and libertines to blaspheme. And now he encourages them to insult me. I will not bear it.

CHARLES. Do not be an idiot, Barbara: Mr Kneller is paying you the greatest compliment in taking you for a model of the universe. The choice would seem to be between a universe of Barbara's curves and a universe of straight lines seduced from their straightness by some purely mathematical attraction. The facts seem to be on the side of the painter. But in a matter of this kind can I, as founder of the Royal Society, rank the painter as a higher authority than the philosopher?

KNELLER. Your Majesty: the world must learn from its artists because God made the world as an artist. Your philosophers steal all their boasted discoveries from the artists; and then pretend they have deduced them from figures which they call equations, invented for that dishonest purpose. This man talks of Copernicus, who pretended to discover that the earth goes round the sun instead of the sun going round the earth. Sir: Copernicus was a painter before he became an astronomer. He found astronomy easier. But his discovery was made by the great Italian painter Leonardo, born twentyone years before him, who told all his intimates that the earth is a moon of the sun.

NEWTON. Did he prove it?

KNELLER. Man: artists do not prove things. They do not need to. They KNOW them.

NEWTON. This is false. Your notion of a spherical universe is borrowed from the heathen Ptolemy, from all the magicians who believed that the only perfect figure is the circle.

KNELLER. Just what such blockheads would believe. The circle is a dead thing like a straight line: no living hand can draw it: you make it by twirling a pair of dividers. Take a sugar loaf and cut it slantwise, and you will get hyperbolas and parabolas, ellipses and ovals, which Leonardo himself could not draw, but which any fool can make with a knife and a lump of sugar. I believe in none of these mechanical forms. The line drawn by the artist's hand, the line that flows, that strikes, that speaks, that reveals! that is the line that shews the divine handiwork.

CHARLES. So you, too, are a philosopher, Mr Kneller!

KNELLER. Sir: when a man has the gift of a painter, that qualification is so magical that you cannot think of him as anything else. Who thinks of Leonardo as an engineer? of Michael Angelo as an inventor or a sonneteer? of me as a scholar and a philosopher? These things are all in our day's work: they come to us without thinking. They are trifles beside our great labor of creation and interpretation.

JAMES. I had a boatswain once in my flagship who thought he knew everything.

FOX. Perhaps he did. Divine grace takes many strange forms. I smell it in this painter. I have met it in common sailors like your boatswain. The cobbler thinks there is nothing like leather—

NELL. Not when you make it into breeches instead of boots, George.

BARBARA. Be decent, woman. One does not mention such garments in well-bred society.

NELL. Orange girls and players and such like poor folk think nothing of mentioning them. They have to mend them, and sometimes to make them; so they have an honest knowledge of them, and are not ashamed like fine ladies who have only a dishonest knowledge of them.

CHARLES. Be quiet, Nelly; you are making Barbara blush.

NELL. Thats more than you have ever been able to do, Rowley darling.

BARBARA. It is well for you that you have all these men to protect you, mistress. Someday when I catch you alone I'll make you wish you had ten pairs of leather breeches on you.

CHARLES. Come come! no quarrelling.

NELL. She began it, Rowley darling.

CHARLES. No matter who began it, no quarrelling, I command.

LOUISE. Charles: the men have been quarrelling all the morning. Does your command apply to them too?

CHARLES. Their quarrels are interesting, Louise.

NELL. Are they? They bore me to distraction.

CHARLES. Much blood has been shed for them; and much more will be after we are gone.

BARBARA. Oh, do not preach, Charles. Leave that to this person who is dressed partly in leather. It is his profession: it is not yours.

CHARLES. The Protestants will not let me do anything else, my dear. But come! Mr Newton has asked us to leave his house many times. And we must not forget that he never asked us to come into it. But I have a duty to fulfil before we go. I must reconcile him with Mr Kneller, who must paint his portrait to hang in the rooms of the Royal Society.

KNELLER. It is natural that your Majesty should desire a work of mine for the Society. And this man's head is unusual, as one would expect from his being a philosopher: that is, half an idiot. I trust your

Majesty was pleased with my sketch of Her Grace of Cleveland.

BARBARA. Your filthy caricature of Her Grace of Cleveland is under your feet. You are walking on it.

KNELLER [*picking up a fragment and turning it over to identify it*] Has the King torn up a work of mine? I leave the country this afternoon.

CHARLES. I would much sooner have torn up Magna Carta. Her Grace tore it up herself.

KNELLER. It is a strange fact, your Majesty, that no living man or woman can endure his or her portrait if it tells all the truth about them.

BARBARA. You lie, you miserable dauber. When our dear Peter Lilly, who has just died, painted me as I really am, did I destroy his portrait? But he was a great painter; and you are fit only to whitewash unmentionable places.

CHARLES. Her Grace's beauty is still so famous that we are all tired of it. She is the handsomest woman in England. She is also the stupidest. Nelly is the wittiest: she is also the kindest. Louise is the loveliest and cleverest. She is also a lady. I should like to have portraits of all three as they are now, not as Lilly painted them.

LOUISE. No, Charles: I do not want to have the whole truth about me handed down to posterity.

NELL. Same here. I prefer the orange girl.

KNELLER. I see I shall not succeed in England as a painter. My master Rembrandt did not think a woman worth painting until she was seventy.

NELL. Well, you shall paint me when I am seventy. In the theatre the young ones are beginning to call me Auntie! When they call me Old Mar Gwyn I shall be ready for you; and I shall look my very best then.

CHARLES. What about your portrait, Mr Fox? You have been silent too long.

FOX. I am dumbfounded by this strange and ungodly talk. To you it may seem mere gossip; but to me it is plain that this painter claims that his hand is the hand of God.

KNELLER. And whose hand is it if not the hand of God? You need hands to scratch your heads and carry food to your mouths. That is all your hands mean to you. But the hand that can draw the images of God and reveal the soul in them, and is inspired to do this and nothing else even if he starves and is cast off by his father and all his family for it: is not his hand the hand used by God, who, being a spirit without body, parts or passions, has no hands?

FOX. So the men of the steeplehouse say; but they lie. Has not God a passion for creation? Is He not all passion of that divine nature?

KNELLER. Sir: I do not know who you are; but I will paint your portrait.

CHARLES. Bravo! We are getting on. How about your portrait, Mr Newton?

NEWTON. Not by a man who lives in a curved universe. He would distort my features.

LOUISE. Perhaps gravitation would distort them equally, Mr Newton.

CHARLES. That is very intelligent of you, Louise.

BARBARA. It takes some intelligence to be both a French spy and a bluestocking. I thank heaven for my stupidity, as you call it.

CHARLES. Barbara: must I throw you downstairs?

LOUISE. In France they call me the English spy. But this is the first time I have been called a bluestocking. All I meant was that Mr Kneller and Mr Newton seem to mean exactly the same thing; only one calls it beauty and the other gravitation; so they need not quarrel. The portrait will be the same both ways.

NEWTON. Can he measure beauty?

KNELLER. No. I can paint a woman's beauty; but I cannot measure it in a pint pot. Beauty is immeasurable.

NEWTON. I can measure gravitation. Nothing exists until it is measured. Fine words are nothing. Do you expect me to go to the Royal Society and tell them that the orbits of a planet are curved because painters think them prettier so? How much are they curved? This man cannot tell you. I can. Where will they be six months hence? He cannot tell you. I can. All he has to say is that the earth is a moon of the sun and that the line of beauty is a curve. Can he measure the path of the moon? Can he draw the curve?

KNELLER. I can draw your portrait. Can you draw mine?

NEWTON. Yes, with a camera obscura; and if I could find a chemical salt sensitive to light I could fix it. Some day portraits will be made at the street corners for sixpence apiece.

KNELLER. A looking glass will make your portrait for nothing. It makes the duchess's portrait fifty times a day.

BARBARA. It does not. I dont look at myself in the glass fifty times a day. Charles never passes one without looking at himself. I have watched him.

CHARLES. It rebukes my vanity every time, Barbara. I am an ugly fellow; yet I always think of myself as an Adonis.

LOUISE. You are not so ugly as you think, Charles. You were an ugly baby; and your wicked mother told you so. You have never got over it. But when I was sent to England to captivate you with my baby face, it was you who captivated me with your seventy inches and your good looks.

BARBARA. Ay, flatter him, flatter him: he loves it.

CHARLES. I cannot bear this. The subject is to be dropped.

LOUISE. But, Charles—

CHARLES. No, no, No. Not a word more. The King commands it.

Dead silence. They sit as if in church, except Fox, who chafes at the silence.

FOX. In the presence of this earthly king all you great nobles become dumb flunkeys. What will you be when the King of Kings calls you from your graves to answer for your lives?

NELL. Trust you, George, to put in a cheerful word. Rowley darling: may we all stop being dumb flunkeys and be human beings again?

CHARLES. Mr Rowley apologizes for his lapse into royalty. Only, the King's person is not to be discussed.

LOUISE. But, Charles, I love you when you put on your royalty. My king, Louis Quatorze, le grand monarque, le roi soleil, never puts off his royalty for a moment even in the most ridiculous circumstances.

BARBARA. Yes; and he looks like a well-to-do grocer, and will never look like anything else.

LOUISE. You would not dare to say so at Versailles, or even to think so. He is always great; and his greatness makes us great also. But it is true that he is not six feet high, and that the grand manner is not quite natural to him. Charles can do it so much better when he chooses. Charles: why dont you choose?

CHARLES. I prefer to keep the crown and the grand manner up my sleeve until I need them. Louis and I played together when we were boys. We know each other too well to be pleasant company; so I take care to keep out of his way. Besides, Louise, when I make you all great you become terrible bores. I like Nelly because nothing can make a courtier of her. Do you know why?

BARBARA. Because the orange girl has the gutter in her blood.

CHARLES. Not at all. Tell her the reason, Nell.

NELL. I dont know it, Rowley darling. I never was an orange girl; but I have the gutter in my blood all right. I think I have everything in my blood; for when I am on the stage I can be anything you please, orange girl or queen. Or even a man. But I dont know the reason why. So you can tell it to her, Rowley darling, if you know it.

CHARLES. It is because in the theatre you are a queen. I tell you the world is full of kings and queens and their little courts. Here is Pastor Fox, a king in his meeting house, though his meetings are against the law. Here is Mr Newton, a king in the new Royal Society. Here is Godfrey Kneller: a king among painters. I can make you duchesses and your sons dukes; but who would be mere dukes or duchesses if they could be kings and queens?

NELL. Dukes will be six a penny if you make all Barbara's sons dukes.

BARBARA. Oh! My sons have gentle blood in their veins, not gutter dirt.

CHARLES. For shame, Nelly! It was illbred of you to reproach her Grace for the most amiable side of her character.

NELL. I beg pardon. God forgive me, I am no better myself.

BARBARA. No better! You impudent slut.

NELL. Well, no worse, if you like. One little duke is enough for me.

LOUISE. Change the subject, Charles. What you were saying about little kings and queens being everywhere was very true. You are very spiritual.

BARBARA. Ha ha! Ha ha ha! He spiritual!

LOUISE. Clever, you call it. I am always in trouble with my English. And Charles is too lazy to learn French properly, though he lived in France so long.

BARBARA. If you mean clever, he is as clever as fifty foxes.

FOX. He may be fifty times as clever as I; but so are many of the blackest villains. Value him rather for his flashes of the inner light? Did he not stop the butchering of the regicides on the ground that if he punished them they could never punish themselves? That was what made me his loyal subject.

BARBARA. I did not mean fifty of you: I meant real foxes. He is so clever that he can always make me seem stupid when it suits him: that is, when I want anything he wont give me. He is as stingy as a miser.

CHARLES. You are like a dairymaid: you think there is no end to a king's money. Here is my Nelly, who is more careful of my money than she is of her own. Well, when I am dying, and all the rest of you are forgotten, my last thought will be of Nelly.

NELL. Rowley darling: dont make me cry. I am not the only one. Louise is very thoughtful about money.

BARBARA. Yes: she knows exactly how much he has: she gets it for him from the King of France.

LOUISE. This subject of conversation is in the worst possible taste. Charles: be a king again; and forbid it.

CHARLES. Nobody but Barbara would have introduced it. I forbid it absolutely.

Mrs Basham returns.

MRS BASHAM. Mr Newton: dinner is served.

BARBARA. You should address yourself to His Majesty. Where are your manners, woman?

MRS BASHAM. In this house Mr Newton comes first. Come along quick, all of you; or your victuals will be cold.

NEWTON [*rising*] Mr Kneller: will you take her Grace of Cleveland, as you are interested in her curves?

BARBARA [*violently*] No. I am the senior duchess: it is my right to be taken in by the King.

CHARLES [*rising and resignedly giving her his arm*] The Duke of York will follow with the junior duchess. Happy man!

All rise, except Fox.

BARBARA. Brute! [*She tries to disengage herself*].

CHARLES [*holding her fast*] You are on the King's arm. Behave yourself. [*He takes her out forcibly*].

MRS BASHAM. Now, your Highness. Now, Madam Carwell.

JAMES [*taking Louise*] You have remembered, I hope, that Madam Carwell is a Catholic?

MRS BASHAM. Yes: there will be enough cod for the two of you.

LOUISE. Provided Charles does not get at it first. Let us hurry. [*She hurries James out*].

MRS BASHAM. Will you take the player woman, Mr Kneller?

NELL. No no. The player woman goes with her dear old Fox. [*She swoops on the Quaker and drags him along*] George: today you will dine with publicans and sinners. You will say grace for them.

FOX. You remind me that where my Master went I must follow. [*They go out*].

MRS BASHAM. There is no one left for you to take in, Mr Kneller. Mr Newton must take me in and come last.

KNELLER. I will go home. I cannot eat in this house of straight lines.

MRS BASHAM. You will do nothing of the sort, Mr Kneller. There is a cover laid for you; and the King expects you.

NEWTON. The lines are not straight, Mr Kneller. Gravitation bends them. And at bottom I know no more about gravitation than you do about beauty.

KNELLER. To you the universe is nothing but a clock that an almighty clockmaker has wound up and set going for all eternity.

NEWTON. Shall I tell you a secret, Mr Beauty-monger? The clock does not keep time. If it did there would be no further need for the Clockmaker. He is wiser than to leave us to our foolish selves in that fashion. When He made a confusion of tongues to prevent the Tower of Babel from reaching to heaven He also contrived a confusion of time to prevent us from doing wholly without Him. The sidereal clock, the clock of the universe, goes wrong. He has to correct it from time to time. Can you, who know everything because you and God are both artists, tell me what is amiss with the perihelion of Mercury?

KNELLER. The what?

NEWTON. The perihelion of Mercury.

KNELLER. I do not know what it is.

NEWTON. I do. But I do not know what is amiss with it. Not until the world finds this out can it do without the Clockmaker in the heavens who can set the hands back or forward, and move the stars with a touch of His almighty finger as He watches over us in the heavens.

KNELLER. In the heavens! In your universe there is no heaven. You have abolished the sky.

NEWTON. Ignoramus: there may be stars beyond our

vision bigger than the whole solar system. When I have perfected my telescope it will give you your choice of a hundred heavens.

MRS BASHAM. Mr Kneller: your dinner will be cold; and you will be late for grace. I cannot have any more of this ungodly talk. Down with you to your dinner at once.

KNELLER. In this house, you said, Mr Newton comes first. But you take good care that he comes last. The mistress of this and every other house is she who cooks the dinner. [*He goes out*].

MRS BASHAM [*taking Newton out*] Thats a funny fellow, sir. But you really should not begin talking about the stars to people just as they are going away quietly. It is a habit that is growing on you. What do they know or care about the perry healing of Mercury that interests you so much? We shall never get these people out of the house if— [*They pass out of hearing*].

There is peace in the deserted room.

[ACT II]

The boudoir of Catherine of Braganza, Charles's queen, in his not too palatial quarters in Newmarket late in the afternoon on the same day. A prie-dieu, and the pictures, which are all devotional, are signs of the queen's piety. Charles, in slippers and breeches, shirt and cravat, wrapped in an Indian silk dressing gown, is asleep on a couch. His coat and boots are on the carpet where he has thrown them. His hat and wig are on a chair with his tall walking stick. The door, opening on a staircase landing, is near the head of the couch, between it and the prie-dieu. There is a clock in the room.

Catherine, aged 42, enters. She contemplates her husband and the untidiness he has made. With a Portuguese shake of the head (about six times) she sets to work to put the room in order by taking up the boots and putting them tidily at the foot of the couch. She then takes out the coat and hangs it on the rail of the landing. Returning, she purposely closes the door with a bang sufficient to wake Charles.

CHARLES. How long have I been asleep?

CATHERINE. I not know. Why leave you your things about all over my room? I have to put them away like a chambermaid.

CHARLES. Why not send for Chiffinch? It is his business to look after my clothes.

CATHERINE. I not wish to be troubled with Chiffinch when we are alone.

CHARLES [*rising*] Belovéd: you should make me put away my clothes myself. Why should you do chambermaid's work for me? [*His "beloved" always has three syllables*].

CATHERINE. I not like to see you without your wig. But I am your wife and must put up with it.

CHARLES [*getting up*] I am your husband; and I count it a great privilege. [*He kisses her*].

CATHERINE. Yes yes; but why choose you my boudoir for your siesta?

CHARLES. Here in our Newmarket lodging it is the only place where the women cannot come after me.

CATHERINE. A wife is some use then, after all.

CHARLES. There is nobody like a wife.

CATHERINE. I hear that Cleveland has come back from Paris. Did you send for her?

CHARLES. Send for her! I had as soon send for the divvle. I finished with Barbara long ago.

CATHERINE. How often have you told me that you are finished with all women! Yet Portsmouth keeps her hold on you, and Nellie the player. And now Cleveland comes back.

CHARLES. Beloved: you do not understand. These women do not keep their hold on me: I keep my hold on them. I have a bit of news for you about Louise. What do you think I caught her at this morning?

CATHERINE. I had rather not guess.

CHARLES. Buying a love potion. That was for me. I do not make love to her enough, it seems. I hold her because she is intelligent and ladylike and keeps me in touch with France and the French court, to say nothing of the money I have to extract from Louis through her.

CATHERINE. And Nelly? She can play the fine lady; but is she one?

CHARLES. Nelly is a good creature; and she amuses me. You know, beloved, one gets tired of court ladies and their conversation, always the same.

CATHERINE. And you really did not send for Cleveland to come back?

CHARLES. Beloved: when I was young I thought that there was only one unbearable sort of woman: the one that could think of nothing but her soul and its salvation. But in Barbara I found something worse: a woman who thought of nothing but her body and its satisfaction, which meant men and money. For both, Barbara is insatiable. Grab, grab, grab. When one is done with Barbara's body—a very fine body, I admit—what is there left?

CATHERINE. And you are done with Barbara's body?

CHARLES. Beloved: I am done with all bodies. They are all alike: all cats are grey in the dark. It is the souls and the brains that are different. In the end one learns to leave the body out. And then Barbara is packed off to Paris, and is not asked back by me, though I have no doubt there is some man in the case.

CATHERINE. Why spend you so much time with me here—so much more than you used to?

CHARLES. Beloved: do I plague you? I am off.

He makes for the door: she runs to it and bars his egress.

CATHERINE. No: that is not what I meant. Go back and sit down.

Charles obediently goes back to the couch, where they sit side by side.

CHARLES. And what did you mean, beloved?

CATHERINE. You spend too much time away from court. Your brother is stealing the court away from you. When he is here his rooms are crowded: yours are empty.

CHARLES: I thank heaven for it. The older I grow, the less I can endure that most tiresome of all animals, the courtier. Even a dissolute court, as they say mine is—I suppose they mean a court where bawdy stories are told out loud instead of whispered—is more tedious than a respectable one. They repeat themselves and repeat themselves endlessly. And I am just as bad with my old stories about my flight after the battle of Worcester. I told the same one twice over within an hour last Tuesday. This morning Barbara called me an old wreck.

CATHERINE [*flaming up*] She dared! Send her to the Tower and let her rot there.

CHARLES. She is not so important as that, beloved. Nor am I. And we must forgive our enemies when we can afford to.

CATHERINE. I forgive my enemies, as you well know, Charles. It is my duty as a Catholic and a Christian. But it is not my duty to forgive y o u r enemies. And you never forgive mine.

CHARLES. An excellent family arrangement for a royal pair. We can exchange our revenges and remain good Christians. But Barbara may be right. When a king is shunned, and his heir is courted, his death is not far off.

CATHERINE. You must not say things like that: I not can bear it. You are stronger in your mind than ever; and nobody can keep up with you walking.

CHARLES. Nevertheless, beloved, I shall drop before you do. What will happen to you then? that is what troubles me. When I am dead you must go back to Portugal, where your brother the king will take care of you. You will never be safe here, because you are a Catholic queen.

CATHERINE. I not think I shall care what becomes of

me when you are gone. But James is a Catholic. When he is king what have I to fear? Or do you believe your son Monmouth will prevent him from succeeding you and become a Protestant king?

CHARLES. No. He will try, poor boy; but Jamie will kill him. He is his mother's son; and his mother was nothing. Then the Protestants will kill Jamie; and the Dutch lad will see his chance and take it. He will be king: a Protestant king. So you must make for Portugal.

CATHERINE. But such things not could happen. Why are you, who are afraid of nothing else, so afraid of the Protestants?

CHARLES. They killed my great grandmother. They killed my father. They would kill you if I were not a little too clever for them: they are trying hard enough, damn them! They are great killers, these Protestants. Jamie has just one chance. They may call in Orange Billy before they kill him; and then it will hardly be decent for Billy to kill his wife's father. But they will get rid of Jamie somehow; so you must make for home the moment I have kissed you goodbye for the last time.

CATHERINE [*almost in tears*] You not must talk of it— [*She breaks down*].

CHARLES [*caressing her*] Beloved: you will only lose the worst of husbands.

CATHERINE. That is a lie: if anyone else said it I would kill her. You are the very best husband that ever lived.

CHARLES [*laughing*] Oh! Oh! Oh! The merry monarch! Beloved: can anything I can ever do make up to you for my unfaithfulness?

CATHERINE. People think of nothing but that, as if that were the whole of life. What care I about your women? your concubines? your handmaidens? the servants of your common pleasures? They have set me free to be something more to you than they are or can ever be. You have never been really unfaithful to me.

CHARLES. Yes, once, with the woman whose image as Britannia is on every British penny, and will perhaps stay there to all eternity. And on my honor nothing came of that: I never touched her. But she had some magic that scattered my wits: she made me listen for a moment to those who were always pressing me to divorce my patient wife and take a Protestant queen. But I could never have done it, though I was furious when she ran away from me and married Richmond.

CATHERINE. Oh, I know, I know: it was the only time I ever was jealous. Well, I forgive you: why should a great man like you be satisfied with a little thing like me?

CHARLES. Stop. I cannot bear that. I am not a great man; and neither are you a little woman. You have more brains and character than all the rest of the court put together.

CATHERINE. I am nothing except what you have made me. What did I know when I came here? Only what the nuns teach a Portuguese princess in their convent.

CHARLES. And what more had I to teach you except what I learnt when I was running away from the battle of Worcester? And when I had learnt that much there was an end of me as a king. I knew too much.

CATHERINE. With what you have taught me I shall govern Portugal if I return to it?

CHARLES. I have no doubt of it, beloved; but whether that will make you any happier I have my doubts. I wish you could govern the English for me.

CATHERINE. No one can govern the English: that is why they will never come to any good. In Portugal there is the holy Church: we know what we believe; and we all believe the same things. But here the Church itself is a heresy; and there are a thousand other heresies: almost as many heresies as there are people. And if you ask any of them what his sect believes he does not know: all he can say is that the men of the other sects should be hanged and their women whipped through the town at the cart's tail. But they are all against the true Church. I do not understand the English; and I do not want to govern them.

CHARLES. You are Portuguese. I am Italian, French, Scottish, hardly at all English. When I want to know how the great lump of my subjects will take anything I tell it to Barbara. Then I tell it to Chiffinch. Then I tell it to Jamie. When I have the responses of Barbara, Chiffinch, and Jamie, I know how Tom, Dick and Harry will take it. And it is never as I take it.

CATHERINE. In Portugal we not have this strange notion that Tom, Dick and Harry matter. What do they know about government?

CHARLES. Nothing; but they hate it. And nobody teaches them how necessary it is. Instead, when we teach them anything we teach them grammar and dead languages. What is the result? Protestantism and parliaments instead of citizenship.

CATHERINE. In Portugal, God be praised, there are no Protestants and no parliaments.

CHARLES. Parliaments are the very divvle. Old Noll began by thinking the world of parliaments. Well, he tried every sort of parliament, finishing with a veritable reign of the saints. And in the end he had to turn them all out of doors, neck and crop, and govern through his major-generals. And when Noll died they went back to their parliament and made such a mess of it that they had to send for me.

CATHERINE. Suppose there had been no you?

CHARLES. There is always somebody. In every nation there must be the makings of a capable council and a capable king three or four times over, if only we knew how to pick them. Nobody has found out how to do it: that is why the world is so vilely governed.

CATHERINE. But if the rulers are of noble birth—

CHARLES. You mean if they are the sons of their fathers. What good is that?

CATHERINE. You are king because you are the son of your father. And you are the best of kings.

CHARLES. Thank you. And your brother Alfonso was king of Portugal because he was the son of his father. Was he also the best of kings?

CATHERINE. Oh, he was dreadful. He was barely fit to be a stable boy; but my brother Pedro took his crown and locked him up; and Pedro also is my father's son.

CHARLES. Just so: six of one and half a dozen of the other. Heredity is no use. Learning Latin is no use: Jack Churchill, who is an ignoramus, is worth fifty scholars. If Orange Billy dies and one of my nieces succeeds him Jack will be King of England.

CATHERINE. Perhaps the Church should select the king—or the queen.

CHARLES. The Church has failed over and over again to select a decent Pope. Alexander Borgia was a jolly fellow; and I am the last man alive to throw stones at him; but he was not a model Pope.

CATHERINE. My father was a great king. He fought the Spaniards and set Portugal free from their yoke. And it was the people who chose him and made him do it. I have sometimes wondered whether the people should not choose their king.

CHARLES. Not the English people. They would choose Titus Oates. No, beloved: the riddle of how to choose a ruler is still unanswered; and it is the riddle of civilization. I tell you again there are in England, or in any other country, the makings of half a dozen decent kings and councils; but they are mostly in prison. If we only knew how to pick them out and label them, then the people could have their choice out of the half dozen. It may end that way, but not until we have learnt how to pick the people who are fit to be chosen before they are chosen. And even then the picked ones will be just those whom the people will not choose. Who is it that said that no nation can bear being well governed for more than three years? Old Noll found that out. Why am I a popular king? Because I am a lazy fellow. I enjoy myself and let the people see me doing it, and leave things as they are, though things as they are will not bear thinking of by those who know what they are. That is what the people like. It is what they would do if they were kings.

CATHERINE. You are not lazy: I wish you were: I should see more of you. You take a great deal too much exercise: you walk and walk and nobody can keep up with you; you are always gardening or sailing or building and talking to gardeners and sailors and shipwrights and bricklayers and masons and people like that, neglecting the court. That is how your brother gathers the court round him and takes it away from you.

CHARLES. Let him. There is nothing to be learnt at court except that a courtier's life is not a happy one. The gardeners and the watermen, the shipwrights and bricklayers and carpenters and masons, are happier and far far more contented. It is the worst of luck to be born a king. Give me a skilled trade and eight or ten shillings a week, and you and I, beloved, would pig along more happily than we have ever been able to do as our majesties.

CATHERINE. I not want to pig along. I was born to rule; and if the worst comes to the worst and I have to go back to my own country I shall shew the world that I can rule, and that I am not the ninny I am made to look like here.

CHARLES. Why dont you do it, beloved? I am not worth staying with.

CATHERINE. I am torn ten different ways. I know that I should make you divorce me and marry a young Protestant wife who would bring you a son to inherit the crown and save all this killing of Monmouth and James and the handing over of your kingdom to the Hollander. I am tempted to do it because then I should return to my own beautiful country and smell the Tagus instead of the dirty Thames, and rule Portugal as my mother used to rule over the head of my worthless brother. I should be somebody then. But I cannot bring myself to leave you: not for all the thrones in the world. And my religion forbids me to put a Protestant on the throne of England when the rightful heir to it is a good Catholic.

CHARLES. You shall not, beloved. I will have no other widow but you.

CATHERINE. Ah! you can coax me so easily.

CHARLES. I treated you very badly when I was a young man because young men have low tastes and think only of themselves. Besides, odsfish! we could not talk to oneanother. The English they taught you in Portugal was a tongue that never was spoke on land or sea; and my Portuguese made you laugh. We must forget our foolish youth: we are grown-up now.

CATHERINE. Happy man! You forget so easily. But think of the difference in our fortunes! All your hopes of being a king were cut off: you were an exile, an outcast, a fugitive. Yet your kingdom dropped into your mouth at last; and you have been a king since you were old enough to use your power. But I! My mother was determined from my birth that I should be a queen: a great queen: Queen of England. Well, she had her way: we were married; and they call me queen. But have I ever reigned? Am I not as much an exile and an outcast as ever you were? I am not Catherine of England: I am Catherine of Bragança: a foreign woman with a funny name that they cannot pronounce. Yet I have the blood of rulers in my veins and the brains of rulers in my head.

CHARLES. They are no use here: the English will not be ruled; and there is nothing they hate like brains. For brains and religion you must go to Scotland; and Scotland is the most damnable country on earth: never shall I forget the life they led me there with their brains and their religion when they made me their boy king to spite Old Noll. I sometimes think religion and brains are the curse of the world. No, beloved, England for me, with all its absurdities!

CATHERINE. There can be only one true religion; and England has fifty.

CHARLES. Well, the more the merrier, if only they could let oneanother live. But they will not do even that.

CATHERINE. Have you no conscience?

CHARLES. I have; and a very troublesome one too. I would give a dukedom to any doctor that would cure me of it. But somehow it is not a conscience of the standard British pattern.

CATHERINE. That is only your witty nonsense. Our

consciences, which come from God, must be all the same.

CHARLES. They are not. Do you think God so stupid that he could invent only one sort of conscience?

CATHERINE [*shocked*] What a dreadful thing to say! I must not listen to you.

CHARLES. No two consciences are the same. No two love affairs are the same. No two marriages are the same. No two illnesses are the same. No two children are the same. No two human beings are the same. What is right for one is wrong for the other. Yet they cannot live together without laws; and a law is something that obliges them all to do the same thing.

CATHERINE. It may be so in England. But in Portugal the Holy Church makes all Catholics the same. My mother ruled them though she was a Spaniard. Why should I not do what my mother did?

CHARLES. Why not, indeed? I daresay you will do it very well, beloved. The Portuguese can believe in a Church and obey a king. The English robbed the Church and destroyed it: if a priest celebrates Mass anywhere in England outside your private chapel he is hanged for it. My great grandmother was a Catholic queen: rather than let her succeed to the throne they chopped her head off. My father was a Protestant king: they chopped his head off for trying to govern them and asking the Midlands to pay for the navy. While the Portuguese were fighting the Spaniards the English were fighting oneanother. You can do nothing with the English. How often have I told you that I am no real king: that the utmost I can do is to keep my crown on my head and my head on my shoulders. How often have you asked me to do some big thing like joining your Church, or some little thing like pardoning a priest or a Quaker condemned to some cruel punishment! And you have found that outside the court, where my smiles and my frowns count for everything, I have no power. The perjured scoundrel, Titus Oates, steeped in unmentionable vices, is lodged in my palace with a pension. If I could have my way he would be lodged on the gallows. There is a preacher named Bunyan who has written a book about the Christian life that is being read, they tell me, all the world over; and I could not release him from Bedford Gaol, where he rotted for years. The world will remember Oates and Bunyan; and I shall be The Merry Monarch. No: give me English birds and English trees, English dogs and Irish horses, English rivers and English ships; but English men! No, NO, NO.

CATHERINE. And Englishwomen?

CHARLES. Ah! there you have me, beloved. One cannot do without women: at least I cannot. But having to manage rascals like Buckingham and Shaftesbury, and dodgers like Halifax, is far worse than having to manage Barbara and Louise.

CATHERINE. Is there really any difference? Shaftesbury is trying to have me beheaded on Tower Hill on a charge of plotting to poison you sworn to by Titus Oates. Barbara is quite ready to support him in that.

CHARLES. No, beloved. The object of having you beheaded is to enable me to marry a Protestant wife and have a Protestant heir. I have pointed out to Barbara that the Protestant wife would not be so kind to her as you are, and would have her out of the kingdom before she could say Jack Robinson. So now she has thrown over Shaftesbury; and when I have thrown him over, as I shall know how to do presently, there will be an end of him. But he will be succeeded by some stupider rascal, or, worse still, some stupid fellow who is not a rascal. The clever rascals are all for sale; but the honest dunderheads are the very divvle.

CATHERINE. I wish you were not so clever.

CHARLES. Beloved: you could not do without my cleverness. That is why you must go back to Portugal when I am gone.

CATHERINE. But it makes your mind twist about so. You are so clever that you think you can do without religion. If only I could win you to the Church I should die perfectly happy; and so would you.

CHARLES. Well, I promise you I will not die a Protestant. You must see to that when the hour strikes for me: the last hour. So my very belovedest will die happy; and that is all I care about. [*Caressing her*] Does that satisfy you?

CATHERINE. If only I could believe it.

CHARLES. You mean I am the king whose word no man relies on.

CATHERINE. No: you are not that sort of king for me. But will it be a real conversion? I think you would turn Turk to please me.

CHARLES. Faith I believe I would. But there is more in it than that. It is not that I have too little religion in me for the Church: I have too much, like a queer fellow I talked with this morning. [*The clock strikes five*]. Odsfish! I have a Council meeting. I must go. [*He throws off his dressing gown*]. My boots! What has become of my boots?

CATHERINE. There are your boots. And wait until I make you decent.

Whilst he pulls his boots on, she fetches his coat and valets him into it. He snatches up his hat and stick and puts the hat on.

CATHERINE. No no: you have forgotten your wig.

[*She takes his hat off and fetches the wig*]. Fancy your going into the Council Chamber like that! Nobody would take you for King Charles the Second without that wig. Now. [*She puts the wig on him; then the hat. A few final pats and pulls complete his toilet*]. Now you look every inch a king. [*Making him a formal curtsey*] Your Majesty's visit has made me very happy. Long live the King!

CHARLES. May the Queen live for ever!

He throws up his arm in a gallant salute and stalks out. She rises and throws herself on her knees at her prie-dieu.

Buoyant Billions:
A Comedy of No Manners

WITH

Preface

The Author Explains

BUOYANT BILLIONS

Composition begun on 17 February 1936; abandoned in August 1937. Re-begun on 2 August 1945; completed 13 July 1947. First published in German translation, as *Zu viel Geld*, Zürich, 1948. First published in English in a limited edition, 1949, and in *Buoyant Billions, Farfetched Fables, & Shakes versus Shav*, 1951. First presented in German at the Schauspielhaus, Zürich, on 21 October 1948. First presented in English at the Festival Theatre, Malvern, on 13 August 1949.

Junius Smith *Denholm Elliott*
His Father *Donald Eccles*
Clementina Alexandra Buoyant ("Babzy" or "Clemmy") *Frances Day*
The Native *Kenneth Mackintosh*
The Chinese Priest *Arthur Hewlett*
Sir Ferdinand Flopper *John Longden*
The Widower (Tom Buoyant) *Dennis Cannan*
Eudoxia Emily ("Darkie") Buoyant *Jasmine Dee*
Mr Secondborn (Dick Buoyant) *Dermot Walsh*
Mrs Secondborn *Sylvia Coleridge*
Mrs Thirdborn (Mrs Harvey Buoyant) *Peggy Burt*
Frederick ("Fiffy") Buoyant *Peter Bartlett*
Bastable ("Old Bill") Buoyant *Maitland Moss*

Period—The Present

ACT I A Study. *The World Betterer*
ACT II A Jungle Clearing in Panama. *The Adventure*

ACT III A Drawing-room in Belgrave Square. *The Discussion*

ACT IV The same. *The End*

On the title-page of the limited edition (1949) of *Buoyant Billions*, which was illustrated by Clare Winsten (with a drawing of Shaw and Mrs Winsten reproduced on the covers of the book), Shaw provided a verse:

Only in dreams my prime returns
And my dead friends forsake their urns
To play with me the queerest scenes
In which we all are but have-beens.
My billions are no longer buoyant
Nor my polemics so foudroyant;
So lest you disappointed be
Let Clare depict my Me and She.

Preface

I commit this to print within a few weeks of completing my 92nd year. At such an age I should apologize for perpetrating another play or presuming to pontificate in any fashion. I can hardly walk through my garden without a tumble or two; and it seems out of all reason to believe that a man who cannot do a simple thing like that can practise the craft of Shakespear. Is it not a serious sign of dotage to talk about oneself, which is precisely what I am now doing? Should it not warn me that my bolt is shot, and my place silent in the chimney corner?

Well, I grant all this; yet I cannot hold my tongue nor my pen. As long as I live I must write. If I stopped writing I should die for want of something to do.

If I am asked why I have written this play I must reply that I do not know. Among the many sects of Peculiar People which England produces so eccentrically and capriciously are the Spiritualists. They believe in personal immortality as far as any mortal can believe in an unimaginable horror. They have a cohort of Slate Writers and Writing Mediums in whose hands a pencil of any sort will, apparently of its own volition, write communications, undreamt-of by the medium, that must, they claim, be supernatural. It is objected to these that they have neither novelty, profundity, literary value nor artistic charm, being well within the capacity of very ordinary mortals, and are therefore dismissed as fraudulent on the ground that it is much more probable that the mediums are pretending and lying than performing miracles.

As trueblue Britons the mediums do not know how to defend themselves. They only argue-bargue. They should simply point out that the same objection may be raised against any famous scripture. For instance, the Peculiars known as Baconians believe, with all the evidence against them, that the plays attributed to Shakespear must have been written by somebody else, being unaccountably beyond his knowledge and capacity. Who that somebody else was is the mystery; for the plays are equally beyond the capacity of Bacon and all the later rival claimants. Our greatest masterpiece of literature is the Jacobean translation of the Bible; and this the Christian Churches declare to be the word of God, supernaturally dictated through Christian mediums and transcribed by them as literally as any letter dictated by a merchant to his typist.

Take my own case. There is nothing in my circumstances or personality to suggest that I differ from any other son of a downstart gentleman driven by lack of unearned income to become an incompetent merchant and harp on his gentility. When I take my pen or sit down to my typewriter, I am as much a medium as Browning's Mr Sludge or Dunglas Home, or as Job or John of Patmos. When I write a play I do not foresee nor intend a page of it from one end to the other: the play writes itself. I may reason out every sentence until I have made it say exactly what it comes to me to say; but whence and how and why it comes to me, or why I persisted, through nine years of unrelieved market failure, in writing instead of in stockbroking or turf bookmaking or peddling, I do not know. You may say it was because I had a talent that way. So I had; but that fact remains inexplicable. What less could Mr Sludge say? or John Hus, who let himself be burnt rather than recant his "I dont know. Instruct me"?

When I was a small boy I saw a professional writing medium, pencil in hand, slash down page after page with astonishing speed without lifting his pencil from the blank paper we fed on to his desk. The fact that he was later transported for forgery did not make his performance and his choice of mediumship as his profession less unaccountable. When I was an elderly man, my mother amused herself with a planchette and a ouija, which under her hands produced what are called spirit writings abundantly. It is true that these screeds might have been called wishful writings (like wishful thinkings) so clearly were they as much her own story-telling inventions as the Waverley novels were Scott's. But why did she choose and practise this senseless activity? Why was I doing essentially the same as a playwright? I do not know. We both got some satisfaction from it or we would not have done it.

This satisfaction, this pleasure, this appetite, is as yet far from being as intense as the sexual orgasm or the ecstasy of a saint, though future cortical evolution may leave them far behind. Yet there are the moments of inexplicable happiness of which Mr J. B. Priestley spoke in a recent broadcast as part of his experience. To me they have come only in dreams not oftener than once every fifteen years or so. I do not know how common they are; for I never heard anyone but Mr Priestley mention them. They have an exalted chronic happiness, as of earth become heaven, proving that such states are possible for us even as we now are.

The happiest moment of my life was when as a child I was told by my mother that we were going to move from our Dublin street to Dalkey Hill in sight of the skies and seas of the two great bays between Howth and Bray, with Dalkey Island in the middle. I had already had a glimpse of them, and of Glencree in the mountains, on Sunday excursions; and they had given me the magic delight Mr Ivor Brown has described as the effect on him of natural scenery. Let who can explain it. Poets only can express it. It is a hard fact, waiting for some scientific genius to make psychology of it.

The professional biologists tell us nothing of all this. It would take them out of the realm of logic into that of magic and miracle, in which they would lose their reputation for omniscience and infallibility. But magic and miracle, as far as they are not flat lies, are not divorced from facts and consequently from science: they are facts: as yet unaccounted for, but none the less facts. As such they raise problems; and genuine scientists must face them at the risk of being classed with Cagliostro instead of with Clerk-Maxwell and Einstein, Galileo and Newton, who, by the way, worked hard at interpreting the Bible, and was ashamed of his invention of the Infinitesimal Calculus until Leibniz made it fashionable.

Now Newton was right in rating the Calculus no higher than a schoolboy's crib, and the interpretation of The Bible as far more important. In this valuation, which seems so queer to us today, he was not in the least lapsing from science into superstition: he was looking for the foundation of literary art in the facts of history. Nothing could be more important or more scientific; and the fact that the result was the most absurd book in the English language (his Chronology) does not invalidate in the least his integrity as a scientific investigator, nor exemplify his extraordinary mental gifts any less than his hypothesis of gravitation, which might have occurred to anyone who had seen an apple fall when he was wondering why moving bodies did not move in straight lines away into space. Newton was no farther off the scientific target in his attribution of infallibility to Archbishop Ussher than most modern biologists and self-styled scientific socialists in their idolatry of Darwin and Marx. The scientist who solves the problem of the prophet Daniel and John of Patmos, and incidentally of Shakespear and myself, will make a longer stride ahead than any solver of physical problems.

My readers keep complaining in private letters and public criticisms that I have not solved all the problems of the universe for them. As I am obviously neither omnipotent, omniscient, nor infallible, being not only not a god nor even the proprietor of The Times (as they all assume), they infuriate me. Instead of reminding them calmly that, like Newton, all I know is but a grain of sand picked up on the verge of the ocean of undiscovered knowledge, I have some difficulty in refraining from some paraphrase of "An evil and idolatrous generation clamors for a miracle." But as Mahomet kept his temper under the same thoughtless pressure, so, I suppose, must I.

This is all I can write by way of preface to a trivial comedy which is the best I can do in my dotage. It is only a prefacette to a comedietta. Forgive it. At least it will not rub into you the miseries and sins of the recent wars, nor even of the next one. History will make little of them; and the sooner we forget them the better. I wonder how many people really prefer bogus war news and police news to smiling comedy with some hope in it! I do not. When they begin I switch off the wireless.

AYOT SAINT LAWRENCE, *July 1947*

ACT I

THE WORLD BETTERER

A modern interior. A well furnished study. Morning light. A father discussing with his son. Father an elderly gentleman, evidently prosperous, but a man of business, thoroughly middle class. Son in his earliest twenties, smart, but artistically unconventional.

FATHER. Junius, my boy, you must make up your mind. I had a long talk with your mother about it last night. You have been tied to her apron string quite long enough. You have been on my hands much too long. Your six brothers all chose their professions when they were years younger than you. I have always expected more from you than from them. So has your mother.

SON. Why?

FATHER. I suppose because you are our seventh son; and I myself was a seventh son. You are the seventh son of a seventh son. You ought to have second sight.

SON. I have. At first sight there is no hope for our civilization. But one can still make money in it. At second sight the world has a future that will make its people look back on us as a mob of starving savages. But second sight does not yet lead to success in business nor in the professions.

FATHER. That is not so. You have done unusually well at everything you have tried. You were a success at school. I was assured that you had the makings of a born leader of men in you.

SON. Yes. They made me a prefect and gave me a cane to beat the boys they were too lazy to beat themselves. That was what they called teaching me leadership.

FATHER. Well, it gave you some sense of responsibility: what more could they do? At the university you did not do so well; but you could have if you had chosen to work for honors instead of joining rather disreputable clubs and working on your own lines, as you called them. As it was, you did not disgrace yourself. We looked to you to outshine your brothers. But they are all doing well; and you are doing nothing.

SON. I know. But the only profession that appeals to me is one that I cannot afford.

FATHER. How do you know that you cannot afford it? Have I ever stinted you in any way? Do you suppose I expect you to establish yourself in a profession or business in five minutes?

SON. No: you have always been a model father. But the profession I contemplate is not one that a model father could recommend to his son.

FATHER. And what profession is that, pray?

SON. One that is always unsuccessful. Marx's profession. Lenin's profession. Stalin's profession. Ruskin's profession. Plato's profession. Confucius, Gautama, Jesus, Mahomet, Luther, William Morris. The profession of world betterer.

FATHER. My boy, great prophets and poets are all very well; but they are not practical men; and what we need are practical men.

SON. We dont get them. We need men who can harness the tides and the tempests, atom splitting engineers, mathematicians, biologists, psychologists. What do we get? Windbag careerists. Proletarians who can value money in shillings but not in millions, and think their trade unions are the world. As a world betterer I shall spend most of my life hiding from their police. And I may finish on the scaffold.

FATHER. Romantic nonsense, boy. You are in a free country, and can advocate any sort of politics you please as long as you do not break the law.

SON. But I want to break the law.

FATHER. You mean change the law. Well, you can advocate any change you please; and if you can persuade us all to agree with you, you can get elected to Parliament and bring your changes before the House of Commons.

SON. Too slow. Class war is rushing on us with tiger springs. The tiger has sprung in Russia, in Persia, in Mexico, in Turkey, in Italy, Spain, Germany, Austria, everywhere if you count national strikes as acts of civil war. We are trying to charm the tiger away by mumbling old spells about liberty, peace, democracy, sanctions, open doors, and closed minds, when it is scientific political reconstruction that is called for. So I propose to become a political reconstructionist. Are you in favor of reconstruction?

FATHER. I do not see any need for it. All the people who are discontented are so because they are poor. I am not poor; and I do not see why I should be discontented.

SON. Well, I am discontented because other people are poor. To me living in a world of poor and unhappy people is like living in hell.

FATHER. You need not speak to them. You need not know them. You do not mix with them. And they are not unhappy.

SON. How am I to get away from them? The streets are full of them. And how do I know that we shall not lose all our money and fall into poverty ourselves? Fancy you and mother ending your days in a workhouse, or trying to live on an old age pension! That happens, you know.

FATHER. In our case it happens the other way. There is no need to mention it outside; but one of my grandfathers, the founder of our present fortune, began as a porter in a hotel. Thanks to his ability and the social system that gave it scope, we are now safely fixed in a social circle where rich men become richer instead of poorer if they are sensible and well conducted. Our system works very satisfactorily. Why reconstruct it?

SON. Many people feel like that. Others feel as I do. If neither of us will budge, and no compromise is possible, what are we to do? Kill oneanother?

FATHER. Nonsense! There are constitutional ways of making all possible political changes.

SON. Voting instead of fighting. No use. The defeated party always fights if it has a dog's chance when the point is worth fighting for and it can find a leader. The defeated dictator always fights unless his successor takes the precaution of murdering him.

FATHER. Not in England. Such things happen only on the Continent. We dont do them here.

SON. We do. We did it in Ireland. We did it in India. It has always been so. We resist changes until the changes break us.

FATHER. Well, what does all this come to? If people wont change what good is there in your being a world betterer, as you call it?

SON. What good is there in going on as we are? Besides, things will not stay as they are. However hard we try to stick in our old grooves, evolution goes on in spite of us. The more we strive to stay as we are, the more we find that we are no longer where we were.

FATHER. Yet we are not always having revolutions.

SON. They occur, though nobody understands them. When the feudal aristocracy collapsed before the plutocratic middle class Henry the Seventh had to fight the battle of Bosworth Field. When the plutocrats got the upper hand of the monarchy Cromwell had to cut off the king's head. The French Revolution tried hard to be Liberal and Parliamentary. No use: the guillotine was overworked until the executioners struck; and Napoleon had to fight all Europe. When the Russians did away with the Tzardom they had to fight not only all the rest of the world but a civil war as well. They first killed all the counter-revolutionists; and then had to kill most of the revolutionists. Revolution is dirty work always. Why should it be?

FATHER. Because it is unconstitutional. Why not do things constitutionally?

SON. Because the object of a revolution is to change the constitution; and to change the constitution is unconstitutional.

FATHER. That is a quibble. It is always possible to vote instead of fighting. All the blood shed in revolutions has been quite unnecessary. All the changes could have been effected without killing anybody. You must listen to reason?

SON. Yes; but reason leads just as clearly to a catholic monarchy as to an American republic, to a Communist Soviet as to Capitalism. What is the use of arguing when the Pope's arguments are as logical as Martin Luther's, and Hilaire Belloc's as H. G. Wells's? Why appeal to the mob when ninetyfive per cent of them do not understand politics, and can do nothing but mischief without leaders? And what sort of leaders do they vote for? For Titus Oates and Lord George Gordon with their Popish plots, for Hitlers who call on them to exterminate Jews, for Mussolinis who rally them to nationalist dreams of glory and empire in which all foreigners are enemies to be subjugated.

FATHER. The people run after wicked leaders only when they cannot find righteous ones. They can always find them in England.

SON. Yes; and when they find them why do they run after them? Only to crucify them. The righteous man takes his life in his hand whenever he utters the truth. Charlemagne, Mahomet, St Dominic: these were righteous men according to their lights; but with Charlemagne it was embrace Christianity instantly or die; with Mahomet the slaying of the infidel was a passport to Heaven; with Dominic and his Dogs of God it was Recant or burn.

FATHER. But these things happened long ago, when people were cruel and uncivilized.

SON. My dear father: within the last thirty years we have had more horrible persecutions and massacres, more diabolical tortures and crucifixions, more slaughter and destruction than Attila and Genghis Khan and all the other scourges of God ever ventured on. I tell you, if people only knew the history of their own times they would die of horror at their own wickedness. Karl Marx changed the mind of the world by simply telling the purseproud nineteenth century its own villainous history. He ruined himself; his infant son died of poverty; and two of his children committed suicide. But he did the trick.

FATHER. The Russian madness will not last. Indeed it has collapsed already. I now invest all my savings in Russian Government Stock. My stockbroker refuses to buy it for me; but my banker assures me that it is the only perfectly safe foreign investment. The Russians pay in their own gold.

SON. And the gold goes to rot in American banks, though whole nations are barely keeping half alive for lack of it.

FATHER. Well, my boy, you are keeping alive pretty comfortably. Why should you saw through the branch you are sitting on?

SON. Because it is cracking; and it seems to me prudent to arrange a soft place to drop to when it snaps.

FATHER. The softest place now is where you are. Listen to me, my boy. You are cleverer than I am. You know more. You know too much. You talk too well. I have thought a good deal over this. I have tried to imagine what old John Shakespear of Stratford-upon-Avon, mayor and alderman and leading citizen of his town, must have felt when he declined into bankruptcy and realized that his good-for-nothing son, who had run away to London after his conviction as a poacher, and being forced to marry a girl he had compromised, was a much greater man than his father had ever been or could hope to be. That is what may happen to me. But there is a difference. Shakespear had a lucrative talent by which he prospered and returned to his native town as a rich man, and bought a property there. You have no such talent. I cannot start you in life with a gift of capital as I started your brothers, because the war taxation has left me barely enough to pay my own way. I can do nothing for you: if you want to better the world you must begin by bettering yourself.

SON. And until I better the world I cannot better myself; for nobody will employ a world betterer as long as there are enough selfseekers for all the paying jobs. Still, some of the world betterers manage to survive. Why not I?

FATHER. They survive because they fit themselves into

the world of today. They marry rich women. They take commercial jobs. They spunge on disciples from whom they beg or borrow. What else can they do except starve or commit suicide? A hundred years ago there were kings to spunge on. Nowadays there are republics everywhere; and their governments are irresistible, because they alone can afford to make atomic bombs, and wipe out a city and all its inhabitants in a thousandth of a second.

SON. What does that matter if they can build it again in ten minutes? All the scientists in the world are at work finding out how to dilute and control and cheapen atomic power until it can be used to boil an egg or sharpen a lead pencil as easily as to destroy a city. Already they tell us that the bomb stuff will make itself for nothing.

FATHER. I hope not. For if every man Jack of us can blow the world to pieces there will be an end of everything. Shakespear's angry ape will see to that.

SON. Will he? He hasnt done so yet. I can go into the nearest oil shop and for less than a shilling buy enough chemical salts to blow this house and all its inhabitants to smithereens. A glass retort, a pestle and mortar, and a wash bottle are all I need to do the trick. But I dont do it.

FATHER. The trade unions did it in Manchester and Sheffield.

SON. They soon dropped it. They did not even destroy the slums they lived in: they only blew up a few of their own people for not joining the unions. No: mankind has not the nerve to go through to the end with murder and suicide. Hiroshima and Nagasaki are already rebuilt; and Japan is all the better for the change. When atom splitting makes it easy for us to support ourselves as well by two hours work as now by two years, we shall move mountains and straighten rivers in a hand's turn. Then the problem of what to do in our spare time will make life enormously more interesting. No more doubt as to whether life is worth living. Then the world betterers will come to their own.

FATHER. The sportsmen will, anyhow. War is a sport. It used to be the sport of kings. Now it is the sport of Labor Parties.

SON. What could kings and parties do without armies of proletarians? War is a sport too ruinous and vicious for men ennobled by immense power and its splendid possibilities.

FATHER. Power corrupts: it does not ennoble.

SON. It does if it is big enough. It is petty power that corrupts petty men. Almighty power will change the world. If the old civilizations, the Sumerians, the Egyptians, the Greeks, the Romans, had discovered it, their civilizations would not have collapsed as they did. There would have been no Dark Ages. The world betterers will get the upper hand.

FATHER. Well, it may be so. But does not that point to your settling down respectably as an atom splitting engineer with the government and the police on your side?

SON. Yes, if only I had any talent for it. But I seem to have no talent for anything but preaching and propaganda. I am a missionary without an endowed established Church.

FATHER. Then how are you to live? You must do something to support yourself when I am gone.

SON. I have thought of insuring your life.

FATHER. How are you to pay the premium?

SON. Borrow it from mother, I suppose.

FATHER. Well, there is some sense in that. But it

would not last your lifetime: it would only give you a start. At what?

SON. I could speak in the parks until I attracted a congregation of my own. Then I could start a proprietary chapel and live on the collections.

FATHER. And this is what I am to tell your mother!

SON. If I were you I wouldnt.

FATHER. Oh, you are incorrigible. I tell you again you are too clever: you know too much: I can do nothing with you. I wonder how many fathers are saying the same to their sons today.

SON. Lots of them. In your time the young were post-Marxists and their fathers pre-Marxists. Today we are all post-Atomists.

FATHER. Damn the atomic bomb!

SON. Bless it say I. It will make world bettering possible. It will begin by ridding the world of the anopheles mosquito, the tsetse fly, the white ant, and the locust. I want to go round the world to investigate that, especially through the Panama Canal. Will you pay my fare?

FATHER. Yes, anything to keep you from tomfooling in the parks. And it will keep your mother quiet for a while.

SON. Better say nothing until I am gone. She would never let me go: her seventh son is her pet. It is a tyranny from which I must escape.

FATHER. And leave me to weather the storm! Well, goodbye.

SON. Goodbye. You are a damned good father; and I shall not forget it.

They kiss; and the son goes.

ACT II

THE ADVENTURE

The shore of a broad water studded with half-submerged trees in a tropical landscape, covered with bush except for a clearance by the waterside, where there is a wooden house on posts, with a ladder from the stoep or verandah to the ground. The roof is of corrugated iron, painted green. The Son, dressed in flannel slacks, a tennis shirt, and a panama hat, is looking about him like a stranger. A young woman, dressed for work in pyjama slacks and a pullover, comes out of the house and, from the top of the steps, proceeds to make the stranger unwelcome.

SHE. Now then. This clearance is private property. Whats your business?

HE. No business, dear lady. Treat me as a passing tramp.

SHE. Well, pass double quick. This isnt a doss house.

HE. No; but in this lonely place the arrival of any stranger must be a godsend. Besides, I am hungry and thirsty.

SHE. Most tramps are. Get out.

HE. No: positively no, until I have had refreshments.

SHE. I have a dog here.

HE. You have not. It would have barked. And dogs love me.

SHE. I have a gun here.

HE. So have I. Both useless, except to commit suicide. Have you a husband?

SHE. What is that to you?

HE. If you have, he is only a man, lady. I also am a man. But you do not look married. Have you any milk in the house? Or a hunk of bread and an onion?

SHE. Not for you.

HE. Why not? Have you any religion?

SHE. No. Get out.

HE. Ah, that complicates matters. I thought you were a hospitable friendly savage. I see you are a commercial minded British snob. Must I insult you by offering to pay for my entertainment? Or impress you by introducing myself as a graduate of Oxford University?

SHE. I know that stunt, my lad. The wandering scholar turns up here about twice a week.

HE. "My lad" eh? That is an endearment. We are getting on. What about the milk?

SHE. You can get a meal where the lake steamers stop, two miles farther on.

HE. Two miles! In this heat! I should die.

SHE [*patiently*] Will you pass on and not come troubling where you are not wanted. [*She goes into the house and slams the door*].

An elderly native arrives with a jar of milk and a basket of bread and fruit. He deposits them on the stoep.

THE NATIVE [*calling to the lady inside*] Ahaiya! Missy's rations. Pink person loafing round.

She opens the door and hands a coin to the native; then slams the door before, after an angry glance at the intruder, leaving the meal on the stoep.

HE [*to the native*] You bring me samee. Half dollar. [*He exhibits the coin*].

THE NATIVE. Too much. Twentyfive cent enough.

HE [*producing a 25c. piece and giving it to him*] The honest man gets paid in advance and has his part in the glory of God.

THE NATIVE. You wait here. No walk about.

HE. Why not?

THE NATIVE. Not good walk about. Gater and snake.

HE. What is gater?

THE NATIVE. Alligator, sir. Much gater, much rattler.

HE. All right. I wait here.

THE NATIVE. Yes, sir. And you no speak holy woman. Speak to her forbidden. She speak with great spirits only. Very strong magics. Put spell on you. Fetch gaters and rattlers with magic tunes on her pipe. Very unlucky speak to her. Very lucky bring her gifts.

HE. Has she husband?

THE NATIVE. No no no no. She holy woman. Live alone. You no speak to her, sir. You wait here. Back quick with chop chop. [*He goes*].

SHE [*opening the door again*] Not gone yet?

HE. The native says you are a holy woman. You are treating me in a very unholy manner. May I suggest that you allow me to consume your meal? You can consume mine yourself after he brings it? I am hungrier than you.

SHE. You are not starving. A fast will do you no harm. You can wait ten minutes more at all events. If you persist in bothering me I will call the gaters and the rattlers.

HE. You have been listening. That is another advance.

SHE. Take care. I can call them.

HE. How?

SHE. In the days of my vanity, when I tried to be happy with men like you, I learnt how to play the soprano saxophone. I have the instrument here. Twenty notes from it will surround you with hissing rattling things, with gaping jaws and slashing tails. I am far better protected against idle gentlemen here than I should be in Piccadilly.

HE. Yes, holy lady; but what about your conscience? A hungry man asks you for food. Dare you throw him to the gaters and rattlers? How will that appear in the great day of reckoning?

SHE. Neither you nor I will matter much when that day comes, if it ever does. But you can eat my lunch to shut your mouth.

HE. Oh, thanks!

SHE. You need not look round for a tumbler and a knife and fork. Drink from the calabash: eat from your fingers.

HE. The simple life, eh? [*He attacks the meal*].

SHE. No. In the simple life you ring for the servants. Everything is done for you; and you learn nothing.

HE. And here you wait until that kindly native comes and feeds you, like Elijah's ravens. What do you learn from that?

SHE. You learn what nice people natives are. But you begin by trying to feed yourself and build your own shack. I have been through all that, and learnt what a helpless creature a civilized woman is.

HE. Quite. That is the advantage of being civilized: everything is done for you by somebody else; and you havnt a notion of how or why, unless you read Karl Marx.

SHE. I read Karl Marx when I was fifteen. That is why I am here instead of in London looking for a rich husband.

HE. We are getting on like old friends. Evidently I please you.

SHE. Why do you want to please me now that you have your meal?

HE. I dont know. Why do we go on talking to one-another?

SHE. I dont know. We are dangerous to oneanother. Finish your food; and pass on.

HE. But you have chosen to live dangerously. So have I. It may break our hearts if I pass on.

SHE. Young man: I spent years waiting for somebody to break my heart before I discovered that I havnt got one. I broke several men's hearts in the process. I came here to get rid of that sort of thing. I can stand almost anything human except an English gentleman.

HE. And I can stand anything except an English lady. That game is up. Dancing and gambling, drinking cocktails, tempting women and running away when they meet you half-way and say "Thats quite all right, sonny: dont apologize." Hunting and shooting is all right; but you need to be a genuine countrified savage for it; and I am a town bird. My father is a chain shopkeeper, not a country squire.

SHE. Same here: my father is a famous lucky financier. Born a proletarian. Neither of us the real thing.

HE. Plenty of money and no roots. No traditions.

SHE. Nonsense. We are rooted in the slums and suburbs, and full of their snobbery. But failures as ladies and gentlemen.

HE. Nothing left but to live on father's money, eh?

SHE. Yes: parasites: that is not living. Yet we have our living selves for all that. And in this wild life you can taste yourself.

HE. Not always a pleasant taste, is it?

SHE. Every animal can bear its own odor.

HE. That remark has completely destroyed my appetite. The coarse realism with which women face physical facts shocks the delicacy of my sex.

SHE. Yes: men are dreamers and drones. So if you can eat no more, get out.

HE. I should much prefer to lie down and sleep in the

friendly shadow of your house until the heat of the day has done its worst.

SHE. If you want a house to shade you, build one for yourself. Leave mine in peace.

HE. That is not natural. In native life the woman keeps the house and works there: the man keeps the woman and rests there.

SHE. You do not keep the woman in this case. She has had enough of you. Get out.

HE. As I see things the woman does not say get out.

SHE. Do you expect her to say come in? As you see things, the man works out of doors. What does he work at, pray?

HE. He hunts, fishes, and fights.

SHE. Have you hunted or fished for me?

HE. No. I hate killing.

SHE. Have you fought for me?

HE. No. I am a timid creature.

SHE. Cowards are no use to women. They need killers. Where are your scalps?

HE. My what?

SHE. Your trophies that you dare kill. The scalps of our enemies.

HE. I have never killed anybody. I dont want to. I want a decent life for everybody because poor people are as tiresome as rich people.

SHE. What is the woman to eat if you do not kill animals for her?

HE. She can be a vegetarian. I am.

SHE. So am I. But I have learnt here that if we vegetarians do not kill animals the animals will kill us. It is the flesh eaters who let the animals live, and feed and nurse them. We vegetarians will make an end of them. No matter what we eat, man is still the killer and woman the life giver. Can you kill or not?

HE. I can shoot a little, though few experienced country gentlemen would care to be next to me at a shoot. But I do not know how to load the gun: I must have a loader. I cannot find the birds: they have to be driven to me by an army of beaters. And I expect a good lunch afterwards. I can also hunt if somebody will fetch me a saddled horse, and stable it for me and take it off my hands again when the hunt is over. I should be afraid not to fight if you put me into an army and convinced me that if I ran away I should be shot at dawn. But of what use are these heroic accomplishments here? No loaders, no beaters, no grooms, no stables, no soldiers, no King and country. I should have to learn to make bows and arrows and assegais; to track game; to catch and break-in wild horses; and to tackle natives armed with poisoned arrows. I should not have a dog's chance. There are only two things I can do as well as any native: eat and sleep. You have enabled me to eat. Why will you not let me sleep?

SHE. Because I want to practise on the saxophone. The rattlers will come and you will never awake.

HE. Then hadnt you better let me sleep indoors?

SHE. The saxophone would keep you awake.

HE. On the contrary, music always sends me fast asleep.

SHE. The only sleep that is possible here when I am playing the saxophone is the sleep of death.

HE [*rising wearily*] You have the last word. You are an inhospitable wretch.

SHE. And you are an infernal nuisance [*she goes into the house and slams the door*].

Ths native returns with another meal. He puts it down near the door, at which he raps.

THE NATIVE [*cries*] Ahaiya! Missy's meal.

HE. Say, John: can you direct me to the nearest witch doctor? Spell maker. One who can put terrible strong magics on this house.

THE NATIVE. Sir: magics are superstitions. Pink trash believe such things: colored man, no.

HE. But havnt you gods and priests who can bring down the anger of the gods on unkind people?

THE NATIVE. Sir: there is but one god, the source of all creation. His dwelling is in the sun: therefore though you can look upon all other things you cannot look at the sun.

HE. What do you call him?

THE NATIVE. Sir: his name is not to be pronounced without great reverence. I have been taught that he has other names in other lands; but here his holy name [*he bends his neck*] is Hoochlipoochli. He has a hundred earthly brides; and she who dwells within is one of them.

HE. Listen to me, John. We white men have a god much much greater than Hoochlipoochli.

THE NATIVE. Sir: that may be so. But you pink men do not believe in your god. We believe in ours. Better have no god at all than a god in whom you do not believe.

HE. What do you mean by our not believing? How do you know we do not believe?

THE NATIVE. He who believes in his god, obeys his commands. You expect your god to obey yours. But pardon me, sir: I am forbidden to converse on such high matters with the unlearned. I perceive by your assurance that you are a highly honorable person among your own people; but here you are a heathen, a barbarian, an infidel. Mentally we are not on the same plane. Conversation between us, except on such simple matters as milk and vegetables, could lead only to bewilderment and strife. I wish you good morning, sir.

HE. Stay, presumptuous one. I would have you to know that I am a Master of Arts of the University of Oxford, the centre of all the learning in the universe. The possession of such a degree places the graduate on the highest mental plane attainable by humanity.

THE NATIVE. How did you obtain that degree, sir, may I respectfully ask?

HE. By paying a solid twenty pounds for it.

THE NATIVE. It is impossible. Knowledge and wisdom cannot be purchased like fashionable garments.

HE. In England they can. A sage teaches us all the questions our examiners are likely to ask us, and the answers they expect from us.

THE NATIVE. One answers questions truthfully only out of one's own wisdom and knowledge.

HE. Not at Oxford. Unless you are a hundred years behind hand in science and seven hundred in history you cannot hope for a degree there.

THE NATIVE. Can it be true that the doctrines of your teachers are less than a thousand years old?

HE. The most advanced of them would have felt quite at home with Richard the Third. I should like to have heard them discussing Columbus with him.

THE NATIVE. Then, sir, you must indeed venerate me; for the doctrines of my teachers have lasted many thousands of centuries. Only the truth could survive so long.

HE. I venerate nobody. Veneration is dead. Oxford doctrine has made a gentleman of me. You, it seems, have been made a sage by a similar process. Are we any the better or wiser?

THE NATIVE. Sir: you have lost your faith; but do not throw the hatchet after the handle. Pink men, when they find that their beliefs are only half true, reject both halves. We colored men are more considerate. My grandfather saw the great evils of this world, and thought they shewed the terrible greatness of Hoochlipoochli. My father saw them also, but could not reconcile the existence of evil with divine justice and benevolence. He therefore believed not only in Hoochlipoochli but in Poochlihoochli, the god of hell, whom you pink men call The Devil. As for me, I cannot believe everything my ancestors believed. I believe as they did that justice and benevolence are mighty powers in the world, but that they have no effective existence save in ourselves, and that except to the extent to which you and I and our like are just and benevolent there is no justice and no benevolence.

HE. And consequently no Hoochlipoochli.

THE NATIVE. Not at all. You are throwing the hatchet after the handle. His kingdom is within us; but it is for us to administer it. Something within me makes me hunger and thirst for righteousness. That something must be Hoochlipoochli.

HE. Was it Hoochlipoochli who set you talking pidgin English to me though you can talk philosopher's English better than most Englishmen?

THE NATIVE. Sir: you began by speaking pidgin to me. You addressed me as John, which is not my name. In courtesy I spoke as you spoke.

HE. Still, when you told me that the woman here is one of Hoochlipoochli's many hundred earthly wives, you were humbugging me.

THE NATIVE. Sir: Hoochlipoochli possesses all of us more or less; and so every woman is his bride. I desired only your good when I bade you beware of her; for it is true that when she plays on her strange instrument the serpents of the bush and the monsters of the lake are charmed, and assemble here to listen.

SHE [*throwing open her door and appearing on the threshold with the saxophone in her hand*] And if you do not stop talking and maddening me with the sound of your cackle I shall strike up.

HE. Strike up by all means. I shall enjoy a little music.

SHE. We shall see. I have had enough of you.

She preludes on the saxophone.

Hissing and rattlings in the bush. An alligator crawls in. The two men fly for their lives.

ACT III

THE DISCUSSION

A drawingroom in Belgrave Square, London, converted into a Chinese temple on a domestic scale, with white walls just enough rose tinted to take the glare off, and a tabernacle in vermilion and gold, on a dais of two broad shallow steps. Divan seats, softly upholstered against the walls, and very comfortable easy chairs of wickerwork, luxuriously cushioned, are also available. There is a sort of bishop's chair at one corner of the tabernacle. The effect is lovely and soothing, as only Chinese art could make it.

A most incongruous figure enters: a middle-aged twentieth century London solicitor, carrying a case of papers. He is accompanied and ushered by a robed Chinese priest, who fits perfectly into the surroundings.

THE SOLICITOR [*looking round him*] Whats all this? I should have been shewn into the library. Do you understand who I am? Sir Ferdinand Flopper, Mr Buoyant's solicitor?

THE PRIEST. It is Mr Buoyant's wish that you should meet his children in this holy place. Did he not mention it in your instructions?

SIR FERDINAND. No. This place is not holy. We are in Belgrave Square, not in Hong Kong.

THE PRIEST. Sir: in many old English houses there is a room set apart as a meditation parlor.

SIR FERDINAND. Pooh! They have been abolished.

THE PRIEST. Yes. The English people no longer meditate.

SIR FERDINAND. Does Mr Buoyant?

THE PRIEST. His soul needs refreshment. He is a mighty man of business: in his hands all things turn into money. Souls perish under such burdens. He comes here and sits for half an hour while I go through my act of worship, of which he does not understand a single word. But he goes out a new man, soothed and serene. You may call this his oratory.

SIR FERDINAND. I shall certainly not call it anything of the sort. His oratory would be a Church of England oratory.

THE PRIEST. He has not found peace in the Church of England.

SIR FERDINAND. And you tell me that he has found it here, in this outlandish apartment where he does not understand a word of the service!

THE PRIEST. In the Church of England he understood too much. He could not believe. And the people in their Sunday clothes were so forbidding!

SIR FERDINAND. Forbidding!!

THE PRIEST. Sunday clothes and poker faces. No peace, no joy. But for the music they would all go mad. That is, perhaps, why you do not go to church.

SIR FERDINAND. Who told you I do not go to church?

THE PRIEST. Nobody told me. But do you?

SIR FERDINAND. I am here on business, and cannot waste my morning on religious discussions. Will you be good enough to direct me to the library?

THE PRIEST. You would find it a rather dismal apartment after this one. And its atmosphere is mentally paralyzing. Mr Buoyant's instructions are that your advice to his family must be given here. But no religious service is to be imposed on you.

SIR FERDINAND. Nothing can be imposed on me. The atmosphere here is most unsuitable. Does the family know I have arrived?

THE PRIEST. Here they are.

The family, consisting of a middle-aged widower, a younger man, two married ladies, an unmarried girl of 20, *and an irreverent youth of* 17, *enters. The widower introduces them.*

THE WIDOWER. Good morning, Sir Ferdinand. We are the family of your client Mr Bastable Buoyant, better known as Old Bill Buoyant the Billionaire. I am a widower. The ladies are my brothers' wives. One brother is absent: he leaves everything to his wife. The two children are our sister Darkie and our brother Fiffy, registered as Eudoxia Emily and Frederick.

They bow to Sir Ferdinand as they are introduced, and seat themselves on the divan, the husbands on opposite sides from their wives.

The two juniors also plant themselves on opposite sides well to the fore. Sir Ferdinand, returning their bows rather stiffly, seats himself in the bishop's chair.

THE PRIEST. I leave you to your deliberations. Peace be with you!

He goes, the family waving him a salute.

SIR FERDINAND. As I have only just been called in, and am a stranger to you all, I am naturally somewhat at a loss. How much do you know already of the business I am to put before you?

DARKIE [*taking the lead at once decisively*] Nothing whatever. Business means money; and none of us knows anything about money because our father knows everything about it. But I know all about housekeeping because our mother knew nothing about it and cared less. She preferred painting. We had extraordinarily clever parents; and the result is that we are a family of helpless duffers.

SECONDBORN. That is true. So much has been done for us we have learnt to do hardly anything for ourselves. I am a bit of a mathematician, but earn nothing by it.

MRS SECONDBORN [*an aggressive woman*] Mathematics; that is his fad. Start a Buoyant on a fad; and he is happy and busy with it for the rest of the year.

THE YOUTH. We are too damnably rich, you see. The boss making billions all the time.

DARKIE. We have bits and scraps of tastes and talents for scholarship, painting, playing musical instruments, writing, and talking. One brother is a champion amateur boxer. Another is a historian and knows eleven languages. He is also a pedestrian and walks 3000 miles every year on principle. We are all more or less like that, because daddy began with eight shillings a week and taught himself to read and write when he was seventeen and wanted to write to his mother. She could read handwriting.

THE WIDOWER. Darkie is explaining to you that as we are entirely dependent on our father for our incomes we can defend ourselves against his tyranny only by acquiring the culture of which an uneducated man stands in awe.

MRS THIRDBORN [*gentle, beautiful, and saintly*] Oh, he is not a tyrant.

THE WIDOWER. He might be, if we were not obviously his social superiors.

MRS SECONDBORN. In justice to the old devil I must say that, as far as I can make out, he has never spoken a cross word to any of you.

DARKIE. I never said he did. I was going on to explain my own exceptional position in the family. Am I boring you, Sir Ferdinand?

SIR FERDINAND. Not at all. We have plenty of time before lunch. So if your position is exceptional, I had better know what it is.

DARKIE. Well, as I am the only female, I am the spoilt darling and pampered pet of the lot. I have no talents, no accomplishments, except what I picked up doing just what I liked and was given everything I asked for. That has been harder than any schooling; and I sometimes blame my parents for not having thrashed the life out of me instead of leaving me to learn life's lessons by breaking my shins against them and falling into every booby trap. I was so over-petted that I had to learn or die. So if there is anything real to be done I have to see to it.

MRS THIRDBORN [*very kindly*] Dont mind her, Sir Ferdinand. She always talks the greatest nonsense about herself.

DARKIE. I daresay I do. Anyhow I have finished now. Go ahead, Sir Ferdinand.

SIR FERDINAND. One question first please. Mr Buoyant must have had legal advice during all these years. Is there not a family solicitor?

THE WIDOWER. No. He does not believe in having the same solicitor every time.

DARKIE. He thinks it is throwing away experience. He always calls in a different doctor when he is ill.

THE YOUTH. He picks up his solicitor for the job, like picking up a taxi.

THE WIDOWER. There is something to be said for his plan. He has learnt much about doctors and solicitors by it.

SECONDBORN. He now advises his doctors and instructs his solicitors.

SIR F. If so, why does he call them in at all?

MRS SECONDBORN. If he didnt, and any of us died, or any money he is trustee for went wrong, he might be prosecuted for negligence or conversion or something.

SIR F. True. But this raises questions of professional etiquet. I have some misgivings as to whether I can act in the case.

THE YOUTH. If the boss says you can, you may bet your bottom dollar it will be all right.

DARKIE. He makes so much money that whatever he says, goes.

SIR F. Not legally.

THE WIDOWER. No doubt. But it works pragmatically.

SIR F. I hardly know what to say. You are such an unusually outspoken family, and your father such an extraordinary man, that I should like to know more of you. You belong to a new generation, quite unlike mine. I am at sea here. May I continue provisionally as a friendly acquaintance rather than as a solicitor?

DARKIE. The very thing!

THE YOUTH. Silence all.

DARKIE. Go ahead, Sir Ferdinand. Whats the latest?

SIR F. You know, I presume, that your father's money, now practically unlimited, has been made, and is still being made, on the money market, by buying stocks and shares and selling them again at a profit. Such profits are not taxed, as they are classed as capital, not as income. Consequently it has been possible for your father to remain enormously rich, although the war taxation has abolished rich men as a class.

THE YOUTH. So much the better for us.

SIR F. Not altogether. The Chancellor of the Exchequer may tax money market incomes, either as such or as gambling. In that case The Buoyant Billions will dry up abruptly. In any case they will stop with his death, which cannot now be far off. Your incomes will be taxed like everyone elses, if you have any incomes. Have you?

THE WIDOWER. All I know is that what money I need appears to my credit in my bank passbook as cash or dividends on the few investments my stockbroker has advised.

SIR F. Does that apply all round?

SECONDBORN. To me, yes.

DARKIE. I told you so, Sir Ferdinand. None of us knows anything about making money because our father knows all about it.

SIR F. Has he never taught you anything about it?

THE WIDOWER. He couldnt. He does not understand it himself. He makes money by instinct, as beavers build dams.

SECONDBORN. Whenever I have taken his financial advice I have lost by it. I now leave it to my banker.

SIR F. Then I am afraid I must warn you all that you will presently become very poor. You will have to let your country houses and live in gate lodges and gardeners' cottages. Your ladies will have to do the housework. Your clothes will have to last you for years. I am here to impress these hard facts on you.

THE WIDOWER. But surely this shortage will not last for ever. The Labor Government, which is responsible for these robberies of the rich, will be defeated at the next election.

SIR F. Do not depend on that. All the king's horses and all the king's men cannot bring back the unearned incomes of the nineteenth century. The Socialists and Trade Unionists will see to that.

DARKIE. None of us women knows how to do housework.

SIR F. I am afraid you will have to learn.

MRS SECONDBORN. The whole thing is utterly ridiculous. The war is over; and there will always be rich and poor. The Chancellor is a beggar on horseback. He will be sent back to the gutter at the next election.

SIR F. Nobody can object to these revolutionary changes more than I do; but they are occurring among my clients every day.

MRS SECONDBORN. Nonsense! We must live. What are we to do?

SIR F. Reduce your expenditure. Live as poorer people than yourselves now live.

MRS SECONDBORN. Oh yes, poor people. But we are not poor people. We cannot live that way.

MRS THIRDBORN. Why not? Our riches have not made us happy. Our Lord's mother was the wife of a carpenter. I have always thought of her as a woman who did her own housework. I am sure I could learn. Is it not easier for a camel to pass through the eye of a needle than for a rich woman to enter the kingdom of heaven?

MRS SECONDBORN. Oh, you are religious. Much good your religion will do us!

THE WIDOWER. Don't let us quarrel about religion.

THE YOUTH. The old man isnt dead yet. He will make billions, taxes or no taxes. Lets make the most of him while he lasts.

SECONDBORN. I find it hard to believe that he will ever die. He is a human calculating machine. Calculating machines dont die.

SIR F. They wear out. He cannot live for ever.

THE WIDOWER. I used to play the cornet fairly well. If only my wife were alive to play my accompaniments on a street piano I should not starve.

SIR F. None of you need starve. On your father's reputation you will live on company directorships. You need not know anything about the businesses; your name on the prospectus will be sufficient. I must now pass on to another matter. Mr Buoyant has added to his instruction this sentence. "My elder daughter is provided for and need not be present. She can take care of herself." Have you a sister, Miss Buoyant?

DARKIE. I have a stepsister.

SIR F. [*surprised*] Was your father twice married?

THE WIDOWER. He was; but we try to forget it. We are ashamed of it.

MRS THIRDBORN. I am not ashamed of it.

MRS SECONDBORN. Thats only your religion: you have no natural feelings. Of course we are ashamed of it.

SIR F. May I ask what was wrong about it?

THE WIDOWER. Nothing wrong. But when our father married he was a very poor man; and he married a very common woman. She had never in her life had a satisfying dinner; and she died of overeating when they could afford it. They had one daughter.

MRS SECONDBORN. A quite impossible person.

SIR F. In what way?

DARKIE. She can do everything we cant do. She can cook. She can make beds. She can make her own clothes. She can sweep and scrub. She can nurse. She learnt it all before she was ten, and was sent to a ladies' school.

MRS SECONDBORN. Nothing could make a real lady of her. She dresses like a lady, and can talk like a lady, and can behave like a lady when she likes; but she does not belong to us. Her ten years of poverty and commonness makes a difference we cannot get over. She knows things a lady ought not to know.

MRS THIRDBORN. Including some things nobody ought to know. But it is not her fault.

MRS SECONDBORN. She has no manners at home, and no education. She keeps them for visitors. No class.

SIR F. My dear good people, you are behind the times. It is now a disgrace to have been born rich. Fashion is led by the wives of Cabinet Ministers whose fathers and husbands began on five shillings a week: they boast of it. Your stepsister is probably ashamed of you. May I ask where she is at present?

THE WIDOWER. In Panama, we believe.

SIR F. Panama!

THE YOUTH. On the banks of the canal all alone in a shack put up by herself and a few natives.

SECONDBORN. An interesting experience. When I feel that I can no longer bear civilized society I retreat into pure mathematics. But I need not go to Panama for that, thank Heaven.

MRS SECONDBORN. No: because I provide a comfortable home for you, where you can see whom you like when you like. This woman lives like a savage in a swamp full of snakes and alligators and natives.

SECONDBORN. My dear: the world is so wicked and ignorant and unreasonable that I must get away from it occasionally.

MRS SECONDBORN. You do it to get away from me. You think I dont know; but I do. Am I wicked and ignorant and unreasonable?

SECONDBORN. Occasionally, my dear. Only occasionally. Not always.

MRS SECONDBORN. Well, of all the monstrous accusations—

SIR F. Need we go into your domestic affairs? We really must not be personal.

MRS SECONDBORN. Whatever is not personal is not human.

The woman from Panama dashes into the temple, in travelling dress, and in a blazing rage.

SHE. What is all this? Why was I not told? [*To Sir F.*] Who are you?

SIR F. I am Mr Buoyant's solicitor, in consultation with his family. May I ask whom I am addressing?

SHE. You are addressing old Bill Buoyant's firstborn, next to himself the head of the family.

SIR F. Then you are expressly excluded from this family council on the ground that you are already provided for. The rest may have to face ruin when your father dies.

SHE. Well, here I am and here I stay. When they are all ruined they will expect me to keep them on my annuity. I cant and wont. So now give me a chair.

THE YOUTH [*giving her his chair*] Here you are, Clemmy. [*He plants it in front of the altar at the side opposite to Sir Ferdinand; fetches another for himself; and resumes his place*].

SIR F. Did you say Clemmy? The name in my instructions is Babzy.

SHE. Babzy is my vulgar father's vulgar pet name for his vulgar first baby. I was christened Clementina Alexandra; but Babzy is shorter: my father would not change it. Clemmy to the others.

MRS SECONDBORN. Have you come home for good?

SHE. That wont matter to you, Julia. For my home is here, in Daddy's house, not in yours. Daddy is growing old; and old men sometimes do foolish things with their money. None of you knows anything about money; so I had better keep an eye on you and him. Where is Daddy?

SIR F. Mr Buoyant is staying away purposely. He has no gift of expression; and his children, he tells me, are too much for him as talkers, and generally arrive at wrong conclusions by talking their feet off the ground. I am quoting his own words. Having done my best to act for him without making the least impression on your very interesting relatives, I really do not know why I am staying, especially as you appear to be taking my place. I had better go.

SHE. No. Stay for the fun of it. Whats your name, by the way?

SIR F. Envelopes should be addressed to Sir Ferdinand Flopper, Bart.

SHE. What! The great Sir Ferdinand?

SIR F. You are good enough to put it that way. Now may I ask you a question?

SHE. Ask a dozen if you like.

SIR F. You did not come back from Panama to attend this meeting. You must have left before it was decided on.

SHE. How clever of you to think of that! I came because I was attacked by the symptoms of a very dangerous disease.

They all shew great concern, exclaiming Oh *in their various ways.*

SIR F. Oh! You came for medical advice. I beg your pardon.

SHE. No. It is not a doctor's job. I found myself what is called falling in love. I had illusions, infatuations, impulses that were utterly unreasonable and irresistible. Desires in which my body was taking command of my soul. And all for a man of whom I knew nothing: a passing vagabond who had begged a meal from me. He came to me next day and said he had fallen in love with me at first sight, and that he was going quite mad about me. He warned me to run away and leave no address, as he would follow me to the ends of the earth if he knew where I was; and we should both make fools of ourselves by getting married. So I fled; and here I am. He does not know my name, nor I his. But when I think of him everything is transfigured and I am magically happy. Unreadable poems like the Song of Solomon delight me: bagatelles by Beethoven deepen into great sonatas: every walk through the country is an exploration of the plains of heaven. My reason tells me that this cannot possibly be real; that the day will come when it will vanish and leave me face to face with reality; perhaps tied to a husband who may be anything from a criminal to an intolerable bore. So I have run away and put the seas between me and this figure that looks like a beautiful and wonderful celestial messenger—a Lohengrin—but really does not exist at all except in my imagination. So now you know, all of you. Let us change the subject.

SIR F. Not, if you please, until I have reminded you that very few men are criminals, and that most married couples spend the whole day apart, the woman in the house, the man in the office or study or workshop. And there is such a possibility as divorce.

THE WIDOWER. Besides, take my case. My late wife and I were so indispensable to oneanother that a separation would have been for us a desolating calamity. Yet I repeatedly found myself irresistibly attracted biologically by females with whom I could not converse seriously for five minutes. My wife needed some romance in her life when I ceased to be romantic to her and became only her matter-of-fact husband. To keep her in good humor and health I had to invite and entertain a succession of interesting young men to keep her supplied with what I call Sunday husbands.

MRS SECONDBORN. That is a perfectly different thing. You have low tastes, which you occasionally gratify. I take an interest in young men; but I do not misconduct myself with them.

SECONDBORN. That, my love, is because your sense of property is stronger than your biological instinct. I am your property. Therefore you are damnably jealous.

MRS SECONDBORN. I deny it. I am not jealous.

THE WIDOWER. I think Sir Ferdinand's mind would be clearer on the subject if, like me, he had been married twice. My first marriage, which was quite biological, was a failure. What people called our love turned into something very like hatred. But biological tastes are not low tastes. Our two children were great successes: beautiful children with good characters. But nobody could live in the same house with their mother.

SIR F. [*very gravely*] Excuse me. I do not think you should speak of your dead wife in such terms.

THE WIDOWER. Oh, she is not dead: I let her divorce me. We are now quite good friends again. But to understand this question it is not enough to have been married once. Henry the Eighth would be the leading authority if he were alive. The prophet Mahomet was married more than fourteen times. And what about Solomon?

SIR F. Do pray let us keep religion out of this discussion. Surely religion is one thing, and the British marriage law another.

All the rest laugh, except Mrs Secondborn, who snorts.

SIR F. What is there to laugh at? Can we not be sensible and practical? We are dealing with the hard cash of your incomes, not with Solomon and Mahomet. We are not Mormons. Their wives in British law were only concubines.

THE WIDOWER. I hold that concubines are a necessary institution. In a nation wellbred biologically there should be concubines as well as wives and husbands. Some marriages are between couples who have no children because they have hereditary ailments which they fear to transmit to their offspring. Others are of shrews and bullies who produce excellent bastards, though domestic life with them is impossible. They should be concubines, not husbands and wives. All concubinages are exactly alike. No two marriages are alike.

SIR F. Nonsense! All marriages are exactly alike in law.

THE WIDOWER. So much the worse for law, I am afraid.

MRS THIRDBORN. No two love affairs are alike. I was in love three times before I married a friend who was not in love with me nor I with him. We were both sane. Yet we can say honestly "Whom God hath joined"—

SIR F. Oh, do please leave God out of the question. Marriage is a legal institution; and God has nothing to do with legal institutions.

MRS THIRDBORN. God keeps butting in somehow.

SIR F. Surely that is not the way to speak of the Almighty. If you must drag in religion, at least do so in becoming language.

MRS THIRDBORN. When you really believe in God

you can make fun of Him. When you are only pretending you pull long faces and call Him Gawd.

MRS SECONDBORN. Dont forget that when you wake up from your dreams and delusions about your husband you have your children to love. You may be only too glad to be rid of your crazy notions about your husband. The kids fill his place.

MRS THIRDBORN. Not after they are six, when they go to school and begin to be independent of you and form a new relation with their teachers. Only husband and wife come to feel that they belong to oneanother and are really parts of oneanother. That is one of the mysteries of marriage.

MRS SECONDBORN. Besides, the illusions dont affect people who have common sense. I never read the Song of Solomon, nor bothered about Beethoven; but I always knew whether it was a fine day or a wet one without any nonsense about the plains of heaven. Dick's weaknesses were as obvious to me then as they are now. But I could put up with them. I liked him because he was so unlike me. [*To her husband*] And it was the same with you, wasnt it, Dick?

SECONDBORN. Not quite. I had my share of the illusions. But when they vanished they did not matter much. I had got used to you. Let us look at this mathematically. The sex illusion is not a fixed quantity: not what mathematicians call a constant. It varies from zero in my wife's case to madness in that of our stepsister. Reason and experience, which hold it in check, are also variable. Our stepsister is highly observant and reasonable. My wife is totally unreasonable.

MRS SECONDBORN. Which of us two is the reasonable one? Who keeps the house for you? Who looks after your clothes? Who sees that you get your meals regularly and do not eat and drink more than is good for you? Reason! I have to reason with you every day, and can get nothing out of you but incomprehensible ravings about variables and functions. Your mind never stays put for ten minutes at a time.

SECONDBORN. My dearest: nothing in the world ever stays put for ten seconds. We can know it only relatively at any moment. Yet most people can think only absolutely. Relatively, variably, mathematically, they cannot think at all. Everything for them is either soot or whitewash. They undertake to make a new world after every war without brains enough to add *a* to *b*.

MRS SECONDBORN. Are you happy with me or are you not?

SECONDBORN. I am never happy. I dont want to be happy. I want to be alive and active. Bothering about happiness is the worst unhappiness.

DARKIE. Oh, let us talk sense. [*To her stepsister*] Clemmy: your room is not ready for you: to clear it will take weeks. And there are no maids to be got now.

SHE. English maids are no use to me. I have brought a Panama native: he will clear my room for me in twenty minutes.

THE WIDOWER. Then our business is finished. Sir Ferdinand has told us that our incomes will stop when our father dies. He has advised us that we can live on directorships on the strength of our famous name and its associations with billions. I hope so. What more is there to be said?

THE YOUTH. What about me? Nobody will make me a director. I am a world betterer.

SIR F. World betterer! What new hare are you starting now?

THE YOUTH. All intelligent men of my age are world betterers today.

SIR F. Pooh! You will drop all that nonsense when you take your university degree.

THE WIDOWER. Impossible. Our father gave us all the money we needed on condition that we would never engage in money making, nor take a university degree.

SIR F. Not go to a university!

SECONDBORN. You misunderstand. We have all spent three years at college. Our father sent us there to acquire the social training the communal life of a university gives. But he insisted on our leaving without a degree.

SIR F. In Heaven's name, why?

SECONDBORN. One of his notions. He holds that dictated mental work on uncongenial subjects is overwork which injures the brain permanently. So we are not university graduates; but we are university men none the less. If a man is known to have been at Oxford or Cambridge nobody ever asks whether he has taken a degree or not.

SIR F. But that does not justify false pretences.

THE YOUTH. University degrees are the falsest of pretences. Graduates as a class are politically and scientifically obsolete and ignorant. Even in the elementary schools children spend nine years without learning how to speak their native language decently or write it easily.

THE WIDOWER. We are not impostors, Sir Ferdinand, because we ran away from our examinations. What culture a university can give, we possess. However, if you have any scruples—

SIR F. I have scruples. I have principles. I have common sense. I have sanity. They seem to have no place in the affairs of this family.

MRS THIRDBORN. Listen to me, Sir Ferdinand. You

must understand that my father-in-law's dearest wish was to be a teacher and a preacher. But as he had original ideas no one would employ him as a preacher nor listen to him as a teacher. He could do nothing but make money: though he regarded it as the curse of his life. He made it in the city all day and returned to his home every evening to forget it, and teach his children to speak their minds always and never to mistake saying the proper thing for the truth.

SIR F. But surely the truth is always the proper thing.

MRS THIRDBORN. Yes; but the proper thing is not always God's truth.

SIR F. [*bothered*] You give things such a twist! We really shall get nowhere unless you will speak in an expected manner.

The Panama native, attired as a British valet, enters hastily and comes straight to Her.

NATIVE. Pink lady: the man has come.

SHE. Here!!!

NATIVE. In this house. He will not be denied. He has divine guidance. He has seen you again at the singing theatre here in London. God led him to Panama.

SHE. Shew him up.

The Native bows his assent and goes out.

SIR F. May I ask who is this man?

SHE. He is the man I am in love with: the object of my illusions, my madness. If he followed me across the Atlantic, and tracked me back again, he must be as mad as I am.

NATIVE [*at the door, announcing*] The man of destiny. [*He withdraws*].

The Son, elegantly dressed, enters.

HE [*to Her, standing in the middle of the temple after looking at the company in dismay*] Am I intruding? I had hoped to find you alone.

SHE. The Buoyants are never alone. Let me introduce you. My stepbrothers, Tom and Dick. Mrs Dick and Mrs Harry: a grass widow. Tom is a widower. Darkie: my unmarried stepsister. Fiffy: the youngest. Sir Ferdinand Whopper, our father's latest and most eminent solicitor.

SIR F. My name is not Whopper: it is Flopper.

SHE. My mistake. They rhyme.

HE. Bon soir la compagnie. This room is like a temple. Are you engaged in an act of worship?

MRS THIRDBORN. All the world is a temple of the Holy Ghost. You may be quite at your ease here, resting your soul.

SIR F. In what capacity do you claim to join us, may I ask?

HE. Only in pursuit of old Bill Buoyant's billions. I am by profession a world betterer. I need money for investigation and experiment. I saw Miss Buoyant one night at the opera. She attracted me so strongly that I did not hear a note of the music. I found out who she was but not what she is. I know nothing of her tastes, her intelligence, her manners, her temper: in short, of anything that would make it possible for me to live with her; yet I feel that I must possess her. For this I have no excuse. Nature has struck this blow at me: I can neither explain it nor resist it: I am mad about her. All I can do is to marry her for her money if I can persuade her to marry me.

SIR F. Do I understand that you propose to marry this lady for her money, and are apologizing for wanting to marry her for love as well?

HE. I said nothing about love. Love means many different things: love of parents and children, love of pet animals, love of whisky or strawberry ices, love of cricket or lawn tennis, also love of money. My case is a specific one of animal magnetism, as inexplicable as the terrestrial magnetism that drags a steel ship to a north or south pole that is not the astronomical pole. The ship can be demagnetized: who can demagnetize me? No one. We have not even a name for this mystery.

SIR F. I should call it the voice of nature.

HE. How much farther does that get you? Calling things names does not explain them: it is the trade of sham scientists who do not know what science means.

SECONDBORN. That is true. Are you a mathematician?

HE. I know the multiplication table, and can do very simple sums: that is all; but though I cannot do equations, I am mathematician enough to know that nothing is stationary: everything is moving and changing.

SHE. What complicates the affair is that I am in love with this man. And I dare not marry a man I love. I should be his slave.

SIR F. Really you are all quite mad. Is not your being in love with him a reason for marrying him if he is in love with you, as he appears to be in spite of his outrageous boast of being a fortune hunter?

SHE. You may leave money out of the question. Though I was brought up never to think of money, I have never spent all my annuity; and with what I could spare I have doubled my income on the money market. I have inherited my father's flair for finance. Money makes itself in my hands in spite of his preaching. When I want a husband I can afford to pay for him.

HE. That is very satisfactory. Why not marry me?

SHE. We might regret it. Love marriages are the most

unreasonable, and probably the most often regretted.

HE. Everything we do can be regretted. There is only one thing that a woman is certain to regret.

SHE. What is that, pray?

HE. Being unmarried.

SHE. I deny it. The day of ridiculous old maids is over. Great men have been bachelors and great women virgins.

HE. They may have regretted it all the same.

SIR F. I must remind you, Miss Buoyant, that though many women have regretted their marriages there is one experience that no woman has ever regretted, and that experience is motherhood. Celibacy for a woman is *il gran rifiuto*, the great refusal of her destiny, of the purpose in life which comes before all personal considerations: the replacing of the dead by the living.

MRS THIRDBORN. For once, dear Sir Ferdinand, you are not talking nonsense. Child bearing is an experience which it is impossible to regret. It is definitely ordained.

SECONDBORN. Regret is essentially mathematical. What are the mathematical probabilities? How many marriages are regretted? How much are they regretted? How long are they regretted? What is the proportion of divorces? The registrar of marriages should have a totalizator balancing these quantities. There should be one in every church. People would then know what chances they are taking. Should first cousins marry? Should Catholics and Protestants marry? Should lepers marry? At what ages should they marry? Without these statistics you cannot give scientific answers to these questions: you have only notions and guesswork to go on.

HE. Our fancies come first: they are irresistible. They must have a meaning and a purpose. Well, I have a strong fancy for your stepsister; and she confesses to a strong fancy for me. Let us chance it.

DARKIE. What about your own experience, Sir Ferdinand?

SHE. Yes. How did your own marriage turn out? Did you marry for love?

SIR F. I am not married. I am a bachelor.

They laugh at him.

SIR F. What are you all laughing at? Am I expected to substitute personal experiences for legal advice? May I not advise women though I am not a woman? I am here to advise a family which I can only describe charitably as a family of lunatics. Does not the value of my advice lie in the fact that I am not myself a lunatic?

THE YOUTH. But you are a lunatic. And you havnt given us any advice.

SECONDBORN. What have you given us? Instead of facts, escapist romance from the cinemas. Instead of mathematical and relative measurements, a three dimensional timeless universe. Instead of logic, association of ideas, mostly nonsensical ideas. Instead of analysis, everything in totalitarian lumps. Nothing scientific.

SIR F. I am a lawyer, not a scientist.

SECONDBORN. Until law and science, politics and religion, are all one, the scientists, the lawyers, the clergymen, the politicians will be foolish tinkers who think they can mend the world because they can mend holes in a saucepan.

DARKIE. Do let us get back to tin tacks. Is Clemmy going to marry him or is she not? If she says yes I bet she will have her own way whatever he does.

THE WIDOWER. The woman always does. I have gone twice to my weddings like a lamb to the slaughter house. My two wives were triumphant. I bought new clothes, oiled and brushed my hair, and was afraid to run away. My second marriage was a success: I knew what to expect. Second marriages are the quietest and happiest. The twice married, if one of them dies, marry a third time even at the most advanced age.

SIR F. Then marriage is not a failure as an institution. With reasonable divorce laws, not at all.

HE [*to Her*] You hear?

SHE. Sit down, will you. Dont stand over me, pontificating.

HE. I beg your pardon. [*He sits down on the altar step in the middle*].

SHE. You make everything beautiful to me. You give me a happiness I have never experienced before. But if I marry you all this will cease. If I dont marry you—if you die—if we never meet again, it may last all my life. And there are rights I will give to no man over me.

SIR F. Conjugal rights. They cannot now be enforced. Not effectively. Do not let them hinder you. What are the gentleman's means? that is the question.

SHE. What am I to do with my means? that also is the question.

HE. What all independent women do with their means. Keep a husband on them.

MRS SECONDBORN. Is a husband a dog or a cat to be kept as a pet? I never heard such nonsense.

HE. Dogs are sometimes better bargains. I am not so sure about cats.

MRS SECONDBORN [*rising*] Come home, Dick. I have had enough of this. It will just end in their getting married like other people. Come home. [*She storms out*].

MRS THIRDBORN [*rising*] Sir Ferdinand's law has failed us. Dick's science has failed us. Fiff's boyish dreams have failed us: he has not yet bettered the world. We must leave it in God's hands [*She goes out*].

SECONDBORN [*rising*] It always comes to that: leave it to God, though we do not know what God is, and are still seeking a general mathematical theory expressing Him. All we know is that He leaves much of it to us; and we make a shocking mess of it. We must be goodnatured and make the best of it. Goodbye, Mr Golddigger. [*He follows his wife out*].

THE WIDOWER [*rising*] As I have no wife to decide for me, I must go of my own accord.

SIR F. [*rising*] As nobody pays the slightest attention to my advice, I will accompany you. [*The three go out*].

DARKIE [*rising*] Come on, Fiff. Lets leave them alone together.

HE. Thank you.

Darkie and Fiff go out.

HE. Well?

SHE. I will think about it.

The Chinese Priest returns, followed by the Native swinging a censer.

THE PRIEST. Will you have the kindness to follow your friends and leave me to purify this temple of peace. It has been terribly profaned for the last hour. Father Buoyant will be here presently for his rest, his meditation, his soothing, his divine recreation. You have poisoned its atmosphere with your wranglings. I must change its air and restore its peace lest it kill Father Buoyant instead of giving him a foretaste of heaven. Go now: you must not breathe here any longer.

SHE [*rising*] Daddy made me sit still and be silent here when I was in my restless teens. I detested it. The scent of incense sickens me. [*To Him*] Come, you. We must think it over.

She goes out. He waves his hand to the Priest and follows.

THE PRIEST. What freaks these pinks are! Belonging neither to the west, like you, nor to the east, like me.

THE NATIVE [*swinging the censer*] Neither to north nor south; but in that they resemble us. They have much to teach us.

THE PRIEST. Yes; but they are themselves unteachable, not understanding what they teach.

THE NATIVE. True: they can teach; but they cannot learn.

THE PRIEST. Freaks. Dangerous freaks. The future is with the learners.

The temple vanishes, blacked out.

ACT IV

THE END

When the temple reappears the censer is on the altar. The Priest and the Native are rearranging the chairs.

Old Bill Buoyant comes in. A greybeard, like any other greybeard; but a gorgeous golden dressing gown and yellow slippers give him a hieratic air.

OLD BILL. Have they all cleared out?

PRIEST. All. The temple is cleansed.

OLD BILL. Good. Who is your friend?

NATIVE. I am the servant of your daughter.

OLD BILL. Which daughter?

NATIVE. From Panama.

OLD BILL. Good. Has she left the house yet?

NATIVE. Not without me. I drive her car.

OLD BILL. Good. Tell her to come and see me here.

NATIVE. At your service, O sage. [*He salaams and goes out*].

OLD BILL. Shall I profane the temple if I kiss my daughter here? I am fond of her.

PRIEST. Truly no. The temple will sanctify your kiss.

OLD BILL. Good. It is curious how happy I always feel here. I am not a religious man. I do not go to church.

PRIEST. You meditate.

OLD BILL. No. Meditation is not in my line: I speculate. And my speculations turn out well when I spend an hour here and just empty my mind.

PRIEST. When the mind is empty the gods take possession. And the gods know.

OLD BILL. Yes: I suppose thats it. But it's a queer business: I thought I was the very last man in the world to put my nose into a temple. However, you know all this. I am repeating myself, and boring you. Leave me to myself. [*He seats himself in the bishop's chair*].

PRIEST. I repeat the service every day; yet it does not bore me: there is always something new in it. They tell me it is the same with your orchestral symphonies: the great ones cannot be heard too often. But as you desire, I leave you to your aftercalm.

OLD BILL. So long, Mahatma.

The Priest nods gravely, and is going when She and He come in.

THE PRIEST. Peace be with you three. [*He goes*].

SHE [*rushing to Old Bill and kissing him*] Daddyest!

OLD BILL [*returning her embrace*] My Babzy! Who is the man?

SHE. I dont know. He wants to marry me.

OLD BILL. Does he indeed? Do you want to marry him?

SHE. I am considering it. I am not dead set against it.

OLD BILL. Whats his name?

SHE. I dont know.

OLD BILL. The devil you dont!

SHE [*to Him*] Whats your name?

HE. Smith. Only Smith. Christened Junius.

OLD BILL. Have you nothing else to say for yourself?

JUNIUS. Nothing whatever.

OLD BILL. Any profession?

HE. World betterer. Nothing paying.

SHE. If I marry him I shall have to keep him and manage for him. But that is not altogether a drawback. I do not mean to be any man's kept slave.

OLD BILL [*to Junius*] What about you? Do you want to be any woman's kept man?

JUNIUS. I dont want anything but your daughter. I dont know why. I know nothing about her; and she knows nothing about me. I am simply mad on the subject.

OLD BILL [*to Her*] Are you mad on the subject?

SHE. Not so mad as he is. I can do without him. If not, I should be his slave.

OLD BILL. Do you hear that, young man? You will be the slave.

JUNIUS. I suppose so. But I must risk it. So must she. You can understand this. You have made your billions by taking risks.

OLD BILL. I have seen men ruined by taking risks. I have a sort of instinct about them which brings me out all right. For old Bill Buoyant there are no risks. But for you, perhaps???

JUNIUS. Well, there may be none for your daughter. She may inherit your genius.

OLD BILL. She does. But my genius tells me not to throw away my daughter on a young lunatic.

JUNIUS. You are jealous, eh? Let me remind you that all parents must see their children walk out sooner or later. Mothers-in-law are stock jokes. Nobody jokes about fathers-in-law; but they are troublesome enough when they hold on too long.

SHE. Parents cannot be turned out into the woods to die. We are not savages. Daddy will always be a part of my life.

JUNIUS. Not always. How long do you intend to live, old man?

OLD BILL. Not for ever: God forbid! [*To Her*] The fellow is right, darling. Leave me out of the question.

SHE. I cant leave you out, Daddy. But you will know

your natural place in my house: you have always known it in your own. I can trust you.

JUNIUS. I have no objection to your father as long as he lasts. He has the billions.

OLD BILL. The billions will stop when I die. Would you be as keen if there were no billions?

JUNIUS. Just as keen. How often must I tell you that I am mad about her? But we shall want the money. I have earned nothing so far.

OLD BILL [*to Her*] He has an eye for facts, this chap. I rather like him.

SHE. Yes: so do I. He has no illusions about himself nor about me. After all, if he turns out badly I can divorce him.

OLD BILL. Well, our parting must come someday; and if you and I were the wisest father and daughter on earth the upshot would be just as much a toss-up as if we were the two damndest fools. Still, there are certain precautions one can take.

JUNIUS. A joint annuity, for instance.

OLD BILL. Your sense of money is very clear, young man. But I have already bought her an annuity for her life. Not for yours. Any further precautions you must take yourself.

JUNIUS. I must agree. The Life Force has got me. I can make no conditions.

OLD BILL [*to Her*] Well, will you marry him?

SHE. I will consider it.

JUNIUS. If you consider it you will refuse. There would be no marriages if the two started considering.

OLD BILL. That is the first stupid thing you have said, young man. All marriages are very anxiously considered; but considering has never yet prevented a marriage. If you are her man she will have you, consideration or no consideration.

SHE. What do you advise, Daddy?

OLD BILL. Oh, take him, take him. I like him; and he will do as well as another. You may regret it; but you will regret it worse if you are afraid to try your luck.

JUNIUS. I am surprised and deeply obliged to you, Mr Buoyant. I expected you to use all your influence against me. You are a model father-in-law.

SHE. I feel as if I were going to commit suicide.

JUNIUS. In a sense, you are. So am I. The chrysalis dies when the dragonfly is born.

SHE. I am no chrysalis. I am a working bee: you are a drone.

JUNIUS. That is nature's arrangement. We cannot change it.

OLD BILL. A working husband is no husband at all. When I had to work, my wife was only my housekeeper: she saw next to nothing of me except when I came home at night hungry and tired and dirty. When I did nothing but send telegrams to my stockbroker—I dont call that work—and buy fancy waistcoats and diamond cravat pins, she began to enjoy her marriage and love me. And long as she has been dead now, I have never been unfaithful to her, nor ever shall be.

JUNIUS. But you married again.

OLD BILL. It was not the same thing. I wanted more children because I was so fond of the one I had. But it was not the same.

JUNIUS. Did you never think of bettering the world with your money?

OLD BILL. What the devil do I care about the world? What did it care about me when I was poor? Dont talk your world bettering cant to me if we are to get on together. I am not going to buy any of your shares.

JUNIUS. I apologize. My shares pay no dividends. I

will not pursue the subject. When are we to get married? Name the day.

OLD BILL. Dont frighten her. When she names it, you will be frightened.

JUNIUS. I am frightened already. But we must dare. By the way, where shall we live? Not in Panama, I hope.

SHE. No. In Panama I should be nervous about you when you were out of my sight. You cannot charm the rattlers and gaters as I can.

JUNIUS. Why not? I can learn the saxophone.

SHE. True; but we should be out of reach of Daddy. We shall live in Park Lane.

JUNIUS. You know, of course, that there are plenty of rattlers and gaters of the human variety in Park Lane?

SHE. Yes; and you may be one of them.

JUNIUS. You have an answer for everything. What a prospect for me!

SHE. We are both taking chances. We shall live where I like.

JUNIUS. Or where I like. I can assert myself.

SHE. So can I. We shall see which of us wins. Stop chattering; and go out and buy a marriage licence.

JUNIUS [*taken aback*] Oh, I say! This is very sudden.

OLD BILL. Frightened, eh? Go. Get it over. You will have to arrange for two witnesses.

JUNIUS. I wish I could arrange for an anesthetist. The operation is terrifying.

SHE. Dont forget to buy a wedding ring. Have you money enough?

JUNIUS. I have what is left of the thousand pounds my father started me with. Panama made a big hole in it.

OLD BILL. Off with you, damn you. You are stealing my daughter from me. I hope she will soon tire of you and come back to me. [*To Her*] Give him one of your rings to get the fit right. Never mind the witnesses: Tom and Dick will do.

JUNIUS [*to Her*] Wouldnt you like to be married in church and have the banns called? That would give us three weeks to think it over.

SHE. No. Now or never.

JUNIUS. I am being rushed.

OLD BILL. You will spend your life being rushed if you live with Babz. Better get used to it at once.

SHE. A ring that will fit your middle finger will be big enough for my third. I have bigger hands. I was brought up to use them. You werent.

JUNIUS. You must put up with that. My hands are those of a philosopher: yours of a charwoman. Oh, why, WHY am I infatuated with you? I know so many apparently superior women.

SHE. Same here. Daddy is worth ten of you.

JUNIUS. You think so. But if you only knew how quickly I can lose money. He can only make it.

OLD BILL. Leave me out of it: I shall not last much longer: you have a lifetime to give her. Away with you to the registry office and stop talking.

JUNIUS. I go. But I'm not sure I shall ever come back. [*He goes out*].

SHE. I half hope he wont.

JUNIUS [*coming back*] By the way, whats your Christian name?

SHE. Clementina Alexandra.

JUNIUS. Righto! [*Making a note of it*] Cle-Men-Tina Alexandra. [*He goes*].

SHE [*throwing her arms round Old Bill's neck and kissing him*] Daddy! Daddy! Daddy!

The Native comes in and closes the door carefully. Babz quickly releases her father.

THE NATIVE [*to Her*] Sir Flopper, the illustrious law

servant of God, has waited until your venerable father is disengaged. May he enter?

OLD BILL. Yes. Shew him in.

THE NATIVE [*looks to Her for confirmation*] ??

SHE. Yes. Shew him in.

THE NATIVE [*throwing the door open*] Enter, Excellency.

Sir Ferdinand comes in. The Native withdraws.

SIR FERDINAND [*to Old Bill*] Pardon. I thought you were alone.

OLD BILL. Get out, Babzy.

SHE. Au revoir, Sir Ferdinand.

He opens the door for her and bows gravely as she passes out, then closes the door, and, after an inviting gesture from Old Bill, sits down in the chair vacated by her.

SIR FERDINAND. First let me say that I am not here professionally.

OLD BILL. Why not? You must live.

SIR FERDINAND. My reason is that I am totally incapable of advising you on the subject of your extraordinary family. They are outside my experience. If I were a medical adviser I should certify them as insane.

OLD BILL. And me?

SIR FERDINAND. Well, hardly yet. Your instructions were rational enough. I put your financial case before your sons as you desired. I was interrupted by the arrival from America of the lady who has just left us. I was interrupted again by the arrival of a young man who proposed to marry her for her money. Your daughter made no objection: she seemed to prefer it to a disinterested proposal. Your family did not demur. I am prepared to learn that you do not demur. In any other family he would have been kicked out of the house.

OLD BILL. I like the fellow.

SIR FERDINAND. Like the fellow! Like an impudent fortune hunter! In Heaven's name, why?

OLD BILL. He asks straight questions and gives straight answers. So does my daughter. I taught her to do it. It was all I could teach her. Didnt you notice it?

SIR FERDINAND. I did indeed. And I have come to tell you I can no longer act as your solicitor. My brother Cyril is a doctor, head of a mental hospital for incurables. He is the man you should consult. Lawyers are useless here.

OLD BILL. Come, come, Flopper! You know as well as I do that people who marry for money are happy together as often as other people. It is the love matches that break down because Providence wants sound children and does not care a snap of its fingers whether the parents are happy or not. It makes them mad about one another until the children are born, and then drops them like hot potatoes. Money guarantees comfort and what you call culture. Love guarantees nothing. I know this. You know it. My daughter knows it. The young man knows it. Are we mad because we act and speak accordingly? Are you sane because you pretend to be shocked by it? It is you who should go to the mental hospital.

SIR FERDINAND. That also is a matter for medical, not legal opinion. I will not discuss it. I have only to tell you that I explained to your second family as you instructed me, that the source of their incomes would dry up at your death, and they must then fend for themselves.

OLD BILL. Good. What did they say to that?

SIR FERDINAND. Nothing. I had to suggest that they should live by directorships founded on your reputation.

OLD BILL. Guinea pigs. No use: that game is up. The new Labor Government gives such jobs to superannuated Trade Union secretaries.

SIR FERDINAND. Then why have you not provided for your second family as you did for your first daughter?

OLD BILL. It is not the same. They dont belong to me as she does.

SIR FERDINAND. They will starve.

OLD BILL. No they wont. They can live on their wives' incomes. I took care of that.

SIR FERDINAND. Well, that is all I have to say. I shall accept no fees for it; but I shall be glad to keep up our acquaintance, if that will be agreeable to you.

OLD BILL. Why?

SIR FERDINAND. Pure curiosity.

OLD BILL. I dont believe you.

SIR FERDINAND [*rising, offended*] Do you accuse me of lying?

OLD BILL. Yes. There must be some attraction. Which woman is it? One of my sons' wives, eh?

SIR FERDINAND [*sitting down again, deflated*] Well, really! No: they are married women. You have two unmarried daughters.

OLD BILL. Darkie? I actually forgot Darkie. Think of that!

SIR FERDINAND. Do not misunderstand me. I am a bachelor, not a libertine. I want a daughter.

OLD BILL. Good. Ive always had an uneasy conscience about Darkie. Ive never been able to give her the affection Ive heaped on Babzy. She has never had a father. Take her; and be a father to her. Come as often as you please: you are one of the family now.

SIR FERDINAND. You take my breath away. This is too sudden. A minute ago I did not know why I wanted to keep on terms with you all. You have shoved it down my throat.

OLD BILL. That is the Buoyant way: it saves a lot of time. Now that you know, you had better stay to lunch.

SIR FERDINAND. No. I must go home and think it over. Never fear: I shall not back out.

Darkie comes in.

OLD BILL. Here she is. Telepathy. It runs in the family.

DARKIE. Oh! I beg your pardon. I did not know you were engaged. It is only to ask whether you will have asparagus or broad beans for lunch.

OLD BILL. Sparrowgrass? Yes: plenty of it. [*She turns to go*]. Wait a bit. Sir Ferdinand Flopper here has fallen for you. He wants to be your father.

DARKIE. I dont want a father. Ive never had a real father: I'm not accustomed to it. I'm only a housekeeper.

OLD BILL. Well, my child, you can have a real father now, a baronet. Try him. You can drop him if he doesnt suit. Somebody to spoil you as Ive spoilt Babzy.

DARKIE. I dont want to be spoilt. I like housekeeping; and I'm not sentimental. If I ever want to be spoilt I shall get married. I am sorry to disappoint you, Sir Ferdinand; but daughtering is a game I have no turn for.

SIR FERDINAND. I see. But at least youll not mind my keeping up my acquaintance with the family.

DARKIE. Not a bit. Let me know what you like to eat and drink: that is all. I must go now to see about father's lunch. Tata.

She goes out.

OLD BILL. Dumbfounded, eh?

SIR FERDINAND. Completely. What a house this is!

She was not a bit surprised, though she was quite unprepared.

OLD BILL. We Buoyants are always prepared for the worst.

SIR FERDINAND. Or the best, I hope. My offer is hardly a misfortune, as I see it.

OLD BILL. It isnt. Dont fancy you have escaped her. She asked about your grub. She is glad to have one more to housekeep for. You may consider yourself adopted.

SIR FERDINAND. I am past considering anything.

OLD BILL. Youll get used to it.

SIR FERDINAND. Yes: I suppose I shall. The curious thing is, I am beginning to like it.

OLD BILL. Good. [*Looking at his watch*] I wonder whether that chap is coming back. He ought to be here by now.

The Widower enters.

THE WIDOWER. Look here, Ee Pee: the young man from Panama says he is going to be married to Clemmy. He wants me and Dick to be witnesses. Is that all right?

OLD BILL. Yes. Quite all right. Has he got the licence?

THE WIDOWER. Yes. And he has borrowed my wife's wedding ring for the ceremony. He was short of pocket money for a new one. The money for the licence cleaned him out.

OLD BILL. Then he has come back?

THE WIDOWER. Yes. A bit upset, naturally; but he means business.

OLD BILL. Good.

SIR FERDINAND. Excuse me: but what does Ee Pee mean? Esteemed Parent?

OLD BILL. No. Earthly Providence. Darkie's invention.

SIR FERDINAND. Ah! Precisely.

The youth Fiffy comes in.

FIFFY. Look here, Ee Pee. Clemmy and the man from Panama are going to marry. He has got the licence.

OLD BILL. Well, what is that to you, you young rip?

FIFFY. Only that the chap is a World Betterer. I thought you had enough of that from me.

OLD BILL. So I have. The pair of you want to better the world when you dont know enough of it to manage a fish and chips business.

FIFFY. True, O king. But we are needed in the world bettering business, not in fish and chips. Still, one World Betterer is enough in one family.

OLD BILL. Keep out of it then, you. You were born to talk and say nothing, to write and do nothing. That pays.

FIFFY. To make sure, I shall marry for money, as the Panama chap is doing. Dont you agree, Sir Ferdinand?

SIR FERDINAND. Yes, if you can find the lady. Dress better; and oil your hair.

Babzy comes back with her two stepsisters-in-law.

SHE. Dick, dear: shall I marry the man from Panama?

SECONDBORN. My dearest Clemmy: I cannot advise you. You must take chances; but they are not calculable mathematically. We have no figures to go on: the proportion of happy love marriages to happy marriages of convenience has never been counted.

MRS SECONDBORN. Do stop talking heartless nonsense, Dick. Has the man any means or expectations? Is he a gentleman? He speaks like a gentleman. He dresses like a gentleman. But he has not the feelings of a gentleman. He says things that no gentleman would dream of saying. That is all we know about him. Dont marry him, Clemmy.

SECONDBORN. My dear: she must take chances or not marry at all.

MRS SECONDBORN. Oh, bother your chances! Chances! Chances! Chances! You are always talking about chances. Talk sense.

SECONDBORN. You tell me so almost every day, dear. I took my chance when I married you. But I do not regret it. You are the stupidest woman on earth; but you are a part of my life.

MRS SECONDBORN. Well, ask Sir Ferdinand which of us is right. Clemmy has low tastes; but that is no reason why she should throw herself away on a nobody.

SIR FERDINAND. I do not think, Mr Buoyant, that you can treat this question altogether as a mathematical one. You must take account of feelings, passions, emotions, intuitions, instincts, as well as cold quantities and figures and logic.

SECONDBORN [*rising to the occasion eloquently*] And who dares say that mathematics and reasoning are not passions? Mathematic perception is the noblest of all the faculties! This cant about their being soulless, dead, inhuman mechanisms is contrary to the plainest facts of life and history. What has carried our minds farther than mathematical foresight? Who has done more for enlightenment and civilization than Giordano Bruno, Copernicus, Galileo, Newton, Descartes, Rutherford, Einstein, all of them far seeing guessers carried away by the passion for measuring truth and knowledge that possessed and drove them? Will you set above this great passion the vulgar concupiscences of Don Juan and Casanova, and the romance of Beatrice and Francesca, of Irish Deirdre, the greatest bores in literature, mere names incidentally immortalized by a few lines in a great poem?

MRS THIRDBORN. They had hearts, Dick.

SECONDBORN. Hearts! What are hearts without brains? You mean that they had glands: pituitary glands, adrenal glands, thyroid glands, pouring hormones into their blood. Do you suppose that there is no mathematical hormone? Our anatomists have not yet discovered it; but it is there, undiscovered and invisible, pouring into our brains, controlled by our enzymes and catalysts as surely as our appetites for beef and brandy. La Rochefoucauld told you two centuries ago that though the appetite we call love is in everybody's mouth very few have ever experienced it. God is not Love: Love is not Enough: the appetite for more truth, more knowledge, for measurement and precision, is far more universal: even the dullest fools have some glimmer of it. My wife here never tires of playing bridge and solving crossword puzzles as she tires of housekeeping. Her love for me is very variable: it turns to hate in its terrible reactions. Mathematical passion alone has no reaction: our pleasure in it promises a development in which life will be an intellectual ecstasy surpassing the ecstasies of saints. Think of that, Clara. Take your chance, Clemmy. Forgive my prolixity. Ive done.

He flings himself back into his chair.

MRS SECONDBORN [*humbled*] Well, Dick, I will say that you are wonderful when you speak your piece, though I never understand a word. You must be the greatest man in the family: you always make me feel like a fool. I am proud of you. I may lose my temper sometimes; but I never hate you.

Darkie comes in.

OLD BILL. Ah! there you are. Youve missed something.

DARKIE. No: Ive been listening at the door.

FIFFY. By George, Dick, you were splendid. World bettering be damned! I shall qualify as a doctor and look for that hormone.

Junius comes in with the licence in his hand.

JUNIUS. Well, Ive come back after all. Here is the licence. Ive got the witnesses. Is it yes or no?

SHE. I suppose I must take my chance. Yes.

DARKIE. What I want to know is how many of you are staying for lunch.

The curtain falls and ends the play.

The Author Explains

(Replies to a questionnaire by Stephen Winsten and Esmé Percy, in holograph facsimile. *World Review*, London, September 1949)

(*1*) *Why did you call your new play a 'Comedy of No Manners' when this is the best-mannered play you have written? In Act I, father and son are exceptionally courteous.*

They are not courteous. They are simply frank, which is the extremity of no manners. This takes the play out of the well category [*sic*] called Comedy of Manners.

(*2*) *If, as the result of taxation, there will be no more wealthy folk, what will Worldbetterers do if they cannot marry 'for money'?*

Just what they do at present when they cannot attract wealthy wives.

(*3*) *All the wisdom seems to have been put into the mouths of native and Eastern. Have you given up hope on the Pinks?*

Read the play again. The pink women are as wise as the yellow men; and none of the white men are nitwits. But east is east and west is west throughout.

(*4*) *In* Good King Charles *Kneller seems to have the*

better of Newton in argument. Here, in Buoyant Billions, *you go all out for the mathematician. Does it mean you have changed your mind?*

I do not go all out for anybody or anything. I am a playwright, not a Soot or Whitewash doctrinaire. I give Newton his own point of view and Kneller his own also. There is neither change nor contradiction on my part.

(5) *In* Buoyant Billions *it is the male who is the pursuing animal: a change from* Man and Superman*?*

There is no pursuing animal in the play. There are two people who fall in love at first sight and are both terrified at finding themselves mad on the subject, and caught in a trap laid by the Life Force. Do you expect me to keep writing Man & Superman over and over again?

(6) *Do you suggest that Buoyant's training of his children made it difficult for them to cope with changed circumstances?*

No. It is difficult for everybody to cope with changed circumstances.

Farfetched Fables

WITH

Preface

Composition begun 17 July 1948; completed August 1948. First published in *Buoyant Billions, Farfetched Fables, & Shakes versus Shav*, 1951 (the first fable had earlier appeared in German, as "Phantastiche Fabel," in the *Neue Schweizer Rundschau*, March 1950). First presented by the Shaw Society at the Watergate Theatre, London, on 6 September 1950.

The First Fable
Park Attendant *Patrick Graucob*
Young Woman *Margaret Manners*
Young Man *Eric Batson*
An Excitable Middle-aged Man *Dominic Clauzel*

Second Fable
Secretary *Rosemary Carvill*
Commander-in-Chief Ulsterbridge *Howard Bourgein*
Lord Oldhand of the Foreign Office *Michael Sherwell*

Third Fable
Girl *Barbara Carter*
Tourist *Charles Rennison*
Matron *Marion Everall*
A Shrewd Middle-aged Man *Eric Batson*
Tramp *Martin Starkie*

Fourth Fable
Commissioner *Esmé Percy*

Fifth Fable

Shamrock *Michael Sherwell*
Rose *Ellen Pollock*
Herm *Esmé Percy*
Thistle *Patrick Graucob*

Sixth Fable

Teacher *Ellen Pollock*
Youth 1 *Charles Rennison*
Maiden 5 *Marion Everall*
Youth 3 *Ray Jackson*
Youth 2 *Geoffrey Sassé*
Maiden 4 *Margaret Manners*
Raphael *Martin Starkie*

THE FIRST FABLE *A Public Park, London*
SECOND FABLE *At the War Office, London*
THIRD FABLE *Outside the Anthropometric Laboratory, Isle of Wight*
FOURTH FABLE *At the Diet Commissioners, Isle of Wight*
FIFTH FABLE *At the Genetic Institute, Isle of Wight*
SIXTH FABLE *Sixth Form School, Isle of Wight*

Preface

As I have now entered my 93rd year, my fans must not expect from me more than a few crumbs dropped from the literary loaves I distributed in my prime, plus a few speculations as to what may happen in the next million light years that are troubling me in the queer second wind that follows second childhood.

Being unable to put everything in the heavens above and on the earth beneath into every page I write, as some of my correspondents seem to expect, I have had to leave some scraps and shavings out; and now I gather up a few of them and present them in the childish form of Farfetched Fables. Philosophic treatises, however precise and lucid, are thrown away on readers who can enjoy and sometimes even understand parables, fairy tales, novels, poems, and prophecies. Proverbs are more memorable than catechisms and creeds. Fictions like The Prodigal Son, The Good Samaritan, The Pilgrim's Progress, and Gulliver's Travels, stick in minds impervious to the Epistles of Paul, the sermons of Bunyan, and the wisecracks of Koheleth and Ecclesiasticus. Hard workers who devour my plays cannot all tackle my prefaces without falling asleep almost at once.

The Panjandrums of literature will no doubt continue to assume that whoever can read anything can read everything, and that whoever can add two and two, bet on a horse, or play whist or bridge, can take in the tensor calculus. I know better, and can only hope that a batch of childish fables may stick in some heads that my graver performances overshoot.

THE NEW PSYCHOBIOLOGY

Nowadays biology is taking a new turn in my direction. What I called metabiology when I wrote The Doctor's Dilemma has made a step towards reality as psychobiology. The medical profession has split violently into psychotherapists and old-fashioned pill and bottle prescribers backed by surgeons practising on our living bodies as flesh plumbers and carpenters. When these surgeons find a tumor or a cancer they just cut it out. When your digestion or excretion goes wrong the bottlemen dose you with hydrochloric acid or chalk-and-opium ("the old mixture") as the case may be. When these treatments fail, or when they are impracticable, they tell you sympathetically that you must die; and die you do, unless you cure yourself or are cured by a disciple of Mrs Eddy practising Christian Science.

The more intelligent, observant, and open-minded apothecaries and Sawboneses, wakened up by an extraordinarily indelicate adventurer named Sigmund Freud, and by the able Scotch doctor Scott Haldane (J. B. S. Haldane's father), become more and more sceptical of the dogma that a healthy body insures a healthy mind (*mens sana in corpore sano*) and more and more inclined to believe that an unhealthy body is the result of a diseased mind. As I write, a treatise on Mental Abnormality by Dr Millais Culpin has just been published. It would have been impossible when I wrote The Doctor's Dilemma. In spite of its author's efforts to be impartial, it is convincing and converting as to his evident belief that the old mechanistic surgery and *materia medica* cost many lives.

AM I A PATHOLOGICAL CASE?

This leads my restlessly speculative mind further than Dr Culpin has ventured. Is literary genius a disease? Shakespear, Walter Scott, Alexandre Dumas, myself: are we all mental cases? Are we simply incorrigible liars? Are players impostors and hypocrites? Were the Bible Christians right when they disowned Bunyan because the incidents he described had never occurred nor the characters of whom he told such circumstantial tales ever existed? He pleaded that Jesus had taught by parables; but this made matters worse; for the Bibliolators never doubted that the Prodigal Son and the Good Samaritan were historical personages whose adventures had actually occurred. To them Bunyan's plea, classing the parables with Esop's Fables and the stories of Reynard the Fox, was a blasphemy. The first Freudians used to recite a string of words to their patients, asking what they suggested, and studying the reaction, until they wormed their way into the sufferer's sub-conscious mind, and unveiled some forgotten trouble that had been worrying him and upsetting his health. By bringing it to light they cured the patient.

When this Freudian technique was tried on me it failed because the words suggested always something fictitious. On the salt marshes of Norfolk I had been struck by the fact that when the horses stood round timidly at a distance, a handsome and intelligent donkey came and conversed with me after its fashion. I still have the photograph I took of this interesting acquaintance. The word Ass would have recalled this experience to any normal person. But when it was put to me, I immediately said Dogberry. I was once shewn the dagger with which Major Sirr killed Lord Edward Fitzgerald; but the word dagger got nothing from me but Macbeth. Highway or stile produced Autolycus, Interpreter the Pilgrim's Progress, blacksmith Joe Gargery. I was living in an imaginary world. Deeply as I was interested in politics, Hamlet and Falstaff were more alive to me than any living politician or even any relative. Can I then be given credit for common sanity? Can I make any effective excuse except Bunyan's excuse, which is no excuse at all? If I plead that I am only doing what More and Bunyan, Dickens and Wells did I do not exonerate myself: I convict them.

All I can plead is that as events as they actually occur mean no more than a passing crowd to a policeman on point duty, they must be arranged in some comprehensible order as stories. Without this there can be no history, no morality, no social conscience. Thus the historian, the story teller, the playwright and his actors, the poet, the mathematician, and the philosopher, are functionaries without whom civilization would not be possible. I conclude that I was born a story teller because one was needed. I am therefore not a disease but a social necessity.

DIVINE PROVIDENCE

Providence, which I call The Life Force, when not

defeated by the imperfection of its mortal instruments, always takes care that the necessary functionaries are born specialized for their job. When no specialization beyond that of common mental ability is needed, millions of "hands" (correctly so called industrially) are born. But as they are helpless without skilled craftsmen and mechanics, without directors and deciders, without legislators and thinkers, these also are provided in the required numbers. Chaucer and Shakespear, Dante and Michael Angelo, Goethe and Ibsen, Newton and Einstein, Adam Smith and Karl Marx arrive only once at intervals of hundreds of years, whilst carpenters and tailors, stockbrokers and parsons, industrialists and traders are all forthcoming in thousands as fast as they are needed.

I present myself therefore as an instrument of the Life Force, writing by what is called inspiration; but as the Life Force proceeds experimentally by Trial-and-Error, and never achieves a 100 per cent success, I may be one of its complete failures, and certainly fall very short not only of perfection but of the Force's former highest achievements. For instance I am much less mentally gifted than, say, Leibniz, and can only have been needed because, as he was so gifted as to be unintelligible to the mob, it remained for some simpler soul like myself to translate his monads and his universal substance, as he called the Life Force, into fables which, however farfetched, can at least interest, amuse, and perhaps enlighten those capable of such entertainment, but baffled by Leibniz's algebraic symbols and his philosophic jargon.

Here I must warn you that you can make no greater mistake in your social thinking than to assume, as too many do, that persons with the rarest mental gifts or specific talents are in any other respect superior beings.

The Life Force, when it gives some needed extraordinary quality to some individual, does not bother about his or her morals. It may even, when some feat is required which a human being can perform only after drinking a pint of brandy, make him a dipsomaniac, like Edmund Kean, Robson, and Dickens on his last American tour. Or, needing a woman capable of bearing first rate children, it may endow her with enchanting sexual attraction yet leave her destitute of the qualities that make married life with her bearable. Apparently its aim is always the attainment of power over circumstances and matter through science, and is to this extent benevolent; but outside this bias it is quite unscrupulous, and lets its agents be equally so. Geniuses are often spendthrifts, drunkards, libertines, liars, dishonest in money matters, backsliders of all sorts, whilst many simple credulous souls are models of integrity and piety, high in the calendar of saints.

MENTAL CAPACITY DIFFERS AND DIVIDES

When reading what follows it must not be forgotten that though we differ widely in practical ability and mental scope, the same basic income, or ration, or minimum wage, or national dividend, or whatever the newspapers call it for the moment, will suffice for mayor and scavenger, for admiral and cabin boy, for judge and executioner, for field marshal and drummer boy, for sexton and archbishop, bank manager and bank porter, sister of charity and prison wardress, and who not. What is more, they are all equally indispensable. An industrial magnate once wrote asking me did I realize that his army of laborers would be destitute and helpless without him. I replied that if he did not realize that without them he would be a nobody he was no gentleman. This closed the correspondence.

Equality of income is an obvious corollary. Yes; but how much income? A national dividend of, say, thirteen shillings a week per family, which was the share agricultural laborers got in the nineteenth century, kept them alive for thirty years or so, but left no surplus for education and culture: in short, for civilization. Now without cultured homes civilization is impossible. Without culture possible in every home democratic civilization is impossible, because equality of opportunity is impossible. The present combination of class culture and general savagery produces civil war, called class war, until strikes, lock-outs, and police batons are succeeded by shot and shell. Then the final destruction of civilization is threatened.

Consequently the basic income to be aimed at must be sufficient to establish culture in every home, and wages must be levelled up, not down, to this quota by increased production. When the quota is achieved, arithmetical inequality will no longer matter; for the eugenic test is general intermarriageability; and though the difference between £5 a week and £50 makes the recipients practically exogamous, millionaires could not marry at all if they scorned brides from homes with £5000 a year. There is no harm in a few people having some spare money, called capital, to experiment with; for the basic income will keep them in the normal grooves.

So much for the economics of the situation produced by differences in mental capacity! Having dealt with it in former writings, I mention it here only for new readers saturated with the common notion that income ought to vary with mental capacity, personal talent, and business ability. Such equations are wildly impossible, and have nothing to do with the insane misdistribution of national income produced by nineteenth century plutocracy. And so I pass on to political ethics.

Most of us so far are ungovernable by abstract thought. Our inborn sense of right and wrong, of grace and sin, must be embodied for us in a supernatural ruler of the universe: omnipotent, omniscient, all wise, all benevolent. In ancient Greece this was called making the word flesh, because the Greeks did not then discriminate between thought and the words that expressed it. The Bible translators have Englished it too literally as the word made flesh.

But as the minds of the masses could not get beyond their trades and their localities, their God could not be omnipresent; and a host of minor gods sprang up. The Greeks added to Zeus and Chronos vocational deities: Vulcan the blacksmith, Athene (Minerva) the thinker, Diana the huntress, Aphrodite (Venus) the sexmistress. They reappear in Christianity as Peter the fisherman, Luke the painter, Joseph the carpenter, Saint Cecilia the musician, and the rest.

But this also was too wide a classification for the very simple souls, who carried the localization of their gods to the extent of claiming exclusive property for their own city in each saint, and waging civil war in the name of the black image of the Blessed Virgin in their parish church against the worshippers of her white image in the next village.

SATANIC SOLUTION OF THE PROBLEM OF EVIL

A difficulty was raised by the fact that evil was in the world as well as good, and often triumphed over the good. Consequently there must be a devil as well as a divinity: Poochlihoochli as well as Hoochlipoochli, Ahriman as well as Ormudz, Lucifer, Beelzebub and Apollyon as well as the Holy Trinity, the Scarlet Woman as well as Our Lady: in short as many demons as saints.

At first, however, this setting up against God of a rival deity with a contrary ideology was resented as a Manichean heresy, because plague, pestilence and famine, battle, murder and sudden death, were not regarded with horror as the work of Shelley's Almighty Fiend, but with awe as evidence of the terrible greatness of God, the fear of him being placed to his credit as the beginning of wisdom. The invention of Satan is a heroic advance on Jahvism. It is an attempt to solve the Problem of Evil, and at least faces the fact that evil *is* evil.

Thus the world, as we imagine it, is crowded with anthropomorphic supernatural beings of whose existence there is no scientific proof. None the less, without such belief the human race cannot be civilized and governed, though the ten per cent or so of persons mentally capable of civilizing and governing are mostly too clever to be imposed on by fairy tales, and in any case have to deal with hard facts as well as fancies and fictions.

MENDACITY COMPULSORY IN KINGCRAFT AND PRIESTCRAFT

This lands them in the quaintest moral dilemmas. It drives them to falsehoods, hypocrisies, and forgeries most distressing to their intellectual consciences. When the people demand miracles, worship relics, and will not obey any authority that does not supply them, the priest must create and nourish their faith by liquefying the blood of Saint Januarius, and saying Mass over a jawbone labelled as that of Saint Anthony of Padua. When the people believe that the earth is flat, immovable, and the centre of the universe, and Copernicus and Leonardo convince both Galileo the scientist and the Vatican that the earth is a planet of the sun, the Pope and the cardinals have to make Galileo recant and pretend that he believes what the people believe, because, if the Church admits that it has ever been mistaken, its whole authority will collapse, and civilization perish in anarchy. If Joshua could not make the sun stand still, there is a blunder in the Bible. When the Protestants blew the gaff to discredit the Vatican, and the secret could no longer be kept by forbidding Catholics to read the Bible, the people were not logical enough to draw subversive inferences. They swallowed the contradiction cheerfully.

Meanwhile the people had to be threatened with a posthumous eternity in a brimstone hell if they behaved in an uncivilized way. As burning brimstone could not hurt a spirit, they had to be assured that their bodies would be resurrected on a great Day of Judgment. But the official translators of the Bible in England were presently staggered by a passage in the Book of Job, in which that prophet declared that as worms would destroy his body, in the flesh he should not see God. Such a heresy, if published, would knock the keystone out of the arch of British civilization. There was nothing for it but to alter the word of God, making Job say that though worms would destroy his body yet in his flesh he should see God. The facts made this forgery necessary; but it was a forgery all the same.

A later difficulty was more easily got over. The

apostles were Communists so Red that St Peter actually struck a man and his wife dead for keeping back money from the common stock. The translators could not pretend that St Peter was a disciple of the unborn Adam Smith rather than of Jesus; so they let the narrative stand, but taught that Ananias and Sapphira were executed for telling a lie and not for any economic misdemeanor. This view was impressed on me in my childhood. I now regard it as a much graver lie than that of Ananias.

"The lie" said Ferdinand Lassalle "is a European Power." He might, however, have added that it is none the worse when it does a necessary job; for I myself have been a faker of miracles. Let me tell one of my old stories over again.

G. B. S. MIRACLE FAKER

When I was a vestryman I had to check the accounts of the Public Health Committee. It was a simple process: I examined one in every ten or so of the receipted accounts and passed it whilst my fellow members did the same; and so enough of the accounts got checked to make their falsification too risky.

As it happened, one which I examined was for sulphur candles to disinfect houses in which cases of fever had occurred. I knew that experiments had proved that the fumes of burning sulphur had no such effect. Pathogenic bacilli like them and multiply on them.

I put the case to the Medical Officer of Health, and asked why the money of the ratepayers should be spent on a useless fumigant. He replied that the sulphur was not useless: it was necessary. But, I urged, the houses are not being disinfected at all. "Oh yes they are" he said. "How?" I persisted. "Soap and water and sunshine" he explained. "Then why sulphur?" "Because the strippers and cleaners will not venture into an infected house unless we make a horrible stink in it with burning sulphur."

I passed the account. It was precisely equivalent to liquefying the blood of Saint Januarius.

Some twenty years later I wrote a play called Saint Joan in which I made an archbishop explain that a miracle is an event that creates faith, even if it is faked for that end. Had I not been a vulgar vestryman as well as a famous playwright I should not have thought of that. All playwrights should know that had I not suspended my artistic activity to write political treatises and work on political committees long enough to have written twenty plays, the Shavian idiosyncrasy which fascinates some of them (or used to) and disgusts the Art For Art's Sake faction, would have missed half its value, such as it is.

PARENTAL DILEMMAS

The first and most intimate of the moral dilemmas that arise from differences in mental ability are not between classes and Churches, but in the daily work of bringing up children. The difference between Einstein and an average ploughman is less troublesome than the difference between children at five, at ten, and at fifteen. At five the Church catechism is only a paradigm: I learnt it at that age and still remember its phrases; but it had no effect on my conduct. I got no farther with it critically than to wonder why it obliged me, when asked what my name was, to reply that it was N or M, which was not true.

What did affect my conduct was my nurse's threat

that if I was naughty or dirty the cock would come down the chimney. I confidently recommend this formula to all parents, nurses, and kindergarten teachers, as it effects its purpose and then dies a natural death, fading from the mind as the child grows out of it without leaving any psychic complexes.

But the same cannot be said for more complicated schemes of infant civilization. If they begin with Law's Serious Call, as many pious parents think they should, they may be worse than no scheme at all. I knew a man whose youth was made miserable by a dread of hell sedulously inculcated from his infancy. His reaction against it carried him into Socialism, whereupon he founded a Labor Church in which all the meetings began by calling on the speakers to pray: a demand which so took aback my Fabian colleagues that one of them began with "Heavenly Father: unaccustomed as I have been many years to address you, I *etc. etc.*" The Labor Church did not last; but the reaction did; and the last I heard of its founder was that he was helping the movement against Victorian prudery in a very practical way as a Nudist photographer, the basis of that prudery being the fact that the clothing, or rather upholstering, of Victorian women was much more aphrodisiac than their unadorned bodies.

As to the Socialist orator who parodied "Unaccustomed as I am to public speaking," he died in the bosom of the Roman Catholic Church.

I tell these anecdotes because they give an impression, better than any abstract argument could, of the way in which highly intelligent children of pious families, or of irreligious ones capable of nothing more intellectual than sport and sex, reacted against their bringing-up. One day, at a rehearsal of one of my plays, an actress who was a Roman Catholic consulted me in some distress because her adolescent son had become an atheist. I advised her not to worry; for as family religions have to be cast off as thoughtless habits before they can be replaced by genuine religious convictions, she might safely leave her son's case to God.

Edmund Gosse was the son of a Plymouth Brother, and was baptized by total immersion, of which he wrote a highly entertaining description in his book called Father and Son. The immersion had washed all the father's pious credulity out of the son. George Eliot, also piously brought up, began her reaction by translating Emil Strauss's Life of Jesus, which divested the worshipped Redeemer of supernatural attributes, and even questioned the sanity of his pretension to them.

THE ALL OR NOTHING COMPLEX

In those days we were all what I called Soot or Whitewash merchants, pilloried as All or Nothings in Ibsen's Brand. When one link in our mental chain snapped we did not pick up the sound links and join them, we threw the chain away as if all its links had snapped. If the story of Noah's Ark was a fable, if Joshua could not have delayed the sunset in the Valley of Ajalon, if the big fish could not have swallowed Jonah nor he survive in its belly, then nothing in the Bible was true. If Jehovah was a barbarous tribal idol, irreconcilable with the God of Micah, then there was no God at all, and the heavens were empty. On the other hand if Galileo, the man of science, knew better than Joshua, and Linneus and Darwin better than Moses, then everything that scientists said was true.

Thus the credulity that believed in the Garden of Eden with its talking serpent, and in the speeches of Balaam's ass, was not cured. It was simply transferred to Herbert Spencer and John Stuart Mill. The transfer was often for the worse, as when baptism by water and the spirit, consecrating the baptized as a soldier and a servant of the Highest, was replaced by the poisonous rite of vaccination on evidence that could not have imposed on any competent statistician, and was picked up by Jenner from a dairy farmer and his milkmaids.

CATHOLICISM IMPRACTICABLE

The lesson of this is that a totally Catholic Church or Communist State is an impossible simplification of social organization. It is contrary to natural history. No Church can reconcile and associate in common worship a Jehovah's Witness with William Blake, who called Jehovah Old Nobodaddy. Napoleon, who pointed to the starry sky and asked "Who made all that?" did not kneel beside those who replied that it made itself, or retorted "We dont know: and neither do you." I, as a Creative Evolutionist, postulate a creative Life Force or Evolutionary Appetite seeking power over circumstances and mental development by the method of Trial and Error, making mistake after mistake, but still winning its finally irresistible way. Where in the world is there a Church that will receive me on such terms, or into which I could honestly consent to be received? There are Shaw Societies; but they are not Catholic Churches in pretence, much less in reality. And this is exactly as it should be, because, as human mental capacity varies from grade to grade, those who cannot find a creed which fits their grade have no established creed at all, and are ungovernable unless they are naturally amiable Vicars of Bray supporting any government that is for the moment established. There are hosts of such creedless voters, acting strongly as a conservative force, and usefully stabilizing government as such. But they make reforms very difficult sometimes.

THE TARES AND THE WHEAT

I therefore appreciate the wisdom of Jesus's warning to his missionaries that if they tore up the weeds they would tear up the wheat as well, meaning that if they tried to substitute his gospel for that of Moses instead of pouring the new wine into the old bottles (forgive the Biblical change of metaphor) nothing would be left of either Jesus or Moses. As I put it, the conversion of savagery to Christianity is the conversion of Christianity to savagery.

This is as true as ever. Not only are the immediate black converts of our missionaries inferior in character both to the unconverted and the born converted, but all the established religions in the world are deeply corrupted by the necessity for adapting their original inspired philosophic creeds to the narrow intelligences of illiterate peasants and of children. Eight thousand years ago religion was carried to the utmost reach of the human mind by the Indian Jainists, who renounced idolatry and blood sacrifice long before Micah, and repudiated every pretence to know the will of God, forbidding even the mention of his name in the magnificent temples they built for their faith.

But go into a Jainist temple today: what do you find? Idols everywhere. Not even anthropomorphic idols but horse idols, cat idols, elephant idols and what not? The statues of the Jainist sages and saints, far from being contemplated as great seers, are worshipped as gods.

THE THIRTYNINE ARTICLES

For such examples it is not necessary to travel to Bombay. The articles of the Church of England begin with the fundamental truth that God has neither body, parts, nor passions, yet presently enjoin the acceptance as divine revelation of a document alleging that God exhibited his hind quarters to one of the prophets, and when he had resolved to destroy the human race as one of his mistakes, was induced to make an exception in the case of Noah and his family by a bribe of roast meat. Later articles instruct us to love our fellow-creatures, yet to obey an injunction to hold accursed all who do good works otherwise than in the name of Christ, such works being sinful. In one article it is at first assumed that the swallowing of a consecrated wafer is only the heathen rite of eating the god (transubstantiation) and as such abominable, and then that it is holy as a memorial of the last recorded supper of Jesus. No man can be ordained a minister of the Church of England unless he swears without any mental reservation that he believes these contradictions. I once held lightly that candidates of irresistible vocation might swear this blamelessly because they were under duress. But one day I was present at the induction of a rector. When the bishop asked the postulant to tell a flat lie which both of them knew to be a lie, and he told it without a blush, the impression made on me was so shocking that I have felt ever since that the Church of England must revise its articles at all hazards if it is to be credited with the intellectual honesty necessary to its influence and authority. Shake that authority, and churchgoing will be nothing more than parading in our best clothes every Sunday.

A HUNDRED RELIGIONS AND ONLY ONE SAUCE

As it is, Christianity has split into sects, persuasions, and Nonconformities in all directions. The Statesman's Year-Book has given up trying to list them. They range from Pillars of Fire, Jehovah's Witnesses, Plymouth Brothers, and Glasites, to Presbyterians, Methodists, Congregationalists, Baptists, Friends (Quakers), and Unitarians. Within the Established Church itself there are Ritualists, Anglo-Catholics who call their services Masses and never mention the Reformation, Laodicean Broad Churchmen, and Low Church Protestants. The Friends abhor ritual and dictated prayers, and repudiate cathedral services and Masses as playacting, whilst the Anglo-Catholics cannot think religiously without them. Presbyterians and Congregationalists differ from the clergy of the Established Church on the political issue of episcopal or lay Church government. The Unitarians reject the Trinity and deny deity to Jesus. Calvinists deny universal atonement, preached by our missionaries, who are practically all Independents.

Common to these irreconcilable faiths is the pretension that each is the true Catholic Church, and should hand over all whom it cannot convert to the State (the Secular Arm) to be exterminated for the crime of heresy by the cruellest possible methods, even to burning alive. This does not mean that all rulers who order such extermination are horribly cruel. "Bloody Mary" believed that heretics must be liquidated; but she was not responsible for the political circumstance that the secular criminal law was atrociously cruel, and that no other agency could effect the liquidation. Calvin agreed that Servetus must be killed; but he objected humanely to his being burned. Charles II, humane (indeed, as some think, too humane in his kindness to his dozen dogs and half dozen mistresses), could not question the necessity for punishing the Regicides with death; but he loathed the butchering of them in the hideous manner ordained centuries earlier for the punishment of William Wallace, and stopped it as soon as he dared. It was still unrepealed during my own lifetime; and has only just (1948) been repealed in Scotland.

So far I have not been imprisoned, as poorer men have been in my time, for blasphemy or apostasy. I am not technically an apostate, as I have never been confirmed; and my godparents are dead. But having torn some of the Thirtynine Articles to rags, I should have been pilloried and had my ears cropped had I lived in the days of the British Inquisition called the Star Chamber. Nowadays Nonconformity and Agnosticism are far too powerful electorally for such persecution. But the Blasphemy Laws are still available and in use against obscure sceptics, whilst I suffer nothing worse than incessant attempts to convert me. All the religions and their sects, Christian or Moslem, Buddhist or Shinto, Jain or Jew, call me to repentance, and ask me for subscriptions. I am not so bigoted as to dismiss their experiences as the inventions of liars and the fancies of noodles. They are evidence like any other human evidence; and they force me to the conclusion that every grade of human intelligence can be civilized by providing it with a frame of reference peculiar to its mental capacity, and called a religion.

THE MARXIST CHURCH

The Marxist Church, called Cominform, is like all the other Churches, Having ceased to believe in the beneficently interfering and overruling God of Adam Smith and Voltaire, no less than in the vicarage of the Pope and his infallibility in council with the College of Cardinals, Cominform makes Karl Marx its Deity and the Kremlin his Vatican. It worships his apostles at its conventicles and in its chapels, with Das Kapital as its Bible and gospel, just as Cobdenist Plutocracy used to make a Bible of Adam Smith's Wealth of Nations with its gospel of The Economic Harmonies and its policy of Free Trade.

I am myself much idolized. I receive almost daily letters from devout Shavians who believe that my income is unlimited, my knowledge and wisdom infinite, my name a guarantee of success for any enterprise, my age that of Jesus at his death, and the entire Press at my command, especially The Times, of which I am assumed to be the proprietor.

If this is not idolatry the word has no meaning. The fact that I am ascertainably, and indeed conspicuously, only a superannuated (not supernatural) journalist and playwright does not shake the faith of my idolaters in the least. Facts count for nothing. I am told that I should be shot in Russia if I dared to pontificate against the Government there as I often do here, and that Freedom of the Press, the glory of England, does not and cannot exist under Communist tyranny.

SHOULD I BE SHOT IN RUSSIA?

As a matter of fact the Russian newspapers are full of complaints and grievances. There is a Government Department whose function it is to receive and deal with such complaints. Here in England I, an old journalist and agitator, know only too well that both platform and press are gagged by such an irresponsible tyranny of partisan newspaper proprietors and shamelessly mendacious advertizers, and by the law against seditious and blasphemous libel, that my speeches were never reported, and my letters and articles inserted only when I could combine what I believed and wanted to say with something that the paper wanted to have said, or when I could disguise it as an attractively readable art criticism, the queer result being that my reputation was made in Conservative papers whilst the Liberal, Radical, and Socialist editors dared not mention my name except in disparagement and repudiation. I owe more of my publicity to The Times than to any other daily newspaper. The same is true of my Fabian colleagues. The Webbs, now in Westminster Abbey, never could get into the British daily newspapers. In Russia, when Fabians were despised there as bourgeois Deviators, the Webbs were translated by Lenin.

As a playwright I was held up as an irreligious pornographer, and as such a public enemy, not to say a thoroughpaced cad, for many years by an irresponsible censorship which could not be challenged in parliament or elsewhere. No such misfortune has happened to me in Russia.

What damns our foreign policy here is our ignorance of history of home affairs. In the imagination of our amateur politicians England is a Utopia in which everything and everybody is "free," and all other countries "police States." I, being Irish, know better.

To return to the inveteracy of idolatry. Ten years ago disciples of a rival celebrity were sending me portraits of an Austrian Messiah named Hitler, described by Mr Winston Churchill as a bloodthirsty guttersnipe, yet more fanatically deified in Germany than Horatio Bottomley in England.

One of the puzzles of history is whether Jesus, denounced by the ladies and gentlemen of his time as a Sabbath breaker, a gluttonous man, and a winebibber, and finally executed for rioting in the temple, really believed in his claim to be Messiah, or was forced to assume that character because he could not make converts on any other terms, just as Mahomet found that he could not govern the Arabs without inventing a very sensual paradise and a very disgusting hell to keep them in order. Whether he invented his conversations with the Archangel Gabriel, or, like Joan of Arc, really heard voices when he listened for the voice of God, we shall never know. I have just had a letter from a man who, having made repeated attempts to give up smoking, had failed, until one day, walking through Hyde Park, he heard a Gospel preacher cry "Listen for the voice of God and it will come to you." This stuck in his mind. He listened, not piously but experimentally; and sure enough a voice said to him "Quit smoking: quit smoking." This time he quitted without the smallest difficulty.

COMPATIBILITIES

Differences of creed must be tolerated, analyzed, discussed, and as far as possible reconciled. My postulate of a provident and purposeful Life Force that proceeds by trial-and-error, and makes mistakes with the best intentions, is not in effect irreconcilable with belief in a supernatural benignant Providence at war with a malignant Satan. We cannot "make our souls" in the same assembly; but in the same building we can. Therefore if our cathedrals and churches are to be open to all faiths, as they in fact are, for contemplation and soul making, their different rituals must be performed at different hours, as they are at the Albert Hall in London, the Usher Hall in Edinburgh, the Free Trade hall in Manchester, the Montford Hall in Leicester, and wherever two or three gathered together may hear Messiah or the great Masses of Bach and Beethoven on Sunday or Monday, and watch a boxing show on Tuesday or Wednesday. The rituals differ, but not enough to provoke their votaries to burn one another at the stake or refuse to dine together on occasion. The sporting peer who becomes famous as the owner of a Derby winner meets the winner of a Nobel Prize without the least embarrassment; and I have never suffered the smallest discourtesy except once in a Manchester club, and then only because my criticisms of Shakespear stopped this side of idolatry.

It may seem that between a Roman Catholic who believes devoutly in Confession and a modern freethinking scientist there can be neither sympathy nor co-operation. Yet there is no essential difference between Confession and modern Psychotherapy. The post-Freudian psychoanalyst relieves his patient of the torments of guilt and shame by extracting a confession of their hidden cause. What else does the priest do in the confessional, though the result is called cure by one and absolution by the other? What I, a Freethinker, call the Life Force, my pious neighbors call Divine Providence: in some respects a better name for it. Bread and wine are changed into living tissue by swallowing and digestion. If this is not transubstantiation what *is* transubstantiation? I have described the surprise of a Fabian lecturer on being asked to open a political meeting with prayer. When I was invited to address the most important Secular Society in England I found that I had to supply the sermon in a ritual of hymns and lessons in all respects like a religious Sunday service except that the lessons were from Browning and the hymns were aspirations to "join the choir invisible." Later on, when I attended a church service in memory of my wife's sister, and was disposed to be moved by it, the lesson was the chapter from the Bible which describes how the Israelites in captivity were instructed by a deified Jonathan Wild to steal the jewelry of the Egyptians before their flight into the desert. The Leicester Atheists were in fact more pious than the Shropshire Anglicans.

BOHEMIAN ANARCHISM

The anarchy which the priests feared when they gagged Galileo actually came to pass much more widely than the epidemics which the Medical Officer of Health dreaded when he gagged me about the sulphur candles. In my early days as a Socialist lecturer I was once opposed by a speaker who had been an apostle of Robert Owen's New Moral World, the first version of British Socialism. His ground was that too many of his fellow apostles took the new moral world as an emancipation from all the obligations of the old moral world, and were dishonest and licentious. Prominent in my own generation of

Marxists was one who, I believe, would have gone as a martyr to the scaffold or the stake rather than admit that God existed, or that Marx and Darwin were fallible. But when money or women were concerned, he was such a conscienceless rascal that he was finally blackballed by all the Socialist societies.

Do not misunderstand me. I am not stigmatizing all Owenites, Marxists, and Darwinists as immoral; but it must be borne in mind that all revolutionary and reform movements are recruited from those who are not good enough for the existing system as well as those who are too good for it. All such movements attract sinners as well as saints by giving them a prominence as platform orators and pamphleteers out of all proportion to their numbers and deserts. They justify their delinquencies as assertions of principle, and thus give Socialism a reputation for anarchism, irreligion, and sexual promiscuity which is association of ideas, not logic. No eminence in a specific department implies even ordinary ability in any other, nor does any specific personal depravity imply general depravity. I may fairly claim to be an adept in literature; but in dozens of other departments I am a duffer. I have often quoted a certain ex-Colonel who said to me "I know for certain that the Rector is the father of his housemaid's illegitimate child; and after that you may tell me that the Bible is true: I shall not believe you." It does not follow that the Colonel was not a military genius, nor the Rector an eloquent preacher and efficient clergyman.

Nevertheless we cannot legislate for every individual separately, nor provide a special policeman to keep him (or her) in order. All civilized persons except certified lunatics and incorrigible criminals must for elementary purposes be held equally capable and responsible. Those who cannot read any book more abstruse than Esop's Fables, nor get beyond the multiplication table (if so far) in mathematics, can understand the Ten Commandments well enough to be legislated for in the mass.

SHAM DEMOCRACY

In the face of these hard facts most of the current interpretations of the word Democracy are dangerous nonsense. The fundamental notion that the voice of the people is the voice of God is a sample. What people? Were Solon and Sully, Voltaire and Adam Smith, Plato and Aristotle, Hobbes and Tom Paine and Marx, the people? Were Lord George Gordon, Titus Oates, and Horatio Bottomley the people? Were General Roberts and Henry Irving, nominated by Gallup poll as ideal rulers, the people? Am I the people? Was Ruskin? Were Moses, Jesus, Peter and Paul, Mahomet, Brigham Young? If their voices were all voices of God, God must be a very accomplished ventriloquist.

Democracy means government in the interest of everybody. It most emphatically does not mean government BY everybody. All recorded attempts at that have not only failed but rapidly developed into despotisms and tyrannies. The trade union secretary elected by everybody in his Union, the pirate captain whose crew can make him walk the plank at any moment, are the most absolute despots on earth. Cromwell tried government by a parliament of elected saints and had to turn it into the street as Bismarck turned the Frankfort Parliament in 1862. He tried an oligarchy of majors general, but finally had to make himself Lord Protector and govern despotically as much as it was possible to govern Englishmen at all, which, as he bitterly complained, was not very much. Much or little, votes for everybody, politically called Adult Suffrage, always produces anarchy, which, being unbearable, produces by reaction overwhelming majorities in favor of Regressions called Restorations, or Napoleonic Emperors and South American dictator-presidents. Democratic government of the people by the people, professed ideologically nowadays by all Governments and Oppositions, has never for a moment existed.

Real democracy leaves wide open the question as to which method best secures it: monarchies, oligarchies, parliaments nominated or elected with or without proportional representation, restricted franchise, intervals between general elections, or other "checks and balances" devised to prevent glaring abuses of virtually irresponsible power. None of them has ever made Voltaire's *Monsieur Tout le Monde* master of the situation. Adult suffrage did not prevent two so-called world wars and a royal abdication on which the people were no more consulted than I was. Political adventurers and "tin Jesuses" rose like rockets to dictatorships and fell to earth like sticks, or were succeeded, as Napoleon was, by Bourbonic bosses. The Russian Bolsheviks, having invented the Soviet System, and brought their country to the verge of ruin and a little over by All or Nothing Catastrophism, were forced by the facts to make room in Bolshevism for more private enterprise than there is in England. The moment it did so, the basic difference between British and Russian economic policy vanished or criss-crossed. Lenin and Stalin had to cry *Laisser-faire* to all the enterprises not yet ripe for nationalization. The Labor Party in England nationalized as many industries as it could manage, and regulated private employers, controlled prices, rationed food and clothing, imposed purchase taxes on luxuries, and increased the bureaucracy both in numbers and power whilst jealously restricting official salaries more grudgingly with a view to equality of income than the Kremlin. Stalin's Russo-Fabian slogan, Socialism in a Single Country, is countered by Churchill's manifestos of Plutocratic Capitalism Everywhere and Down with Communism, which is more than Trotsky claimed for international Marxism.

With all this staring them in the face, and no intention whatever of going back to turnpike roads, toll bridges, private detectives and prizefighters for police, sixpenny linkmen for municipal electric lighting, cadis under palm trees for judges, condottieri and privateers for national defence, profiteers for Exchequer Chancellors: in short, the substitution of private enterprise for the omnipresent Communism without which our civilization could not endure for a week, our politicians and partisans keep shouting their abhorrence of Communism as if their Parties were cannibal tribes fighting and eating one another instead of civilized men driven by sheer pressure of facts into sane co-operation.

THE POLITICAL TIME LAG

The worst features of our sham-democratic misgovernment are caused, not by incurable mental incapacity, but by an ignorance that is essentially mathematical. None of our politicians seems to know that political action, like all earthly action, must take place in a world of four dimensions, not three. The fourth dimension is that of Time. To ignore it is to be pre-Einstein, which is as out-of-date as to be pre-Marx. Fortunately it can be taught, just as the theories of rent and value can be taught; and those who learn it see that our British parliamentary system is far too slow for twentieth century social organization. The Soviet system in Russia outstrips it because, being faster, it is more immediately responsive to the continual need for reforms and adaptations to changing circumstances. It includes all the conventional democratic checks and safeguards against despotism now so illusory, and gives them as much effectiveness as their airy nature is capable of. Incidentally it gives Stalin the best right of any living statesman to the vacant Nobel peace prize, and our diplomatists the worst. This will shock our ignoramuses as a stupendous heresy and a mad paradox. Let us see.

When the horrors of unregulated selfish private enterprise forced both Conservatives and Cobdenists to devise and pass the Factory Acts, it took the British Parliament a time lag of 50 years to make them effective. Home Rule for Ireland took thirty years to get through Parliament, and was decided after all by a sanguinary civil war.

In the simplest home affairs the time lag extends to centuries. For instance, the practice of earth burial, with its cemeteries crowding the living out by the dead, its poisonous slow putrefactions, its risk of burial alive, and its cost, should be forbidden and replaced by cremation. It was discussed 80 years ago when I was a boy. Yet not even the cremation of an Archbishop (Temple: one of our best) has overcome our dread of doing anything that everyone else is not yet doing, nor the bigoted opposition of the Churches which preach the Resurrection of The Body without considering that a body can be resurrected from dust and ashes as feasibly as from a heap of maggots. Our crematory gardens of rest are still countable only in dozens, and cremations only in thousands, even in big cities. In lesser towns the figure is zero.

ADULT SUFFRAGE IS MOBOCRACY

Adult Suffrage is supposed to be a substitute for civil war. The idea is that if two bodies of citizens differ on any public point they should not fight it out, but count heads and leave the decision to the majority. The snag in this is that as the majority is always against any change, and it takes at least thirty years to convert it, whilst only ten per cent or thereabouts of the population has sufficient mental capacity to foresee its necessity or desirability, a time lag is created during which the majority is always out-of-date. It would be more sensible to leave the decision to the minority if a qualified one could be selected and empanelled. Democratic government needs a Cabinet of Thinkers (Politbureau) as well as a Cabinet of Administrators (Commissars). Adult Suffrage can never supply this, especially in England, where intellect is hated and dreaded, not wholly without reason, as it is dangerous unless disciplined and politically educated; whilst acting and oratory, professional and amateur, are popular, and are the keys to success in elections.

THE MARXIST CLASS WAR

The conflict of economic interest between proprietors and proletarians was described by H. G. Wells as past and obsolete when it had in fact just flamed up in Spain from a bandying of strikes and lock-outs into raging sanguinary civil war, as it had already done in Russia, with the difference that in Russia the proletarians won, whereas in Spain they were utterly defeated through lack of competent ministers and commanders.

The struggle is confused by a cross conflict between feudal and plutocratic ideologies. The feudal proprietariat is all for well policed private property and *Laisser-faire*, the proletariat all for State industry with abolition of feudal privilege and replacement of private or "real" property by property on social conditions; so that a proprietor shall hold his land, his shares, his spare money (called capital) on the same terms as his umbrella: namely that he shall not use it to break his neighbor's head nor evict him from his country and homestead to make room for sheep or deer.

Both parties insist on the supreme necessity for increased production; but as the Plutocrats do all they can to sabotage State industry, and the Proletarians to sabotage private enterprise, the effect is to hinder production to the utmost and demonstrate the vanity of two-party government.

WHAT IS TO BE DONE?

I am asked every week what is my immediate practical remedy for all this. Also what is my solution of the riddle of the universe? When I reply that I dont know, and have no panacea, I am told that I am not constructive, implying that practical people are constructive and do know. If they are and do, why are we in our present perilous muddle?

I can only suggest certain definite and practicable experiments in social organization, on a provisional hypothesis or frame of reference (a necessary tool of thought) that will serve also as a credible religion. For nomenclatory purpose I may be called a Fabian Communist and Creative Evolutionist if I must have a label of some sort. At present I am stuck all over with labels like a tourist's trunk. I cannot call myself the Way and the Life, having only a questionable hypothesis or two to offer; but that is the heroic label that all Worldbetterers aspire to, and some have even dared to claim.

Some 30 years or so ago I wrote a play called As Far As Thought Can Reach. Perhaps I should have called it as far as my thought could reach; but I left this to be taken for granted.

POLITICAL MATHEMATICS

What we need desperately is an anthropometric slide-rule by which we can classify and select our rulers, most of whom are at present either rich nonentities, venal careerists, or round pegs in square holes. Now it is no use my singing at the top of my voice that democracy is impossible without scientific anthropometry. I might as well be the Town Crier offering a reward for an imaginary lost dog. How are we to begin?

Sixty years ago Sidney Webb created a Progressive Party on the new County Councils by sending to all the candidates at the first election a catechism setting forth a program of Socialist reforms, and demanding whether they were in favor of them or not. As Nature abhors a vacuum the program flew into empty heads and won the election for them. This, as far as I know, was the first non-party test ever applied to membership of a public authority in England since benefit of clergy was legal and the professions were closed to all but members of the Church of England. This at least provided some evidence as to whether the candidate could read, write, and even translate a little dog Latin. It was better than no test at all.

But it is now quite insufficient in view of the enormous increase of public functions involved by modern Socialism. We already have in our professional and university examinations virtual panels of persons tested and registered as qualified to exercise ruling functions as Astronomers Royal, Archbishops, Lord Chief Justices, and public schoolmasters. Even police constables are instructed. Yet for the ministers who are supported to direct and control them we have no guarantee that they can read or write, or could manage a baked potato stall successfully.

Now people who cannot manage baked potato stalls nor peddle bootlaces successfully cannot manage public departments manned with school-tested permanent executives. Consequently these executives constitute a bureaucracy, not a democracy. Elections do not touch them: the people have no choice. When they have passed the competitive examinations by which they are tested, they are there for life, practically irremovable. And so government goes on.

Unfortunately the tests tend to exclude born rulers. Knowledge of languages, dead and foreign, puts a Mezzofanti, useless as a legislator or administrator, above a Solon who knows no language but his own. It puts facility in doing set sums in algebra by rule of thumb above inborn mathematical comprehension by statesmen who cannot add up their washing bills accurately. Examinations by elderly men of youths are at least thirty years out of date: in economics, for instance, the candidate who has been taught that the latest views are those of Bastiat and Cobden, ignoring those of Cairnes and Mill, is successful, especially if he ranks those of Karl Marx as blasphemous, and history as ending with Macaulay. The questions that will be asked and the problems set at the examinations, with the answers and solutions that will be accepted by the elderly examiners, soon become known, enabling professional crammers to coach any sixth form schoolboy to pass in them to the exclusion of up-to-date candidates who are ploughed because they know better than their examiners, yet are as unconscious of their mental superiority as a baby is of the chemistry by which it performs the complicated chemical operation of digesting its food.

Evidently the present curriculum and method should be radically changed. When I say this, the reply is "Granted; but how?" Unfortunately I dont know; and neither does anyone else; but as somebody must make a beginning here are a few of the best suggestions I can think of.

RENT AND VALUE THE ASS'S BRIDGES

First, there is the economic Ass's Bridge: the theory of rent, and with it inextricably the theory of exchange value. Unless a postulant for first class honors in politics can write an essay shewing that he (or she) has completely mastered these impartial physical and mathematical theories, the top panel must be closed against him. This would plough Adam Smith, Ricardo, Ruskin, and Marx; but they could read up the subject and return to the charge. Stanley Jevons would pass it, though after he had knocked out Ricardo and the rest with his correct mathematical theory he taught that a State parcel post is an impossibility. For when he returned to England after serving in the Gold Escort in Australia, and became a university professor, he taught anything and everything the old examiners expected him to teach, and so might have failed in a character test.

STATISTICS VITAL

The panel for health authorities should require a stringent test in statistics. At present the most unbearable tyranny is that of the State doctor who has been taught to prescribe digitalis and immobilization, plus a diet of alcoholic stimulants, for heart disease, and to amputate limbs and extirpate tonsils as carpenters and plumbers deal with faulty chair legs and leaking pipes. He may, like Jenner, be so ignorant of the rudiments of statistics as to believe that the coincidence of a decrease in the number of deaths from a specific disease following the introduction of an alleged prophylactic proves that the prophylactic is infallible and that compulsion to use it will abolish the disease. Statisticians, checking the figures by the comparisons they call controls, may prove up to the hilt that the prophylactic not only fails to cure but kills. When vaccination was made compulsory as a preventive of smallpox the controls were cholera, typhus, and endemic fever: all three rampant when I was born. They were wiped out by sanitation; whilst under compulsory vaccination, enforced by ruthless persecution, smallpox persisted and culminated in two appalling epidemics (1871 and 1881) which gave vaccination its deathblow, though its ghost still walks because doctors are ignorant of statistics, and, I must add, because it is lucrative, as it calls in the doctor when the patient is not ill. In the army some thirty inoculations are practically compulsory; and vaccination is made a condition of admission to the United States and other similarly deluded countries. The personal outrage involved is so intolerable that it will not be in the least surprising if vaccination officers are resisted, not with facts and figures but with fists, if not pistols.

The remedy, however, is not to compel medical students to qualify as statisticians, but to establish a Ministry of Statistics with formidable powers of dealing with lying advertisements of panaceas, prophylactics, elixirs, immunizers, vaccines, antitoxins, vitamins, and professedly hygienic foods and drugs and drinks of all sorts. Such a public department should be manned not by chemists analyzing the advertized wares and determining their therapeutical value, but by mathematicians criticizing their statistical pretensions. As there is an enormous trade in such wares at present the opposition to such a Ministry will be lavishly financed; but the need for it is too urgent to allow any consideration to stand in its way; for the popular demand for miracles and deities has been transferred to "marvels of science" and doctors, by dupes who think they are emancipating themselves from what in their abysmal ignorance they call medieval barbarism when they are in fact exalting every laboratory vivisector and quack immunizer above Jesus and St James. Mrs Eddy, a much sounder hygienist than Jenner, Pasteur, Lister, and their disciples, had to call her doctrine Christian Science instead of calling the popular faith in pseudo-scientific quackery Anti-Christian Nonsense.

THE ESTHETIC TEST

The next test I propose may prove more surprising. For the top panel I would have postulants taken into a gallery of unlabelled reproductions of the famous pictures of the world, and asked how many of the painters they can name at sight, and whether they have anything to say about them, or are in any way interested in them. They should then be taken into a music room furnished with a piano, and asked to sing or whistle or hum or play as many of the leading themes of the symphonies, concertos, string quartets, and opera tunes of Mozart and Beethoven, and the Leitmotifs of Wagner, as they can remember. Their performances may be execrable; but that will not matter: the object is not to test their executive skill but to ascertain their knowledge of the best music and their interest in and enjoyment of it, if any.

I would have them taken then into a library stocked with the masterpieces of literature. They should be asked which of them they had ever read, and whether they read anything but newspapers and detective stories. If the answer be Yes, they can be invited to indicate the books they know.

I am quite aware of the possibility of misleading results. Dr Inge, an unquestionably top notcher, when he was Dean of St Paul's and had to deal with the music there, expressed a doubt whether the Almighty really enjoys "this perpetual serenading." William Morris, equally *honoris causa*, could not tolerate a piano in his house. When one was played in his hearing by his neighbors, he would throw up his window and roar curses at them.

But if Dr Inge had been brought up on Beethoven instead of on Jackson's Te Deum, he might have preferred Wagner to Plotinus; and Morris was deeply affected by medieval music, and quite right in loathing the modern steel grand piano of his day as a noisy nuisance. Still, some of the postulants will be tone deaf or color blind. Their comments may be none the less valuable as evidence of their mental capacity.

SUBCONSCIOUS CAPACITIES

More baffling at present are the cases in which the judges will be faced with apparently vacant minds, and met, not with an epigram of which no mediocrity would be capable, but with a blank "I dont know what you are talking about." This will not prove that the postulant is a nitwit: it will raise the question whether the question is beyond his mental powers or so far within them that he is unconscious of them. Ask anyone how water tastes, and you will get the reply of Pinero's Baron Croodle "Water is a doglike and revolting beverage" or simply "Water has no taste," or, intelligently, "Water has no taste for me, because it is always in my mouth." Ask an idle child what it is doing, and it will not claim that it is breathing and circulating its blood: it will say it is doing nothing. When we co-ordinate our two eyes to look at anything, we do not notice that the images of everything else within our range of vision are doubled. When we listen to an orchestra or an organ we are deaf to the accompanying thunder of beats, partials, and harmonics. Attention is a condition of consciousness. Without it we may miss many "self-evident truths." How then are we to distinguish between the unconscious genius and the idiot?

Again, I do not know; but we can at least call in the professional psychotherapists whose business it is to dig up the buried factors of the mind and bring them to light and consciousness. The technique of this therapy has developed since the days when, being asked what the word Ass suggested to me, I replied

Dogberry and Balaam. It suggested, not facts and experiences, but fictions. Put the word Calculus to a surgeon and he will name the disease called stone, from which Newton suffered. Put it to a mathematician and he will cite the method of measurement Newton and Leibniz elaborated.

EXAMINATIONS AND SCHOOLMASTERS

I avoid calling the tests examinations because the word suggests the schoolmaster, the enemy of mankind at present, though when by the rarest chance he happens to be a born teacher, he is a priceless social treasure. I have met only one who accepted my challenge to say to his pupils "If I bore you you may go out and play." Set an average schoolmaster or schoolmarm to test for the panels, and the result will be a set of examination papers with such questions and problems as "Define the square root of minus one in Peano terms; and if an empty aeroplane travelling at supersonic speed takes a thousand light years to reach the nearest star, how long will it take a London motor bus keeping schedule time to travel from Millbank to Westminster Bridge with a full complement of passengers? Give the name, date, and locality of the birth of Beethoven's great grandmother's cousin's stepsister; and write a tonal fugue on the following theme. Give the family names of Domenichino and Titian; and write an essay not exceeding 32 words on their respective styles and influence on Renaissance art. Give the dates of six of Shakespear's plays, with the acreage occupied by (*a*) the Globe Theatre, (*b*) the Shoreditch Curtain theatre, and (*c*) the Blackfriars theatre. Estimate the age of Ann Hathaway at her marriage with Shakespear.

Enumerate the discrepancies between the narratives of Homer, Plutarch, Holinshed, and Shakespear. Was Bacon the author of Shakespear's plays (5000 words)?"

THE WRONG SORT OF MEMORY

And so on. The schoolmaster does not teach. He canes or impositions or "keeps in" the pupils who cannot answer pointless questions devised to catch them out. Such questions test memory, but secure victory in examinations for the indiscriminate encyclopedic memory, which is the most disabling of all memories. Universities are infested with pedants who have all recorded history at their tongues' ends, but can make no use of it except to disqualify examinees with the priceless gift of forgetting all events that do not matter. Were I to keep always in mind every experience of my 93 years living and reading I should go mad. I am often amazed when, having to refer to old papers filed away and forgotten, I am reminded of transactions which I could have sworn had never occurred, and meetings with notable persons I have no recollection of having ever seen. But this does not disconcert me. Kipling's "Lest we forget" is often less urgent than "Lest we remember."

Certainly, those who forget everything are impossible politically; and I have often wished I had the memory of Macaulay or Sidney Webb, or the patience of my player collaborators who have to memorize speeches I have myself written but of which at rehearsal I cannot quote two words correctly; but on the whole the people who remember everything they ought to forget are, if given any authority, more dangerous than those who forget some things they had better remember. Dr Inge, commenting on the Irish question, pointed out how difficult is the common government of a nation which never remembers and one which never forgets.

Anyhow, we must keep schoolmasters away from the panel tests. My own school experience has biased me on this point. When the time came to teach me mathematics I was taught simply nothing: I was set to explain Euclid's diagrams and theorems without a word as to their use or history or nature. I found it so easy to pick this up in class that at the end of the half year I was expected to come out well in the examinations. I entirely disgraced myself because the questions did not pose the propositions but gave only their numbers, of which I could recollect only the first five and the one about the square of the hypothenuse.

The next step was algebra, again without a word of definition or explanation. I was simply expected to do the sums in Colenso's schoolbook.

Now an uninstructed child does not dissociate numbers or their symbols from the material objects it knows quite well how to count. To me *a* and *b*, when they meant numbers, were senseless unless they mean butter and eggs and a pound of cheese. I had enough mathematical faculty to infer that if $a=b$ and $b=c$, a must equal c. But I had wit enough to infer that if a quart of brandy equals three Bibles, and three Bibles the Apostles' Creed, the Creed is worth a quart of brandy, manifestly a *reductio ad absurdum.*

My schoolmaster was only the common enemy of me and my schoolfellows. In his presence I was forbidden to move, or to speak except in answer to his questions. Only by stealth could I relieve the torture of immobility by stealthily exchanging punches (called "the coward's blow") with the boy next me. Had my so-called teacher been my father, and I a child under six, I could have asked him questions, and had the matter explained to me. As it was, I did exactly what the Vatican felt everybody would do if Galileo picked a hole in the Bible. I concluded that mathematics are blazing nonsense, and thereafter made a fool of myself even in my twenties when I made the acquaintance of the editor of Biometrika, Karl Pearson, who maintained that no theory could be valid until it was proved mathematically. I threw in his teeth my conviction that his specialty was an absurdity. Instead of enlightening me he laughed (he had an engaging smile and was a most attractive man) and left me encouraged in my ignorance by my observation that though he was scrupulous and sceptical when counting and correlating, he was as credulous and careless as any ordinary mortal in selecting the facts to be counted. Not until Graham Wallas, a born teacher, enlightened me, did I understand mathematics and realize their enormous importance.

SOME RESULTS

Is it to be wondered at that with such school methods masquerading as education, millions of scholars pass to their graves unhonored and unsung whilst men and women totally illiterate, or at most selftaught to read and write in their late teens, rise to eminence whilst "university engineers" are drugs in the labor market compared to those who go straight from their elementary schools to the factory, speaking slum English and signing with a mark. Experienced employers tell us they prefer uneducated workmen. Senior Wranglers and Double-Firsts and Ireland Scholars see no more than costermongers in the fact that a saving of 1 per cent per minute of time in writing English means 525,000 per cent per year, and that ten times that much could be saved by adding 15 letters to the alphabet. It took a world war to establish summer time after it had been contemptuously rejected by our pundits as a negligible fad. The fact that by adding two digits to our arithmetic tables we could make 16 figures do the work of twenty (a colossal saving of time for the world's bookkeeping) appeals no more to winners of the mathematical tripos than the infinitesimal calculus to a newly born infant. Political controversy is now (1949) raging on the nationalization of our industries; yet not one word is said nor a figure given as to its basic advantage in the fact that coal can be had in Sunderland for the trouble of picking it up from the sands at low tide, whilst in Whitehaven it has to be hewn out under the sea, miles from the pit head, or that land in the City of London fetches fabulous prices per square foot and twenty miles off will hardly support a goose on the common, thus making it impossible without nationalization to substitute cost-of-production prices, averaged over the whole country, for prices loaded with enormous rents for the proprietors of London land and Seaham mines, not equivalently surtaxed. Doctors and dental surgeons who excuse their high fees on the ground that they are working until half past four in the afternoon earning rent for their landlords, and only the rest of the day for themselves and their families, are so incapable of putting two and two together politically that they vote like sheep for the landlords, and denounce land municipalization as robbery. Had the late famous President Franklin Roosevelt, a thoroughly schooled gentleman-amateur Socialist, been taught the law of rent, his first attempts at The New Deal would not have failed so often. I could cite dozens of examples of how what our Cabinet ministers call Democracy, and what I call Mobocracy, places in authority would-be rulers who assure us that they can govern England, plus the Commonwealth, plus Western Europe, and finally the world, when as a matter of fact they could not manage a village shop successfully.

CAPITAL ACCUMULATION

Capital is spare money saved by postponement of consumption. To effect this in a private property system some people must be made so rich that when they are satiated with every purchasable luxury they have still a surplus which they can invest without privation. In the nineteenth century this arrangement was accepted as final and inevitable by able and benevolent public men like Thomas de Quincey, Macaulay, Austin, Cobden, and Bright, until Karl Marx dealt it a mortal blow by shewing from official records that its delusive prosperity masked an abyss of plague, pestilence and famine, battle, murder, compulsory prostitution, and premature death. Ferdinand Lassalle in Germany had already demonstrated the injustice of its "iron law of wages."

ENGLAND'S SHAMEFACED LEADERSHIP

England was by no means silent on the subject. Marx's invective, though it rivalled Jeremiah's, was pale beside the fierce diatribes of Ruskin, who puzzled his readers by describing himself as an old Tory and the Reddest of Red Communists. Carlyle called our boasted commercial prosperity shooting Niagara, and dismissed Cobdenist Free Trade as Godforsaken nonsense. The pious Conservative Lord Shaftesbury and the Radical atheist demagogue Bradlaugh were at one in their agitation for Acts in restraint of the prevalent ruthless exploitation of labor. Robert Owen had called for a New Moral world as loudly as any of our present post war Chadbands. It was he who made current the word Socialism as the alternative to Capitalist plutocracy. When the Russian Bolsheviks went ruinously wrong by ignoring "the inevitability of gradualness" and attempting a catastrophic transfer of industry and agriculture from private to public ownership, it was the Englishman Sidney Webb and his Fabians who corrected them and devised the new economic policy Lenin had to announce, and Stalin to put in practice. Thus Englishmen can claim to have been pioneers in the revolutionary development of political organization since Cobdenism conquered us.

Unfortunately, whenever English parties effect an advance, they are so ashamed of it that they immediately throw away all credit for it by protesting that they are respectable citizens who would never dream of changing anything, and shouting their abhorrence of all the wicked foreigners who are in effect taking their advice. And then they are surprised when their disciples, especially in Russia, regard them as enemies, and the Marxist Left wins more and more votes from them.

THE THREATENING FUTURE: HOMILIES NO USE

While the time lag lasts the future remains threatening. The problem of optimum wealth distribution, which Plutocracy, with its inherent class warfare, has hopelessly failed to solve, will not yield to the well-intentioned Utopian amateurs who infest our parliaments and parties, imagining that it can be solved by giving all of us according to our needs and balancing the account by taking from each of us according to our productive capacity. They might as well decree that we shall do unto others as we would have them do to us, or achieve the greatest good for the greatest number, or soothe our souls with exhortations to love oneanother. Homilies cut no ice in administrative councils: the literary talent and pulpit eloquence that has always been calling for a better world has never succeeded, though it has stolen credit for many changes forced on it by circumstances and natural selection. The satirical humor of Aristophanes, the wisecracks of Confucius, the precepts of the Buddha, the parables of Jesus, the theses of Luther, the *jeux d'esprit* of Erasmus and Montaigne, the Utopias of More and Fourier and Wells, the allegories of Voltaire, Rousseau, and Bunyan, the polemics of Leibniz and Spinoza, the poems of Goethe, Shelley, and Byron, the manifesto of Marx and Engels, Mozart's Magic Flute and Beethoven's Ode to Joy, with the music dramas of Wagner, to say nothing of living seers of visions and dreamers of dreams: none of these esthetic feats have made Reformations or Revolutions; and most of them, as far as they have been thrown into the hands of the common people as the Protestant Reformation threw the Bible, have been followed by massacres, witch hunts, civil and international wars of religion, and all forms of persecution, from petty boycotts to legalized burnings at the stake and breakings on the wheel, highly popular as public entertainments. The nineteenth century, which believed itself to be the climax of civilization, of Liberty, Equality, and Fraternity, was convicted by Karl Marx of being the worst and wickedest on record; and the twentieth, not yet half through, has been ravaged by two so-called world wars culminating in the atrocity of the atomic bomb.

As long as atomic bomb manufacture remains a trade secret known to only one State, it will be the mainstay of Peace because all the States (including the one) will be afraid of it. When the secret is out atomic warfare will be barred as poison gas was in 1938–45; and war will be possible as before. How that may happen is the subject of the first two farfetched fables that follow.

AYOT SAINT LAWRENCE, *1948–9*

FIRST FABLE

A public park on a fine summer afternoon. Chairs for hire scattered about the sward.

A young woman of respectable appearance arrives and seats herself. A park attendant approaches her; takes two-pence from her; says "Kew," short for "Thank-you"; and gives her a ticket.

A well-dressed young man enters and takes the nearest chair. The attendant takes two-pence as before, and passes on.

YOUNG MAN. Excuse me. Would you rather I sat farther away?

YOUNG WOMAN. As you please. I dont care where you sit.

YOUNG MAN. I hope you dont think me intrusive?

YOUNG WOMAN. I am not thinking about you at all. But you may talk to me if you want to. I dont mind.

YOUNG MAN. Well, I certainly do want to talk to you. In fact that is why I took this chair.

YOUNG WOMAN. I thought so. Well, talk away. What have you to say to me?

YOUNG MAN. Ive never seen you before. But at first sight I find you irresistibly attractive.

YOUNG WOMAN. Lots of men do. What of it?

YOUNG MAN. Some women find me attractive. Are you married?

YOUNG WOMAN. No. Are you?

YOUNG MAN. No. Are you engaged?

YOUNG WOMAN. No. What is it to you whether I am engaged or not?

YOUNG MAN. Need you ask? Ive got into this conversation with a view to our possible marriage.

YOUNG WOMAN. Nothing doing. I'll not marry.

YOUNG MAN. It is odd that so many attractive women are unmarried. Dull ugly frumps never seem to have any difficulty in finding mates. Why wont you marry? I am available.

YOUNG WOMAN. My father was shot in the Great War that now seems such a little one. My eldest brother was killed in Normandy when we were liberating France there. His wife and children were blown to bits by a bomb that wrecked the whole street they lived in. Do you think I'll bear children for that?

YOUNG MAN. They died for England. They made war to end war. Dont you admire bravery? Dont you love your country?

YOUNG WOMAN. What use is bravery now when any coward can launch an atomic bomb? Until men are wise and women civilized they had better not be born. At all events I shall not bring them into this wicked world to kill and be killed.

An excited middle-aged man comes along waving a newspaper and cheering.

M. A. M. Hurrah! Have you heard the news?

YOUNG MAN. No. Whats happened?

M. A. M. No more war. The United Nations have abolished it.

YOUNG MAN [*disparagingly*] Hmm! May I have a look at your paper?

M. A. M. Here it is in black and white. You may keep it. I'll buy another. Hurrah! hurrah!! hurrah!!!

He hands over the paper and rushes away, cheering.

YOUNG WOMAN. What does it say?

YOUNG MAN [*reading the headlines*] "THE WORLD AT PEACE AT LAST. WASHINGTON AGREES. MOSCOW AGREES. CHINA AGREES. THE WESTERN UNION AGREES. THE FEDERALISTS AGREE. THE COMMUNISTS AGREE. THE FASCISTS AGREE. ATOMIC BOMB MANUFACTURE MADE A CAPITAL CRIME. UNIVERSAL SECURITY GUARANTEED."

YOUNG WOMAN. Have the armies been disbanded? Have the military academies been closed? Has conscription been abolished?

YOUNG MAN. It doesnt say. Oh yes: here is a stop press paragraph. "ARMIES WILL IN FUTURE BE CALLED WORLD POLICE. NO MORE CONSCRIPTION." Hm!

YOUNG WOMAN. You dont seem pleased.

YOUNG MAN. I dont swallow all that rot about no more war. Men will always fight even if they have nothing to fight with but their fists. And the women will egg them on.

YOUNG WOMAN. What does the leading article say?

YOUNG MAN [*turning to the leader page and quoting*] "Truce of God begins a new chapter in the history of the globe. The atomic bomb has reduced war to absurdity; for it threatens not only both victors and vanquished but the whole neutral world. We do not as yet know for certain that the bomb that disintegrated Hiroshima is not still at work disintegrating. The weather has been curiously unusual ever since. But no nation will ever venture on atomic warfare again."

YOUNG WOMAN. Do you believe that?

YOUNG MAN. Yes; but it wont stop war. In 1914 the Germans tried poison gas; and so did we. But the airmen who dropped it on the cities could not stay in the air for long; and when they had to come down they found the streets full of the gas, because poison gas is heavier than air and takes many days to disperse. So in the last war gas was not used; and atomic bombs wont be used in the next one.

YOUNG WOMAN. Oh! So you think there will be a next one.

YOUNG MAN. Of course there will, but not with atomic bombs. There is no satisfaction in seeing the world lit up by a blinding flash, and being burnt to dust before you have time to think about it, with every stick and stone for miles around falling and crumbling, all the drains and telephones and electrics torn up and flung into the air, and people who are too far off to be burnt die of radiation. Besides, bombs kill women. Killing men does not matter: the women can replace them; but kill the women and you kill the human race.

YOUNG WOMAN. That wont stop war. Somebody will discover a poison gas lighter than air! It may kill the inhabitants of a city; but it will leave the city standing and in working order.

YOUNG MAN [*thoughtfully, letting the newspaper drop on his knees*] That is an idea.

YOUNG WOMAN. What idea?

YOUNG MAN. Yours. There is a lot of money in it. The Government gave £100,000 to the man who found out how to land our army in Normandy in 1945.

YOUNG WOMAN. Governments will pay millions for any new devilment, though they wont pay twopence for a washing machine. When a Jewish chemist found out how to make high explosive cheaply we made him a present of Jerusalem, which didn't belong to us.

YOUNG MAN [*hopefully*] Yes, by George! So we did.

YOUNG WOMAN. Well, what of it?

YOUNG MAN. I'm a chemist.

YOUNG WOMAN. Does that mean that you are in the atomic bomb business?

YOUNG MAN. No; but I'm on the staff in a chlorine gas factory. The atomic bomb people may be barking up the wrong tree.

YOUNG WOMAN [*rising wrathfully*] So that is what you are! One of these scientific devils who are destroying us! Well, you shall not sit next me again. Go where you belong: to hell. Good day to you.

She goes away.

YOUNG MAN [*still thoughtful*] Lighter than air, eh? [*Slower*] Ligh—ter—than—air?

The scene fades out.

SECOND FABLE

A room in the War Office in London. The Commander-in-Chief at work reading letters. A secretary opening them. The telephone rings. The secretary answers it.

SEC. Yes?... [*To the C.-in-C.*] Lord Oldhand from the Foreign Office.

C.-IN-C. Shew him up; and get out.

SEC. He is shewing himself up. He must have heard—

Lord O. bursts in. The secretary hurries out.

OLDHAND. Ulsterbridge: have you heard the news?

C.-IN-C. Of course Ive heard the news. Here in the War Office we have to get the news in six minutes. At the Foreign Office six years is soon enough for you. Sit down.

OLDHAND [*seating himself*] Is this a time for your Irish jokes? What the devil are we to do? How much do you know?

C.-IN-C. Only that there is not one of God's creatures left alive in the Isle of Wight. I shall have to send every soldier in England to cremate the dead or throw them into the sea. The Home Office will have to find 88,454 civilians to dust the houses with vacuum cleaners and keep the banks and the telephone services and the wireless and water supplies and the lighting and the markets and all the rest of it going.

OLDHAND. Precisely. And all this is your fault.

C.-IN-C. Oldhand: you lie, categorically. How my fault?

OLDHAND. Do you forget that when that fellow who found out how to make volatile poison gas offered us his discovery it was you who turned him down?

C.-IN-C. That cockney blighter? He wanted a hundred thousand pounds for it. And the scientific authorities assured me that every penny spent on anything but atomic research would be wasted.

OLDHAND. Well, he sold it to the South African negro Hitler, Ketchewayo the Second, for a hundred and fifty thousand. Ketch could afford it: his backyard is chock full of diamonds. The fellow made a Declaration of Independence for Zululand with himself as emperor. Capetown, Natal, and Rhodesia went to war with him and involved us in it. That made it your job, didnt it?

C.-IN-C. Not a bit of it. Ketch is far too cunning to go to war with us. He did not go to war with anybody. He dropped his bombs on the Isle of Wight just to shew Capetown and the rest that the world was at his mercy. He selected the Isle of Wight because it's a safe distance from his own people, just as we selected Hiroshima in 1945. He thinks islands are out-of-the-way little places that dont matter to us. But he maintains that his relations with the Commonwealth are friendly; and as you have not declared war on him we are still technically at peace. That makes it your job, not mine, though as usual when there is anything to be done except what was done last time, I shall have to do it.

OLDHAND. You have a very important diplomatic point there, I admit; but it must stand over. Meanwhile let us put our heads together and get to work. The first practical step is to hang this traitor who has sold his accursed invention to the enemy.

C.-IN-C. What! Dont you know that he went to live

in the Isle of Wight as the safest civilized place in the world, and is now lying dead there, killed by his own poison gas?

OLDHAND. Serve the scoundrel right! there is the hand of God in this. But your mistake in turning the fellow down was none the less a mistake because he is dead and you are alive—so far. You may be dead tomorrow.

C.-IN-C. So may you.

OLDHAND. Yes; and it will be your doing.

C.-IN-C. How was I to know that the gas was any good? I get dozens of such inventions every week, all guaranteed to make an end of war and establish heaven on earth. I'm a soldier, not a chemist. I have to go by what the scientific authorities tell me. Youre a diplomatist, not a laboratory bloke. Do you know what an isotype is? Do you know what a meson is? I dont: neither do you. What could you have done except what I did? kick the fellow out.

OLDHAND. Listen to me. I am, as you say, a diplomatist; and I think youll admit that I know my job after my fifteen years in the Foreign Office. You know your job too as a soldier: I dont question it. That gives us one great principle in common.

C.-IN-C. And what is that, may I ask?

OLDHAND. It is to regard all our allies as Powers that may at any moment become our enemies. The public thinks it is the other way about; but we know better. We must be prepared for war before everything.

C.-IN-C. We never are, thanks to the damned taxpayers who wont vote us the money. But of course I agree in principle. What then?

OLDHAND. I'll tell you what then. What sort of fellow was this volatile gas man? You interviewed him. What did you make of him?

C.-IN-C. Oh, a middleclass cad through and through. Out for money and nothing else. Big money.

OLDHAND. Just so. Well, what security have we that after selling his invention to Ketchewayo in Africa he did not sell it over again in Europe? All he had to do was to hand over half a sheet of notepaper with a prescription on it and pocket another hundred and fifty thousand. Every State in Europe and America except ourselves may have it up its sleeve for all we know. The gas may come in at that window while we are talking.

C.-IN-C. That is true: it may. Let us hope it wont.

OLDHAND. Hope wont help us if it does. Our first duty is at all cost to get hold of that receipt, and make the gas ourselves. When the other States know that we have plenty of it none of them will dare to start using it. Meanwhile—

C.-IN-C. Meanwhile I have to provide gas masks for everybody in the country, and make wearing of them compulsory. I have to bury the dead; and I cant spare enough soldiers to do it. Youll have to buy a million vultures from Bombay to pick the bones of the dead before they stink us out. We must make every house in the country gas-proof, and rigidly enforce the closing of all windows. We must—[*he is interrupted by a siren alarm, followed by an artillery salvo*]. What the devil is that?

OLDHAND. Nothing. We have ordered a salute of five guns to celebrate the hundred and first birthday of the President of the Board of Trade.

The siren screams again.

C.-IN-C. [*singing drowsily*]:

"Oh we dont want to lose you;
But we think you ought to go."

He collapses, apparently into a deep sleep.

SHOUTS WITHOUT. Shut the windows! Shut the windows! Gas! Gas! *Another salvo.*

Oldhand rises and rushes toward the open window to shut it. He staggers, and can only clutch at the sill to steady himself.

OLDHAND [*with a vacant grin which develops into a smile of radiant happiness, sings*] "It's a long way to Tipperary—"

He falls dead.

THIRD FABLE

A pleasant spot in the Isle of Wight. A building of steel and glass is inscribed ANTHROPOMETRIC LABORATORY. *On the terrace before it a bench and chairs. Seated in conference are a middle-aged gentleman in a gay pullover and broadly striped nylon trousers, and two women: a comely matron in a purple academic gown, and a junior in short-skirted overall and blue slacks.*

A tourist comes along. His embroidered smock and trimmed beard proclaim the would-be artist. He stops on seeing the three, and produces a camera.

THE GIRL. Hello! What are you doing here?
THE TOURIST. Only hiking round the island. May I take a snapshot?
THE GIRL. You have no business to be here. You have no business to be on the Isle of Wight at all. Who let you land?
THE TOURIST. I came in my own boat. I landed on the beach. What harm am I doing?
THE GIRL. This is a colony of the Upper Ten. Anybodies are not allowed here.
THE TOURIST. I'm not an Anybody: I'm classed as a Mediocrity.
THE GIRL. Neither Mediocrities nor Anybodies are admitted. Go back to your boat; and clear out.
THE MATRON. Stop. You say you are classed as a Mediocrity. Did you pass with honors?

THE TOURIST. No. They were grossly unfair to me. I'm not a Mediocrity: I'm a genius.

THE MATRON. Indeed! Have you a job of any sort?

THE TOURIST. No. They offered me a job as hospital porter because I'm physically strong. How utterly beneath me! When I told them I am a genius and shewed them my drawings, they offered to make me a housepainter. I dont want to paint houses: my destiny is to paint temples in fresco.

THE GENTLEMAN [*amused*] Like Michael Angelo, eh?

THE TOURIST. Oh, I can do better work than Michael Angelo. He is out of date. I am ultra-modern.

THE GENTLEMAN [*to the Matron*] The very man for us.

THE MATRON [*to the Tourist*] You are quite sure that you are a genius, are you?

THE TOURIST. Quite. I dont look like a bank clerk, do I?

THE MATRON. Well, we have no temples here for you to paint; but we can offer you a job that will enable you to support yourself and have enough leisure to paint what you like until the world recognizes your genius.

THE TOURIST. What sort of work will I have to do? I warn you I cant pass examinations; and I hate being regulated and disciplined. I must have perfect freedom.

THE MATRON. Anthropometric work is what we do here. Classifying men and women according to their abilities. Filling up their qualification certificates. Analyzing their secretions and reactions and so on. Quite easy laboratory work.

THE TOURIST. That will suit me down to the ground. I'm a first-rate judge of character.

THE MATRON. Splendid. Take this in to the office

at the end of the passage on the right. You can have tea in the canteen when they have settled with you. [*She hands him a ticket*].

THE TOURIST [*hungrily*] Thank you.

He takes the ticket and goes into the laboratory.

THE GENTLEMAN. He will be a heaven-sent treasure.

THE GIRL. I dont agree. He seems to me to be a conceited fool who thinks himself a genius.

THE GENTLEMAN. Exactly. We shall go by his secretions and reactions: not by his own notions.

A young man in rags, unshaven, and disreputable looking, comes along.

THE GIRL. Who is this awful looking tramp? [*To him*] Hello! Who are you; and what are you doing here?

HE. I'm doing nothing here because nobody will give me anything to do. I'm devilishly hungry. Have you by any chance a crust of bread to spare?

THE MATRON. How did you get into this island? Why were you allowed to land?

HE. I was a stowaway, madam. They wanted to send me back; but the captain of the return boat would not take me: he said I was too dirty and probably infectious and verminous. The medical officer quarantined me; but I convinced him that I am only a harmless tramp, fit for nothing better; so he let me go. And here I am.

THE MATRON. Do you do nothing to earn your bread?

THE TRAMP. I ask for it. People mostly give it to me. If not, I sing for it. Then they give me a penny or two to stop singing and go away. It's a way of life like any other. It suits me. I'm good for nothing else.

THE GENTLEMAN. How do you know you are good for nothing else?

THE TRAMP. Well, what else am I good for? You

an take me into your laboratory and try if you like. There is a canteen there, isnt there?

THE GENTLEMAN. I see you are not unintelligent. You are not uneducated. You could surely work for your living.

THE TRAMP. No. Anything but that. Working is not living. If you are on that tack you wont give me anything: I know your sort. Good morning. [*He starts to go*].

THE GIRL. Stop. You are hungry. I'll get you some bread. [*She goes into the laboratory*].

THE TRAMP. Look at that, now! Ask; and it shall be given to you.

THE GENTLEMAN. Listen to me. I'll give you five guineas if youll submit to a test of your capacity in our laboratory.

THE TRAMP. It would be robbing you. I tell you I have no capacity. I'm an out-and-out Goodfor-nothing. And five guineas is too much to give a tramp. I must live from hand to mouth. All the joy of life goes when you have five guineas in your pocket.

THE GENTLEMAN. You need not keep it in your pocket. You can buy a decent suit of clothes with it. You need one badly. You are in rags.

THE TRAMP. Of course I'm in rags. Who would give alms to a well-dressed man? It's my business to be in rags.

THE GENTLEMAN. Very well. I'll have you arrested and put through the laboratory and classified. That is the law, compulsory for everybody. If you refuse you may be classed as irresponsible. That means that youll be enlisted in the military police or kept under tutelage in a Labor Brigade. Or you may be classed as dangerous and incorrigible, in which case youll be liquidated.

THE TRAMP. I know all that. What good will it do you? Why are you offering me five guineas when you have only to call the police and put me through the mill for nothing?

THE GENTLEMAN. You have ability enough to cross-examine me. You may have administrative ability, and be cunning enough to shirk its responsibilities. You may be one of the Artful Dodgers who know that begging is easier and happier than bossing.

THE TRAMP. Ha! ha! ha! You suspect me of being a heaven-born genius! Very well: test me til you are black in the face. Youll only be wasting your time; but that wont hurt me, because time is of no value to me: it's my profession to waste it. Youll find I can do nothing. Mind: I'm not a fool: youre quite right there; but I'm a duffer, a hopeless duffer. I can always see what the other fellows ought to do; but I cant do it. Ive tried my hand at everything: no use: Ive failed every time. Ive tastes but no talents. I'd like to be a Shakespear; but I cant write plays. I'd like to be a Michael Angelo or a Raphael; but I can neither draw nor paint. I'd love to be a Mozart or a Beethoven; but I can neither compose a symphony nor play a concerto. I envy Einstein his mathematical genius; but beyond the pence table I cant add two and two together. I know a lot, and can do nothing. When I tell the clever chaps what to do, they wont do it, and tell me I'm ignorant and crazy. And so I am: I know it only too well. Youd better give me a meal or the price of one, and let me jog on the footpath way. My name's not Prospero: it's Autolycus.

THE GENTLEMAN. If you know what other people ought to do, youll be too busy telling them, and making laws for them, to do any of it yourself. In with you into the canteen; and get your bread there.

THE TRAMP. I fly for the bread. You are the boss here: the archpriest, chooser of rulers, lord of human destiny. And your choice is a government of tramps! Ha! ha! ha! ha! ha! ha! ha! [*He goes into the laboratory roaring with laughter*].

THE GENTLEMAN. Two big catches for today. A nincompoop who thinks he's a genius; and a genius who thinks he's a nincompoop.

THE MATRON. I prefer nincompoops. I can always depend on them to do what was done last time. But I never know what a genius will be up to next, except that it will be something upsetting.

FOURTH FABLE

The same place in the Isle of Wight: but the building is now inscribed DIET COMMISSIONERS. *A Commissioner in cap and gown sits at a writing table talking into a dictaphone. He has earphones hanging from his ears.*

COMMISSIONER. What I am going to dictate is for the printer; so keep a carbon copy. It is for the new edition of my book on Human Diet. Are you ready? . . . Right. The heading is Chapter four. Living on Air. Now for the text. Ahem!

In the twentieth century the tribes of New Zealand had, under the influence of British colonists, left off eating their prisoners of war. The British themselves, influenced by a prophet whose name has come down to us in various forms as Shelley, Shakespear, and Shavius, had already, after some centuries of restricted cannibalism in which only fishes, frogs, birds, sheep, cows, pigs, rabbits, and whales were eaten, been gradually persuaded to abstain from these also, and to live on plants and fruits, and even on grass, honey, and nuts: a diet which they called vegetarian. Full stop. New paragraph. Ahem!

As this change saved the labor of breeding animals for food, and supported human health and longevity quite as well, if not better, than the eating of dead animals, it was for some time unchallenged as a step forward in civilization. But some unforeseen consequences followed. When cattle were no longer bred and slaughtered for food, milk and butter, cheese and eggs, were no longer to be had. Grass, leaves, and nettles became the staple diet. This was sufficient for rude physical health. At the Olympic Games grass eating athletes broke all the records. This was not surprising, as it had long been known that bulls and elephants, fed on grass and leaves, were the strongest, most fertile, most passionate animals known. But they were also the most ferocious, being so dangerous that nobody dared cross a field in which a bull was loose, and every elephant had to have an armed keeper to restrain it. It had also been noticed that human vegetarians were restless, pugnacious, and savagely abusive in their continual controversies with the remaining meat eaters, who found it easy and pleasant to lead sedentary lives in stuffy rooms whilst the vegetarians could not live without much exercise in the fresh air. When grass eating became general men became more ferocious and dangerous than bulls. Happily they also became less capable of organized action of any kind. They could not or would not make political alliances, nor engage in industrial mass production or wage world wars. Atomic bombs and poison gases and the like were quite beyond their powers of co-operation: their ferocities and animosities, like those of the bull, did not go beyond trespassers within sight and reach. With the ending of wars their numbers increased enormously; but to the few born thinkers who still cropped up among them and ruled them as far as they were capable of being ruled, it was apparent that they were changing into supergorillas through eating grass and leaves. And though they lived longer than the meat eaters, they still suffered from certain deadly diseases and from decay of teeth, failure of eyesight, and decrepitude in old age. Their ablest biologists had to agree that the human race, having tried eating everything on earth that was eatable, had found no food that did not sooner or later poison them. This was challenged by a Russian woman, a noted vegetarian athlete. She pointed out that there was a diet that had not been tried: namely, living on air and water. The supergorillas ridiculed her, alleging that air is not food: it is nothing; and mankind cannot live on nothing in empty space. But a famous mathematician shewed just then that there is no such thing as nothing, and that space is not emptiness and in fact does not exist. There is substance, called matter, everywhere: in fact, the universe consists of nothing else; but whether we can perceive it, or eat and drink it, depends on temperature, rate of radiation, and the sensitiveness of the instruments for detecting and measuring it. As temperature rises, water changes from solid ice to liquid fluid, from liquid fluid to steam, from steam to gas; but it is none the less substantial even at temperatures that are quite immeasurable and hardly conceivable. It followed logically that living on air is as possible as living on flesh or on grass and chopped carrots, though as men cannot live under water, nor fishes out of it, each phase of substance has its appropriate form of life and diet and set of habits. Such creatures as angels are as possible as whales and minnows, elephants and microbes.

The Russian woman claimed that she had lived for months on air and water, but on condition that the air was fresh and that she took the hardest physical exercise daily. It was already known that the vigils and fasts of saints did not weaken them when their spiritual activity was intense enough to produce a state of ecstasy. Full stop: new paragraph.

This briefly is the history of the epoch-making change in social organization produced by the ending of the food problem which had through all recorded history made men the slaves of nature, and defeated all their aspirations to be free to do what they like instead of what they must. The world became a world of athletes, artists, craftsmen, physicists, and mathematicians, instead of farmers, millers, bakers, butchers, bar tenders, brewers, and distillers. Hunger and thirst, which had for centuries meant the need for bread and onions, cheese and beer, beef and mutton, became a search for knowledge of nature and power over it, and a desire for truth and righteousness. The supergorilla became the soldier and servant of Creative Evolution. Full stop. Postscript.

Stop typing and listen to instructions. What I have just dictated is for the tenth edition of my primer for infant schools in the rudimentary biology series. I have dictated only the full stops at the end of the paragraphs. I will fill in the commas and colons and semicolons on the typescript. Leave the type and the format and the illustrations to the printer: he is a better artist in books than I am. He will need paper for two hundred million copies. Goodbye.

He takes off his headphones; puts the cover on the dictaphone; sighs with relief at having done a tedious job; and goes into the building.

FIFTH FABLE

The scene is unchanged; but the building is now labelled GENETIC INSTITUTE. *On the terrace, seated round a table loaded with old books, are four persons of uncertain age, apparently in the prime of life. Two of them are male, one female, the fourth a hermaphrodite. They wear white sleeveless tunics like heralds' tabards on which are embroidered different flower designs, the two men being distinguished by a thistle and a shamrock respectively, the woman by a rose, and the hermaphrodite by an elm with a vine round its trunk. The sleeves of the men are red, of the women green, of the hermaphrodite the two colors in a chequered harlequin pattern. The men are close-cropped and cleanshaven: the woman's hair is dressed like that of the Milo Venus. They are in animated discussion, each with an open book on which they occasionally thump to emphasize their points.*

SHAMROCK. I cannot make head or tail of this nineteenth century stuff. They seem to have considered our business unmentionable, and tried to write books about it in which it was not mentioned. [*He shuts the book impatiently*].

ROSE. That seems hardly possible. Our business is the very first business of any human society: the reproduction of the human race, the most mentionable subject in the world and the most important.

SHAMROCK. Well, Ive been through every scrap of nineteenth century writing that remains; and I tell you that their textbooks on physiology dont mention the reproductive organs nor hint at such a thing as sex. You would not guess from them that it existed.

HERM. To say nothing of hermaphrodites. Being myself a hermaphrodite I have looked myself up in the nineteenth century books; and I simply wasnt there.

THISTLE. Oh, they were the damnedest fools: it is impossible to understand how they kept going for a week, much less for years. They had not brains enough to make an alphabet capable of spelling their language. They counted their goods in twelves but could not count their money in more than tens because they had only ten fingers and could not invent the two missing figures. They could not change their working hours by the sun oftener than twice a year; and it took one of the worst of the killing matches they called wars to make them go even that far. Their calendar is incomprehensible: they could not fix their festivals nor make their months tally with the moon. In music their keyboards had only twelve notes in the octave instead of our sixty-four. One would think they might at least have managed nineteen to play their babyish thirds and sixths bearably in tune. They wasted millions of hours every day because they could not or would not do the simplest things; and when their five per cent of geniuses made wonderful machines for them: big machines that could rise from the ground and fly, and little ones that could think and calculate, they accepted them as gifts from some imaginary paradise they called heaven. When one of their bodily organs went wrong they did not set it right: they just cut it out, and left the patient to recover from the shock or die. When the patient was ill all over and could not be cut to pieces they dosed him with poisons: I hunted out a case of a well-known woman who was given nine different poisons for some trouble they called typhoid. The amazing thing is that she survived it. She must have had the constitution of a bear. It was in the nineteenth century that they gave up believing in idols and priests, and took to believing in medicine men and surgeons. Let us drop digging into this past that is unconceivable, and start from what we really know of the present.

He shuts his book and throws it away.

SHAMROCK [*shutting his book*] Agreed. But why did they consider sex unmentionable?

ROSE. Simply because their methods were so disgusting that they had no decent language for them. You think their methods were like ours, and their passions like ours. You could not make a greater mistake. The seminal fluids which our chemists make in the laboratory, and which it is our business to experiment with, were unknown to them: they had to use glandular excretions from the living body to perpetuate the race. To initiate births they had to practice personal contacts which I would rather not describe. Strangest of all, they seem to have experienced in such contacts the ecstasies which are normal with us in our pursuit of knowledge and power, and culminate in our explorations and discoveries. The religions they believed in were so wildly absurd that one would suppose they could believe anything.

SHAMROCK. Oh, come! They must have had some common sense or they couldnt have lived.

ROSE. They had gleams of it. In spite of their sensual ecstasies, they had decency enough to reserve their highest veneration for persons who abstained from them, exalting them under the special titles of saints, nuns, priests, angels, gods and the like.

HERM. Not always. There were people called Greeks who had dozens of gods whose adventures were scandalously sensual. They poisoned an old man for trying to teach their young men to reason. Serve him right, too; for some of his reasonings were sheer logomachies: in England called puns.

ROSE. True. Another set of them, called Jews or Israelites, tortured a young man to death for trying to persuade them that the divinity they worshipped was in themselves, and promising that if they killed him he would rise from the dead and establish a kingdom of righteousness not among angels in the clouds but on earth among human men and women.

HERM. That was not why they killed him: they believed anyone who promised that much. They killed him because he made a riot in their temple and drove out the money changers, whom he mistook for thieves, being too young and not enough of a financier to know how useful and necessary they were to pilgrims. His name was Hitler, poor chap!

ROSE. All the same, utterly as we are unlike these primitive savages, we are descended from them; and though we manufacture ourselves scientifically, we are not yet agreed as to the sort of mankind we ought to make, nor how many at a time, nor how long they ought to last. We all want the Just Man Made Perfect; but when our chemists ask us for an exact prescription of the necessary protoplasms, hormones, vitamins, enzymes and the rest, we never agree on the last milligram of each ingredient; and it is that milligram that determines whether the resulting product will be a poet or a mathematician.

HERM. I'm against all that. It revolts me. I tell you again and again we shall never make decent human beings out of chemical salts. We must get rid of our physical bodies altogether, except for stuffed specimens in the Natural History Museum. I dont want to be a body: I want to be a mind and nothing but a mind. In the sixteenth century men made it their first article of religion to worship a god who had neither body, parts, nor passions: sensual passions. Even in the dark ages of the nineteenth and twentieth centuries there was a man who aspired to be a vortex in thought, and a woman who declared that the mind made the body and not the body the mind. Demolish all the laboratories. Build temples in which we can pray and pray and pray for deliverance from our bodies until the change occurs naturally as all real changes do.

ROSE. My child, how much farther would that take us? We should still be unable to agree on what sort of mind we needed. Prayer, we know, is a great creative power; but to pray effectively you must know what to pray for. In the sixteenth century there was a famous mathematician who declared that our utmost knowledge was no more than a grain of sand picked up on the margin of the ocean of our ignorance. He was a silly fellow who thought that the world was only forty centuries old and that straight lines were ethically right; but the utmost that we know is still no more than his grain of sand. I would like to be a mind without a body; but that has not happened to me yet; and meanwhile, as another sixteenth [century] sage said, the world must be peopled; and as we can no longer endure the old unmentionable methods we must make material citizens out of material substances in biochemical laboratories. I was manufactured that way myself; and so were you, my boy.

HERM. My body was, and my mind such as it is. But my desire to get rid of my body was not. Where did that come from? Can you tell me?

ROSE. No; but when we know even that, it will be only another grain of sand on the seashore. But it will be worth picking up; and so will all the other grains.

SHAMROCK: In the infinity of time, when the oceans dry up and make no more sand, we shall pick them all up. What then?

ROSE. The pursuit of knowledge and power will never end.

SIXTH AND LAST FABLE

As before, except that the building is now labelled

SIXTH FORM SCHOOL
SCHEDULED HISTORIC MONUMENT

On the terrace are five students in class, wearing uniforms with six sleeve stripes. Their individual numbers are on their caps. Numbers 1, 2, 3, are youths. 4 and 5 are maidens. Number 1 is older than number 2, number 4 than number 5.

The teacher, a matron, in cap and gown, enters from the building and takes her place.

TEACHER. Let me introduce myself. You have just been promoted to the sixth form. I am your teacher. Explain to me how and why the sixth form differs from the fifth.

YOUTH 1. We shall explain nothing to you. If you are our teacher it is for us to question you: not for you to question us.

MAIDEN 5. Do not be prehistoric. Savages thousands of years ago schooled their children by asking them conundrums and beating them if they could not answer them. You are not going to start that game on us, are you?

YOUTH 3. If you do, Mother Hubbard, youll not have a happy time with us.

TEACHER. You are quite right. It is what I expected

you to say. My question was a test. Three of you have shewn that you understand the relation between us as teacher and pupils in the sixth form. The rest of you, if you also agree, will signify the same in the usual manner.

All the students raise their hands in assent.

TEACHER. Good. Now fire away. Ask your questions.

YOUTH 3. What questions shall we ask?

TEACHER. Aha! You see it is not so easy to ask questions. Is there nothing you want to know? If not, the sixth form is not for you: it is out of your mental range; and you can go back to the fifth form and take your leaving certificate.

YOUTH 3. Oh I say! Give me time to think of something.

TEACHER. Two minutes; or back to the fifth you go.

YOUTH 2 [*prompting*] Ask her whether when a pine cone disappears into the ground it is the ground that wraps the pine cone up or the cone that buries itself into the clay.

TEACHER. Good, Number Two. I dont know; and neither does anyone else. And you, Number Three, do you really want to know?

YOUTH 3. No. I didnt know that cones bury themselves; and I dont care a dump whether they do or not.

TEACHER. Dont care a dump is vulgar. You should say dont care a dam.

YOUTH 3. Oh, I'm not literary. What does dam mean?

TEACHER. It means a negligible trifle.

YOUTH 2. Wrong, Teacher. My Dark Ages dictionary defines it as a form of profanity in use among clergymen.

TEACHER. In the sixth form, the teacher is always wrong.

YOUTH I. You are both wrong. It means an animal's mother.

MAIDEN 5. No it doesnt. It means a wall across a river valley to pen it up as a lake.

YOUTH 3. All I meant is what the teacher says.

TEACHER. And so the teacher is always right. For announcing this, Number Three, I'll give you another minute to ask me a question that you do really care about.

YOUTH 3. Why are you so down on me? I am not the only one who hasnt a question ready for you.

TEACHER. The sixth form should be bursting with questions. I'll come to the others presently. I pick on you because your looks do not suggest more than fifth form brains.

YOUTH I. Dont look at his face. Look at his fingers.

TEACHER. Fingers are not brains.

YOUTH 3. Yes they are. My brains are in my fingers: yours are only in your head. Have you ever invented a machine and constructed it?

TEACHER. No. Have you?

YOUTH 3. Yes.

TEACHER. How?

YOUTH 3. I dont know. I cant find words for it: I'm no talker. But I can do things. And I wont go down to the fifth. Here I am and here I stick, whatever you say.

TEACHER. So you shall. You know your own mind, though you cannot speak it.

YOUTH 3. I have no mind. I can only do things.

MAIDEN 4. I have a question, Teacher.

TEACHER. Out with it.

MAIDEN 4. How is it that the things that come into Number Three's head never come into mine? Why can he do things that I cant do? Why can I do things that he cant do? I can write an essay: he cant write even a specification of the machines he invents. If you ask him to, he can only twiddle his fingers as if they were wheels and levers? He has to employ a Third Form patent agent to describe it for him.

TEACHER. Ah, now we are coming to the riddle of the universe. You young things always ask it, and will not take "I dont know" for an answer. Can any of you tell me the story of the Sphinx?

MAIDEN 5. I can. The Sphinx was a quadruped with a woman's head and breasts, who put conundrums to everyone who came along, and devoured them if they could not answer them.

TEACHER. Yes: that is the story. But where is the interest of it for you?

MAIDEN 5. Well, a story is a story. I like stories.

MAIDEN 4. She does, Teacher: she is always reading them. And she tells stories about herself. All lies.

YOUTH 2. Why does she tell lies? That is what I want to know.

YOUTH 3. The Sphinx story is rot. Why should the Sphinx eat everybody who couldnt answer its riddles?

YOUTH 1. Why should it kill itself if anyone did answer them? Tell me that.

TEACHER. Never ask why. Ask what, when, where, how, who, which; but never why. Only first form children, who think their parents know everything, ask why. In the sixth form you are supposed to know that why is unanswerable.

YOUTH 3. Nonsense. Why is not unanswerable. Why does water boil? Because its temperature has been raised to 100 Centigrade. What is wrong with that?

TEACHER. That is not why: it is how. Why was it boiled?

YOUTH 2. Because some fellow wanted to boil an egg and eat it. That is why.

TEACHER. Why did he want to eat it?

YOUTH 2. Because he wanted to live and not starve.

TEACHER. That is a fact, not a reason. Why did he want to live?

YOUTH 2. Like everybody else, I suppose.

TEACHER. Why does everybody want to live, however unhappily? Why does anybody want to live?

YOUTH 3. How the devil does anybody know? You dont know. I dont know.

TEACHER. Why dont we know?

YOUTH 2. Because we dont. Thats why.

TEACHER. No. Why is beyond knowledge. All the whys lead to the great interrogation mark that shines for ever across the sky like a rainbow. Why do we exist? Why does the universe exist?

YOUTH 1. If you ask me I should say the universe is a big joke.

MAIDEN 4. I do not see any fun in it. I should say it is a big mistake.

YOUTH 2. A joke must have a joker. A mistake must have a blunderer. If the world exists it must have a creator.

TEACHER. Must it? How do you know? One of the ancient gods, named Napoleon, pointed to the sky full of stars and said "Who made all that?" His soothsayers replied "Whoever it was, who made Him?"

MAIDEN 4. Or Her? Why—

TEACHER. Order, order! Let us have no more whys. They only set you chasing your own tails, like cats. Let us get to work. I call for questions beginning with how.

MAIDEN 5. How do thoughts come into our heads? I dont have a lot of thoughts like Number Four here. She is a highbrow; but I was born quite emptyheaded. Yet I get thoughts that nobody ever suggested to me. Where did they come from?

TEACHER. As to that, there are many theories. Have you none of your own, any of you?

YOUTH 2. My grandfather lectured about the theory of the Disembodied Races. I picked it up from him when I was a kid. Of course the old man is now out-of-date: I dont take him seriously; but the theory sticks in my head because Ive never thought of anything better.

YOUTH I. Our biology professor in the fifth swore by it. But I cannot quite stomach it.

TEACHER. Can you give me a reason for that?

YOUTH I. Well, I was brought up to consider that we are the vanguard of civilization, the last step in creative evolution. But according to the theory we are only a survival of the sort of mankind that existed in the twentieth century, no better than black beetles compared to the supermen who evolved into the disembodied. I am not a black beetle.

YOUTH 3. Rot! If we were black beetles, the supermen would have tramped on us and killed us, or poisoned us with phosphorus.

YOUTH I. They may be keeping us for their amusement, as we keep our pets. I told you the universe is a joke. That is my theory.

MAIDEN 5. But where do our thoughts come from? They must be flying about in the air. My father never said "I think." He always said "It strikes me." When I was a child I thought that something in the air had hit him.

YOUTH I. What is the use of talking such utter nonsense? How could people get rid of their bodies?

TEACHER. People actually did get rid of their bodies. They got rid of their tails, of their fur, of their teeth. They acquired thumbs and enlarged their brains. They seem to have done what they liked with their bodies.

YOUTH 2. Anyhow, they had to eat and drink. They couldnt have done so without stomachs and bowels.

TEACHER. Yes they could: at least so the histories say. They found they could live on air, and that eating and drinking caused diseases of which their bodies died.

YOUTH 2. You believe that!!!

TEACHER. I believe nothing. But there is the same evidence for it as for anything else that happened millions of years before we were born. It is so written and recorded. As I can neither witness the past nor foresee the future I must take such history as there is as part of my framework of thought. Without such a framework I cannot think any more than a carpenter can cut wood without a saw.

YOUTH 2. Now you are getting beyond me, Teacher. I dont understand.

TEACHER. Do not try to understand. You must be content with such brains as you have until more understanding comes to you. Your question is where our thoughts come from and how they strike us, as Number Five's father put it. The theory is that the Disembodied Races still exist as Thought Vortexes, and are penetrating our thick skulls in their continual pursuit of knowledge and power, since they need our hands and brains as tools in that pursuit.

MAIDEN 4. Some of our thoughts are damnably mischievous. We slaughter one another and destroy the cities we build. What puts that into our heads? Not the pursuit of knowledge and power.

TEACHER. Yes; for the pursuit of knowledge and power involves the slaughter and destruction of everything that opposes it. The disembodied must inspire the soldier and the hunter as well as the pacifist and philanthropist.

YOUTH 1. But why should anybody oppose it if all thoughts come from well meaning vortexes?

TEACHER. Because even the vortexes have to do their work by trial and error. They have to learn by mistakes as well as by successes. We have to destroy the locust and the hook worm and the Colorado beetle because, if we did not, they would destroy us. We have to execute criminals who have no conscience and are incorrigible. They are old experiments of the Life Force. They were well intentioned and perhaps necessary at the time. But they are no longer either useful or necessary, and must now be exterminated. They cannot be exterminated by disembodied thought. The mongoose must be inspired to kill the cobra, the chemist to distil poisons, the physicist to make nuclear bombs, others to be big game hunters, judges, executioners, and killers of all sorts, often the most amiable of mortals outside their specific functions as destroyers of vermin. The ruthless foxhunter loves dogs: the physicist and chemists adore their children and keep animals as pets.

YOUTH 2. Look here, Teacher. Talk sense. Do these disembodied thoughts die when their number is up, as we do? If not, there can hardly be room for them in the universe after all these millions of centuries.

MAIDEN 5. Yes: that is what I want to know. How old is the world?

TEACHER. We do not know. We lost count in the dark ages that followed the twentieth century. There are traces of many civilizations that followed; and we may yet discover traces of many more. Some of them were atavistic.

MAIDEN 5. At a what?

TEACHER. Atavistic. Not an advance on the civilization before it, but a throw-back to an earlier one. Like those children of ours who cannot get beyond the First Form, and grow up to be idiots or savages. We kill them. But we are ourselves a throw-back to the twentieth century, and may be killed as idiots and savages if we meet a later and higher civilization.

YOUTH I. I dont believe it. We are the highest form of life and the most advanced civilization yet evolved.

YOUTH 2. Same here. Who can believe this fairy tale about disembodied thoughts? There is not a scrap of evidence for it. Nobody can believe it.

MAIDEN 4. Steady, Number Two: steady. Lots of us can believe it and do believe it. Our schoolfellows who have never got beyond the third or fourth form believe in what they call the immortality of the soul.

YOUTH I [*contemptuously*] Yes, because they are afraid to die.

TEACHER. That makes no difference. What is an immortal soul but a disembodied thought? I have received this morning a letter from a man who tells me he was for nineteen years a chain smoker of cigarets. He had no religious faith; but one day he chanced on a religious meeting in the park, and heard the preacher exhorting his flock to listen to the voice of God. He said it would surely come to them and guide them. The smoker tried the experiment of listening just for fun; and soon his head was filled with the words "Quit smoking. Quit smoking." He quitted without the least difficulty, and has never smoked since, though he had tried before and always failed. What was that but the prompting of a disembodied thought? Millions of our third and fourth form people believe it.

YOUTH 2. Well, I am sixth form; and I dont believe it. Your correspondent is just a liar.

MAIDEN 4. What rubbish you talk, Number Two! Do

fourth form people let themselves be eaten by lions in the circus, burnt at the stake, or live lives of unselfish charity rather than stop telling lies? It is much more likely that you are a fool.

YOUTH 2. May be; but that does not answer the question.

MAIDEN 5. Hear hear! The smoker may be a liar or Number Two a fool; but where did the thoughts come from? What puts them into our heads? The preachers say they are whispered by God. Anyhow they are whispered; and I want to know exactly how.

TEACHER. Like all young things you want to begin by knowing everything. I can give you only the advice of the preachers: listen until you are told.

A youth, clothed in feathers like a bird, appears suddenly.

TEACHER. Hullo! Who are you? What are you doing here?

THE FEATHERED ONE. I am an embodied thought. I am what you call the word made flesh.

YOUTH 3. Rats! How did you get here? Not by your wings: you havnt got any. You are a Cockyolly Bird.

THE FEATHERED ONE. I do not fly: I levitate. Call me Cockyolly if you like. But it would be more respectful to call me Raphael.

MAIDEN 4. Why should we respect you in that ridiculous costume?

THE TEACHER. Do you seriously wish us to believe that you are one of the disembodied, again incarnate?

RAPHAEL. Why not? Evolution can go backwards as well as forwards. If the body can become a vortex, the vortex can also become a body.

THE TEACHER. And you are such a body?

RAPHAEL. I am curious to know what it is like to be a body. Curiosity never dies.

MAIDEN 4. How do you like it so far?

RAPHAEL. I do not like nor dislike. I experience.

YOUTH 3. That nonsense will not go down here, Cocky. It sounds smart enough; but it means nothing. Why should we respect you?

RAPHAEL. You had better. I am restraining my magnetic field. If I turned it on it would kill you.

MAIDEN 5. Dont provoke him, Number Three. I feel awful.

MAIDEN 4. You cannot experience bodied life unless you have a girl, and marry, and have children, as we do. Have you brought a girl with you?

RAPHAEL. No. I stop short of your eating and drinking and so forth, and of your reproductive methods. They revolt me.

MAIDEN 4. No passions, then?

RAPHAEL. On the contrary: intellectual passion, mathematical passion, passion for discovery and exploration: the mightiest of all the passions.

THE TEACHER. But none of our passions?

RAPHAEL. Yes. Your passion for teaching.

YOUTH 2. Then you have come to teach us?

RAPHAEL. No. I am here to learn, not to teach. I pass on. [*He vanishes*].

ALL [*screaming*] Hi! Stop! Come back! We have a lot to ask you. Dont go yet. Wait a bit, Raphael.

YOUTH 3. No use. He has invented some trick of vanishing before he is found out. He is only a Confidence Trick man.

THE TEACHER. Nonsense! He did not ask us for anything.

MAIDEN 4. He was just sampling us.

YOUTH 1. He told us nothing. We know nothing.

YOUTH 3. Rot! You want to know too much. We know how to make cyclotrons and hundred inch telescopes. We have harnessed atomic energy. He couldnt make a safety pin or a wheelbarrow to save his life.

THE TEACHER. Enough. We can never want to know too much. Attention! [*All rise*]. You will get at the schoolbook counter copies of an old poem called The Book of Job. You will read it through; and—

YOUTH 2. I read it through when I was thirteen. It was an argument between an old josser named Job and one of the old gods, who pretended he had made the universe. Job said if so he had made it very unfairly. But what use is all that to me? I dont believe the old god made the universe.

TEACHER You will read the book over again from the point of view that the old god made no such pretence, and crushed Job by shewing that he could put ten times as many unanswerable questions to Job as Job could put to him. It will teach you that I can do the same to you. All will read the book and ask questions or write essays before next Friday.

A jubilant march is heard.

TEACHER. Lunch. March. [*Beating time*] Left-right, left-right, left-right.

They tramp out rhythmically.

Shakes Versus Shav:
A Puppet Play

WITH

Preface

Composition begun 20 January 1949; completed 23 January 1949. Published in the *Arts Council Bulletin*, September 1949. First collected in *Buoyant Billions, Farfetched Fables, & Shakes versus Shav*, 1951. First presented by the Waldo Lanchester Marionette Theatre at the Lyttelton Hall, Malvern, on 9 August 1949.

Puppets' voices recorded by:

Shakespear *Lewis Casson*
Shaw *Ernest Thesiger*
Macbeth *Russell Thorndike*
Rob Roy *Archie Duncan*
Captain Shotover *Cecil Trouncer*
Ellie Dunn *Isabel Dean*

Period—Summer 1949

Scene: *A Theatre in Malvern*

Preface

This in all actuarial probability is my last play and the climax of my eminence, such as it is. I thought my career as a playwright was finished when Waldo Lanchester of the Malvern Marionette Theatre, our chief living puppet master, sent me figures of two puppets, Shakespear and myself, with a request that I should supply one of my famous dramas for them, not to last longer than ten minutes or thereabouts. I accomplished this feat, and was gratified by Mr Lanchester's immediate approval.

I have learnt part of my craft as conductor of rehearsals (producer, they call it) from puppets. Their unvarying intensity of facial expression, impossible for living actors, keeps the imagination of the spectators continuously stimulated. When one of them is speaking or tumbling and the rest left aside, these, though in full view, are invisible, as they should be. Living actors have to learn that they too must be invisible while the protagonists are conversing, and therefore must not move a muscle nor change their expression, instead of, as beginners mostly do, playing to them and robbing them of the audience's undivided attention.

Puppets have also a fascination of their own, because there is nothing wonderful in a living actor moving and speaking, but that wooden headed dolls should do so is a marvel that never palls.

And they can survive treatment that would kill live actors. When I first saw them in my boyhood nothing delighted me more than when all the puppets went up in a balloon and presently dropped from the skies with an appalling crash on the floor.

Nowadays the development of stagecraft into film-craft may destroy the idiosyncratic puppet charm. Televised puppets could enjoy the scenic backgrounds of the cinema. Sound recording could enable the puppet master to give all his attention to the strings he is manipulating, the dialogue being spoken by a company of first-rate speakers as in the theatre. The old puppet master spoke all the parts himself in accents which he differentiated by Punch-and-Judy squeaks and the like. I can imagine the puppets simulating living performers so perfectly that the spectators will be completely illuded. The result would be the death of puppetry; for it would lose its charm with its magic. So let reformers beware.

Nothing can extinguish my interest in Shakespear. It began when I was a small boy, and extends to Stratford-upon-Avon, where I have attended so many bardic festivals that I have come to regard it almost as a supplementary birthplace of my own.

No year passes without the arrival of a batch of books contending that Shakespear was somebody else. The argument is always the same. Such early works as Venus and Adonis, Lucrece, and Love's Labour's Lost, could not possibly have been written by an illiterate clown and poacher who could hardly write his own name. This is unquestionably true. But the inference that Shakespear did not write them does not follow. What does follow is that Shakespear was not an illiterate clown but a well read grammar-schooled son in a family of good middle-class standing, cultured enough to be habitual playgoers and private entertainers of the players.

This, on investigation, proves to be exactly what Shakespear was. His father, John Shakespear, Gent, was an alderman who demanded a coat of arms which was finally granted. His mother was of equal rank and social pretension. John finally failed commercially, having no doubt let his artistic turn get the better of his mercantile occupation, and leave him unable to afford a university education for William, had he ever wanted to make a professional scholar of him.

These circumstances interest me because they are just like my own. They were a considerable cut above those of Bunyan and Cobbett, both great masters of language, who nevertheless could not have written Venus and Adonis nor Love's Labour's Lost. One does not forget Bunyan's "The Latin I borrow." Shakespear's standing was nearer to Ruskin's, whose splendid style owes much more to his mother's insistence on his learning the Bible by heart than to his Oxford degree.

So much for Bacon-Shakespear and all the other fables founded on that entirely fictitious figure Shaxper or Shagsper the illiterate bumpkin.

Enough too for my feeling that the real Shakespear might have been myself, and for the shallow mistaking of it for mere professional jealousy.

AYOT SAINT LAWRENCE, *1949*

Shakes enters and salutes the audience with a flourish of his hat.

SHAKES. Now is the winter of our discontent
Made glorious summer by the Malvern sun.
I, William Shakes, was born in Stratford town,
Where every year a festival is held
To honour my renown not for an age
But for all time. Hither I raging come
An infamous impostor to chastize,
Who in an ecstasy of self-conceit
Shortens my name to Shav, and dares pretend
Here to reincarnate my very self,
And in your stately playhouse to set up
A festival, and plant a mulberry
In most presumptuous mockery of mine.
Tell me, ye citizens of Malvern,
Where I may find this caitiff. Face to face
Set but this fiend of Ireland and myself;
And leave the rest to me. [*Shav enters*]. Who art thou?
That rearst a forehead almost rivalling mine?

SHAV. Nay, who art thou, that knowest not these features
Pictured throughout the globe? Who should I be
But G. B. S.?

SHAKES. What! Stand, thou shameless fraud.
For one or both of us the hour is come.
Put up your hands.

SHAV. Come on.

They spar. Shakes knocks Shav down with a straight left and begins counting him out, stooping over him and beating the seconds with his finger.

SHAKES. Hackerty-backerty one, Hackerty-backerty two,
Hackerty-backerty three... Hackerty-backerty nine—

At the count of nine Shav springs up and knocks Shakes down with a right to the chin.

SHAV [*counting*] Hackerty-backerty one,... Hackerty-backerty ten. Out.

SHAKES. Out! And by thee! Never. [*He rises*].
Younger you are
By full three hundred years, and therefore carry
A heavier punch than mine; but what of that?
Death will soon finish you; but as for me,
Not marble nor the gilded monuments
Of princes—

SHAV. —shall outlive your powerful rhymes.
So you have told us: I have read your sonnets.

SHAKES. Couldst write Macbeth?

SHAV. No need. He has been bettered
By Walter Scott's Rob Roy. Behold, and blush.

Roy Roy and Macbeth appear, Rob in Highland tartan and kilt with claymore, Macbeth in kingly costume.

MACBETH. Thus far into the bowels of the land
Have we marched on without impediment.
Shall I still call you Campbell?

ROB [*in a strong Scotch accent*] Caumill me no Caumills.
Ma fet is on ma native heath: ma name's Macgregor.

MACBETH. I have no words. My voice is in my sword.
Lay on, Rob Roy;
And damned be he that proves the smaller boy.

He draws and stands on guard. Rob draws; spins round several times like a man throwing a hammer; and finally cuts off Macbeth's head at one stroke.

ROB. Whaur's your Wullie Shaxper the noo?

Bagpipe and drum music, to which Rob dances off.

MACBETH [*headless*] I will return to Stratford: the hotels
Are cheaper there. [*He picks up his head, and goes off with it under his arm to the tune of British Grenadiers*].

SHAKES. Call you this cateran
Better than my Macbeth, one line from whom
Is worth a thousand of your piffling plays.

SHAV. Quote one. Just one. I challenge thee. One line.

SHAKES. "The shardborne beetle with his drowsy hum."

SHAV. Hast never heard of Adam Lindsay Gordon?

SHAKES. A name that sings. What of him?

SHAV. He eclipsed
Thy shardborne beetle. Hear his mighty lines.
[*Reciting*]
"The beetle booms adown the glooms
And bumps among the clumps."

SHAKES [*roaring with laughter*] Ha ha! Ho ho! My lungs like chanticleer
Must crow their fill. This fellow hath an ear.
How does it run? "The beetle booms—

SHAV. Adown the glooms—

SHAKES. And bumps—

SHAV. Among the clumps." Well done, Australia!

Shav laughs.

SHAKES. Laughest thou at thyself? Pullst thou my leg?

SHAV. There is more fun in heaven and earth, sweet William,
Than is dreamt of in your philosophy.

SHAKES. Where is thy Hamlet? Couldst thou write King Lear?

SHAV. Aye, with his daughters all complete. Coulds thou
Have written Heartbreak House? Behold my Lear.

A transparency is suddenly lit up, shewing Captain

Shotover seated, as in Millais' picture called North-West Passage, with a young woman of virginal beauty.

SHOTOVER [*raising his hand and intoning*] I builded a house for my daughters and opened the doors thereof
That men might come for their choosing, and their betters spring from their love;
But one of them married a numskull: the other a liar wed;
And now she must lie beside him even as she made her bed.

THE VIRGIN. "Yes: this silly house, this strangely happy house, this agonizing house, this house without foundations. I shall call it Heartbreak House."

SHOTOVER. Enough. Enough. Let the heart break in silence.

The picture vanishes.

SHAKES. You stole that word from me: did I not write
"The heartache and the thousand natural woes
That flesh is heir to"?

SHAV. You were not the first
To sing of broken hearts. I was the first
That taught your faithless Timons how to mend them.

SHAKES. Taught what you could not know. Sing if you can
My cloud capped towers, my gorgeous palaces,
My solemn temples. The great globe itself,
Yea, all which it inherit, shall dissolve—

SHAV. —and like this foolish little show of ours
Leave not a wrack behind. So you have said.
I say the world will long outlast our day.
Tomorrow and tomorrow and tomorrow
We puppets shall replay our scene. Meanwhile,
Immortal William dead and turned to clay
May stop a hole to keep the wind away.

Oh that that earth which kept the world in awe
Should patch a wall t' expel the winter's flaw!
SHAKES. These words are mine, not thine.
SHAV. Peace, jealous Bard:
We both are mortal. For a moment suffer
My glimmering light to shine.

A light appears between them.

SHAKES. Out, out, brief candle! [*He puffs it out*].

Darkness. The play ends.

THE END

Appendix

Uncollected Dramatic Writings

Introductory Note
Passion Play
Un Petit Drame
The Cassone
The Gadfly
The Inauguration Speech: An Interlude
Suggested Act III Ending for Barker's The Madras House
Beauty's Duty
Macbeth Skit
Glastonbury Skit
Skit for The Tiptaft Revue
The War Indemnities
The Yahoos
The Garden of the Hesperides
The Girl With the Golden Voice
Arthur and the Acetone
Sequence for The King's People
A New Ending for Clemence Dane's Cousin Muriel
Sequence for A Pageant of Plays and Players
Why She Would Not

Introductory Note

The dramatic writings of Bernard Shaw which appear in this appendix were excluded from his published canon either because they were abandoned fragments or because their author considered them to be occasional pieces of too specialised or ephemeral a nature to be of interest to the general reader. Yet, if Shaw spoke disparagingly of his early literary efforts as "all jejune and rotten" and dismissed the occasional pieces as trifles not fit to be published even among the "Tomfooleries" or the "Scraps and Shavings" of his Collected Edition, he still throughout his lifetime carefully preserved many of the fading holograph manuscripts and the typescripts, some of which bear signs of repeated, painstaking revision subsequent to original composition. And before he died Shaw bequeathed them to the British Museum for permanent preservation and availability to researchers.

For various reasons not all of the extant material is presented here. The scenario for a suggested play for G. K. Chesterton, *The Devil and St Augustine*, has recently been published in the *Collected Letters of Bernard Shaw 1898–1910*; two or three "dialogues" written as appendages to private correspondence have been reserved for later volumes of the *Collected Letters*; and under the terms and conditions of Shaw's will, his Trustees are enjoined from permitting, in a Collected Edition of his plays, the publication of discarded draft materials pertaining to those plays.

All of the surviving fragments of the unfinished plays have, however, been included, as well as all of the published (and a few unpublished) occasional pieces, plus the dramatization of Ethel Voynich's novel *The Gadfly*. These materials are published here, not because they are considered to be undiscovered masterpieces, but because they flesh out the portrait of Shaw as a creative artist, and present to the student of Shaw the working materials for a comprehensive study of his dramatic development.

It is ironic that Shaw should not have completed a play until 1892, his thirty-seventh year, when all evidence points to his dramatic instinct having surfaced before he had reached his teens. In his native Dublin he was an habitual patron of the Theatre Royal, where he gaped at the touring stars from the crowded pit, and familiarized himself with the repertoire of the local stock company. Later he frequented the newly-built Gaiety Theatre, where he made his first acquaintance with Gilbert and Sullivan through *Trial by Jury*.

At home he indulged in voluminous correspondence with his friend Matthew Edward McNulty, to whom he entrusted neatly penned copies of the burlesque dramas, the "unreserved soul histories," and the gory verse plays which he worked out, on a table in his room, with the aid of a toy theatre and cut-out scenes and characters from plays like Robert T. Conrad's *Jack Cade, the Captain of the Commons*, purchased in a small shop opposite the Queen's Theatre. And at school, when the teacher was absent from the room, Shaw entertained his eager deskmates in the Arithmetic class—Louis and Henry M'Intosh and David Tinkler—with stories from *The Iliad*, coloured with schoolboy vernacular and vigorously embellished with dramatic sketches depicting the puckish activities of a newly-introduced character named Lobjoe, in some ways akin to the Vice in the miracle plays, who constantly bedevilled the ancient heroes, tying strings across the path to ensnare the burly Ajax, crawling under the table to knot Nestor's beard around one of its legs, and pouring earth brimful into the helmet of Agamemnon.

After leaving school at fifteen and obtaining employment as a clerk in a land agent's office, Shaw's aspirations shifted for a brief time to the musical stage, he having envisaged himself as an opera singer. Thereafter, for a year or two, he gave consideration to a career in art. Following his emigration to London, however, his dramatic interests revived. After toying briefly in 1877 with the idea of writing "An Essay on Repartee. by Jesus Christ" he set seriously to work in February 1878 on a verse drama which at first he called *Household of Joseph*, but which subsequently came to be known simply as *Passion Play*.

Although he was to forsake the play in the midst of its second act, the surviving fragment indicates that, in spite of the difficulties Shaw was having with the verse form—and with Scripture (confusing Mary of Bethany with Magdalen), he had already begun to reveal such hallmarks of his creative genius as unorthodox, humanized treatment of historic characters, the technique of ironic inversion, the use of what he eventually would call "Shavio-Socratic" dialectic, and the creation of a dramatic dichotomy by setting up "mighty opposites" to voice the bifurcations of his argument. And in the play's thesis, that man by gradual improvement would lead himself to his own salvation, he had introduced the major element of his lifelong philosophy of Creative Evolution.

For half a dozen years after he set aside the scriptural play Shaw busied himself with fiction-writing, producing five novels and a fragment of a sixth before conceding that this was not his ideal métier.

In 1884 he was encouraged by William Archer to collaborate on a play which, eight years later and by now Archerless, was to emerge as *Widowers' Houses*, but not before it had been discarded and rewritten and discarded again and revised, while he continued to toy with other dramatic projects. In February 1886 he outlined a scheme for a comedy for the Kendals and their company at the St James's Theatre, but did not elaborate on it. And in 1889, moved by an incident (never clarified) involving William Archer and Janet Achurch, whom he had met a month previously, after her performance as Nora in *A Doll's House*, Shaw commenced a preliminary sketch—on the very night the Ibsen play closed—for a comedy of intrigue, *The Cassone*, whose characters indubitably were modelled after Archer, Mrs Archer, Janet Achurch, her husband Charles Charrington, and the bachelor Shaw.

In August of the same year he began an expanded treatment of the scenario, modifying it in many ways, and compressing all of the outline material for the first two acts into a single scene. The characters were remodelled and amplified, the conflicts more sharply defined, and the conventions of situation comedy given a series of unorthodox and even diabolical twists in the disjointed dialogues that Shaw scribbled into his notebook between the acts of a play, on joggling trains, in vegetarian restaurants, and on Socialist lecture platforms. The dialogues, he informed a journalist friend Tighe Hopkins, "are all working up to a certain end (a sermon, of course) . . . When I have a few hundred of these dialogues worked up and interlocked, then a drama will be the result—a moral, instructive, suggestive comedy of modern society, guaranteed correct in philosophic & economic detail, and unactably independent of theatrical considerations. . . . My business is to incarnate the Zeitgeist, whereby I experience its impulse and universality . . ."

He had incredible self-confidence that he would succeed as a dramatist. "Never fear," he told Hopkins in a second letter, "my comedy will not be unactable when the time comes for it to be acted . . . I have the instinct of an artist; and the impracticable is loathsome to me. But not only has the comedy to be made, but the actors, the manager, the theatre & the audience. Somebody must do these things—somebody whose prodigious conceit towers over all ordinary notions of success . . ."

Nevertheless, the inspiration for *The Cassone* quickly palled. After three efforts early in September and four in November, Shaw set the play aside, returning to it only to sketch in an unrelated dialogue in February 1890 and to make an effort the following November to expand the scene he had abandoned a year before. A leaf at the end is dated 14 April 1892, suggesting that he momentarily attempted to return to the play shortly before the successful completion and first production of *Widowers' Houses* in the same year, but its blankness is mute testimony to his final rejection of the work.

By the time Shaw gallantly undertook to dramatize Ethel Voynich's novel *The Gadfly*, he was a skilled playwright with eight completed works to his credit. The adaptation was designed to aid Mrs Voynich in fulfilling the requirements of the copyright law, at that time, for a public performance in a theatre in order to protect dramatic rights. It was composed hurriedly, under stress, squeezed into a fortnight in January 1898 which, as Shaw informed Ellen Terry, also included "three first nights, two County Council election meetings, four Vestry committees, one Fabian committee, a pamphlet to write about the Southwark police business . . . the Julius Cæsar article, and one frightful headache." The romantic tale, with its sprawl of time and place and its panoply of ritual and ceremony, was foreshortened, compressed, simplified —"a shocking travesty," Shaw called it in 1945, "sufficient to secure the copyright but quite unworthy of its original." The play as written is certainly unfeasible for performance, yet paradoxically the scenes which are dramatically the strongest and artistically the most effective in the play are those which are drawn largely, not from actual scenes in the novel, but from Shaw's imagination. The play, moreover, in many ways owes as much to *The Devil's Disciple*, written a year earlier, as to the novel.

The texts of *Passion Play* and *The Cassone* have been reproduced here from their original holograph manuscripts, as have several of the occasional pieces, with editorial emendations of punctuation as deemed necessary. *The Gadfly* has been set, also with editorial touches, from the surviving typescript. The remaining occasional pieces are reprinted from their original newspaper or magazine appearances, exactly as published. In all of the works emphasis in the dialogue has been indicated by spaced lettering rather than by italics.

D.H.L.

Passion Play

[Fragment, provisionally called *Household of Joseph*, written in February 1878. First published in a limited edition by the Windhover Press, University of Iowa, 1971. Reproduced here from the holograph manuscript in the British Museum: Add. Mss. 50593.]

PERSONS IN THE DRAMA

Jesus *illegitimate son of Mary*
Judas Iscariot *a rich nobleman*
Pontius Pilate *the Roman governor in Jerusalem*
Saul *one of his officers*
Joseph *a carpenter in Nazareth*
John *his son, a student*
James *brother to John, a child*
Peter *a fisherman, follower of Jesus*
John *a nobleman, follower of Jesus*
Barabbas *a robber*
Lazarus *a drunkard, brother to Martha and Mary Magdalen*
Mary *mother of Jesus, wife to Joseph*
Mary Magdalen } *sisters to Lazarus*
Martha }
Rahab *a Nazarene peasant*

ALSO Publicans, Roman Soldiers, Money Changers, Merchants, a Centurion.

ACT I

NAZARETH

SCENE I. *A workshop. Joseph and James discovered at work. Enter Mary.*

JOSEPH. I want my dinner.
MARY. Yes! You want your dinner.
Work for your dinner then. A thriftless sot!
Why did I marry thee?
JOSEPH. God knows, not I!
MARY. Small good I ever have received by thee.
JOSEPH. Ne'er hast thou had quarter so good a thing
As thy first born son; and him I swear
Thou never hadst by me.
MARY. Aye! you do well.
Flout me again before my child. Unmanly
Drunken and brutal, often hast thou left me
To toil in the parched field lest thou shouldst want.
Didst thou but hear the neighbours' wives comment
Upon thy vices, and my self denial,
Thou'dst blush.
JOSEPH. Well, tell me. What hast thou denied thyself?
Truly saith Jesu, there is but one luxury
Which thy self-sodden ignorance can appreciate;
That one, to use thy tongue. Thou plaguing bittern,
Deniest thou thyself that? No, though thou rob
My toilsome days of health, my rest of peace,
Still dost thou brawl, and in a house, alas!
Not wide, but narrower than to spare a room
Of refuge from thee. Solomon, oh Solomon,

Wisest of ancestors!—Seven hundred wives!
Wrathful Jehovah!—and three hundred—

MARY. Dog!
So wouldst thou have six hundred, if my eye
Relaxed from watching thee. 'Tis ever thus!
Talking of ancestors whom thou disgracest
When thou should'st work to feed my pretty James
And pay the Rabbi for instructing John.
Aye! you look sulky.

JOSEPH. Wife! to call me dog!
It is no wonder that the neighbours' dames
Point with derision at me. Go, get dinner.
The Rabbi's coffer shall be ready for him.
The fruit of four days' toil should pay him well
For teaching nonsense to a fool.

MARY. Now wert thou not
My wedded husband, I would have thee stoned
For thus blaspheming.

JOSEPH. Who first set my mind to't?
Your bastard! Heaven forgive me for reproaching
him.
No better boy alive.

MARY. Fit pet for thee!
A proud and good-for-nothing vagabond,
One who was born my shame, and lives to scorn me.
If he stay past his hour again today,
Though he be starving, he shall have no dinner.
No, not a sop.

JOSEPH. Would God 'twere ready!

JAMES. Mother,
I see John coming.

MARY. Dearest boy, how hard
He toils at learning. 'Tis a goodly thing
T'expound the prophets, sit among the wise
And be respected. In my family

The men were always clever.

Enter John.

JOHN. Mother, hail!
Blessing and length of days upon thy head
And—

JOSEPH. —Dinner?

MARY. Mind him not, my goodly son.
Let us hear more wise words.

JOHN. Nay, 'tis my duty
To bow before my father. What am I?
What are we all? Heaven is above us all.
We cannot count the stars, or tread upon
The restless sea, yet in the desert grey
Elijah needed not to starve.

JOSEPH. Who gainsays it?
Our carrion birds are kinder than our wives!
I want my dinner. I will have it too,
Or by the holy—

JOHN. Peace! forbear such words.
Rabbi ben Hadad, wisest of the wise,
Expressly saith—

JOSEPH. I will not have ben Hadad,
Ben Moses, nor ben ninety thousand devils,
But jolly Esau and sound common sense.
Wife, get the meat; or at thy shrewish head
This jackplane will I launch.

MARY. Durst thou but touch me,
Thou dry and drunken withered-palm—

JOHN. Nay, nay,
Good mother. Get the meal, *I* am enhungered.
I will convince my father's ignorance
With goodly precepts. These presumptuous scoffs
And boastful praises of the godless Edomite
Taught him by Jesus, can I with a breath
Learnedly vanquish. But to dinner now.

After, we will discourse. As for my brother,
We need not wait for him. As I came home
Behold the fields new stripped of golden grain,
Its drooping sheaves burdening the sluggish wain,
And midst a group of work-forgetting gleaners
Whose lewd large eyes applaud his heathen tales
Lies Jesus in the stubble on his back
Pouring forth volumes of delusive words.

MARY. Would I were near them, and him too—
the jades!
I doubt the wisdom of the gleaning law,
But things were otherwise when I was young.

JOSEPH. Curse your book talk and reminiscences.

Exit Joseph, kicking James out of his way. John follows him. James begins to cry.

MARY. My pet, my precious one, my darling child,
Come to your mother. Did he kick thee, dearest?
Hush, let me see it, did he bruise thee?—Ha!
Is this the garment that I gave thee yesterday,
Then new and spotless? Where hast thou been
climbing,
Thou peevish disobedient little mischief!
But this shall teach thee [*beats him violently*].

JAMES [*roaring*] Oh! Oh! Oh! Oh!! Oh!!!

[*Exeunt*]

Enter Jesus with a basket of carpenter's tools, which he flings into a corner. He walks noisily about the shop.

JESUS. Now to the purple grave of this wild day
Hies fast the inflaming sun. Damnable climate!
Thou makest my blood to boil. My teeming brain
As rich in purpose as my heart in love
Will scarce contain itself till time revenge
The evening's madness with the dawn's dejection.

He takes a turn round the shop.

Kind little Ruth!—she does admire too much.

Her goodness makes her wax somewhat insipid.
But Rahab! Gracious Heaven, there's a woman!
A fiery devil, sempiternally
Doomed to the roaring flames of Grecian Tartarus.
Whoosh! quoth the scholar. Oh! her snaky hair;
Her black, profound, unfathomable eye
Liquid as Shechem's well.
And the pert Deborah,
A sallow daughter of Jerusalem
Who thinks me mad. So indeed do they all.
They see me only in my mirthful rage;
And e'en when wretchedness hath closed his claw
Deep in my heart, then my sarcastic misery
Outlaughs the loudest. Hold, am I drooping? No!
I think on Rahab and my mocking spirit
Flies fiercely up, and 'mid the singing stars
Ecstatically dances. *Squabbling within*
Down again!
Grovel in domestic baseness, which will not
Permit thee to forget the thing thou art:
No son of fire and air, but the base issue
Of a poor workman's shrew. Tush, boy! no matter.
Where is my dinner? [*calling*] Goodman! mother!
Rabbi!

Enter Judas Iscariot.

JUDAS. Art thou a carpenter?

JESUS. At your service, sir.

JUDAS. I have a cabinet of cunning work
Which in my journey hither hath sustained
Some damage to its fastenings. Can'st thou work
In metals, for the clasps are made of brass?

Enter Mary, unobserved.

JESUS. To tell the truth, we are indifferent workmen.
We can fit stable doors and nail up fences,
Or hew out feeding troughs and pens for pigs,

But artists are we none. This ark of yours
Is, you say, costly. Better take it elsewhere.
We would but botch it.
JUDAS. How!
JESUS. Mistake me not.
I do not scorn your hire, but would not injure you,
By feigning—to the ruin of your ark—
A craftsmanship to which I have no claim.
JUDAS. Is there not one here who hath skill to carve?
JESUS. My brother thinks he can.
JUDAS. Art thou a fool?
Usest thou all thy customers like this?
How dost thou live?
MARY [*coming forward*] By sloth and idleness.
Great sir, this ragged fellow—
JESUS. Peace, be still!
Avoid thee. Sir, if you have any work
Befitting our attainments, we'll be thankful for't.
If not, wrong not yourself to buy us bread
As this, my mother, fain would have you do.
MARY. Thou filthy liar! Oh sir, heed him not.
Aught that you have to do can be done here
And, though I say it, no place better to
Be found in Galilee. 'Botch it'! Thou plague,
Thou pig, thou shalt eat husks which swine revolt from.
JUDAS. Be patient, pray! Good woman, this thy son
Seems an odd fellow.
MARY. He's the very worst
Of sons since Cain. Lo thee, his brothers, and
My husband.

Enter Joseph, James and John, who become extraordinarily obsequious on perceiving Judas.

JOSEPH. Sir, your very humble servant.

JOHN. Peace, corn and wine for ever be thy portion.
JUDAS. A student?
JOHN. Yea! a modest one.
JUDAS. Indeed!
Say, master carpenter, hast thou a hand
Accustomed to the fragrant southern woods
From which are carved those curious ointment boxes
Made in the east? One of them I possess
And I have broken it.
JOHN. To speak thus balmily
Thou surely hailest from Jerusalem.
JUDAS. Even so.
JESUS [*aside*] Jerusalem!
JOSEPH. Most gracious patron,
Apt wilt thou find us to excel in work
Such as thou speakest of.
JUDAS. It is from Persia
And delicately carved.
JOSEPH. We for such work
Employ our eldest son. He hath a taste
For moulding knobs and carving images.
Good Jesus, go. Attend this worthy stranger.
JUDAS. Why, he himself told me a moment since
That neither thou nor any of thy men
Can hold a saw.
JOSEPH. It is his modesty.
He's somewhat strange. Oft speaks he in this wise.
[*aside*] Plague on his conscience.
JUDAS. He shall come tomorrow
An hour after noon. Young man, thou knowest
The Way of Darkness, near the synagogue?
JESUS. It is a broad and pleasant path, wherein
Many do enter. I'll attend you, sir.
JUDAS. Farewell!
JOHN. All hail!

MARY. Beautiful sir, adieu!

JOSEPH. Safe be the journey of the gracious stranger.

JUDAS. Thanks, carpenter. Let not thy son forget.

[*Exit*]

JOSEPH. What is this thou hast told to yonder man?

MARY. What dost thou mean, to waste our daily bread?

JOHN. Dost thou not know thy duty to thy father?

Exit Jesus.

MARY. Thou dost most manfully to let him scorn thee.

JOSEPH. Rate him thyself. Thou canst do little else.

MARY. Thou hoary and debauchèd miscreant,
Take that! [*striking him*]

JOSEPH. Holy Elijah! [*beats her*]

JOHN [*interposing*] Jesus, ho!
Come help me here. Thus are my prospects ruined
By public brawling in the open shop.
How strongly have I striven to raise myself
Out of these vulgar shavings, and ye still
Make me the neighbours' scorn with your quarrels.
Oh mother, carest thou nothing for thy son?

MARY. I am lost, slain, clean undone. Now art thou satisfied?
Thou'st done't at last. Bury me with—

JOSEPH. Jehovah!
I did not mean to hurt thee, wife. Alas!

JOHN. What, Jesus, ho! Come hither, for God's sake!
Mother is dead. Come forth!

A pause.

MARY. Thou villain, thou!
Dost thou not sorrow for thy mother's death?

JESUS [*entering*] Thou bitter brawler, get thee to thy house

And mock with cleanliness the close domain
Which thou hast made a hell. Over thy grave
Shall fall no drops of heartfelt lamentation.
The noisy crying of the hired mourner
Shall, as a wolf, halloo thee to thy rest.
Duty! sayst thou? For me what hast thou done
More than a leopard for her whelp? What less
Than in the courtesy of the commonest stranger
I daily find? All! Thou hast been to me
An evil shade, to drive with oaths and blows
Or maudlin kisses scarce less despicable
All noble aspiration from my head
And poetry from my heart. 'Tis well for thee
Thou canst plead ignorance and thy maker's hand,
Else would the world, horrified at thy venom,
Tired of thy boasts, and at thy ignorance
Disgusted past expression, lift its hand
And sweep thee off, or hang thee up in chains
So that thy husband might no longer fear thee
And other shrews be warned. Hence to thy broom!
Nay, drop thine eyebrows; use has too much staled
That pitiful pretence of wonderment.
I will not hear thy clamour. 'Gainst my return
Which may hap after midnight, leave some supper
Where I may find it to my hand. Farewell! [*Exit*]

MARY [*weeping*]

Oh never, never since the world was made
Was woman so ill used as I by Jesus.
To think of all that I have done for him—
The sacrifices made, prayers offered up;
I have sat up four nights to watch his cradle
When he was ill with cold upon his chest
Caught as we rode from Bethlehem on an ass.

JOSEPH. Happy wert thou that hadst an ass to ride on.

I walked, and cursed be the soul of Herod
That put me to it.

MARY. Not in Nazareth
A kinder mother.

JOHN. In the law 'tis written
Honor thy father and thy mother. Jesus
Hath now transgressed the law, lifting his voice
Impiously against thee. He shall be punished.

MARY. I will not have him harmed.

JOHN. Nor would I.
But in him is a stiffnecked doubting devil
Which should be cast. The priests will reason with him.
Their gentle exhortation may do much,
Their stern authority will make him listen.

JOSEPH. I will not meddle in the undertaking.
Where priests are found, there mischief makes her bed.

MARY. An ingrate!—I am cut to the heart.—
Come in. [*Exeunt*]

SCENE II. *A field of stubble, lit by the harvest moon. Rahab discovered standing near the gate.*

RAHAB. I will go home. I'll not be served so lightly
Or wait for any man. Hist! Here he comes.
I'll pretend not to see him. [*Looks at the moon with affected carelessness*].

Judas appears behind the gate.

JUDAS. Exquisite night,
Thy harvest balm is heaven to my soul
After the parched stones of Jerusalem.
[*He uncovers his head and fans himself*].
Creation seldom seems so beautiful

And such a night as this illumes the grey
Of sceptical philosophy.

[*He covers himself, springs over the gate, and comes forward*].

Now to the winds
With speculations cramped and reasons close.
Leave to the pillared hall the pointed epigram
And here plunge headlong in a bath divine
Of moon lighted romance. Once—in my youth—
I hoped to be a poet, ere my pride
In reason's empire made me a philosopher;
And still the perfume of my early dreams
Smacks in my brain, responsive to the call
Of this enchanting scene. Judas! I love thee.
Thou art a rare fellow—now in Pilate's hall
An earthy libertine, and anon in Nazareth
Ethereal and sublime, a wanderer 'midst
The radiant stars. And yet a sorry creature
Without a crumb of knowledge to replace
The anchor, Faith, which thou hast cast away.
Pah!—A beastly world!—better believe in nothing
Than old wives' tales and murder-stained Jehovahs.
Avaunt, ye trains of logic. Up, Iscariot!
Be irresponsible, sublime, and young.
Enjoy, enjoy, bask in the sultry wind
And worship beauty even in ruthless Nature—

RAHAB [*aside*]
Pray will the fool stand muttering there all night?

JUDAS. Ha! 'Tis a woman. Alas! thou poor poor poet,
Grovelling already. Shall I retire? No!
The subtle devilry of this delights me,
A sarcasm on myself. She's beautiful,
Voluptuous as Jezebel. She sees me
And feigns to stargaze. They are all alike,

Mere brood cattle. [*Crosses the gate, and approaches her*]. Now for it. Prithee, dearest—
RAHAB. Oh Heaven! It is not Jesus.
JUDAS [*feigning surprise*] Strange mistake!
I took thee for Rebecca. Pray you, pardon me,
You are so beauteous.
RAHAB. Man!
JUDAS. Be not unkind,
Daughter of Galilee, to a sojourner
Upon thy borders. Weary from Jerusalem
By toilsome ways I came unto this place
Seeking beneath these gentle skies a respite
From threatening death. Art thou an Arab?
RAHAB [*with dignity*] Sir,
Jew of the Jews am I.
JUDAS. A Jew! but then
Thou canst not be a queen.
RAHAB. You mock me, sir.
JUDAS. Not I. Thy robe hangs on thee like a purple,
And majesty sits native on thy brow.
Vouchsafe me then to look a little while,
To touch your hand.
RAHAB. Your distance keep, I pray.
Thou stealing, midnight man, I do not know thee.
JUDAS. Know me then as thy slave, thy treasury
Of jewels rich and love profound as ocean.
No longer in the stubble shalt thou toil
No longer shall a hard and vulgar pallet
Receive those goddess limbs. The village girls
Shall envy thee, the rich and great shall court thee.
In gold and purple thou shalt press the grape
And sweep the city with a train of slaves.
The Roman governor shall kiss thy hand—
Say, hast thou ever seen Jerusalem?

RAHAB. The night goes on, I thank you for your words.
Your servant, sir, farewell!

JUDAS. Ah! clever one,
Wilt thou not be beguiled? Nay, stay a while.
We'll chat together. Thou art very competent
To guard thyself. Then, in the name of sense,
Don't, for a custom, steal a pleasant hour
From both of us. Come on across the fields,
We'll have a romp and talk about ourselves,
Thou of this village, I of any place,
For I've been everywhere. Thou doubtst me still?

RAHAB. I do not fear you.

JUDAS. No, nor need not to.
Let's have a race.

RAHAB. I will, for devilment.
Ha! ha! Come on.

JUDAS [*aside*] Modest young creature.

They are running off, arm in arm, when they are met by Jesus, who runs against them.

JESUS. Rahab!

JUDAS. How dost thou, master carpenter?

JESUS. Oh shameless!
Dost thou betray me for the first rich stranger
That offers thee vile gold and viler words?

RAHAB. Pray, who art thou, that dar'st to question me?
Thou carpenter! [*to Judas*] Sir, do not heed this fellow.
Because at some of his impertinences
I have laughed in the fields, he thus makes bold with me.

JUDAS [*to Jesus*] If thou'rt too honest for a carpenter,
How hast thou ventured to essay the lover

Who should be full of lies? Imperious Rahab,
Relent, and let him go with us.

RAHAB. Indeed!

JESUS. I do not need your lordship's intercession.

RAHAB. I will go home.

JUDAS. Good night!

A pause, and exit Rahab angrily.

Well, friend. Thou starest.

JESUS. Why did'st thou let her go?

JUDAS. Marry, because
I value her more justly than thou dost.
My friend, thou art young, and in a woman's eyes
Thou findest unimaginable things:
Sympathy, purity, kinship into heaven,
A divine something far beyond the scope
Of sordid man—Alas! It is not so.
All she possesses is contained in thee
And forms that portion of thy disposition
Which most thou dost mistrust, hate, and despise,
Glorying in that of which she nothing hath
And cannot understand.

JESUS. I pity thee,
Thou joyless cynic, ne'er canst thou have loved.

JUDAS. Dost thou love Rahab?

JESUS. No.

JUDAS. Hast ever loved?

JESUS. I have not yet met—

JUDAS. The ideal woman,
Nor wilt thou ever. Look into thine heart.
How far from that ideal art thou thyself?
And yet, I tell thee, never such a paragon
Existed amongst women as could boast
Half of thy worth. Deal with me candidly,
Hast ever found a woman that would stand
The test of intimacy?

JESUS. I know naught
Of the great world beyond this wretched village.
JUDAS. This wretched village, as thou call'st it
(Thou man exceeding young), is a true image
Of all the world. The women of Jerusalem
An extra vice or so can boast, and they
Would stab thee with a somewhat subtler wit
Than Rahab. But it is the method only
That differs in them. Heart of womankind
Is the same shallow thing from Dan to Beersheba,
And woe betide thee if thou build thy future
On any supposition of their goodness.
'Twill not be then to wince, as thou didst now
When the offended jade spat out her venom
Of 'carpenter' and 'Do not heed this fellow';
But bitter, lasting disappointment, gnashing
Of teeth a while, then lifelong sourness.
A prospect green.
JESUS. Touching what Rahab said,
I am not offended; what care I for such?
JUDAS. Your mind runs on it rather?
JESUS. Not at all.
Thou need'st not smile. [*a pause*]
Stranger, I had resolved
That cost me what it would, I ne'er would stoop
Even to think a lie. Now have I told one.
I feel her insult stinging none the less
Because I know it to be coarse and worthless.
This I denied to thee, and in thy face
Saw that the lie was futile. I mistook.
I thought because to tell the truth o' the shop
And of our household brawls was easy to me,
Nay, flattering to my vanity, as it made me
Marked out as singular, I could be just
In other things as well; but I was wrong.

Common things touched me not, I soared above them.
Yet this—alas!—I thought it was below me
And it strikes home. I am a weak creature.
She hath turned the sky black.
JUDAS. Tush! Enough of her.
Thou art no common man, why dost thou rot
In this forgotten corner.
JESUS. Be it curst.
I sometimes wish, by Heaven, I had the power
To extinguish it like Sodom—leave not one
Of all who know my wretched history
Alive to blight me with contemptuous memories.
I know 'tis peevish, impious, and selfish,
But sometimes cannot help it.
JUDAS. Hearken gravely.
I recognise the course thou hast started on;
But strong must be thy brain, and clear thy mind
If thou would'st reach the seeming wintry goal
Undaunted. Ere thou see the crooked straight
And the rough places plain, thou may'st recoil
Before the bloody teeth of monstrous nature.
Think for thyself, and it must come to this:
That the great God will seem a silly idol;
The prophets, raving and hysteric madmen,
Poets driven wild by their corrupt surroundings;
Creation will retire behind a veil,
Riddle inexplicable!
Then must thou
Learn to stand absolutely by thyself,
Leaning on nothing, satisfied that thou
Can'st nothing know, responsible to nothing,
Fearing no power and being within thyself
A little independent universe.
JESUS. But this is atheism.
JUDAS. 'Tis so. What then?

JESUS. Behold the world. Somebody must have made it.
JUDAS. Somebody must have made this somebody.
JESUS. Some cause must have existed from all time.
JUDAS. I may as easily say the world has too.
But friend, thou reasonest like a carpenter.
Thou makest coffers; ergo, all visible coffers
Must have been made by hands intelligent
As thine are. But behold yon sheaves of wheat.
They were not planed nor sawn; from a small grain
They grew, containing in themselves the principle
That thou would'st force on an eternal craftsman.
And since thou can'st not cause a box to grow
Thou must conclude the cause of all creation
Is something wholly different from thy craft.
Thou can'st make nothing, thou can'st only fashion
What thou find'st made already. Why dost thou then
Believe a God created in thine image?
JESUS. God can do all things.
JUDAS. To patch up thy doctrine?
Or wantonly to baffle questioning man?
JESUS. If thou believest naught, I cannot argue.
Thou hast no basis.
JUDAS. Take then for thy basis
All thou hast ever seen of man or world.
What would'st thou wider?
JESUS. Basis this is none,
For what I see I cannot understand.
JUDAS. Why dost thou then pretend to understand it?
'Tis thou dictat'st to me how all was made.
I tell thee thou know'st naught concerning it.
JESUS. I prithee, hold; over this weary ground
Often in meditation have I travelled.
I am better used to be called 'Infidel!'

Than, as by thee, accused of superstition.
For, till this day, I never met a man
Who believed less than I. I do confess
The God of Scripture is a gloomy tyrant
On whom I cannot bring myself to look.
But, were I to believe no God at all
I would, despairing, die; I could not face
A stony blank of vegetable life
Preying upon itself. No! I believe
A grand, ineffable, benevolent Power
Throned in the clouds, and all composed of Love
Whose influence, though obscured by death and sin
(The origin of these inexplicable),
Yet gives us all that's noble in our nature
And draws our souls, aspiring, to its majesty.
Death is to me the portal to this presence.
And sure am I, though worms destroy this body
God shall not suffer me to see corruption.
JUDAS. Art thou so learned? Thou hast read the Scripture.
I'll not debate with thee, for I perceive
Thou art a poet, and hast made a refuge
In rosy bowers of imagination
Where thy o'erburdened, questioning soul may rest.
Yet would I not exchange the mail of proof,
Hard though it be, in which I combat destiny
For the soft woven but delusive robe
In which thou dost so meekly wrap thyself.
JESUS. It may be, yet I marvel what thou livest for.
My vision of a sempiternal state
Of love and universal brotherhood
Is as a goal and beacon to my path.
But what hast thou to seek?
JUDAS. Only the truth.
How selfish are all creeds! The atheist only,

Thirsting for truth and knowledge, sternly waives
All paradise for himself. Of all mankind
He is the only man who dares to die:
The rest must bolster up their wormy lives
With flattering lies and heavens specially made
For their delight. Therefore I thank kind nature
For giving me such an unruly mind
That all the splendours of the temple failed
To tempt me to accept it for my prison.
And still I find the open fields without
The freest and the happiest.
JESUS. But thy hopes?
Hast thou no more disquiet than the bees?
JUDAS. Man, as thou know'st, can suffer and enjoy,
Though, for the most part, betwixt these extremes
He vegetates indifferently. Now, to me
The fittest study for a feeling man
Is ceaseless observation of his fellows,
Whereby he comes to know himself by them
Having first learnt their nature from his own.
This knowledge reached, the student straight becomes
A solitary watcher of the world,
A man whose sympathies are so enlarged
That he is lost above the vulgar crowd,
Who straight cry 'Joyless cynic,' 'Atheist!'
In parrot fashion. But the man, unmoved,
Feeling the stream of happiness steadily rising
Though but an inch gained midst a hundred ebbs,
Exultingly foresees the distant age
When man shall conquer pain, and on the brow
Of Death place an imperishable wreath.
And what more rosy vision can'st thou conjure
With thy o'ershadowing, slave-suggested God
Than this that I have of a time to come
When Man, impenetrable, calm, and knowing,

Shall carry life so loftily, that pleasure
Will almost lose its meaning, and the horror
Of writhen Pain be as a thing unknown.
By the sure warrant of mine eyes and History
I know that this will come to pass at last
Unless the earth dissolve first. This, to thee
I know, is too remote and unsubstantial
To satisfy thy craving for perfection.
And thou, a hot and sentimental youth,
Would'st cut the knot by a poetic myth
Which will shew grim enough when scrutinized,
But which reserves unto thyself a share
Of the soft sunset-colored lovers' rapture
Thou dreamest of. Now I, a man unblinded
And trained to shun the snare of self delusion,
Know that my very dust will scarce exist
When man shall have no reason to despise himself.
I live, almost content, and set my hand
To pick a pebble from the mighty mountain
Whose giant shadow keeps the world in darkness,
Heaped, like the Pyramid, by throngs of slaves
Whose hands, to glorify their master, Ignorance,
Piled this dull ground of superstition up.
Thus I to reason trust, and thou to dreams.
But, save that I ask no part for myself
Except the foretaste which my mind supplies,
We look to the same end. Then let's take hands.
I do not often meet a man like thee
And fain would be thy friend.

JESUS. I scarce can follow
Thy strange and abstract form of philosophy,
For so it seems to me. I am a carpenter,
By birth a bastard, in my workday nature
A man with all the failings of a man.
Thou seemest of high caste, and thy booklearning

Far beyond mine. Wilt thou then take my hand?
JUDAS. I will indeed. Henceforth, thy gentle faith
Shall travel hand in hand with hard negation,
Tempering its unsympathetic edge
And learning somewhat from its breadth of vision.
Trust me not, though, too quickly. Man is fickle,
And all that I have said under these stars
Tomorrow I may laugh at. But fear nothing:
I will not laugh at thee. What are thy plans?
JESUS. I have formed none. The more I strive to solve it
The more perplexed my future fate appears.
I am not learned. Carpentry I hate.
The people will not listen to my preaching—
JUDAS. What! Thou can'st preach! I will find listeners for thee.
No longer must thy life be wasted here;
Thou must come with me to Jerusalem.
There is a man of whom thou mayst have heard
Called John the Baptist. By the Jordan side
He preaches and baptizes, and hath stirred
The groaning and Rome-ridden mob so deeply—
They thirst for knowledge, change, liberty, anything!
And there are certain things which he hath dropped
Hints of—one who shall soon come after him—
Which will secure the peoples' willing ears
To any man who hath ability
To seize the chance. We'll plan the matter further
When we are on the scene. Say, wilt thou come?
JESUS. I cannot grasp this project all at once.
Give me some time to think. And yet what needs it?
I must begin to live and work.
JUDAS. Not soon
Will such another chance present itself.
JESUS. I am resolved. I'll go.

JUDAS. Sensibly said.
Meet me hard by at dawn.
JESUS. I will. Farewell!
I cannot stay to talk. This resolution
Is like a sudden plunge into a flood;
It leaves me blind and breathless.
JUDAS. Then farewell.
Exeunt severally.

SCENE III. *The same. Early morning. A crowd of idlers on the highway watching Jesus and Judas, who ride by. Also Rahab.*

SOME BYSTANDERS.
Hail prophet! Goest thou to seek thy father?
OTHERS. Where did'st thou steal that ass?
OTHERS. Beware, beware,
Thy mother follows thee. She wields a strap.
JESUS. In Heaven's name, let us hasten.
RAHAB. See the carpenter
In haste to make his fortune.
MOB. Stone them! Stone them!
Exeunt Jesus and Judas, followed by some of the mob.
A REAPER. Why, Rahab girl. Thou bit'st thy lip.
Thou'rt weeping.
RAHAB. Let me alone. I always hated him.
He thought he duped—
THE REAPER. Peace, here his mother comes.
Enter Mary, distractedly, followed by Joseph.
BOYS. Hail Mary! Hail Mother Mary the shrew!
When didst thou last flog Joseph? Long-tongued Mary!
JOSEPH. Avaunt, ye curs. Where's my apprentice gone?

MARY. My son! My son! He has left me. Where is he?
REAPER. Gone not long since at full speed on an ass
With the rich stranger and his cavalcade.
MARY. Alas! my child. He never will come back.
From such a mother gone—
RAHAB. Thou stinging adder,
'Tis thou hast driven him hence; but for thy tongue
He had stayed with me.
JOSEPH. Good Rahab, no more words.
Wife, come thou home. He shortly must come back.
MARY. *I* driven him hence! I will come home no more. [*she faints*]

Curtain. End of Act I

ACT II

JERUSALEM

SCENE I. *Interior of the Temple, presenting the appearance of a great bazaar. The followers of Barabbas bartering their spoils. Judas is seen pointing out the various sights to Peter and John.*

BARABBAS. Ho, friend! Did we not meet at Betharaba?
A PUBLICAN. Aye, I remember. How of the savage prophet?
BARABBAS. A surly fool. After we met, one day,
I found him at the old tricks of his trade
Calling the people vipers, threatening hell
Till the old women shook again. Then I,
Accosting him, inquired what I should do
To keep my bones clear of his brimstone lake.
'Soldier,' says he, 'do violence to no man.
See thou accuse none falsely. With thy wages
Be even content.' At which I thrust my tongue
Between my teeth, and roared a jolly stave
That drowned his preaching.
A ROMAN SOLDIER. Why! the man is mad.
What is the soldier's trade but violence,
And plunder, to eke out his scanty dole?
PUBLICAN. Fantastic and impracticable youths,
Bred to no trade, do often air such crotchets.
My business having brought me to the Jordan
I asked this John the Baptist for advice.
Quoth he 'Exact no more than is appointed.'

A fool could say as much.
R. SOLDIER. Yet many think
He is Elias.
BARABBAS. Pooh! He's out of fashion.
The newest man is entering Jerusalem.
I passed him on the way; the girls are mad
And dance before his donkey, strewing garlands,
Crying 'Hosanna to the Son of David'
And whispering 'What a goodly man it is.'
Yet he is but a paltry Nazarene
Who made a fortune by a great picnic.
They say he fed ten thousand followers
Upon a dozen loaves, and at a wedding
Turned water into wine. Amongst the Gadarenes
He played the devil with two thousand pigs
And is—to boot—a potent quack. He cures
All ills, from warts to blindness.
A MERCHANT. Yea! 'tis true.
This is avouched by men of the first credit.
BARABBAS. Marvels and ghosts will ne'er lack witnesses.
Why must a prophet be a conjuror?
Were he to raise Adam and Eve to life
It would not prove his sayings to be true.
These miracles turn reason into foolishness
'Stead of convincing reason. And at last
The prophets are destroyed, and cannot save themselves
With all their tricks. They make a fool of God!
The others draw away from him.
What? Are ye frightened at plain speaking? Jesus
—That's the new prophet's name—will give ye plenty of it.
He says, we must return good for evil,
Blessing for cursing, and cast out the law

Of eye for eye, and tooth for tooth.
PETER. Good friend,
Thou talkest ignorantly.
BARABBAS. Wilt thou teach me better?
What art thou? Friends, behold a fisher fellow
Come up to preach i' the Temple.
PETER. Blusterer,
Soon shalt thou know—
JUDAS. Peace, friend; thou art not now
Expounding on thy native beach. Discretion
Alone can serve the master's cause. Barabbas, [thou]
Hail from the mountains. Hast had luck last foray?
BARABBAS. Rejoiced am I to see Iscariot here.
But pray beware the priests. When in the city
I talk not loudly about my profession,
For prejudice still holds. Your follower
Seems somewhat hotheaded.
JUDAS. No need to heed him.
He follows Jesus, whose precepts upon
The doctrine of revenge are much belied.
And hearing you echo the common cry
It moved him.
BARABBAS. Well, let him explain his point.
PETER. What our Lord saith is this. He that returns
Evil for evil, good for good, as use
All men to do, for this can claim no credit.
For 'tis their interest and inclination,
And even so also do the publicans.
But if man seek reward beyond the world,
Then must he render good beyond the world
And benefit his foes. This is sheer virtue
With no terrene set off, and such may claim
Reward in Heaven.
BARABBAS. Doctrine most excellent!
Would those I rob would act on it. Yet no.

For all the world would turn to brigandage.
Hark! what a hubbub. What is here? Close up!

A crowd enters the Temple. Great confusion ensues, the merchants defending their stalls, and a few Roman soldiers endeavoring to preserve order. Then enter Jesus, excitedly.

JESUS. Yea! They have told me truly—

JUDAS. Art thou mad?
—Leprosy seize these pushers!—Jesus! Friend!
I cannot reach him, and his blood is boiling,
The crack brained fool.

JESUS. Beneath this roof august,
Ordained a house of prayer for all the people,
I had hoped that truth might find a peaceful hearing.
I have come; and lo! I find a den of thieves.

MONEY CHANGER.
Stand from my gold, thou daylight drunkard!

JESUS [*overthrowing the table*] Slave!
Hence with thy lucre. I will purge this fane
From thy corruption.

BARABBAS. Bravely said. What ho!
Turn out the bloodsuckers!

PUBLICANS. Treason! Sedition! Murder!

MONEY CH. My gold. Thieves! Murder!

SOLDIERS [*struggling amidst a general riot with the followers of Barabbas, who seize money and merchandize*]
Peace, in Cæsar's name!

BARABBAS [*taking a money changer's purse*]
Usurious dog, yield thy illgotten gain!

ROMAN SOLDIER [*pushing him back*]
Peace, thou unruly fellow.

BARABBAS. May hell swallow thee!

[*Kills him with a blow of his mace. The rioters pause, terror stricken, and the soldiers seize Barabbas.*]

Rescue me, ho! [*no one responds*] Ye curs, suffer ye this?

A SOLDIER [*striking him on the mouth*]
Silence, thou bloody man.
JUDAS. Truly, Barabbas,
Thou art caught at last. I think they will spread-eagle thee.
BARABBAS. Aye! I am netted, curse them. Prithee give
Some money to the gaoler, lest I starve.
CENTURION. Drag off the murderer.
JESUS. Nay, but let him go.
Iniquity, breeding iniquity,
Through me hath caused this riot. Let me suffer.
A PRIEST. He hath confessed. He did begin it. Seize him!
JUDAS [*to the centurion*]
Thou wilt lose both the prisoners if thou stay'st.
The mob is waking.
CENTURION [*to Jesus*] At some other time
I hope to drag thee, prophet, to the tree.
Away to prison.

Exeunt Centurion and soldiers, with Barabbas and the body of their comrade. The rest follow curiously, and Jesus is left alone with Judas. The former is greatly dejected, the latter walks softly about in thought, occasionally laughing to himself.

JUDAS. Humph! How very easy
It is to knock the life out of a man,
Considering how tedious 'tis to make one.
Heavens! just to see the fellow turn green and drop!
The rascal's mace fell like a thunderbolt
Fair on his temple.
JESUS [*shuddering*] Would I had seen it!
JUDAS [*surprised*] Why?
JESUS. To save me from my fancy, which fills up
The outline thou hast limned, so sick'ningly

It frightens me.
JUDAS. Indeed, it seems so. Come!
Cheer up, my friend. You look as sad as Job
Plunged in cutaneous misery on his dunghill.
JESUS. And thou canst laugh! Is murder mirth to thee?
Dost thou forget that at my hands this blood
Will be required. Oh miserable vanity!
Oh wretched worm, that came to mend the world
Having served apprenticeship to mending sticks;
That came to drive corruption from the temple
And in its sacred hall let loose foul murder.
His friend an atheist, his flock a rabble,
Himself an ignorant bastard. Bitter lesson!
Torturing rebuke!—But I am cured of madness.
I will go forth and wander with the lepers,
My features veiled, my presence shunned of man,
My memory cursed—
JUDAS. Tush! man. Enough of this.
How wilt thou bear to see corruption writhe
And the deep rooted faith of Abraham
Tramped in the dust, if thou dost blench before
The vulgar murder of a hired homicide?
The man was not immortal—would have died
Perhaps in torture, had not yon stern bandit
Forestalled Death's arrow with his iron mace.
If 'twas ordained, it was not so by thee;
If chance, it lay far beyond thy control.
No faith or truth has ever yet been preached
But has been made by rascals a pretext
To serve their ends; and hop'st thou to escape
This healthy ordeal, which truth survives,
But beneath which falsehood and vanity
Collapse in rottenness and black oblivion.
Why, if thy doctrines live, the world will see

Not single men, but fertile provinces
Ravaged by fire and sword for thy name's sake
As horribly as Canaan. Let us go.
Arise and waste no thought on the slain jackal.
JESUS. How easy 'tis to slander those we injure!
An hour ago we owed that soldier nothing,
Durst not have used him but with courtesy.
Yet, having stolen his life and slain his soul
By tripping up his sanguinary rage,
We loudly call him 'murderer' and 'oppressor'
As though his guilt, even were it proved and known
Instead of our invention and excuse,
Could lighten our responsibility.
But thou art right. Ours be the common plea
We are no worse than others. Even so,
What if we were in deed, my aim is good.
That thought shall chase my squeamishness away.
I have too much boy left in me. Come! We'll go
And seek a lodging house without the city
According to our plan.
JUDAS. Thy fits of gloom
Are beyond reason. Thy recoveries
Beyond belief. Never was such a man
For wild extremes as thou. Now in the clouds
A raptured prophet: and anon in hell
Gnashing thy teeth in horrible despair.
Thou dost disgust me with thine instability.
When I am sad, heaven might throw wide its gate,
I could not lift my head.
JESUS. Talk thou no more.
Come on.
JUDAS. To Bethany!
JESUS. Why there?
JUDAS. Because
I have bespoken lodging for thee there.

Two sisters keep the household for their brother.
The very man for thee, a desperate sot,
Who drinks himself to death's door thrice a week.
Thou canst reform him, perhaps Mary too—
That may prove perilous though.

JESUS. What is this Mary?

JUDAS. A modern Eve. A petulant impenitent,
A lovely woman, friend. Her hair's of Ophir,
Her eyes are sapphire made instinct with life—
But thou must see her. Do not touch her though,
This rose of Sharon, for she's dangerous
And snares the wisest and the purest men.
She once snared me.

JESUS. Indeed?

JUDAS. What! Thou sarcastic!
The man who never smiles. Yet I was pure,
And, for my age, wise. But I was too young
To shun the bait, although I saw the snare.
I freed myself at last, and felt as though
I had left half my soul behind. At present
I am none the worse, and almost think the dream
Was worth the waking.

JESUS. If she softened thee
She is a wonder. We had best be going.
The sun will soon be setting. As we go
I will be glad to hear about thy weakness.
'Twill be a change from thy philosophy,
To hear thee talk of which one would suppose
Thou had'st a heart of flint. Let us set forth.

[*Exeunt.*]

Enter severally. Peter and John the Apostle.

JOHN. Where is the master?

PETER. What is that to thee?
It is for thee to follow, not to question.
Thou art too forward, stripling. I have noted thee.

Thoud'st be, forsooth, the master's favorite.
JOHN. I strive at least to keep the master's doctrine.
Why dost thou rail upon me thus?
PETER. Why not?
Pray who art thou, that mayst not be bespoke
But cap in hand. Know, thou vainglorious upstart,
I am as good as thou in sight of heaven.
JOHN. Well, who gainsays it?
PETER. Do not thou.
JOHN. And wherefore?
PETER. Because I will not brook it from thee.
JOHN. Fellow!
Beware thou threaten not. Do not presume,
Because thou wast a netmender, to think
Thou canst abuse all men of gentler nurture—
PETER. Indeed? The little lord is growing angry.
JOHN. Go to, thou art a fool. Hope not to foist
Thy devil's temper upon me.
PETER. Our Lord
Hath said that he who calls his brother fool
Shall suffer hell.
JOHN. Yea! but when said he
That Peter was my brother?
PETER. Am I then
Not good enough for thee?
JOHN. Thy pride again,
Troublesome hound!
PETER [*seizing him*] By Baal, I'll murder thee.

They wrestle and buffet one another. A March. Enter a guard of Roman soldiers, followed by an open litter in which is Mary Magdalen. Pontius Pilate walks beside. Soldiers, musicians, mob &c follow. Also Saul. The soldiers seize Peter and John, and separate them.

PILATE. What are these?
A GUARD [*holding Peter*] Galileans, sir, to judge

By this one's tongue.

PILATE. Bear them away and scourge them.

JOHN. In the name of justice—madam—

PILATE. Take them hence.

MARY. Nay, bring them back. Let's hold a court i' the temple.
I will be judge, and thou shalt be my lictor.

PILATE. But what a scandal—

MARY. Darest thou delay?

PILATE. Sweet, thou art mad. No matter. If thou wilt
Thou shalt be governor. Set down the litter.
Bring up the men.

Peter and John are set before Mary and Pilate.

Now, sirrahs, answer us.
Are there no temples in Capernaum
Where ye can brawl and—

MARY [*to Pilate*] Lictor, hold your peace.
[*to John*] Hast thou a wife?

JOHN. No, madam.

MARY. Ah! Poor boy!
Thou need'st not blush.

JOHN. Madam, I am not used
To see in holy places women's heads
Uncovered.

PILATE. Fellow, best bridle thy wit.

MARY. Bridle thy tongue, oh saucy governor,
The prisoner's a goodlier fellow than thou.
Now, of your condescension, pretty youth,
Tell us what was your quarrel with your elder?

John hesitates and remains silent.

Lictor, command the captive to reply.

PILATE. Hebrew, obey the court.

PETER. He cannot tell
For shame. I, being his senior, did reprove him

For bearing arrogantly on his fellows.
Whereon he gave me foul words, and we quarrelled.
MARY. I do not like thee, fellow.
SAUL. Please you, madam,
These men are followers of Jesus.
PILATE. Are they?
How know'st thou that? The new risen Elias
Preaches not fisticuffs.
SAUL. They marched beside him
This morning when he entered. In the gate
I watched, and saw them.
PILATE. Are ye Christians?
PETER, JOHN [*after a moment's hesitation*] Yea!

A great laughing.

PILATE. A peaceful and an honorable sect.
PETER. Unworthy as we are—
MARY. I tire of this.
Send them away, I prithee. Hurt them not,
For the sake o' the younger.
PILATE. Hark ye, rioters.
For centuries your fathers cursed the earth
With blood and rapine, lust and public stonings,
And the old leaven still is strong enough
To breed sedition, and forgetfulness
Of Roman discipline. But be advised.
Ye killed a man this morning on these flags.
For the next twelvemonth shew but half a tooth
I'll fling your carcases to the four winds,
Your daughters to my soldiers; tear your streets up
And make your temple smoke. Hence with you all,
Vile rabble, and but dare to breathe a murmur
And look for massacre.

The mob sneak off.

[*to Peter and John*] What wait ye for?

Were ye not bid begone? Go tell your master
What ye have done for him, and say his head
Were safer thrust within a lion's jaws
Than breeding mischief in my jurisdiction.
No words. Away!

They are driven out.

Fairest, forgive my wrath.
Of all the irksome tasks a man can have,
This kennel keeping is the worst. I would
That Cæsar cracked the whip himself. I am weary of it.

MARY. Poor governor. Why does it not resign?

PILATE. Thou would'st not come to Rome. So I should lose thee.

MARY. Thou hast thy wife.

PILATE. Come! This is idle talk.
Having harangued the people, I'll not stay
To prate with priests. The banquet is appointed
For the twelfth hour. We will dance and sing
And drink the stars asleep.

Exeunt.

SCENE II. *Bethany. Sunset. A garden before the house of Lazarus. Jesus seated, watching the sky. Judas standing near.*

JUDAS. Now, ere we part, hast thou made up thy mind

JESUS. Yea.

JUDAS. Well?

JESUS. How wearisome are these details!
I am well content with the lodging. It is peaceful.
The garden's pretty, and my chamber looks on it.
This Martha seems a kind and quiet woman

And keeps the house well swept. Take rest tonight
For on the morrow thou must go with me,
Shew me the public places of resort,
And help me to select some hillside near,
Where I may set to work without delay.

JUDAS. Dost thou not, looking yonder, feel thy plans
Snatch a factitious glory from that sky
Of flawed purple? 'Tis a curious habit
To let our hearts die with the setting sun
And keep our tearsprings fruitful. Poor King Ahab,
What with an arrowhead, a failing battle,
And sentimentally gazing on Phoebus,
Killed himself outright. Once I travelled west
And found that there the sun sunk gloriously
In gold and crimson billows shored around
By banks of green like emerald. Yet I think
The ineffable purple native to our land
Transcends it far. By Heaven, I revel in it.
It makes me feel colossal, fire created,
Sublime! There is a taste of tragedy
In thinking that the day we bid farewell
Never returns again.

JESUS. Is not that sad?

JUDAS. No, it is grand, inspiring. Filthy earth
Breeds sadness in the hearts of girls and boys
And bitterness in men. But rhapsody
Finds sentiments like these too small for it
And swells itself with fancies vast as chaos
Magnified out of crotchets—silly enough
Too, when you analyse them. Fare thee well.

Exit.

JESUS. I never think that man a genius but
He straightway shews himself a mountebank.

Re-enter Judas.

JUDAS. In my anxiety to cap my speech

With an appropriate vanishing, I forgot
A word I meant to say.

JESUS. Out with it, then.

JUDAS. This woman—Martha's sister—she I told you of—

JESUS. You said you loved her.

JUDAS. I am now in earnest.
If she should fall in love with thee—

JESUS. With me!

JUDAS. Remember thou art not the first or fiftieth
Nor wilt thou be the last of her light passions.

JESUS. Thou need'st not fear.

JUDAS. Natheless I do fear much.
Wait till thou see'st her.

JESUS. Good!

JUDAS. First let me tell thee
That she hath followed the contemned profession,
Antique and popular, of—

JESUS. Prithee stay.
Use with me every privilege of a brother.
Criticise, ridicule me, if you will,
But do not talk licentiously to me.
How, with such converse ringing in mine ears,
Can I exhort the people?

JUDAS. Dreamer. Good night!
I doubt the world will prove too hard for thee.
Ponder my words.

JESUS. Good night! I will remember.

Exit Judas. The sun has disappeared, and the scene darkens. The galloping of a horse breaks the twilight silence. Enter Saul hurriedly.

SAUL. Sot, is thy sister here?

JESUS. Friend, you mistake me,
I have no sister. I am newly lodged here.

SAUL. Knowest thou Mary, sister to thine host?

JESUS. By reputation only.

SAUL. Is she here?
Speak, man!

JESUS. Good youth, be patient. Go within.
There they perchance will tell thee what thou seekest.

Enter Mary Magdalen.

SAUL. If thou canst tell me anything of her
Or get me access to her, here is gold.
The governor hath promised me my troop,
So I get speech of her.

MARY. Whom dost thou seek?

SAUL. Madam, the governor— [*he hesitates*]

MARY. Well, what says he?
What must his message be, when even his parasite
Finds his tongue stumbling o'er it?

SAUL. Gracious lady,
He begs you will return and grace his banquet.

MARY. Ha! and what further?

SAUL. That you will forgive
His thoughtless speech, which on his sacred word
He swears had no import that could offend you.
And as a token of his deep contrition
He sends this jewel—

MARY. Get you gone.

SAUL. Dear Lady!—

MARY. Sycophant, hence! Take thy bribe back. Thy patron
Shall know that dreamer of the day of wrath,
His wife, is not the type of all her sex
Nor I his slave. Begone! If thou delay
I will unloose the dogs upon thee. Go!

SAUL. I deserve this, for stooping to do errands
To such as thou. I will report your words.

[*Exit.*]

MARY [*falling on her knees, and swaying to and fro as if in pain*]

I will drink that man's blood! God of my fathers,
Grant me his death! Strike him with leprosy
And me with lightning! In their drunken orgies
Confound the unwholesome horde of revellers!
Stamp out this city from man's memory!
Be Magdalen and misery forgot
As things that never were! Let me escape
A moment from myself, even though the way
Lie through the gates of hell! Its pangs were bliss
To the remorse and rage that racks my heart.
Oh! I'll not think on it, lest I go mad.
I wonder who's within!—What do I care?
If they reproach me by a word—a look—
I will sit covered in the city gate
And shame them publicly. Those who respect not
At least shall fear to pity me, who am
The most unhappy woman in the world.

[Text ends here]

Un Petit Drame

[Written on 7 October 1884 as an exercise for Edith (Mrs Pakenham) Beatty, from whom Shaw was receiving French lessons. Based on intimate knowledge of the Beattys and their acquaintances, the play makes reference to the poet (and heavy drinker) Pakenham Beatty, his brother Octavius, the family physician Dr Henry S. Wilson, and Shaw's young friend Dr J. Kingston Barton of St Bartholomew Hospital, as well as to Shaw himself, frequently referred to by the Beattys as "old man Shaw" or "old grandfather Shaw." For additional details, read the headnotes to and the texts of the numerous letters to the Beattys in the *Collected Letters of Bernard Shaw 1874–1897* (1965). *Un Petit Drame* was first published in *Esquire Magazine*, Chicago, December 1959. Reproduced here (with all of Shaw's errors intact) from the holograph manuscript in the Humanities Research Center of the University of Texas at Austin.]

36 Rue d'Osnaburg
7 Octobre 1884

Chère Madame

Voici un petit drame.

West Kensington. Un salon. Madame Malade attend le medecin.

UNE DOMESTIQUE [*courante, toute éplurée*] Ah, madame. Monsieur le docteur il est meurtre—Donc-Dieu! D—Oui, jen suis sur. Cet ange de douceur—cet

—ah, pardonnez moi, madame, mais j'en pleure, j'en pleure. Le voici [*Elle sort*].

L'ONCLE ARRI [*il s'avance des pas lents. Un feu humide brûle dans ses yeux. Il rappelle Amleth, un peu usé.*]

MADAME MALADE. Ah mon cher docteur comment ça va t-il ? Madame Wilson va bi—[*Il chancelle—puis fait une chute terrible*] Dieu merci ! quelle secousse effroyable ! Monsieur le docteur—Arri, dites que vous n'etes pas mort. Ah mon Dieu, qu'avez vous ?

ARRI [*se levant, appuyé sur l'épaule de Madame*] Calmez vous, madame. Je suis excessivement habile à cette espèce de gymnastique.

MADAME MALADE. Comment ?

ARRI. Je me suis terrassé comme ça deja dix fois au moins aujourdhui. Mais votre tapis est bien touffu. [*avec un sourire amère*] Ne cachez votre pensée, madame. Parlez à haute voix. Percez mon coeur. Dites 'Il n'est pas encore revenu de son ivresse.' Dites—

MADAME MALADE. Docteur, je vous jure solenellement—sur ma parole d'honneur—

ARRI. Ivre comme une soupe. [*Il tombe sur un fauteuil*] Oh Dieu de bonté, moi ivre ! moi !

MADAME MALADE. Jamais, jamais. Qui a osé répandre des mensonges pareils ?

ARRI [*sanglotant*] Abandonné, désolé, ruiné—tout disparu—ma femme—mes enfants—mes meubles—tous—tous ! Au cimetière—allons ! Ah, je suis en délire. Ma Cecile, ma fille elle m'a quitté. Sa bouche—jai mille fois baisé cette bouche avec les saintes extases d'un père. Elle a rangé cette bouche exprès pour moi—c'était un peu louche, vous savez, madame. Et ma femme : elle m'a quitté aussi—c'est ma seule consolation. Et mon Fairleigh—il m'a traité unfairly, je crois. Et mes meubles, il ne me reste pas même mon lit: je dors sur le plancher. Il fait froid là-bas; mais ça ne durera pas longtemps. La porte du tombeau est entrehaillée.

MADAME MALADE. Ne parlez pas ainsi mon cher Dr Wilson, vous me dechirez le coeur. Mais est il possible que Madame Wilson vous a quitté? Et qu'elle a pris ses enfants! C'est singuliére: les enfants sont generalement de trop en ces occasions. Mais pourquoi s'est elle sauvé. Vous avez commis quelque mechanceté. Aha, gros farceur, avouez donc.

ARRI [*se levant terrible*] Ah, vous vous moquez de moi—vous, à qui j'ai surtout—mais assez de ça. Au tombeau! Au cercueil! Il y a encore du poison—j'ai posé le flaçon tout pret sur la guèridon—

MADAME MALADE. Elle n'a pas pris le guèridon.

ARRI. Il reste encore le poison, le gueridon, et l'honneur. Bientot le gueridon et les restes du poison seront à mes heriturs. Mais mon honneur, madame, mes principes!—j'ai des principes inouies—Dieu, que j'ai soif!

MADAME MALADE. Ah, que je suis coupable d'oublier votre faiblesse. Prenez, cher docteur, prenez un petit peu. [*elle verse du brandy*]. Ne me refusez pas, mon cher ami. Ça vous ferez du bon.

ARRI. Tres peu, madame, tres peu. Merci, merci, assez [*elle remplit son verre: il le vide.*] Ah madame, vous ne pouvez pas imaginer les choses que ma femme a dit de moi, pour s'excuser. Pourtant elle m'aimait. Malheureusement on s'ennuie quand on est aime par sa propre femme. Mais les choses qu'elle a dit! Peut on croire qu'elle a osé dire que je suis ivrogne—moi!

MADAME MALADE. Ah, par exemple!

ARRI. J'ai peut-etre mes fautes—mais comme mari—comme père—je suis un modèle. Que jai plaint les femmes qui souffrent des ivrogneries de ses maris. Il y a ma nièce Aida, lié à un monstre furıbond, qui a fait des avances, je crois, a ma belle Cècile. Il est ivre tous les jours, et son Aida, pauvre innocent, croit que c'est l'état normal des hommes. Ivrogne, dit-elle; qu'est que c'est que ça? Mon âme, il répond, c'est un homme qui ne balbutie pas quand il parle, qui se porte sans chanceler, qui ne voit que un seul objét quand un homme sobre voit deux—enfin, un homme comme Oncle 'Arri. Et comme bien des autres, dit la pauvre Aida. Malhereusement oui, ma petite. Le père Shaw et moi-même savons bien user avec sobrieté les plaisirs de la vie, mais pour les autres!—Vous connaisez le père Shaw, madame?

MADAME MALADE. Je crois que je l'ai vu. Il porté des bottes qui sont à mettre sous verre.

ARRI. C'est lui. Il ne manque pas un certain esprit, mais il est presque toujours ivre. C'est affreux de voir les jeunes hommes abimé par cette habitude fatale. Je les ai prié, je les ai averti, mais en vain. Octave, le frère aussi: il a du talent, mais il est souvent tellement ivre qu'il ne saurait desserrer les dents. Que la vie est amère pour une femme autouré d'ivrognes! Ah, quelle belle femme! Quoiqu'elle m'ait souvent blessé—elle m'a absolument supplanté par un carabin nommé Barton—un franc ivrogne, qui a peu près tua le pauvre petit—elle a une espiéglerie si ravissante—si calinante—qu'on la pardonne tout! Le père Shaw l'admire, je crois; mais il est un vrai Don Juan: il est épris de Kitty, ma femme. Il faut du courage pour ça; c'est un lion. Plût-à-Dieu qu'il l'enlevasse.

MADAME MALADE [*froidement*] À mon gout, Madame Beatty n'est pas grand chose.

ARRI. Elle n'est pas sympathique comme vous, c'est vrai. Elle m'a abandonné. Ah oui, chez elle à Eastbourne le luxe: chez moi ici, la misère—le tombeau. Je suis medecin—eh bien: faut une voiture. Je vais chercher un corbillard. [*Il sort*]

MADAME MALADE. Et moi, je vais écrire à Madame Beatty. Pauvre homme, il est tout éperdu. C'est monstrueux.

—Rideau—

The Cassone: I

[Outline for the play, reproduced from the holograph manuscript in the Humanities Research Center of the University of Texas at Austin.]

29/6/89 —For Play—

A = Kampenfeldt, the married man

B = Hill, his friend bachelor

[Deleted: Z = Lady Florence Balham woman of fashion—demirep—manslayer]

Y = Mrs Kampenfeldt (Lucy) A's wife, pretty, affectionate, conventional but doesnt know it.

To be Established

Point 1

That A & Y are very happy together. This must be sympathized with. There must be young children—not brought on the stage.

Point 2

That B, free of the household, believes that A's marriage has clipped his wings & that Y is really his evil genius, her very sweetness making her the more dangerous.

This is developed in Act I at Kampenfeldt's home, the characters of the 3 being clearly brought out. It should also appear that B has got on Y's nerves & that she only cultivates him out of love for A, though she thinks highly of him all the same.

The action (Act I) must consist in a difference of opinion between A & B as to A's taking the step (to be invented hereafter) which is to throw him in Act II into contact with Z. Evidently this step is accepting an invitation to |—| Ho[use]. That step is to be resisted by B as being a step downward. A is to refer the question to Y, who will decide him in favor of it because it is a worldly, prudent & delicately courteous step. B, beaten, thereupon definitely resolves to fight Y for A's soul.

Act II

Quite a new sort of household

X = Z's mother, soapy old lady

Z = Lady Florence Balham bad lot husband also bad lot [Indecipherable] driving her—manslayer & knows it. Very rich

C = Balham, ignorant, gambler. Z treats him as a boy. He prefers going with loose women to asking for his marital rights. Rather a pet of X's.

D = Impresario—snob—Jew—hankers after Z—pets C—truckles.

Points to be Established

That Z has a romantically high opinion of A—and is curious about him.

That she either knows nothing of B or has a low opinion of him.

Scene

House of X, who is a widow. Swell country house.

Action

1. Anticipation of A & Y's visit.
2. Unexpected arrival of B in some capacity or other.
3. Arrival of A & Y.
4. Z speaks well of A to B. He is suddenly struck with the notion of using her to counteract Y.

The Cassone: II

[Fragment: a series of disjointed dialogues, begun on 28 August 1889, and finally abandoned toward the end of 1890. Reproduced here from the holograph manuscript in the British Museum: Add. Mss. 50595A.]

28/8/89

LADY SYBIL. Teddy: I want to speak to you rather particularly for a few minutes.

TEDDY. Oh bother! What is it? Ive got some things to look after.

LADY S. Yes: you have got something to look after; and I am going to tell you what it is. Sit down there; and stop fiddling with your hat.

TEDDY [*sits*] Oh bother!

LADY S. Your wife—

TEDDY. Oh damn! [*rises*] I dont want to hear anything about her: I have enough of her.

LADY S. Dont talk like a fool, Teddy. I—

TEDDY. Oh, you be—

LADY S. Very well, then, Teddy. Now you just take yourself and your wife and all your belongings out of this—today, mind. I have had enough of you both.

TEDDY. What do I care? You dont suppose I am dependent on you for house room, do you? I didnt ask to come here: you invited me. I might have gone plenty of other places with a darned sight more fun at them than in this old hole. What have you to complain of? I havent done anything. I've kept my pipe out in the house; and I've left Shot at the stables in case he'd worry that beastly little Persian kitten of yours. What more can I do?

LADY S. You can answer civilly when you are spoken to; and you can make up your mind that I will not stand being sworn at.

TEDDY. Oh, you are precious particular. Very well, then. I beg your pardon. Now are you satisfied?

LADY S. No. Sit down and listen to me.

TEDDY. Oh be—

LADY S. Sit down! [*he sits*] I dont mind your being here: you are no trouble. But I do object strongly to Eleanor's proceedings, and you must interfere.

TEDDY. Interfere! Catch me at it! Interfere yourself if you object: I dont care if she drowned herself so long as she keeps out of my way. Why dont you turn her out? *I* dont care.

LADY S. Dont you? Have you sense enough to understand that you would have to go too?

TEDDY. Why?

LADY S. Would you stay in a house which your wife had been turned out of?

TEDDY. Yes, by George, and be much more comfortable than in a house that she had been turned into. You bet, Sissy.

LADY S. I have no doubt you are quite capable of that or anything else. But has it occurred to you that in [a] family like ours something must be done for the sake of appearances?

TEDDY. Bosh! Who cares about appearances?

LADY S. You may not. Other people do.

TEDDY. More fools they.

LADY S. Well, Teddy: fools or not, I am afraid you must make up your mind to insist on Eleanor's throwing some sort of veil over her peculiar notions of domestic morality. It is nothing to me what she does provided she does it decently whilst she is staying with us. But I really will not have her ostentatiously proclaiming her contempt for you and—

TEDDY. I dont care a damn about her contempt.

LADY S. It pierces the thickest skin, they say, Otto*. However, it would be very hard for any woman to keep up much show of respect for a man with the tastes of the stables and the temper and strength of will of the nursery [*he interjects a contemptuous snort*] But I will have no more discussions on free love with Mr Ashton across my dinner table, and if she will not let Mr Castlemane alone, she must pack; and you must go too, for the sake of appearances.

TEDDY. What do you mean by letting Castlemane alone?

LADY S. I mean that she is drawing him on to flirt with her for no other purpose than to make poor little Mrs Castlemane miserable.

TEDDY. Well, I dont think she will get much change out of that chap. He's too straitlaced. [*He thinks for a moment & then bursts into a chuckling laugh*] Egad, Sissy, I'd like to see Nell coming Potiphar's wife over old Castlemane.

LADY S. [*rises*] That is how you look at it, is it? Teddy: have you a spark of manhood in you? Have you any capacity for shame? Do you like having your name dragged through the mud by a woman for whom you dont even pretend to care?

TEDDY. Look here, Sissy. Dont you begin talking tommy rot because you think it's a good enough stick to beat a dog with. If you want my opinion of Nell, it is that with all her style & swagger, it was a poor thing of her to marry me just to get a handle to her name and the liberty of a married woman. You and Margaret and

*This was the original name of the character, subsequently altered throughout the manuscript to "Teddy," but overlooked in this instance.

she put up that job between you; and no doubt you thought yourself very clever to get me married to a woman of her style and save me from throwing myself away on somebody less to your taste. But you were too cock sure about my being a nonentity; and so was she. Between the lot of you I had come to think that I had no right to consideration and no chance of affection; and for two mortal years after we were married I was sneak enough to think her better than myself, and be cowed by her airs, and when I wanted a kiss go dodging and hankering after her like a cur putting in for a bone that he's afraid to steal. And she knew that I felt small; and she rubbed it into me until I felt twice as small. So did you and Margaret whenever you got the chance. You were all ashamed of me; and you helped one another to take it out of me all you could. And now, because Eleanor is cutting out your pet Mrs Ashton you want me to turn dignified and read her a lecture—do the outraged husband and the master of the house and all the rest of it.

LADY S. I want you to tell her—

TEDDY. Tell her yourself, whatever it is. Do you remember when I went up to London with Jack, and met Polly Chambers at the Canterbury?

LADY S. Dont dare—dont DARE to mention that woman to me.

TEDDY. Yes I will; and I wont hear anything against her either. Poll is as good a woman as you, and a darned sight better than Eleanor. You two and Margaret made a sneak and a cur of me: Poll made a man of me. I've got a home with her; I've got a wife in her; I'm somebody in our little crib down at Stoke Newington. It's she that has the right to the title and the position, not Eleanor. Why dont Eleanor divorce me? She knows about Polly well enough. If she wants cruelty to make up a case I'm ready to chuck the milk jug at her head any morning before you all—or the fireirons for the matter of that if she prefers them. She knows I dont care for her; and she has no right to expect me to; for she never cared for me. I've had no respect for her since I met Polly. [30/8/89] I've found you all out since I came to know her; and I've found this house out too: you think this is a home; but that's all you know about it. I—

LADY S. Yes; and you will find your Poll out too in the course of time, I have no doubt. You will find that there is more sense in my worldly tommy rot than in your sentimental tommy rot, Teddy.

TEDDY. You think you know a lot about it, dont you, Sissy. But you superior people lose a good deal more than you imagine. All that makes life worth living—[*she bursts out laughing at him. He stops and mimics her angrily*] Yah, you fool! You know as much about a man's wants and feelings as that cat does. I pity your husband. [*She puts her elbows on the table, interlaces her fingers, rests her chin on her knuckles, and looks at him with cynical amusement*] If you want me to clear out, I'll go when Eleanor goes: it wouldnt be proper, as you say, for me to stay after her. If you want her to go you can tell her so and give her a lecture yourself, if you have the pluck. [*She takes her arms off the table quickly, vexed*] See? [*He snaps his fingers at her, and exit*].

GIRL. Which is the swells, Gee-orge?

GEORGE. You see that door?

GIRL. Yes.

GEORGE. That door is built too low. When you see a gent knock his 'ed and say damn, he's a [Howard ?]* They all say damn. Everybody wot passes that door

*The square brackets are Shaw's.

knocks their 'ed. Well, you keep your eye on it and watch the quality going through.

GIRL. Git out. They dont talk like that.

GEORGE. Dont they. You wait & see.

GIRL. Well, I think you'll find them a cut above sayin' damn. Mind you point out which is young 's wife, Leddy Eleanor. They say she's the heaviest swell of the lot.

GEORGE. You'll know her the same way. She'll say damn too.

GIRL. Yah! What are you talking about? A leddy say damn.

GEORGE. You wait and see if she dont. The bishop'll say Dear me; but you'll know him by his togs. But you look out when the old man knocks his 'ed. Wait'll you hear him call me names and swear at me. He has the real old blood in him.

4/9/89 [*Drawing of staircase and platform, with decorated shields at left and right*]

The whole scene has been enacted with the most impressive stateliness, softened by the most exquisite aristocratic grace. The visitors withdraw, Henry, the youngest boy, holding the door for them. Mrs |—| is much affected. All slowly follow the departing ones with their eyes. The instant the outer door is heard to shut, there is a wild reaction. Henry stands on his head on the mat—or if he cannot, puts his thumb to his nose.

LADY SYBIL [*starts up snapping her fingers*] Give us a kiss, Eleanor. [*They rush excitedly into one another's arms and kiss*]

ELEANOR. Three cheers for the family, Hip hip—

ALL [*except Mrs |—| and the father*] Hooray!

ELEANOR. Family war dance! Come along, Uncle Ginger [*whirls off the Judge*].

TEDDY. Hooray. Come along, mother [*all fall to dancing*].

MOTHER. Oh no, Teddy: I'm too stiff—oh dear, dont [*is whirled off*].

FATHER [*furious*] Stop, you parcel of fools. Stop, I say. D'ye hear [*they all take hands and make a ring round his chair, where he stands raging at them*].

ALL [*singing & going round*]

> Old Daddy Long Legs
> Wouldnt say his prayers.
> Take him by the long legs
> And throw him downstairs.

Mrs |—| *stands aloof, bewildered.** *Sybil suddenly lets go Eleanor's hand, catches Mrs* |—| *& pulls her in, Eleanor closing up cleverly.*

MRS |—|. Oh no, no, no, please—[*is whirled away. Loud dinner bell. All stop*].

ELEANOR. What's that, Henry? Grub?

HENRY. Yes. The dressing bell.

ELEANOR. Come along! [*All except the Judge, and the Mother, who have fallen panting into chairs, & the Father, who is still beside himself. Henry rushing up first, stumbles & falls*].

ELEANOR [*picking him up by the waistband and making a sound as if to a horse*] Wo up, Johnny!

FATHER [*below, as they disperse along the balcony*] Gerrrrrrrr—you pack of in-f e r-nal idiots.

SYBIL [*derisively, leaning over*] What de matter wud deah old daddum?

FATHER. Pish! Ga'long. Grrrrrr.

TEDDY [*who has just reached the top stair, turns facing the audience*] Stop, ladies & gents: your eyes on me

*Small drawing of circle indicating one character within it and another outside it, to the right.

[*conducts with the evening paper rolled up*] Old Stingo.

ALL [*taking up the chorus*]

Old Stingo. Old Stingo. Old Stingo.
A b'ar he war & he war a b'ar
And a barry warry b'ar war Stingo

Curtain

8/9/89

For the entry of Lady Sybil in Act II. The Judge is on the stage holding a dialogue in which he is repeatedly & obsequiously addressed as Sir Agincourt. Exit his interlocutor & enter Lady Sybil from a door on to the gallery. She leans over the rail, and calls "Uncle Ginger."

10/9/89

Lady Eleanor. Guy Cohen. [*Small drawing of the setting*]

Guy in evening dress, hat in hand, inverness on shoulders. She sitting at the table (L) with the lamp on it. He mortally afraid: she mortally insolent.

COHEN. Good evening, Lady Teddy [*proffers his hand shamefacedly: she puts forward her left hand, palm downward. He shakes it as well as he can under the circumstances, venturing to sit down, uninvited*] Wont you allow me to send you a box for next Saturday? The production of Tristan would be incomplete without Lady Teddy.

ELEANOR. Oh yes, if you wish to. Mrs |—| will no doubt be glad to go if I dont.

COHEN. I have another favor—a great favor—to ask you.

ELEANOR. Indeed?

COHEN. If I might. [*She stares coolly at him without offering the slightest encouragement. Then she takes up the paper*] The fact is, we are giving a little reception at Kingston on Sunday afternoon.

ELEANOR. Who is "we"?

COHEN. Oh, I, of course. I. At my place at Kingston. A few of my artists—the pick of them—will be there. We shall have a little music. All first rate people—except perhaps one or two pressmen; but then you dont mind pressmen.

ELEANOR. Dont I? I suppose you want me to come.

COHEN. I want the gathering to be a social success.

ELEANOR. And you propose to make use of me to that end, eh?

COHEN. Not make use of you. Take advantage of your kindness, and your interest in art, and the privilege of knowing you. I am afraid I have taken a liberty; but—

ELEANOR. You have. You begin by calling me Lady Teddy, a title which I suppose, from your using it, people are in the habit of honoring me with, though I need hardly say they know better than to address me by it to my face. [*C mortified*] Then you ask me to your house on the strength of my uncle being one of your guarantors against bankruptcy at the opera. Do you ask everybody who takes a box for the season?

COHEN. I am very sorry, Lady [Eleanor]. I did not

think you would have been offended. I offer you my sincere apology—

ELEANOR. Oh dont apologize. You are quite right to do things of that sort: that is the way for you to get on. I suppose if I say I'll come, you will get plenty of other people to come too by offering me as another guarantor.

COHEN [*rather wounded but still obsequious*] I should be sorry your ladyship should come if you did not wish to.

ELEANOR. Be quite easy about that. I certainly shant come if I dont wish it. And please dont rush to the other extreme of calling me "my ladyship." "Be thou familiar, but by no means vulgar," Mr Cohen.

COHEN. I have not always been accustomed to your la—to society, Lady [Eleanor]. I have had to make my own way in the world; and—and your ladyship is perhaps a little hard to please. I—

Enter Servant.

SERVANT [*presenting card*] Gentleman said to give your ladyship this and say he was waiting.

ELEANOR. Let him wait. Give him a chair in the hall [*Exit servant. E*[*leanor*] *turns to Cohen with a marked accession of sweetness*] Never mind, Mr Cohen: you do very well. I am sure we all admire your *savoir faire.*

COHEN. Your ladyship is laughing at me. I am afraid I am detaining you.

ELEANOR. Not the least bit in the world. The man downstairs can wait: it is only a business appointment. Did you say next Sunday?

COHEN. Next Sunday, at four—or when you please. I should be only too glad if you only came for a moment & went away as soon as possible.

ELEANOR. Thank you, Mr Cohen: very happily put

[*noting the appointment on her tablets*]; but if I might stay a little longer—

COHEN. Oh, you are too hard on me. You know I meant—

Re-enter Servant.

SERVANT. Gentleman wont wait, your ladyship.

ELEANOR [*angry*] What!

SERVANT. Says he must come some other day when your ladyship is disengaged.

ELEANOR. Dont let him go. Shew him in. Did anyone ever hear of such a thing!

SERVANT. He's gone, your ladyship.

ELEANOR. Send after him—bring him back—quick! [*Exit Servant. Cohen rises*] Goodbye. Dont forget the box.

COHEN. Any place in the house you wish is always at your disposal, Lady [Eleanor]. I am deeply obliged to you. Goodbye. [*She checks his effusion by giving him her left hand as before. Ashton enters just in time to witness this. Exit Cohen: he and* [*Ashton*] *taking stock of one another as they pass*].

7/11/89

ASHTON. That's Cohen, the impresario, is it not?

ELEANOR [*after a pause of haughty astonishment*] Yes.

ASHTON. Why does he crawl like that? Is he afraid of you?

ELEANOR. It is very kind of you to take such an interest in my visitors, Mr Ashton. When you are quite ready, perhaps you will allow me to mention the business on which I asked you to call. I wish—

ASHTON. Stop, I am not quite ready. I want to know about Cohen. It has been proposed that I should decorate his theatre; and I want to know whether he is an honest man. Why does he crawl? Why did you give him your left hand and treat him as if he were a dog?

[*Irritably*] I hate to see anybody treated like that: it makes me feel as if it were being done to me. [*He shivers & takes a short turn up the room*] Well, never mind. What is it—the business, I mean?

ELEANOR. You have been recommended to me by your friend Mr Castlemane as—

ASHTON [*restless again*] He's coming here, isnt he?

ELEANOR. Not that I know of.

ASHTON. [rising] What! Do you mean that he has refused the invitation?

ELEANOR. Really, Mr Ashton, I am not at present discussing my sister's invitations—

ASHTON. No, I know that. You are talking about some business that you have with me on Castlemane's introduction. I quite understand. But I want to know whether he is coming here or not: he told me he would. What objection have you to tell me?

ELEANOR. Oh, none in the world. I believe Mr Castlemane is coming here. Is there anything else you would like to ask?

ASHTON. His wife is here already, is she not?

ELEANOR. Yes.

ASHTON. Hm! [*thinks a moment*] Do you like her?

ELEANOR. Mr Ashton: what business is that of yours?

ASHTON. Does she like you?

ELEANOR. You had better ask her. You are perhaps better acquainted with her than with me, and so perhaps she will not regard your questions as impertinences.

ASHTON. He has no business to come here. He belongs to the opposite camp. Politics are not what they were: formerly nobody was any the worse off personally for the success of his political opponent's policy; but Castlemane's object is practically to reduce your income—to heap taxation on it with the express object of taking it from you and giving it back to the people whose labor earned it.

ELEANOR. If you are going to talk politics, you must really excuse me. [*rises, vexed*] Good evening, Mr Ashton.

ASHTON. Good evening, good evening, Mrs—Lady—I beg your pardon [*perplexed*] Er [*she turns on her way to door R.U.*] What did I come for? I totally forget. Didnt you say something about—what was it? I'm afraid my mind has been running so on this visit of Castlemane's—he really ought not to come—that I am afraid I have forgotten what you told me. Or did you tell me?—you've got a black smudge on the side of your nose—no, the other side: that's it: now it's off.

ELEANOR. Thank you, I'm sure [*She sits again. He takes a chair*] I want you to design a cassone for me.

9/11/89

ASHTON. Oh! One of those chests like an altar—an ark in fact, to hold things. A wedding present, I suppose.

ELEANOR. Yes, I suppose ark is the proper name of it. I hate calling things by foreign names. I called it a cassone because I could think of no English word meaning the same thing; and now you have found me one—such a beautiful one, too! I want to give a wedding present—a golden wedding present—to my husband's uncle, Lord ı—ı. Other people will give all sorts of stupid, ugly things that the ı—ıers have plenty of already. Fish slices & dispatch boxes & rubbish.

ASHTON. And you want to cut them out—to be original, artistic, inventive, distinguished.

ELEANOR [*angrily*] I dont want a criticism of my motives: I want a design for a cassone.

ASHTON. An ark.

ELEANOR. Well, an ark. Do you ever lose your temper, Mr Ashton ? I do.

ASHTON. Yes, I know you do. I suppose it's my fault; but I really dont do it intentionally. This affair of—eh, well, go on about the cassone.

ELEANOR. The ark.

ASHTON [*in a momentary flash of rage*] I say the cassone. What do you mean by taking me up like that ? [*subsiding*] What is your idea of the—the whatyoumaycallhim ?

All through the following speech, A[*shton*], instead of *listening, fidgets, preoccupied by some quite foreign train of thought.*

ELEANOR. It must be a beautifully formed box—noble and beautiful and Grecian, and gilt all over with pure gold. The panels must have pictures in gesso, in deep, rich, heartfelt colors. There must be nothing cold, and nothing reasonable—logical—you know what I mean. Then, in the quaintest lettering possible, cut into the gold—not like print, you know; but as if a great artist had carved it for his amusement with a penknife, I want some verses, spoken right out of the heart without any head or calculation in them—just pure deep feeling in words and rhymes—something—

ASHTON [*springing up*] I have it. An inspiration!

ELEANOR. A design!—for the cassone ?

ASHTON. Nonsense! bother the cassone! Listen. Men fall in love with you, dont they ? If they dont you can make 'em, eh ?

ELEANOR. What on earth do you mean ?

ASHTON. Do you like adventures—plots—traps to catch men's souls ?

12/11/89

ELEANOR. What has that to do with people falling in love with me ?

ASHTON. Why, suppose I lay a trap for a man's soul!

ELEANOR. Yes?

ASHTON. I shall want a bait.

ELEANOR. A bait?

ASHTON. A tempting bait—an irresistible bait—one that no man has ever rejected. A woman.

ELEANOR. Ah, I see. A handsome woman.

ASHTON. No, not necessarily a handsome woman. I have known them devilishly ugly—coarse—vulgar—stupid, except at manslaying—never with the true beauty, the divine, heroic beauty. But then that is a man's beauty: women havent got it—yet.

ELEANOR [*angry*] And who, pray, is the ugly, coarse and stupid person who is to bait your trap?—your trap to catch the soul of some divine heroic man?

ASHTON. You may well mock: we deserve it. But my bait must have something heroic in her; for I am trapping this soul not to destroy, but to save it.

ELEANOR [*pleased*] Oh! Tell me all about it [*leaning towards him on the table*].

ASHTON. You know all about it already. Castlemane is the man.

ELEANOR. His wife is here on a visit. She is our guest.

ASHTON. Then you know her. What do you think of her?

ELEANOR. Oh, I dont know. How?

ASHTON. Pretty—affectionate—domestic—sensible—clever little woman, eh?

ELEANOR [*turns up her nose*].

ASHTON. Exactly. Now just imagine a man with one cardinal weakness—that of sentimental chivalry towards women—placed in a position in which his whole salvation depended on his standing out like a rock against all the common social prejudice as to how men should be treated and how women should be treated. You cant separate the man question from the woman question. Castlemane is in such a position. Well, he is sound on the man question, but weak on the woman question. And he goes & marries this little woman. Immediately he sets to work to prevent the winds of heaven visiting her pretty little face too harshly. Those comrades of his who are rough on the outside, or who are free with their heterodox opinions, are gradually made to feel that they must not visit him any more for his wife's sake. He holds his own tongue in private life, to spare her feelings & those of her chosen friends. But still it is hard for her to get into society as the wife of a paid labor member unless he courts it a little—also for his sake. Why should she be cut off from all gaiety on a/c [account] of his opinions? [13.11.89] Should he hesitate to make her happy at the cost of a little reticence—a reticence which is, after all, demanded by good taste. You know what good taste means.

ELEANOR. Yes: moral cowardice.

ASHTON. You are a jewel of a woman: you understand the whole situation.

ELEANOR. Not exactly. I dont understand the man trap.

ASHTON. Yes you do. You are the man trap.

ELEANOR. Oh, I thought I was only the bait.

ASHTON. Dont quibble: it is the same thing. His wife made him come here in spite of his inner conviction. She would have it. Well, let her have it.

ELEANOR. Have what?

ASHTON. Jealousy—of you.

ELEANOR [*remorseful*] Jealousy is a horrible feeling.

ASHTON. Exactly.

ELEANOR [*shuddering*] Oh! I see you are cruel, like all clever people.

ASHTON. No: I abhor cruelty. But if your foot were frozen and senseless, would it be more cruel to warm it, though the life of it would return with keen pain, or to let it drop off? Well, here is a woman whose heart is frozen. Shall we let it die or bring back the blood to it?

ELEANOR. Suppose we let it alone, as being no business of ours.

ASHTON. By all means—if we can, now that the idea has got into our heads.

ELEANOR. I certainly can, and will, if I choose to.

ASHTON. You had better; for this sort of vivisection is as villainous, perhaps, as the other sort: at any rate there is a suspicious resemblance in the arguments by which they are justified. But if your predatory instincts get the better of you, and you find yourself unable to let him alone—or to let her alone—

ELEANOR. Stop. I will have nothing to do with it. My instincts are not predatory.

ASHTON. Then if they are not, you will encourage him to be himself; to stand out against drawingroom lionizing; to do whatever his wife advises him not to do—

ELEANOR. Stop, I tell you. I pledge you my word that I will not say one word to Mr Castlemane beyond what bare civility demands, or cultivate his acquaintance or meddle in his affairs in any way whatever.

ASHTON. Ah! that settles it, doesnt it? And now, since the subject is dismissed, what were we talking about when you ran off on this affair of Castlemane's?

ELEANOR. When *I* ran off! Oh, I see: you are trying to get a rise out of me; but it wont do. Will you do the cassone for me?

ASHTON. Done already, my dear madame. I finished the design in my head quarter of an hour ago whilst you were lecturing on moral cowardice.

ELEANOR. I dont believe a word of it.

ASHTON. I will draw it for you before I leave the house if you will put me somewhere by myself with a pen & a sheet of notepaper for—say twenty minutes.

ELEANOR [*incredulously*] Really?

ASHTON. Try.

ELEANOR. I will. I dont believe you have thought out a line of it; but I may as well catch you whilst you are in the vein. [*She goes to the door & looks through*] There is no one in the library: there never is at this hour. You will find pens & paper on the writing table. I suppose it will take you ever so long.

ASHTON. About forty minutes. You shall see. [*Exit into Library*].

Enter Lady Sybil & Mrs Castlemane, in bonnets & gloves, from a walk.

E. [*to S.*] If you think I am going to stand home truths from you, you are very much mistaken.

14/11/89

FATHER. And when we went, as my brother the Bishop said, there was not a damned one of them to be seen.

BISHOP. No, no. I did not say that.

FATHER. Oh we-e-ell—not those exact words, perhaps. But that was what you meant.

BISHOP. Really—

FATHER. Well, have it your own way. I dont know what you meant. I only know what you said.

16/2/90 —Another—

Judge shouting in the poor house in which he has had to

take refuge by accident. At a table with him, 2 or 3 gentlemen, and the girl of the house . . . [Shorthand fragment: partly indecipherable.] *Judge relates some retort aside to him.*

R.N. Oh I say! That was a corker, wasnt it?

Later on.

R.N. Werent you awful angry when she said that to you?

Later on.

JUDGE. But those two men?

R.N. Well, perhaps Bill wont be there; and Jim's no good. Tell him you'll land him one on the jaw if he dont shut up. But Bill wouldnt stand that; and he's two stone too heavy for you. Besides, he's a young un; and youth will be served, sir, wont it?

JUDGE [*ruefully*] I suppose so.

26.11.90

Lady Eleanor (alone). She has purposely left the library door partly open. She moves toward the other door L.U., hesitates, & turns with the intention of peeping into the library. He, within, shuts the door. She recoils. She stands for a moment: the keyhole suggests itself to her: she refrains. She stands undecided, rapt. Castlemane enters; is puzzled by her intent attitude; comes closer; looks inquisitive; then says:

CASTLEMANE. What's the matter?

ELEANOR [*great shiver*] Oh!!! Mr Castlemane, how could you? You have startled me.

CASTLEMANE. I beg your pardon. Is there—[*checks himself; looks at library door; then at her; finds that she is watching him; is taken aback*].

ELEANOR. Is there what?

CASTLE. Well, I—I—I thought there was something

up, perhaps. I mean that I am in the way. Let me— [*going*].

ELEANOR. Nothing in the world, I assure you. On the contrary, I want to talk—about the cassone, you know. What sort of person is this Mr Ashton?

CASTLE. Oh well, he's—he's not any particular sort of fellow, you understand. I mean, of course, to look at.

ELEANOR. Do you consider him a great friend of yours?

CASTLE. Certainly. He is one of our most intimate friends.

ELEANOR. Then he is a great friend of your wife's, too?

CASTLE. Well, of course, it was through me that she came to know him.

ELEANOR. Does she like him?

CASTLE. I suppose she does.

ELEANOR [*mocking*] Is it to please you or for his own sweet sake, Mr Castlemane?

CASTLE. [*uncomfortable*] I dont constrain her inclinations in any way.

ELEANOR. Mr Castlemane: I have seen this friend of yours; and he has given me a commission concerning you—one that will very considerably interest Mrs Castlemane.

CASTLE. Indeed? Lily will be down presently. Will you wait until she comes to tell us about it?

ELEANOR. No: I had rather leave it to you to tell her, if you think fit.

CASTLE. Oh! something unpleasant, do you mean?

ELEANOR. I do not know how it will strike you. Mr Ashton has come to the conclusion that your soul needs saving. He has kindly suggested that I might help him to effect that desirable result. Shall I tell you how this friend of yours & your wife's proposed to set me to work in your household five minutes after meeting me for the first time, and at a purely business interview, remember?

CASTLE. I know. By making me fall in love with you. He's mad on the subject. He told me he was going to do it.

ELEANOR [*furious*] He told you! Actually told you—to your face!!!

CASTLE. I'm really extremely sorry, Lady Eleanor: it's quite inexcusable in him; but he has some insane theory about it. He falls in love with every woman he sees, and says that it does him good—keeps him from becoming the slave of his ordinary intelligence, he says. You see his theory is like this. He declares that it is never prudent to take a step in advance, because you cannot be sure of what will happen to you where you have never been before.

ELEANOR. That's true.

CASTLE. Exactly. Therefore every step in advance is an imprudence—a folly. That's clear, isn't it?

ELEANOR. Yes.

CASTLE. Very well. Now, says [Ashton], no man will deliberately commit a folly except under the impulse of a feeling that is too strong for his common sense. Consequently he will never advance except under a series of impulses from feeling. But no feeling overpowers a man's common sense so effectually as love: none is so pleasant: none acts with such certainty on all sorts of people. Therefore if you want to keep going—advancing, you understand—you must keep constantly falling in love.

ELEANOR. With a fresh person every time?

CASTLE. That's just the point of my case according to Ashton. He declares that since I married, a sense of duty & a reluctance to hurt my wife's feelings have restrained me from allowing myself to form any fresh attachments; whilst my affection for Lily has become a matter of habit, and lost its stimulating power—otherwise its power of getting the better of my common sense. Necessarily therefore, according to him, I have ceased to advance. All married men, he says, suffer in the same way, for the same reason. So he has set his heart on finding somebody to fascinate me.

ELEANOR. I feel honored, I am sure, at being selected.

CASTLE. Oh, you must not mind him. You are not the first victim: he has tried several times. [*E. enraged: C. does not notice it*] The worst of it is that he has no notion of keeping anything to himself: he blurts his plan out in the first five minutes, instead of laying his trap scientifically. And then he is so vain that he runs to tell me how cleverly he has done it. So what with my being forewarned, and the lady being naturally mad at his coolness, nothing ever comes of it.

ELEANOR. Mr Castlemane: this is intolerable. How dare your friend propose to make use of me in such a way? How dare he presume so on your introduction?

CASTLE. I am really sorry—more than sorry, Lady Eleanor. I have no control over him; and I had no idea that he would venture to carry out his absurd proposal in your case. But if he was not afraid of you, would anything mortal restrain him, do you think? [*E. rather mollified by this*] I thought it best to be quite frank.

ELEANOR. Yes, I suppose it always is best to be frank; but it is rather annoying, all the same. I cannot say that I appreciate the theories of your friend. Perhaps you could contrive to tell him so, and save me from any further experiments.

CASTLE. I will tell him that you are—shall I say offended?

ELEANOR. Yes. Say angry—exceedingly angry. Will he mind much?

CASTLE. [*dubiously*] He must feel it to some extent, I should think.

ELEANOR [*watching him—intelligently & quickly*] Will he laugh?

CASTLE. Well—frankly, I am afraid he will. But he must feel it, you know, all the same.

ELEANOR. Pleasant—to be laughed at! May I ask is he never abashed by the failure of his plans? They do fail, I presume.

CASTLE. Invariably. But that is where my theory comes in. Excuse my mentioning it: I fancy you have had rather more than enough of our theories.

ELEANOR. Oh, dont mention it, pray. It is always best to be frank.

CASTLE. Well, it is only this. Ashton is quite as shy as other people under ordinary circumstances. He is only bold with the people who stimulate him.

ELEANOR. How?

CASTLE. According to his own theory. Stimulate him by attracting him—making him fall in love. He is an extraordinarily susceptible chap. But his complexion is the opposite of mine: consequently the women who attract him do not attract me—not in that way, at least. Now you see how it works. All the women whom he sets at me—if you will excuse my putting it in that odious way—are selected by him because he is smitten with them himself; so that I get off heartwhole, and he generally makes himself more or less ridiculous about them.

ELEANOR. *You leave me to infer—I really dont know

*Balance of text is scribbled in pencil, presumably at a later date.

which of you has the more tact—that I have had the happiness of pleasing Mr Ashton at first sight.

CASTLE. Not a doubt of it. You can punish him to your heart's content for his audacity—and his meddlesomeness.

ELEANOR. Do you think I have nothing better to do than that, Mr Castlemane? I wonder at you.

CASTLE. I only thought—

ELEANOR. That is just what you did not do. If you had thought for a moment, you would never have told me of all this nonsense.

CASTLE. Well—but I did not broach the subject. Still, I am sorry—

ELEANOR. It does not matter. But I must ask you to tell your friend what has taken place between us, so that he may quite understand what I think of his proposal.

CASTLE. But for Heaven's sake, Lady Eleanor, say nothing until the cassone design is ready. Unless he is in love with you, he will have no interest in showing off before you; and nothing but the desire to show off will ever induce him to set about it in earnest. If you snub him, it is all up with the cassone.

ELEANOR. I value my self respect more highly than the cassone.

CASTLE. But surely it will not hurt your self respect to be a source of inspiration to an artist. It is not as if he wanted you as a model—

ELEANOR. Mr Castlemane: I positively decline to pursue the subject.

[*Text ends here*]

The Gadfly

OR

THE SON OF THE CARDINAL

An adaptation of the novel by Ethel Voynich, published in 1897. Composition begun and completed late in January 1898. Copyright performance at the Victoria Hall (Bijou Theatre), Bayswater, on 23 March 1898, with *You Never Can Tell.*

The Gadfly (Arthur Burton, *alias* Felice Rivarez) *H. M. Paget*
Cardinal Montanelli *R. Brimley Johnson*
Ferrari, Grassini, Michele, Officer *Percy Addleshaw*
Martini, Officers, Police, &c. *J. M. Hoar*
Signora Grassini *Violet Paget*
Gemma Bolla *Mrs Beaufort*
Zita Reni *Florence Farr*
Gipsy Woman *Annie Horniman*
Also Count Soltykov, Priest, Carabineers, Peasants, Servants, &c.

Period—1846. Italy

ACT I *The Conversazione at Grassini's. Florence, a night in July*
ACT II *The Steps of the Cathedral. Brisighella, sunset*
ACT III *A Room in the Cardinal's Palace. Brisighella*

ACT IV Scene 1: *The condemned cell. Brisighella, night*
Scene 2: *The Courtyard of the Prison*

ACT I

Scene: The Conversazione at Grassini's. Florence 1846. A night in July. The terrace gardens of Grassini's house. The house is seen on the left, accessible through the brilliantly lighted windows, which open on a terrace with a balustrade and a flight of steps leading down to the gardens.

Music within.

The guests pass in and out, chatting and laughing. Some of them are leaning over the balustrade, looking away across the valley to the distant hills, or peering down into the street immediately below. Among these, Grassini and Gemma.

Enter the Signora Grassini (the hostess) on the arm of Martini. She is a coquettish chatterbox of about 35. Martini, a grave middle-aged man, looks anxious.

SIGNORA GRASSINI. What's the matter, Martini? Why are you so sulky?

MARTINI. May I be frank with you?

SIGNORA GRASSINI. Oh dear, yes.

MARTINI. I came here to take part in a conspiracy; I find a conversazione. Why are these people here?

SIGNORA GRASSINI. To prevent anyone overhearing us, of course. Look round you; everyone is talking; nobody is listening. When we have secrets to discuss we invite all Florence. [*Calling to one of the gentlemen looking over the balustrade*] Grassini!

Grassini comes forward.

SIGNORA GRASSINI. Our friend Martini doubts whether it is safe to plot anything here.

GRASSINI. Quite safe, Martini, provided you plot at the top of your voice. Have you brought the Gadfly?

SIGNORA GRASSINI. The Gadfly! What's that? A newspaper?

MARTINI. No, Signora: a man. A comrade.

SIGNORA GRASSINI. A young man?

MARTINI [*taking out a paper*] Here is a description of him—a police description [*offering it*].

SIGNORA GRASSINI. No: we mustn't pass papers about. Read it.

GRASSINI. At the top of your voice, please.

MARTINI [*reads*] "Felice Rivarez, called 'the Gadfly.' Age about 30, birthplace and parentage unknown, probably South American; profession, journalist. Short in stature with black hair, black beard and dark skin. Eyes blue; forehead broad and square; nose, mouth, chin"—but I am preventing this lady [*indicating Gemma, who has come forward from the balustrade and is listening*] from speaking to her hostess.

GRASSINI. Don't be afraid—a fellow conspirator [*introduces them*] the Signora Bolla: Doctor Martini.

MARTINI. Your husband, Signora, was an old friend of mine.

SIGNORA GRASSINI. Yes; but go on about the Gadfly. What else does it say?

MARTINI [*reads*] "Special marks: right foot lame; left arm twisted; two fingers missing on left hand; recent sabre cut across face; stammers." Then there's a note put: [*reads*] "Very expert shot; care should be taken in arresting."

SIGNORA GRASSINI. How horrid! I hope he'll come.

GEMMA [*gravely*] I hope he will not.

A manservant whispers to Grassini.

GRASSINI [*excitedly*] My love, the new tenor has come.

SIGNORA GRASSINI. The tenor! Stop the band. Clear everything off the piano. Has he brought an accompanist?

She rushes into the house.

GRASSINI [*following*] Shut all the windows tight. Put screens before all the doors. Light a fire in the cloak room.

He follows her—The Guests crowd into the house after them, and the windows are shut.

Martini remains behind with Gemma.

MARTINI. Signora Bolla: why do you hope that the Gadfly may not come?

GEMMA. He belongs to a society called the Occoltellatori—the Knifers. We are revolutionists, not assassins.

MARTINI. The knife is sometimes the only remedy.

GEMMA. You say that very glibly. Did you ever kill a man?

MARTINI. [*starting*] Heaven forbid!

GEMMA. Ah! I thought so. I did.

MARTINI. You!

GEMMA. Yes, I. It was the man who betrayed Bolla.

MARTINI [*horrified*] You brought your hand to use a knife!

GEMMA. No. I struck him in the face with my open hand; that was all. We were very young. I had been his friend; and I suppose he loved me. He went away and drowned himself.

MARTINI. Do you call that killing a man?

GEMMA. What do *you* call it?

MARTINI. Serve the young traitor right!

GEMMA. But you have not heard the end of the story. He was innocent.

MARTINI. Then why did he not clear himself?

GEMMA. He could not. He had betrayed us in the confessional. The priest was a spy.

MARTINI. The fellow must have been a fool to be caught in such a trap as that.

GEMMA. No, only a boy. He was pious and credulous, full of faith and enthusiasm, incapable of realizing the cruelty and treachery of our enemies. I killed him; there is no getting away from that. And Bolla escaped after all, and married me, and died in his bed in England.

MARTINI [*sympathetically*] You mustn't let your mind dwell on any remorseful notions.

GEMMA. Oh, I quite understand all that. You need not be afraid of my making any morbid fuss over so old a story. But I will have nothing to do with assassins. If your Gadfly attempts to bring the knife into our propaganda, I shall withdraw at once.

MARTINI. Never fear. It is his tongue and pen we want; they are both sharper than most men's daggers.

GEMMA. What need have we of him at all?

MARTINI. To destroy Cardinal Montanelli.

GEMMA. Destroy?

MARTINI. Oh don't be alarmed. We had better cut our own throats than scratch the skin of the good Cardinal. It would be a martyrdom; the people think him a saint.

GEMMA. What will you do to him, then?

MARTINI. Make him ridiculous. That's what the Gadfly is for; the Cardinal's saintliness will wither up into the dotage of an old fool when the Gadfly begins to sting. The creature is all venom—ouf! I wish we could do without him; I am not sure that the dagger is not a manlier weapon after all.

GEMMA. No; for with the dagger the lowest wretch

can end the highest life; but if Montanelli is really a saint, your Gadfly will get the worst of it. [*She passes her hand over her brow*] Strange! that we should get talking of Montanelli now!

MARTINI. Why?

GEMMA. He was the Confessor of the boy I killed.

MARTINI [*indignantly*] What! Was he the spy?

GEMMA. Oh, no, no, no. He was away when that happened; otherwise Arthur would have been alive today.

MARTINI. The boy's name was Arthur?

GEMMA. Yes. Montanelli loved him as if he were his own son. He had known Arthur's mother.

MARTINI [*significantly*] Oh, indeed!

GEMMA. What do you mean by that?

MARTINI. Oh, nothing, nothing. Montanelli knew Arthur's mother: Montanelli loved Arthur as if he were his own son. That seems to me extremely natural.

GEMMA. Are you as cynical as the rest of them?

MARTINI. Do you really think that it is cynical to give a priest credit for being a human being? At all events, Signora, you are sufficiently a woman of the world to understand that if the Gadfly gets hold of this story it will put a little extra venom into his sting.

GEMMA [*revolted*] Dr Martini, what I have told you is sacred. [*Martini bows*] Even if Arthur were not dead, a calumny that cannot be proved—

MARTINI. —Is better than a dagger that cannot be driven home; but you are right: it is a blackguard's weapon. At the same time—

GEMMA [*quickly*] At the same time?

MARTINI. I wish Arthur were not dead.

GEMMA [*with deep feeling*] So do I. But what difference would it make to you?

MARTINI. I think that possibly, if he were alive, your

influence with him, and his influence with the Cardinal, might help us: that's all. [*A burst of applause heard within the house*] Ah, that's the end of the tenor's song.

GEMMA. No matter; he will sing another: at least he will be very much offended if they don't insist on it.

MARTINI. But won't you come in and hear him? I've been selfishly keeping you out here.

GEMMA. I am on duty here; all our friends stroll out to look at the moon.

The centre window opens just enough to allow a man to slip through. The Gadfly appears and closes the window softly behind him.

MARTINI. Here comes one of them. Yes: he's looking at the moon as hard as he can.

GEMMA. Hush, no. I don't know him.

The Gadfly, who has thrust his hands in his pockets and stopped to stare listlessly at the moon, comes down the steps from the terrace, kicking them discontentedly with his heels. He is as swarthy as a mulatto, and, notwithstanding his lameness, as agile as a cat. His whole personality is oddly suggestive of a black jaguar. The forehead and left cheek are terribly disfigured by the long crooked scar of an old sabre cut. He is handsome in a restless, uncomfortable way: with a tendency to foppishness in dress and a veiled insolence of expression and manner.

Gemma moves quietly out into the light.

He starts violently on seeing her, and puts up his hand as if to ward off a blow.

GADFLY [*hastily*] You needn't strike me again: blows don't hurt me now.

MARTINI [*puzzled*] Signore—

GADFLY [*recovering himself*] Eh? Oh, I beg your pardon. I suppose the lady is not a ghost then; I thought she was.

MARTINI. I am happy to say that the lady is alive and in excellent health.

GADFLY. Ah yes; that must be a curious sensation. To be in excellent health; to walk straight; to have your full allowance of fingers; and to have no bullet-holes in your lungs. I congratulate you, Signora. By the way, are you a conspirator? There are only two sorts of people in Florence at present; conspirators and spies, mostly spies; some of the latter, attractive ladies. I am a conspirator myself. Pray, which are you?

GEMMA. I can tell you one thing more about the people of Florence at present, Signore; and that is that the gentleman who announces himself frankly as a conspirator is invariably a spy.

GADFLY. Good. That speech is unmistakeable; you're a conspirator. I am Felice Rivarez, alias The Gadfly, at your service. Which of us is your friend? Is he Martini?

MARTINI. At your service.

GEMMA. I am—

GADFLY. Of course you are; I know. Well, here I am to take the field against the pious Montanelli. What are the lines of battle to be, Signora? Shall I attack his theology or his personal character?

GEMMA. His personal character is above attack.

GADFLY. Oho! How did he take in so clever a woman as you are? But you are right: only, what you mean, I suppose, is that all these fellows, from the Sacristans to the Cardinals, are such notorious rascals that their bad characters are taken for granted. You can't collect a crowd to see a river running down hill.

GEMMA. Vulgar prejudice, Signor Rivarez. They say the same thing of us. Don't make the foolish mistake of underrating your enemy.

GADFLY. Ah, well, if Monsignor Montanelli is all you

say he is, so much too good for this world that he ought to be politely escorted into the next. I am sure he would cause as great a sensation there as he has done here; there are probably many old-established ghosts who have never seen such a thing as an honest Cardinal.

GEMMA [*impatiently*] Signor Rivarez, if you have only come here to talk the usual scandal about priests, and to hint at daggers and stuff of that kind, you will be of no use to us; we have only too many people of that sort. Doctor Martini, we may as well go in and listen to the tenor after all; we are wasting our time here.

She turns her back on the Gadfly and goes, with Martini, towards the windows. There is another burst of applause. The windows are opened and the guests come out laughing and chattering about the singing. The Signora Grassini is with them in high spirits.

SIGNORA GRASSINI [*to Gemma as she comes down the steps*] He sang twice for us—the darling!—though he has five more engagements this evening. And you actually stole away, Rivarez. If he had seen you he would never have forgiven me. What do you mean by such conduct?

GADFLY. It seems wasteful and inhuman to me to set a man to make that sort of noise when a goat would do it so much better.

SIGNORA GRASSINI. What a terrible critic you are! So cynical!

Grassini comes from the house.

GRASSINI. He's gone. He went like lightning; he has fourteen other engagements. Ah, Rivarez! How are you; delighted. I saw you come in, but couldn't get to you through the crowd round the piano. Your charming friend, Madame Zita Reni, is looking for you everywhere. She has promised to sing for us. I must tell her where you are; I promised to find you for her.

He hurries indoors.

GEMMA [*to the Gadfly*] Excuse me, Signor Rivarez; do you present Madame Zita Reni as one of our friends?

GADFLY. Signora, I don't present her at all. She is unpresentable.

GEMMA. Oh nonsense, sir; I am speaking to you seriously. Please keep your wit until we have got through our business. Who is Madame Reni?

GADFLY. An improper person at present attached to me, but not to the revolutionary cause. She would sell it, myself included, for a dozen pairs of scarlet silk stockings.

Grassini appears on the terrace with Zita on his arm. She is gorgeously dressed in amber and scarlet, and looks like a tropical bird among sparrows and starlings. She is handsome with a vivid, animal, unintelligent beauty; but the perfect harmony and freedom of her movements are delightful to see. Her forehead is low and narrow, and her expression unsympathetic, almost cruel. Count Soltykov, a very young gentleman, evidently hopelessly in love with her, enters with her, dancing attendance on her; but she pays hardly any attention to him or to Grassini as she stops on the terrace, looking jealously about for the Gadfly.

GEMMA [*to the Gadfly—looking at Zita as if she were some vulgar article of luxury*] Oh! You can afford that, can you? I thought you were as poor as the rest of us.

GADFLY. So I am.

GEMMA. Then you have spoken treacherously of that woman, or else she is a spy. If she stays with you, it must be either for money or love. If it is money, it must come from the government if it does not come from you. If it is love, you had better say so instead of making vulgar jokes about silk stockings.

GADFLY. What a genius I have for making people despise me! Yes: she loves me enough to be most amusingly jealous. But no doubt she is paid by the government too. Most women have business faculty enough to combine pleasure with profit.

ZITA [*detecting him at last and coming down from the terrace*] Monsieur Rivarez, I have been looking for you everywhere. Count Soltykov wants to know whether you can go to his villa tomorrow night, there will be dancing.

GADFLY [*spinning round so as to show his lameness*] Dancing! How charming for me!

ZITA [*jealously*] Is this lady one of your friends?

GADFLY. She permits me to confer with her. Signora Bolla: allow me to introduce to you Madame Zita Reni.

The women bow to one another.

ZITA. Confer with her? What does that mean?

GADFLY. A diplomatic expression.

Grassini has gone into the house and returned with a mandoline.

GRASSINI [*pleadingly offering her the instrument*] Will Madame Reni be persuaded?

ZITA. Felice: my castanets.

The Gadfly produces the castanets from his pocket, inviting Gemma's attention sardonically to his servitude by a grimace.

Zita takes them from him.

GADFLY [*aside to Gemma*] I should be made to play them if I had fingers enough.

ZITA. Felice, where are you going? Stay here: I'm going to sing. Soltykov, do you play the mandoline? I want my hands for the castanets. The bolero.

Song and dance.

GADFLY. Brava! Bravissima! [*to Gemma*] What would you not give to be able to do that? [*He turns to Zita and puts the castanets in his pocket*].

SIGNORA GRASSINI. How delightful! What a gift! Even Signor Rivarez, who ran away from our greatest tenor, had to listen!

GADFLY. Rapt! Spellbound!

ZITA [*to the Gadfly*] I want something to drink after that. Take me in.

GADFLY. Try Soltykov instead. I have business here.

ZITA. You want to speak to that woman.

GADFLY. Of course I do [*lowering his voice*] If you dare make a scene, I'll hand you over to Soltykov altogether [*aloud*] Soltykov: Madame Reni wants you to take her in to supper.

Soltykov takes her in, wounded and angry, but afraid to refuse. The guests follow, Signora Grassini bringing up the rear on a gentleman's arm. Martini, Gemma, Grassini, and the Gadfly remain behind.

GRASSINI. Now is our time for business. What news have you for us, Martini?

MARTINI. Nothing, except that we are convinced in Genoa that it is too late for all this pamphleteering and scheming to undermine the influence of the Cardinal. Things have come to a head with a rush within the last fortnight. We all believe that a rising cannot be prevented now, even if we wanted to prevent it. Before the end of the month we shall be at it, hammer and tongs, on the barricades.

GADFLY. Piff, paff, poof! [*He rattles the castanets*].

GEMMA. In that case, this gentleman can be of no use to us.

GADFLY [*with mock affection*] Dear lady!

GEMMA. We must have men of action—earnest men.

GRASSINI. Domenichino?

GEMMA. Yes, Domenichino. But he is only one. He must stay here in command. Who is to undertake the distribution of the weapons?

MARTINI. Where are they?

GEMMA [*looking mistrustfully at the Gadfly*] I will not tell you just now.

GADFLY. I will. They are hidden in the caves in the hills near Brisighella. They must be got out and distributed in the towns—in Brisighella itself first, under the Cardinal's nose. Don't send anyone you love, Signora Bolla. He'll be killed—or taken, which comes to the same thing.

GEMMA. We are not likely to send anyone who is not prepared for that. We all are, and we shall not find a man who is not loved by somebody.

GADFLY. True, Signora: every pot finds its cover. Even I am adored by Zita.

MARTINI. Where is the man who convoyed the weapons from Genoa to the caves?

GRASSINI. Egad, yes. That was a man in a thousand. We have a splendid disguise for him. Passport and all complete.

GADFLY. What is it?

GRASSINI. An old Spanish pilgrim—a repentant brigand from the Sierras who killed his son and made a pilgrimage to Rome for absolution. He fell ill in Ancona last year; and one of our friends took him on board a trading-vessel out of charity, and set him down in Venice where he had friends. He left his papers with us to show his gratitude. In that disguise the man who convoyed the weapons for us could distribute them.

GEMMA. Yes; he would do. Unfortunately, we don't know him.

MARTINI. Do you, Rivarez?

GADFLY. Oh, a despicable fellow, I assure you, you wouldn't like him, Signora.

GEMMA. He did his work. He was a doer, not a scribbler and slanderer.

GADFLY. How do you know?

GEMMA. By his deeds. We will not think ill of a proved comrade to amuse you, Signor Rivarez.

GRASSINI. Come, come! Business, business! Whom shall we send?

MARTINI. Whom can we best spare, Signora Bolla?

GADFLY. Me, me, me. There is no doubt about that.

GEMMA. You must win our confidence first. I vote against your being sent.

MARTINI. So do I.

GRASSINI. Excuse me, Rivarez. But really so do I.

GADFLY. You flatter me. I propose, then, as an alternative, that you send the man who convoyed the weapons from Genoa to the caves—the despicable fellow.

GEMMA. I agree, if we can find him.

MARTINI. Agreed!

GRASSINI. Agreed.

GADFLY. Carried *nem con.* He shall start the day after tomorrow.

Signora Grassini runs from the house and hurries down to them.

SIGNORA GRASSINI. Domenichino is arrested.

They all rise in consternation.

GADFLY. Our man must start tonight. Away with you and warn everybody.

They hurry towards the house.

Signora Bolla. [*She stops—the rest go into the house*] You must stay with me to send this man off.

GEMMA. I!

GADFLY. He goes to his death. Is he to have no kinder word at parting than mine?

GEMMA. Is he a sentimentalist, then?

GADFLY. Yes, a grovelling sentimentalist.

GEMMA. What is his name?

GADFLY. Arthur.

GEMMA. Arthur!

GADFLY. An English name.

GEMMA. I know. I once knew someone of that name.

GADFLY. Indeed?

GEMMA. Do you know anything of his history?

GADFLY. Nothing that would amuse you. The poor wretch has been kicked about the world, mostly in South America—beaten and maimed, shot and chased, half drowned, drudged and degraded and devil knows what—even slapped across the face.

GEMMA. What do you mean by that?

GADFLY. Nothing, my dear lady, nothing. He has left it all behind now, and wants to hear nothing more of it.

GEMMA. I want to see this man. What is his other name? Where is he to be found?

GADFLY. Oh, he has lots of other names—Rivarez, the Gadfly—plenty of them. [*The Angelus rings*] Sh! Listen! That's his death knell. [*He takes out the castanets and marks the bolero rhythm softly with them, mocking the bell*].

GEMMA. Stop clacking those horrible things. Do you mean that you are—

GADFLY. The man that convoyed the arms from Genoa to the caves? Precisely. And I am nobody else. And I shall soon be nobody at all. So bid me adieu, beautiful widow of Bolla the Betrayed.

GEMMA. Adieu. But remember, the revolution wants men who intend to live for it and not to die for it.

GADFLY [*seriously*] I shall do my best with what is left of me.

GEMMA. If you are taken at Brisighella, appeal to Montanelli. He is merciful.

GADFLY. The more fool he!

GEMMA. We will do all we can ourselves.

GADFLY. Oh, look after the revolution, not after me. When the rush comes there will be no time to stop to pick me up. Besides, I have had all I wanted now. It was not much—only a fancy to see somebody again. And I hate this cursed world, with its infamous cruelties and tyrannies, its slaves and cowards, holding each other down for priests and kings to devour. [*relapsing into his flippant tone*] Ah! excuse my talking shop.

GEMMA. It becomes you better than the other sort of talk. Goodbye. And remember, Montanelli once knew an Arthur whom he loved like his own son.

GADFLY [*implacably*] And whose mother he probably betrayed.

GEMMA. Do you never forgive old injuries?

GADFLY. Only when I have deserved them. I kiss the hands I have betrayed [*he kisses her hand suddenly and lightly*]—not the hands that betrayed me. And now off to Brisighella where I will test my disguise by confessing myself with all speed to Montanelli—to Father Montanelli. Goodbye, Gemma.

He embraces her and then hurries away up the steps. As he reaches the terrace, Zita is heard singing within. He stops and looks quaintly back at Gemma; then goes off accompanying the song with the castanets.

End of Act I.

ACT II

The steps of the Cathedral at Brisighella. Sunset. The Gadfly, disguised in ragged white locks as an old Spanish pilgrim, is sitting on the steps. The square in front of the Cathedral is crowded with peasants and pilgrims. Michele, disguised as a hawker of rosaries, medals, pious chap-books and tapers, approaches the Gadfly and sets down his basket before him.

MICHELE. Are you one of the pilgrims, Father?
GADFLY [*loudly*] I am a miserable sinner. [*privately*] Well, where do we meet?
MICHELE. In the market-place in front of the Cardinal's Palace.
GADFLY. Oh! he manages to live in a Palace, then, in spite of being a saint.
MICHELE. He lives in one wing of it and has turned the rest into a hospital. He is inside there now [*pointing to the Cathedral*].

The Cathedral doors open and the organ is heard.

THE CROWD. His Eminence—His Eminence is coming out. Stand aside, His Eminence is coming.
MICHELE. Pray for me when you get to Rome, Father.

He gets out of the way.

The Cardinal appears at the Cathedral doors in his violet Lenten robe and scarlet cap, blessing the people with outstretched arms. He comes slowly down the steps. The people crowd about him to kiss his hands. Some kneel down and put the hem of his cassock to their lips.

The Gadfly sits motionless with his teeth clenched and his eyes on the ground.

MONTANELLI. Peace be with you, my children.

A WOMAN [*lifting her child*] His Eminence will bless you as the dear Lord blessed the children.

The Gadfly groans.

MONTANELLI. Are you a pilgrim?

GADFLY. I am a miserable sinner.

POLICE OFFICIAL [*stepping forward*] Forgive my intruding, your Eminence. I think the old man is not quite sound in his mind. He is perfectly harmless, and his papers are in order; so we don't interfere with him. He has been in penal servitude for a great crime, and is now doing penance.

GADFLY [*shaking his head slowly*] A great crime.

MONTANELLI. Thank you, Captain. [*to the people*] Stand aside a little, please. [*to the Gadfly*] My friend, nothing is hopeless if a man has sincerely repented. Will you not come to me this evening?

GADFLY. Would your Eminence receive a man who is answerable for the death of his own son?

MONTANELLI [*solemnly*] Is not God Himself answerable for the death of His own Son? If you will come to me I will receive you as I pray that He may one day receive me.

GADFLY [*stretching out his hands with sudden passion*] Listen! [*to the people*] And listen all of you, Christians! If a man has killed his own son—his son who loved and trusted him, who was flesh of his flesh and bone of his bone; if he has led his son into a death-trap with lies and deceit, is there hope for that man in earth or Heaven?

MONTANELLI. It is written: "A broken and contrite heart shalt thou not despise."

The Gadfly bends his head to receive the benediction.

Go to Rome, and ask the blessing of the Holy Father. Peace be with you. [*His voice falters, and becomes almost entreating*] When you receive the Holy Eucharist in Rome, pray for one in deep affliction—for one on whose soul the hand of the Lord is heavy.

GADFLY [*sanctimoniously*] Who am I, that He should hear my prayers? A leper and an outcast! If I could bring to His throne, as your Eminence can, the offering of a holy life—of a soul without spot or secret shame—

MONTANELLI [*turning abruptly away—in a voice of agony*] I have only one offering to give—a broken heart.

The organ is heard.

Montanelli goes on his way, the people following him. It is getting dark. When they are gone, the gipsy woman is seen near the Gadfly, who has seated himself on the steps. She is old, and poorly dressed, with a brown wrinkled face and keen black eyes; a bright-coloured scarf is twisted round her head.

GIPSY. I have brought you a message from Zita Reni.

GADFLY. Who are you?

GIPSY. It's no business of yours who I am. I have come to tell you that Zita Reni has gone away with my son.

GADFLY. With your son!

GIPSY. Yes, sir. If you don't know how to keep your mistress when you've got her, you can't complain if other men take her. My son has blood in his veins, not milk and water; he comes of the Romany folk.

GADFLY [*thoughtfully*] Ah! you're a gipsy, are you? Zita has gone back to her own people then?

GIPSY [*puzzled at his dispassionate way of taking it*] What sort of stuff are you made of, that she should stay with you? Our women may lend themselves to you a bit for a girl's fancy, or if you pay them well;

but the Romany blood comes back to the Romany folk.

GADFLY [*coldly*] Has she gone away to stroll with a gipsy camp, or merely to live with your son?

GIPSY [*laughing tauntingly*] Do you think of following her and trying to win her back? It's too late, Sir; you should have thought of that before!

GADFLY. No; I only want to know the truth, if you will tell it to me.

GIPSY. The truth is, then, that she met my son in the road the day you left her, and spoke to him in the Romany tongue; and when he saw she was one of our folk, he thought nothing of her fine clothes, but fell in love with her bonny face, as o u r men fall in love, and took her to our camp. She told us all her trouble, and sat crying and sobbing, poor lassie, till our hearts were sore for her. We comforted her as best we could; and at last she took off her finery and put on the things our lasses wear, and gave herself to my son to be his woman and to have him for her man. He won't say to her "I don't love you," and "I've other things to do." When a woman is young she wants a man; and what sort of man are you, that you can't even kiss a handsome girl when she puts her arms round your neck, and—

GADFLY [*interrupting*] You said you had brought me a message from her.

GIPSY. Yes. She told me to say she has had enough of your folk and their sluggish blood; and that she wants to get back to her own people and be free. "Tell him," she said, "that I am a woman, and that I loved him, and that is why I would not sell myself to him any longer." The lassie was right to come away. There's no harm in a girl getting a bit of money out of her good looks if she can—that's what good looks are for; but a Romany lass has nothing to do with loving a man of your race.

GADFLY. Is that all the message?

GIPSY. Yes.

GADFLY. Then tell her, please, that I think she has done right, and that I hope she will be happy. Goodnight.

The Gipsy, with a gesture of contempt, goes.

The moon has now risen.

[*On the Cathedral steps*] Another blow on the cheek! Is no rag of pride to be left to me—no shred of self-respect? Surely I've suffered everything that man can endure; my very heart has been dragged in the mud and trampled under the feet of the passers-by; there is no spot in my soul where someone's contempt is not branded in, where someone's mockery has not left its iron trace. And now this gipsy girl I picked up by the wayside—even she has the whip in her hand!

The crowd returns, excited. Among them is Michele. He goes to the Gadfly.

MICHELE [*whining*] Let your piety and charity go hand in hand and buy a blessed candle from the poor man. [*aside*] Get out of this place at once: the soldiers are coming. [*aloud*] Most Holy Queen of Heaven, Maiden undefiled—[*aside*] It's you they're after, Rivarez; they'll be here in two minutes—[*aloud*] And so may the saints reward you—[*aside*] You'll have to make a dash for it: there are spies at the corners. It's no use trying to slip away without being seen.

Exit.

The Gadfly makes a dash to escape on the right; but is met by a body of soldiers entering. He turns and attempts to get away on the left but is stopped there too by other soldiers. He retreats to the Cathedral steps.

OFFICER. Let no one leave the square. Where is the Spanish pilgrim?

GADFLY [*producing a pistol*] At your service, Captain! [*He shoots the Officer, wounding him only. The soldiers with a yell of fury rush to the steps*] Take care! [*He fires again. A soldier falls. The rest hesitate*].

WOUNDED OFFICER. Shoot him down, you fools. Shoot.

The soldiers present their carbines: the Cardinal rushes through them and mounts the steps.

MONTANELLI. What are you doing, my son?

The Gadfly lowers his pistol. The soldiers immediately rush on him with a triumphant shout and drag him down the steps.

WOUNDED OFFICER. We are greatly indebted to your Eminence.

MONTANELLI. Why?

GADFLY. For capturing me so neatly for them, of course. [*He laughs mockingly*].

The soldiers, infuriated, drag him fiercely away. The Cardinal covers his eyes with his hands.

End of Act II.

ACT III

A room in the Cardinal's Palace at Brisighella. Montanelli is seated at his writing-table giving audience to the Military Governor, Colonel Ferrari, who is standing. A Sergeant is waiting at the door. A crucifix hangs on the wall.

FERRARI. And I once more earnestly assure your Eminence that your refusal is endangering the peace of the town. If you knew what I and my assistants have put up with from this man you would feel differently about the matter. His is an exceptional case; and it calls for exceptional measures.

MONTANELLI. There is no case which calls for injustice; and to condemn a civilian by the judgement of a secret military tribunal is both unjust and illegal.

FERRARI. The case amounts to this, your Eminence. The prisoner is manifestly guilty of several capital crimes. He is known to be an influential member of one of the most pestilent secret societies in the country. He has offered armed resistance to authority and seriously wounded two officials in the discharge of their duty; and he is now a standing menace to the peace and order of the town.

MONTANELLI. Whatever the man has done he has the right to be judged according to law.

FERRARI. The ordinary course of law involves delay, your Eminence; and in this case every moment is precious. There's a remarkable amount of devilry—I beg pardon; but really this man is enough to try the patience of a saint. It's hardly credible; but I have to conduct all the interrogations myself; for the regular officer cannot stand it any longer.

MONTANELLI. How is that?

FERRARI. It's difficult to explain, your Eminence, but you would understand if you had once heard the way he goes on. One might think the interrogating officer were the criminal and he the judge. If your Eminence would only be present at one of the interrogations, I am sure you would agree with me. He needn't know anything about it. You might overhear him from—

MONTANELLI [*interrupting haughtily*] I am a minister of religion, Colonel Ferrari, not a police-spy; and eavesdropping forms no part of my professional duties.

FERRARI. I—I didn't mean to give offence—

MONTANELLI. I think we shall not get any good out of discussing this question further. Bring the prisoner in. I will have a talk with him.

FERRARI. I venture very respectfully to advise your Eminence not to attempt it. The man is perfectly incorrigible. It would be both safer and wiser to overstep the letter of the law for this once, and get rid of him before he does any more mischief. It is with great diffidence that I venture to press the point after what your Eminence has said; but after all I am responsible to Monsignor the Legate for the order of the town—

MONTANELLI. And I am responsible to God and His Holiness that there shall be no underhand dealing in my diocese. Since you press me in the matter, Colonel, I take my stand upon my privilege as Cardinal. I will not allow a secret Court-Martial in this town in peace-time.

FERRARI [*resentfully*] As your Eminence pleases. [*to the Sergeant*] Bring the prisoner in. [*He sits down*].

MONTANELLI. Colonel Ferrari, I propose to see the prisoner alone.

FERRARI [*rising stiffly*] You do not wish me to be present?

MONTANELLI. I do not wish anybody to be present.

FERRARI. What! No guards!

MONTANELLI. Certainly not.

FERRARI. Then, with your Eminence's permission, I shall clear out. And I warn you that I take no responsibility for the risk you are going to run.

MONTANELLI. I do not ask you to do so. You will find there is no risk.

FERRARI. Oho! You think so. [*lowering his voice*] Listen to me, your Eminence. I have been obliged to be rather strict with him—especially as it is a military prison. The other day I thought that perhaps a little indulgence might have a good effect. I offered to relax the discipline considerably if he would behave in a reasonable manner; and how does your Eminence suppose he answered me? He lay looking at me a minute, like a wolf in a cage, and then said quite softly: "Colonel, I can't get up and strangle you, but my teeth are pretty good: you had better take your throat a little further off." He is as savage as a wild cat.

MONTANELLI. I am not surprised to hear it. I will give you my answer as to the Court-Martial when I have seen the prisoner.

FERRARI. I have no doubt, your Eminence, he will convince you of the necessity of getting rid of him better than I can.

As he goes to the door, it opens, and the Gadfly enters, escorted by the Sergeant and four soldiers. The Gadfly instantly makes a spring at Ferrari. The soldiers drag him off. The Cardinal rises, white and shocked.

FERRARI. Now, your Eminence, I hope you believe me. You have seen for yourself.

GADFLY [*coolly*] I am bitterly disappointed, your Eminence. I was within an inch of getting a good bite when these foolish fellows stopped me.

FERRARI. I leave him in your Eminence's hands. I wish your Eminence a pleasant interview.

Exit.

MONTANELLI [*to the guards*] I wish to be alone with the prisoner. You can wait downstairs.

SERGEANT. But, your Eminence—

MONTANELLI [*peremptorily*] You are to wait downstairs, all of you. Go.

The Sergeant, overawed, takes his men out.

[*to Gadfly*] Sit down, please.

The Gadfly sits.

Signor Rivarez, I wish to ask you a few questions, and shall be very much obliged to you if you will answer them.

GADFLY. My chief occupation at present is to be asked questions.

MONTANELLI. And—not to answer them? So I have heard, but those questions are put by officials who are investigating your case and whose duty is to use your answers as evidence.

GADFLY [*with covert insolence*] And those of your Eminence?

MONTANELLI [*quietly*] Mine, whether you answer them or not, will remain between you and me. If they should trench upon your political secrets, of course you will not answer. Otherwise, though we are complete strangers to each other, I hope that you will answer frankly, as a personal favour to me.

GADFLY [*icily*] I am entirely at your Eminence's service.

MONTANELLI. First, then, you are said to have been smuggling firearms into this district. What are they wanted for?

GADFLY. To kill rats with.

MONTANELLI. That is a terrible answer. Are all your fellow men rats in your eyes if they cannot think as you do?

GADFLY. Some of them.

MONTANELLI [*suddenly, after a pause*] What is that on your hand?

GADFLY [*glancing at his left hand*] Old marks from the teeth of some of the rats.

MONTANELLI. Excuse me: I was speaking of the other hand. That is a fresh hurt.

GADFLY [*holding up his right hand with the wrist badly cut and bruised*] It is a mere trifle, as you see. When I was arrested the other day, thanks to your Eminence [*he makes a little bow*], one of the soldiers stamped on it.

MONTANELLI [*taking the hand and examining it*] How does it come to be in such a state now, after three weeks? It is all inflamed.

GADFLY. Possibly the pressure of the iron has not done it much good.

MONTANELLI [*frowning*] Have they been putting irons on a fresh wound?

GADFLY. Naturally, your Eminence; that's what fresh wounds are for. Old wounds are not much use. They will only ache: you can't make them burn properly.

MONTANELLI [*looks at him closely, then rises and opens a drawer full of surgical appliances*] Give me the hand. [*He bathes the injured place and bandages it carefully*] I will speak about the irons. Now I want to ask you another question. What do you propose to do?

GADFLY. That is very simply answered, your Eminence. To escape if I can; and if I can't, to die.

MONTANELLI. Why "to die"?

GADFLY. Because if the Governor doesn't succeed in getting me shot, I shall be sent to the galleys; and for me that comes to the same thing. I haven't got the health to live through it.

MONTANELLI [*after a pause*] Suppose you succeed in escaping, what will you do with your life?

GADFLY. I have already told your Eminence; I shall kill rats.

MONTANELLI. That is to say, that if I let you escape from here now—supposing I had the power to do so—you would use your freedom to foster violence and bloodshed instead of preventing them?

GADFLY [*raising his eyes to the crucifix on the wall*] "Not peace but a sword"—at least I should be in good company. For my own part, though, I prefer pistols.

MONTANELLI [*rising*] Signor Rivarez, I am old, and no doubt have not much longer to live. I would go down to my grave without blood on my hands. But Heaven has put upon me the terrible duty of deciding whether you shall live or die. Everything I know of your career seems to me bad and mischievous: but during this last fortnight you have shown that you are a brave man, and that you can be faithful to your friends. You must have in you something better than you show outside. To that better self in you I appeal, and solemnly entreat you, on your conscience, to tell me truthfully: in my place what would you do?

GADFLY [*with sudden, violent passion*] At least I would decide my own actions for myself, and take the consequences of them. I would not come sneaking to other people, in the cowardly Christian way, asking them to make up my mind for me. We atheists understand that if a man has a thing to bear he must bear it as best he can: if he sinks under it, why, so much the worse for him! But a Christian comes whining to his God, or his Saints; or, if they won't help him, to his enemies—he can always find a back to shift his burdens on to. Heavens and earth, man, haven't I enough as it is, without your laying your responsibilities on my shoulders? [*He breaks off, panting, then bursts out again*] "Sign your own death sentence, please; I'm too tender-hearted to do it myself": that's what you're saying to me now. Oh! it would take a Christian to hit on that—a gentle, compassionate Christian, that turns pale at the sight of a scuffle and a couple of bullet wounds. I might have known when you began to play the angel of mercy that the real thing was going to begin! Why do you look at me that way? Consent, man, of course; and go to your dinner: the thing's not worth all this fuss. Tell your colonel he can have me shot, or hanged, or whatever comes handiest—roasted alive, if it's any amusement to him —and be done with it!

Montanelli, with austere dignity, strikes the bell. The soldiers enter instantly, showing that they have been waiting immediately outside. Ferrari follows them.

MONTANELLI. You can take back the prisoner.

GADFLY [*with mock sweetness as he is led out*] Good afternoon, Colonel Ferrari. So sorry to have frightened you.

He is taken out.

MONTANELLI [*to Ferrari*] Do you honestly believe that the presence of Rivarez in the prison here is a serious danger to the peace of the district?

FERRARI. Most certainly I do, your Eminence.

MONTANELLI. You think that, to prevent the risk of

bloodshed, it is absolutely necessary that he should somehow be got rid of before Corpus Domini?

FERRARI. I can only repeat that if he is here on Thursday, I do not expect the festival to pass over without a fight, and I think it likely to be a serious one.

MONTANELLI [*forcibly, after an impressive pause*] Colonel Ferrari: do you believe in God?

FERRARI. !!!! Your Eminence!!

MONTANELLI [*rising and looking at him searchingly*] Do you believe in God?

FERRARI [*also rising*] Your Eminence, I am a Christian man, and have never yet been refused absolution.

MONTANELLI [*lifting the cross on his breast*] Then swear on the cross of the Redeemer Who died for you, that you have been speaking the truth to me.

Ferrari gazes at him blankly.

You have asked me to give my consent to a man's death. Kiss the cross, if you dare; and tell me that you believe there is no other way to prevent greater bloodshed. And remember that if you tell me a lie you are imperilling your immortal soul.

FERRARI [*after a pause, bends down and puts the cross to his lips*] I believe it.

A priest, Montanelli's secretary, enters.

MONTANELLI. Why am I interrupted?

PRIEST. The woman, your Eminence.

MONTANELLI. What woman?

PRIEST. The woman who wrote to your Eminence this morning. On a matter of life and death. Your Eminence's orders were that she should be admitted instantly.

MONTANELLI. Tell her that my present business is also of life and death. She must wait.

FERRARI. One moment, your Eminence. It may be the

same business. I should like to see this woman, if your Eminence will be so good as to admit her before I leave the room.

MONTANELLI. Colonel Ferrari: must I again remind you that my palace is not a police office.

FERRARI [*bluntly*] Your Eminence: it is a place where men are sentenced to death. Will your Eminence take this whole business, fighting and all, on yourself from beginning to end?

MONTANELLI. You know that that is impossible.

FERRARI. Well, will you leave it altogether in my hands?

MONTANELLI. No: I must bear the burden of my own duties.

FERRARI. Then Church and State are partners; and they must treat one another reasonably. This woman can come to no harm if she deserves your protection. If your Eminence will not let me see or hear, I must have her watched: that is all.

MONTANELLI [*to the Priest*] Let her come in.

PRIEST [*opening the door*] You are to come in.

Gemma enters.

FERRARI [*rising*] Ah, I thought so. That is all I wanted, your Eminence. This is Signora Gemma Bolla. If we knew as much about this sedition as Signora Bolla does, we should make short work of it. I take my leave of your Eminence.

The Cardinal dismisses him with a gesture. Gemma watches him as he goes to the door. On the threshold he stops and turns.

Oh, by the way, your Eminence, I was forgetting what I came for. I have not had your Eminence's final answer about the Court-Martial.

GEMMA. I beg your Eminence not to give that answer until you have heard what I have to say to you.

MONTANELLI. In that case, Colonel Ferrari, the lady's business is public and concerns us both. You had better wait.

GEMMA. No: it is private—deeply private business. Private business concerning your Eminence personally.

MONTANELLI. In that case, since no private considerations can alter my public duty, you can take my final answer now, Colonel. I consent to the Court-Martial.

GEMMA. What are you doing—

FERRARI [*cutting her short exultantly*] I thank your Eminence. Your orders shall be carried out at once.

He goes out.

GEMMA. I am glad to see that Cardinal Montanelli is more attached to his duty than Canon Montanelli, Father Director of the Theological Seminary in Pisa, and confessor to Arthur Burton.

MONTANELLI [*turning white*] What do you know of Arthur Burton?

GEMMA. I know that he confessed to only two priests in all his life. The one was a police spy. The other was his own father, the betrayer of his mother.

MONTANELLI [*controlling himself*] What do you want with me, my daughter?

GEMMA. Have you seen Rivarez?

MONTANELLI. Yes.

GEMMA. You know then that he does not believe in priests?

MONTANELLI. I know that he does not believe in anything.

GEMMA. Not even in women?

MONTANELLI. A man who does not believe in priests, my daughter, is not likely to believe in women.

GEMMA. Arthur Burton believed in women until his

girl comrade struck him in the face because he trusted a political secret to a priest.

MONTANELLI. And drove him to his death by that act. Thank God, it was not the priest's sin that broke his heart!

GEMMA. Are you sure that he is dead?

MONTANELLI. He drowned himself.

GEMMA. Did you find his body?

MONTANELLI. He left word that it would not be found.

GEMMA. How did he know that it would not be found?

MONTANELLI [*trembling*] Signora Bolla: you are doing a thing to me that a man born of a woman should hesitate to do to his worst enemy. You are turning the greatest sorrow of my life into a political weapon to save your fellow conspirator. You are trying to persuade me that Rivarez learnt his wickedness from Arthur.

GEMMA. Cardinal: Rivarez is Arthur.

MONTANELLI [*springing up*] In God's name, no!

GEMMA. As surely as it was this hand that struck him. He chose this dangerous duty because he longed to see you. He loves you.

MONTANELLI. No, no, no.

GEMMA. Your duty was nothing to you when you brought him into the world. Is it so sacred now that you must send him out of it?

MONTANELLI. Yes, yes, a thousand times yes. It is the vengeance of God that has fallen on me as it fell upon David. I have defiled his sanctuary, and taken the body of the Lord into polluted hands. He has been very patient with me; but now it has come. "For thou didst it secretly, but I will do this thing before all

Israel and before the sun: the child that is born unto thee shall surely die!"

He falls insensible. Gemma runs to him and stoops over his body.

End of Act III.

ACT IV

SCENE I

Scene. The condemned cell. Night. The Gadfly asleep on a pallet. His coat is hanging on a chair beside it. A gaoler enters with a lamp, followed by Montanelli, who dismisses him.

MONTANELLI [*seating himself beside the pallet and bending over the sleeper*] Arthur.

GADFLY [*rousing himself*] Yes! I am ready. Is it time? [*He recognizes Montanelli, and utters a cry of delight*].

MONTANELLI. Have you come back to me from the dead?

GADFLY [*shivering*] From the dead?

MONTANELLI. You have come back—you have come back at last.

GADFLY [*sighing wearily*] Yes—and you have to fight me, or to kill me.

MONTANELLI. Oh, hush, Carino! We have been like two children lost in the dark, mistaking one another for phantoms. My poor boy, how changed you are—how changed! You look as if all the ocean of the world's misery had passed over your head—you! who used to be so full of the joy of life! Arthur, is it really you? Remember, I thought I had killed you.

GADFLY. You have that still to do.

MONTANELLI [*in terror*] Arthur!

GADFLY. Let us be honest, whatever we do, and not shilly-shally. There can be nothing between us but war, and war, and war. What do you want to hold my hand for ? Can't you see that while you believe in your Cause, we can't be anything but enemies ?

MONTANELLI. As you will, Arthur; but I will do what I can. I will arrange your escape; and when you are safe you shall have your revenge. I will have an accident in the mountains, or take the wrong sleeping-draught by mistake—whatever you like to choose. Will that content you ? It is all I can do. It is a great sin; but I think He will forgive me. He is more merciful—

GADFLY [*with a sharp cry*] Oh, that is too much! What have I done that you should think of me that way? What right have you—as if I wanted to be revenged on you! Can't you see that I only want to save you ? Will you never understand that I love you? [*He catches hold of Montanelli's hands and kisses them*] Padre! come away with us. What have you to do with this dead world of priests and idols ? They are full of the dust of bygone ages; they are rotten; they are pestilent and foul! Come out of this plague-stricken Church—come away with us into the light! Padre, it is we that are life and youth; it is we that are the everlasting springtime; it is we that are the future. Padre, the dawn is close upon us—will you miss your part in the sunrise ? Wake up; and let us forget the horrible nightmares; wake up; and we will begin our life again! Padre, I have always loved you—always, even when you killed me. Will you kill me again ?

MONTANELLI [*tearing his hands away*] Oh, God have mercy on me! You have your mother's eyes! [*a silence*] Have you anything more to say ? Any hope to give me ?

GADFLY. No. My life is of no use to me except to

fight priests. I am not a man; I am a knife. If you let me live, you sanction knives.

MONTANELLI [*falling on his knees and raising his clasped hands to heaven*] Hear me, O God—[*A clash of muskets interrupts him as the door opens and the soldiers enter, commanded by the wounded officer, whose arm is in a sling*].

GADFLY [*springing up and putting on his coat*] Well answered, and promptly!

OFFICER. The time has come, Rivarez.

GADFLY [*turning to the kneeling Montanelli, and placing his hand affectionately on his shoulder*] There is no use in talking any more. [*Montanelli rises like a man in a dream*] [*The Gadfly points upward*] You still believe?

MONTANELLI. Though He slay me, I will trust in Him.

GADFLY [*confidentially*] He understands me. [*Whispering*] I don't want to live. [*He turns to the soldiers*] March!

They go out—Montanelli stands like a man before his God. The scene changes.

SCENE 2

The Courtyard of the prison, lighted by torches. A fig tree at the back, a little to the right, with an open grave newly dug, close to it. A gate in the middle. A firing party of six Carabineers on the left in front. At the other side Ferrari, the wounded officer, priest, and a doctor, in a group on the right. The Gadfly enters in custody of the Sergeant and his four soldiers. He marches firmly to the tree.

GADFLY [*brightly*] Shall I stand here, Sergeant? Good morning, gentlemen! Ah, and his reverence is up so early too! How do you do, Captain? This is a pleasanter occasion for you than our former meeting, isn't it? I see your arm is still in a sling; that's because I bungled my work. These good fellows will do their's better—won't you, lads? There'll be no need of slings this time, anyway. There, there; you needn't look so doleful over it! Put your heels together and show how straight you can shoot. Before long there'll be more work cut out for you than you'll know how to get through; and there's nothing like practice beforehand.

PRIEST. My son, in a few minutes you must enter into the presence of your Maker. Will you approach His awful throne with a jest upon your lips?

GADFLY. A jest, your reverence? Friend Ferrari there will not find it so. When our turn comes, we shall use field-guns instead of half a dozen second-hand carbines; and then you'll see how much we're in jest.

PRIEST. You will use field-guns! Oh, unhappy man! Have you still not realized on what frightful brink you stand?

GADFLY [*glancing over his shoulder at the grave*] And so your reverence thinks that when you have put me down there, you will have done with me! True, I shall lie as still as a mouse, just where you put me. But, all the same, we shall use field-guns.

PRIEST. Merciful God, forgive this wretched man!

SERGEANT. Amen. [*He produces a bandage for the prisoner's eyes*].

GADFLY. Colonel Ferrari: I have your promise that I shall look my death in the face.

FERRARI. It is true. Never mind the bandage.

SERGEANT. It's hard on the men, sir, to see his face, if they are to shoot straight.

FERRARI. That's his affair, not ours. Obey your orders. Are you ready, there?

GADFLY. I am quite ready.

WOUNDED OFFICER. Ready—Present—Fire!

They fire. He—the Gadfly—staggers a little but recovers his balance. He is wounded in the face; the blood drops on his cravat. He raises his mutilated hand to wipe it away. He is smiling.

GADFLY. A bad shot, men! Have another try.

SERGEANT [*to his squad of four*] Change carbines with them, quick. Load for them.

WOUNDED OFFICER. Pull yourselves together, will you?

The squad changes carbines with the firing party, which is reformed.

GADFLY. You have brought out the awkward squad this morning, Colonel. Let me see if I can manage them better. Now men. Are you all straight? Now then. Ready. Present—

FERRARI. Fire.

The gates open and the Cardinal rushes in. The Gadfly falls into his arms.

Is your Eminence hurt? That was a frightfully dangerous thing to do. Let the fellow drop; he is dead.

GADFLY [*with an effort*] Not quite yet, Colonel.

The soldiers utter a groan of horror. The wounded officer draws a pistol, but hesitates.

FERRARI [*snatching it from him*] Make an end of him, in God's name. [*He raises the pistol*].

MONTANELLI [*solemnly*] In God's name—no absolution for you if you do. [*Ferrari's hand drops*].

GADFLY. It is all over; my blood is choking me; but I smell the sunrise. [*He falls*].

The soldiers, throwing down their weapons and falling on their knees, cry.

SOLDIERS. Absolution, absolution.

MONTANELLI [*raising his fingers in benediction*] In the name of the Father, and of the Son—the son who died for the people, the Father who gave his son to be slain!

Curtain

The Inauguration Speech: An Interlude

[Written on 13 January 1907 to be performed by Cyril Maude and his wife Winifred Emery at the opening of the renovated Playhouse, London, on 28 January. It was retained in the bill for all subsequent performances that week. First published in the *Daily Mail*, London, 29 January 1907; reprinted in Cyril Maude's *Behind the Scenes with Cyril Maude* (American edition titled *Lest I Forget*), 1928. Reproduced here from the holograph manuscript in the British Museum: Add. Mss. 50643, ff. 98–109.]

Opening night. Brilliant first night audience assembled. Conclusion of overture. In each program a slip has been distributed, stating that before the play begins the Manager will address a few words to the audience.

The float is turned up. Lights down in auditorium. Expectancy. Silence.

The act drop is swung back. Evidently somebody is coming forward to make a speech.

Enter before the curtain the Manager's wife, with one of the program slips in her hand.

THE MANAGER'S WIFE. Ladies and gentlemen. [*She hesitates, overcome with nervousness; then plunges ahead*] About this speech—you know—this little slip in your programs—it says that Edwin—I mean Mr Goldsmith—I am so frightfully nervous—I—[*she begins tearing up the slip carefully into very small pieces*] I have to get this finished before he comes up from his dressing room, because he doesnt know what I'm doing. If he did—! Well, what I want to say is—of course I am saying it very badly because I never could speak in public; but the fact is, neither can Edwin. Excuse my calling him Edwin; I know I should speak of him as Mr Goldsmith; but—but—perhaps I had better explain that we are married; and the force of habit is so strong—er—yes, isnt it? You see, it's like this. At least what I wanted to say is—is—is—er—. A little applause would encourage me, perhaps, if you dont mind. Thank you. Of course its so ridiculous to be nervous like this, among friends, isnt it? but I have had such a dreadful week at home over this speech of Edwin's. He gets so angry with me when I tell him that he can't make speeches, and that nobody wants him to make one! I only wanted to encourage him; but he is so irritable when he has to build a theatre! Of course you wouldnt think so, seeing him act; but you dont know what he is at home. Well, dear ladies and gentlemen, will you be very nice and kind to him when he is speaking, and if he is nervous, dont notice it? And please dont make any noise: the least sound upsets him and puts his speech out of his head. It is really a very good speech: he has not let me see the manuscript, and he thinks I know nothing about it; but I have heard him make it four times in his sleep. He does it very well when he is asleep—quite like an orator; but unfortunately he is awake now, and in a fearful state of nerves. I felt I must come out and ask you to be kind to him—after all, we are old friends, arn't we? [*Applause*] Oh thank you, thank you: that is your promise to me to be kind to him. Now I will run away. Please dont tell him I dared to do this. [*Going*] And, please, PLEASE, not the least noise. If a hairpin drops, all is lost. [*Coming back to centre*] Oh, and Mr Conductor: would you be so very good, when he comes to the pathetic part, to give him a little slow music. Something affecting, you know.

THE CONDUCTOR. Certainly, Mrs Goldsmith, certainly.

THE MANAGER'S WIFE. Thank you. You know, it is one of the great sorrows of his life that the managers will not give him an engagement in melodrama. Not that he likes melodrama; but he says that the slow music is such a support on the stage; and he needs all the support he can get tonight, poor fellow! The—

A CARPENTER [*from the side, putting his head round the edge of the curtain*] Tsst! ma'am, tsst!

THE MANAGER'S WIFE. Eh? Whats the matter?

THE CARPENTER. The governor's dressed & coming up, ma'am.

THE MANAGER'S WIFE. Oh! [*To the audience*] Not a word. [*She hurries off, with her finger on her lips*].

The warning for the band sounds. Auld Lang Syne is softly played. The curtain rises and discovers a reading table, with an elaborate triple decked folding desk on it. A thick manuscript of unbound sheets is on the desk. A tumbler & decanter, with water, and two candles, shaded from the audience, are on the table. Right of table, a chair, in which the Manager's wife is seated. Another chair, empty, left of table. At the desk stands the Manager, ghastly pale. Applause. When silence is restored, he makes two or three visible efforts to speak.

THE MANAGER'S WIFE [*aside*] Courage, dear.

THE MANAGER [*smiling with effort*] Oh quite so, quite so. Dont be frightened, dearest. I am quite self-possessed. It would be very silly for me to—er—there is no occasion for nervousness—I—er—quite accustomed to public life—er—Ahem! [*He opens the manuscript, raises his head, & takes breath*] Er—[*He flattens the manuscript out with his hand, affecting the ease and large gesture of an orator. The desk collapses with an appalling clatter. He collapses, shaking with nervousness, into the chair*].

THE MANAGER'S WIFE [*running to him solicitously*] Never mind, dear, it was only the desk. Come. Come now. You're better now, arnt you? The audience is waiting.

THE MANAGER. I thought it was the station.

THE MANAGER'S WIFE. There's no station there now, dear; its quite safe.* [*Replacing the* MS *on the desk*] There! Thats right. [*She sits down & composes herself to listen*].

THE MANAGER [*beginning his speech*] Dear friends—I wish I could call you ladies and gentlemen—

THE MANAGER'S WIFE. Hm! hm! hm!

THE MANAGER. What's the matter?

THE MANAGER'S WIFE [*prompting him*] Ladies and gentlemen—I wish I could call you dear friends—

THE MANAGER. Well, what did I say?

THE MANAGER'S WIFE. You said it the other way about. No matter. Go on. They will understand.

THE MANAGER. Well, what difference does it make? [*Testily*] How am I to make a speech if I am to be interrupted in this way? [*To the audience*] Excuse my poor wife, ladies and gentlemen. She is naturally a little nervous tonight. You will overlook a woman's

* After assuming the management of the Avenue Theatre in January 1905, Maude undertook a complete reconstruction of the interior. Just before the work was completed, on 5 December 1905, a part of the overhead Charing Cross railway station collapsed onto the theatre, which was badly damaged. The entire interior had to be rebuilt before Maude was able to reopen the theatre, which he newly named the Playhouse.

weakness. [*To his wife*] Compose yourself, my dear. Ahem! [*He returns to the* MS] The piece of land on which our theatre is built is mentioned in Domesday Book; and you will be glad to hear that I have succeeded in tracing its history almost year by year for the 800 years that have elapsed since that Book—perhaps the most interesting of all English books—was written. That history I now propose to impart to you.—Angelina, I really cannot make a speech if you look at your watch. If you think I am going on too long, say so.

THE MANAGER'S WIFE. Not at all, dear. But our friends may not be so fond of history as you are.

THE MANAGER. Why not? I am surprised at you, Angelina. Do you suppose that this is an ordinary frivolous audience of mere playgoers? You are behind the times. Look at our friend Tree, making a fortune out of Roman history! Look at the Court Theatre: they listen to this sort of thing for three hours at a stretch there. Look at the Royal Institution, the Statistical Society, the House of Commons! Are we less scholarly, less cultured, less serious than the audiences there? I say nothing of my own humble powers; but am I less entertaining than an average Cabinet Minister? You shew great ignorance of the times we live in, Angelina; and if my speech bores you, that only shews that you are not in the movement. I am determined that this theatre shall be in the movement.

THE MANAGER'S WIFE. Well, all I can tell you is that if you dont get a little more movement into your speech, there wont be time for Pickles.*

* Maude was performing *Toddles*, an adaptation by Clyde Fitch from the French of Tristan Bernard and André Godferneaux.

THE MANAGER. That does not matter. We can omit Pickles if necessary. I have played Pickles before. If you suppose I am burning to play Pickles again you are very much mistaken. If the true nature of my talent were understood I should be playing Hamlet. Ask the audience whether they would not like to see me play Hamlet. [*Enthusiastic assent*] There! You ask me why I dont play Hamlet instead of Pickles.

THE MANAGER'S WIFE. I never asked you anything of the kind.

THE MANAGER. Please dont contradict me, Angelina—at least not in public. I say you ask me why I dont play Hamlet instead of Pickles. Well, the reason is that anybody can play Hamlet, but it takes me to play Pickles. I leave Hamlet to those who can provide no livelier form of entertainment. [*Resolutely returning to the* MS] I am now going back to the year eleven hundred.

THE STAGE MANAGER [*coming on in desperation*] No, sir, you cant go back all that way. You promised me you would be done in ten minutes. Ive got to set for the first act.

THE MANAGER. Well, is it my fault? My wife wont let me speak. I have not been able to get in a word edgeways. [*Coaxing*] Come! there's a dear good chap: just let me have another twenty minutes or so. The audience wants to hear my speech: you wouldnt disappoint them, would you?

THE STAGE MANAGER [*going*] Well, its as you please, sir, not as I please. Only dont blame me if the audience loses its last train and comes back to sleep in the theatre: that's all. [*He goes off with the air of a man who is prepared for the worst*].

During the conversation with the Stage Manager, the Manager's wife, unobserved by her husband, steals the

MS*; replaces the last two leaves of it on the desk; puts the rest on her chair and sits down on it.*

THE MANAGER. That man is hopelessly frivolous: I really must get a more cultured staff. [*To the audience*] Ladies & gentlemen, I'm extremely sorry for these unfortunate interruptions and delays: you can see that they are not my fault. [*Returning to the desk*] Ahem! Er—hallo! I am getting along faster than I thought. I shall not keep you much longer now. [*Resuming his oration*] Ladies & gentlemen, I have dealt with our little playhouse in its historical aspect. I have dealt with it in its political aspect, in its financial aspect, in its artistic aspect, in its social aspect, in its County Council aspect, in its biological and psychological aspects. You have listened to me with patience & sympathy: you have followed my arguments with intelligence & accepted my conclusions with indulgence. I have explained to you why I [have] given our new theatre its pleasant old name; why I selected Pickles as the opening piece. I have told you of our future plans, of the engagements we have made, the pieces we intend to produce, the policy we are resolved to pursue. [*With graver emphasis*] There remains only one word more. [*With pathos*] If that word has a personal note in it, you will forgive me. [*With deeper pathos*] If the note is a deeper and tenderer one than I usually venture to sound on the stage, I hope you will not think it out of what I believe is called my line. [*With emotion*] Ladies and Gentlemen: it is now more than twenty years since I and my dear wife—[*Violins tremolando: flute solo Auld Lang Syne*] What's that noise? Stop. What do you mean by this?

The band is silent.

THE MANAGER'S WIFE. They are only supporting you, Edwin. Nothing could be more appropriate.

THE MANAGER. Supporting me! They have emptied my soul of all its welling pathos. I never heard anything so ridiculous. Just as I was going to pile it on about *you*, too.

THE MANAGER'S WIFE. Go on, dear. The audience was just getting interested.

THE MANAGER. So was I. And then the band starts on me. Is this Drury Lane or is it The [Playhouse] ? Now, I havnt the heart to go on.

THE MANAGER'S WIFE. Oh please do. You were getting on so nicely.

THE MANAGER. Of course I was. I had just got everybody into a thoroughly serious frame of mind, and then the silly band sets everybody laughing—just like the latest fashion in tragedy. All my trouble gone for nothing! There's nothing left of my speech now; it might as well be the Education Bill.

THE MANAGER'S WIFE. But you must finish it, dear.

THE MANAGER. I wont. Finish it yourself.

Exit in high dudgeon.

THE MANAGER'S WIFE [*rising & coming* C] Ladies and Gentlemen: perhaps I *had* better finish it. You see, what my husband and I have been trying to do is a very difficult thing. We have some friends here—some old and valued friends—some young ones, too, we hope—but we also have for the first time in this house of ours the great public. We dare not call ourselves the friends of the public: we are only its servants; and like all servants, we are very much afraid of seeming disrespectful if we allow ourselves to be too familiar; and we are most at our ease when we are doing our work. We rather dread occasions like these, when we are allowed, and even expected, to step out of our place, and speak in our own persons of our own affairs —even for a moment, perhaps, *very* discreetly, of our own feelings. Well, what can we do? We recite a little verse; we make a little speech; we are shy; in the end, we put ourselves out of countenance, put you out of countenance, and strain your attitude of kindness and welcome until it becomes an attitude of wishing that it was all over. Well, we resolved not to do that to-night if we could help it. After all, you know how glad we are to see you; for you have the advantage of us: you can do without us: we cannot do without you. I will not say that

The drama's laws the drama's patrons give
And we who live to please must please to live.

because that is not true; and it never has been true. The drama's laws have a higher source than your caprice or ours; and in this [Playhouse] of ours we will not please you except on terms honorable to ourselves and to you. But on those terms we hope that you may spend many pleasant hours here, and we as many hardworking ones, as at our old home in the [Haymarket]. And now may I run away and tell Edwin that his speech has been a great success after all, and that you are quite ready for Pickles? [*Assent & Applause*] Thank you. [*Exit*].

Suggested Act III Ending for Barker's *The Madras House*

[Written late in 1909 or early in 1910. A holograph note by Shaw on the third leaf of the typescript in the Humanities Research Center, University of Texas, indicates: "This was written when [Charles] Frohman and [J.M.] Barrie were driven to desperation by [Harley] Granville Barker's delay in finishing the third act of The Madras House when the date of production [9 March 1910] was imminent. They appealed to me to reason with him. I took a shorter way by finishing the act myself and giving the woman the best of it (his sympathy was with the man). He was infuriated, and finished the act in his own way at once." First published in *Educational Theatre Journal*, Washington, D.C., May 1972.]

Constantine. Miss Knagg, ci devant Yates. Constantine is going out with Huxtable. Miss Knagg enters.

CONSTANTINE. Oh. Just wait for me a moment downstairs, Harry. This lady wants a word with me.

MISS KNAGG. I dont. I didnt know you were here. I came to see Mr Philip. Please dont detain Mr Huxtable on my account.

CONSTANTINE [*thinking that she is playing propriety*] Quite so. I should have said I wanted a word with you Miss Knagg. Harry: will you—

HUXTABLE. All right. All right. I'll wait for you. [*He goes out*].

CONSTANTINE. Very nice of you. Very stupid of me. I apologise. Thank you. Ive been looking for you. You didnt think, I hope, that I was going to leave you in the lurch?

MISS KNAGG. What do you want with me, Mr Constantine? I didnt expect anything from you. I dont want anything from you.

CONSTANTINE. But I understood that—that—

MISS KNAGG. What did you understand?

CONSTANTINE. Well, that there were consequences.

MISS KNAGG. Thats true. There are consequences; and Im out of employment through them. Thats what I want to see Mr Philip about. But the consequences dont concern you.

CONSTANTINE. Of course they concern me. Whats the matter? Are you angry with me?

MISS KNAGG. Not the least in the world. I really dont care that much about your part of it, Mr Constantine. Dont you worry yourself. I shall be able to take care of myself.

CONSTANTINE. But I cant let you. Dont you know that? It's a debt of honor.

MISS KNAGG. Oh. As the lady says in the play, I dont think honor has much to do with it. Anyhow, though I cant afford to go in for high falutin about honor, Ive my own ideas of self-respect and independence. If ever I have to explain to my child, I dont want to have to end by saying I was paid off. So if you dont mind, we'll drop the subject. Is Mr Philip here?

CONSTANTINE. But in justice to yourself—

MISS KNAGG. Please drop the subject, Mr Constantine. I ask you to, as a gentleman.

CONSTANTINE. Well of course if you—but no, I—

Oh, this is impossible. What sort of position are you putting me in? How could I ever hold up my head again? Youve no right to do this.

MISS KNAGG [*patiently*] Please, is Mr Philip in?

CONSTANTINE. Philip's gone.

MISS KNAGG. Thank you. Then I'll go too. [*She turns to go*].

CONSTANTINE [*stopping her*] No: I cant allow this. Youve no right to refuse to accept the consequences of your position in this way. It was a perfectly well understood affair. Youre no baby. You understood it as well as I did. When I buy an article, youve no right to force it on me as a gift.

MISS KNAGG. Thats very plain speaking. Thank you. But youre not very complimentary to yourself, Mr Constantine. I didnt do it because I wanted money. I did it because I wanted to—because at the moment I wanted you, if youll excuse my presumption.

CONSTANTINE. That doesnt give you any claim on me.

MISS KNAGG. I havent made any. I thought you were trying to fasten a claim on me.

CONSTANTINE. This is ridiculous, humiliating, absurd. It's not becoming that you should settle the proper course to take. Thats my business and my place. My honor is concerned in it. I insist on making proper provision for you and for the child. Youve no right to refuse it if it were only for the child's sake. Besides, youre entitled to it.

MISS KNAGG. I know what Im entitled to. Five shillings a week it is, I think. No thank you. It's no use, Mr Constantine. You dont respect me; and you want to go on not respecting me. Youre afraid that if I dont take anything from you, youll have to respect me; and you cant stand that. Well, youll have to stand it. Goodbye. I'll take a shakehands if you like.

CONSTANTINE. No, damme if I will. Thank God, I belong now to a country where women are kept in their place. [*Huxtable returns*].

HUXTABLE. Look here—

CONSTANTINE. Yes, Harry: I know. Im sorry for keeping you waiting. Im coming. [*He turns irresolutely to Miss Knagg*].

MISS KNAGG. It's too late now. You cant do it before Mr Huxtable.

CONSTANTINE [*with suppressed wrath*] I can do as I please. Goodbye. [*He takes her hand and shakes it savagely; then goes out with Huxtable*].

Curtain

Beauty's Duty

[Written on 17 February 1913. First published in *Short Stories, Scraps, and Shavings*, 1932.]

In a solicitor's private office. A client is stamping up and down. Both are youngish men.

CLIENT. No, Arthur: a separation. I'll put up with it no longer.

SOLICITOR. Listen to me, Horace.

CLIENT. I wont listen to you. I wont listen to anybody. My wife and I have come to the parting of the ways.

SOLICITOR. But, my dear Horace, you have nothing against her.

CLIENT. Nothing against her. Nothing ag—

SOLICITOR. I tell you, nothing. You dont complain of her temper: you dont complain of her housekeeping: you dont complain of anything except that she makes you jealous.

CLIENT. I'm not jealous. But if I could stoop to such a feeling, I should have cause for it.

SOLICITOR. Look here, Horace. If you have cause for a separation on that ground, you have cause for a divorce.

CLIENT. I am perfectly willing to be divorced—I mean to divorce her. But you keep telling me I cant.

SOLICITOR. Neither can you. You dont allege misconduct: but allege talk. Talk isnt good enough.

CLIENT. You mean it isnt bad enough. That shews how little you know about it.

SOLICITOR [*out of patience*] O well then, have it your own way. What do you complain of?

CLIENT. Whats that to you?

SOLICITOR. To me! Why, man, Ive got to tackle your wife here in this room this very morning, and explain to her that you are determined to separate from her. Do you suppose I am going to do that without giving her a reason?

CLIENT. I dont mind telling you this. No other man would have stood—

SOLICITOR. Thats no good. What did you stand? You neednt have any delicacy about telling me. Thats what I'm for. You pay a solicitor for the privilege of telling him all your most private affairs. Just forget that we're old friends, and remember only that I'm your solicitor. Besides, you will tell me nothing that I havnt been told fifty times by husbands sitting in that chair. Dont suppose youre the only man in the world that doesnt get on with his wife.

CLIENT. I bet you what you like youve never heard of a case like mine before.

SOLICITOR. I shall be able to judge of that when you tell me what your case is.

CLIENT. Well, look here. Did you ever hear of a woman coming to her husband and saying that Nature had gifted her with such an extraordinary talent for making people fall in love with her that she considered it a sin not to exercise it.

SOLICITOR. But she has you to make fall in love with her.

CLIENT. Yes: but she's done that; and she says it's so nice, and has improved me so much that she wants to do it again and improve somebody else. She says it's like a genius for bringing up children. The women who have that, she says, keep schools. They are so good at it that they have to be unfaithful to their own children and run after other people's, she says. And in just the same way, she maintains, a woman with a genius for improving men by love ought to improve them by the dozen. What do you think of that?

SOLICITOR [*rather taken with the idea*] Theres something in that, you know.

CLIENT. What!

SOLICITOR. I mean of course, logically. It's improper; but it makes good sense. I wonder whats the proper answer to it?

CLIENT. Thats what she says.

SOLICITOR. Oh. And what do you say to her?

CLIENT. I tell her that the proper answer to it is that she ought to be ashamed of herself.

SOLICITOR. Does that do any good?

CLIENT. No.

SOLICITOR. Has she ceased to care for you?

CLIENT. No. She says she will practise on me to keep her hand in; but that she is getting tired of me and must have some new interest in life. Now what do you say to your paragon?

SOLICITOR. My paragon! Have I said a word in her defence?

CLIENT. Have you said a word in mine?

SOLICITOR. But dont you see what the consequences will be if you separate? You will lose all control over her; and then there will be a divorce.

CLIENT. I havnt any control over her at present.

The Junior Clerk enters.

JUNIOR CLERK. A lady to see you, sir. [*With emotion*] She is a very beautiful lady. Oh, sir, if she is in any trouble, will you help her. If she is accused, do not believe a word against her. I'll stake my life on her innocence.

SOLICITOR [*almost speechless*] Well—! Really, Mr Guppy! [*recovering himself a little*] What name?

JUNIOR CLERK. I forgot to ascertain her name, sir.

SOLICITOR. Perhaps you will be so kind as to repair that omission.

JUNIOR CLERK. I hardly dare ask her, sir. It will seem a profanation. But I think—I hope—she will forgive me. [*He goes out*].

CLIENT. It's my wife. She's been trying it on that young lunatic.

Macbeth Skit

[Written on 10 January 1916 for Lillah McCarthy and Gerald du Maurier to be performed at a war charity matinée. "There must not be the faintest hint," Shaw wrote to Lillah McCarthy on 11 January, "that the thing is not quite serious: the audience must believe up to the moment that he opens his mouth that Macbeth is G's first attempt to shew his quality as the successor of Irving. . . . Of course nothing must get out about me." The skit, which was not performed, was first published in the *Educational Theatre Journal*, Washington, D.C., October 1967. Reproduced here from the corrected typescript in the Humanities Research Center of the University of Texas at Austin.]

ACT I. SCENE V.

Inverness. Macbeth's castle. Enter Lady Macbeth, reading a letter.

LADY MACBETH. "They met me in the day of success; and I have learned by the perfectest report, they have more in them than mortal knowledge. When I burned in desire to question them further, they made themselves air, into which they vanished. Whiles I stood rapt in the wonder of it, came missives from the king, who all hailed me 'Thane of Cawdor;' by which title, before, these weird sisters saluted me, and referred me to the coming on of time, with 'Hail, king that shalt be!' This have I thought good to deliver thee, my dearest partner of greatness, that thou mightst not lose the dues of rejoicing, by being ignorant of what greatness is promised thee. Lay it to thy heart, and farewell."

Glamis thou art, and Cawdor, and shalt be
What thou art promised: yet do I fear thy nature;
It is too full o' the milk of human kindness
To catch the nearest way: thou wouldst be great;
Art not without ambition, but without
The illness should attend it: what thou wouldst highly,
That wouldst thou holily; wouldst not play false,
And yet wouldst wrongly win: thou'ldst have, great Glamis,
That which cries "Thus thou must do, if thou have it;
And that which rather thou dost fear to do
Than wishest should be undone." Hie thee hither,
That I may pour my spirits in thine ear,
And chastise with the valour of my tongue
All that impedes thee from the golden round,
Which fate and metaphysical aid doth seem
To have thee crown'd withal.

Enter a Messenger.

What is your tidings?

MESSENGER. The king comes here to-night.

LADY MACBETH. Thou'rt mad to say it:
Is not thy master with him? who, were't so,
Would have inform'd for preparation.

MESSENGER. So please you, it is true: our thane is coming:
One of my fellows had the speed of him,
Who, almost dead for breath, had scarcely more
Than would make up his message.

LADY MACBETH. Give him tending;
He brings great news. [*Exit Messenger*].

The raven himself is hoarse
That croaks the fatal entrance of Duncan
Under my battlements. Come, you spirits
That tend on mortal thoughts, unsex me here,
And fill me, from the crown to the toe, top-full
Of direst cruelty! make thick my blood,
Stop up the access and passage to remorse,
That no compunctious visitings of nature
Shake my fell purpose, nor keep peace between
The effect and it! Come to my woman's breasts,
And take my milk for gall, you murdering ministers,
Wherever in your sightless substances
You wait on nature's mischief! Come thick night,
And pall thee in the dunnest smoke of hell,
That my keen knife see not the wound it makes,
Nor heaven peep through the blanket of the dark,
To cry "Hold, hold!"

Enter Macbeth.

Great Glamis! worthy Cawdor!
Greater than both, by the all-hail hereafter!
Thy letters have transported me beyond
This ignorant present, and I feel now
The future in the instant

MACBETH. My dearest girl;
I am never tired of hearing you
Express yourself in that magnificent way.
Duncan comes here tonight.

LADY MACBETH. And when goes hence?

MACBETH. Tomorrow: so the old man says.

LADY MACBETH. O, never
Shall sun that morrow see!
Your face, my thane, is as a book where men
May read strange matters. To beguile the time,
Look like the time; bear welcome in your eye,
Your hand, your tongue: look like the innocent flower,

But be the serpent under't. He that's coming
Must be provided for: and you shall put
This night's great business into my dispatch;
Which shall to all our nights and days to come
Give solely sovereign sway and masterdom.

During this speech Macbeth tries to play up to it. When she says, "Look like the time" he takes out a turnip watch; bears welcome in his eye and hand and tongue; looks like the innocent flower and then like the serpent under it.

MACBETH. We will proceed no further in this business—you see, deary, I am trying to put it in your style, though its rather out of my line. We will, as I was saying, proceed no further in this business—in short, chuck it. The old man has been fearfully good to me; and ever since I cut that man in two in the war, everybody has been uncommonly kind to me. I enjoy being popular. You dont, I know: but I do. It may be a weakness; but if I were to murder the old man the very first night he is staying with us, I should lose sympathy. I really dont think people would like it.

LADY MACBETH. Was the hope drunk
Wherein you dress'd yourself? hath it slept since?
And wakes it now, to look so green and pale
At what it did so freely? From this time
Such I account thy love. Art thou afeard
To be the same in thine own act and valour
As thou art in desire? Wouldst thou have that
Which thou esteem'st the ornament of life,
And live a coward in thine own esteem,
Letting "I dare not" wait upon "I would,"
Like the poor cat i' the adage?

MACBETH. Like what?

LADY MACBETH [*louder*] Like the cat.

MACBETH. Oh, the cat. In the what, did you say?

LADY MACBETH. In the adage.

MACBETH. Never heard of it. Your language is beyond me, my dear girl. However, if you want to know what I am afraid of, I'm afraid of the police. I dare do all that may become a man—a law-abiding man, you understand—without getting him into trouble. Who dares do more is—well, he isnt me.

LADY MACBETH. What beast was't then
That made you break this enterprise to me?
When you durst do it, then you were a man;
And, to be more than what you were, you would
Be so much more the man.

MACBETH. Look here: I dont follow this.

LADY MACBETH. Nor time nor place
Did then adhere, and yet you would make both, and
They have made themselves, and that their fitness now
Does unmake you. I have given suck, and know
How tender 'tis to love the babe that milks me:
I would, while it was smiling in my face,
Have pluck'd my nipple from his boneless gums,
And dash'd the brains out, had I so sworn as you
Have done to this.

MACBETH. No you wouldnt, darling. It sounds all right; but one doesnt do these things, believe me. Besides, Duncan wont behave in that way: he was weaned about 75 years ago. Suppose we fail?

LADY MACBETH. We fail!!

MACBETH [*prosaically*] Yes, fail.

LADY MACBETH. But screw your courage to the sticking-place,
And we'll not fail. When Duncan is asleep—
Whereto the rather shall his day's hard journey
Soundly invite him—his two chamberlains
Will I with wine and wassail so convince,

That memory, the warder of the brain,
Shall be a fume, and the receipt of reason
A limbec only:

MACBETH. What the devil is a limbec?

LADY MACBETH [*putting her hand over his mouth to shut him up, and proceeding*]
when in swinish sleep
Their drenched natures lie as in a death,
What cannot you and I perform upon
The unguarded Duncan? What not put upon
His spongy officers, who shall bear the guilt
Of our great quell?

MACBETH [*reflecting*] A limbec must be an alembic; and an alembic is the sort of thing you see in an apothecary's shop—a sort of illicit still. But hang me if I know what you mean by this great quell. I never met a woman who could talk over my head as you do What do you expect me to say, darling?

LADY MACBETH. Bring forth men-children only;
For thy undaunted mettle should compose
Nothing but males.

MACBETH. Capital! Just how I wanted to turn it. As I understand you, the two Johnnies who sleep in the room with Duncan will be drunk. By the way, you neednt trouble to make them drunk: you can depend on them for that: they havnt been sober after nine o'clock since they were children. The old man cant keep awake for ten minutes at any hour, even when you are talking to him. All I have to do is to stick their dirks into him. It's great. By George, it's immense! How do you think of such things? Everybody'll say they did it. Eh? What?

LADY MACBETH. Who dares receive it other,
As we shall make our griefs and clamour roar
Upon his death?

MACBETH [*tragically*] I am settled (I mean Duncan is)

And buck up each—each—each—

LADY MACBETH. Each corporal agent to this terrible feat—

MACBETH. Yes—give us a chance, old girl—

[*again tragically*]

Each corporal agent to these terrible feet—Look here: what's wrong with my feet?

MISS MCCARTHY. Gerald: come off it. I shall never make a Shakespearian actor of you. [*She leads him ignominiously from the stage*].

Curtain

Glastonbury Skit

[Written in late August 1916 as an interpolation in Frederick Austin's joke-play "The Glastonbury Travesty," performed on the last night of the Glastonbury Festival, 26 August, by the composer Rutland Boughton, the novelist Frederick Austin, and a local resident (and councillor?) John Bostock. Published, under the pseudonym of Walter Wombwell, in "Conclusion of the Festival," *Central Somerset Gazette*, 1 September 1916; reprinted in part in Michael Hurd's *Immortal Hour*, 1962. Reproduced here from the holograph manuscript in the British Museum: Add. Mss. 50643, ff. 186–189.]

BOSTOCK [*rising*] Stop. Ladies & gentlemen: I rise to protest against this performance. I am sorry to interrupt; but I have a public duty to perform. Men of Glastonbury: you all know me. I—

AUSTIN [*who has come on the stage*] May I ask you to address yourself to me, Mr Bostock. We all know you and have the greatest respect for you. We will listen to you with the greatest patience. What do you wish to say?

BOSTOCK. I protest against this performance.

AUSTIN. In what capacity do you protest, Mr Bostock?

BOSTOCK. As a member of the Committee—as a ratepayer—

CHORUS MAN. That's quite right, Mr Bostock. The rates in this town are something disgraceful—

AUSTIN [*suppressing him*] Order, please. Mr Bostock is not protesting against the rates: he is protesting against the performance.

CHORUS MAN. Then, if you ask me, he dont know when he's well off.

AUSTIN. I did not ask you, sir; and I dont believe you have paid your rates. Besides, you are only the chorus: you have no right to assume a principal part. Now, Mr Bostock.

BOSTOCK. What I say is that classical music should not be burlesqued. I say that the beautiful, glorious, tuneful music of Iphigenia should not be burlesqued. I speak with feeling. I say that it should not be burlesqued. I go further. I say that no music should be burlesqued.

AUSTIN. Do I understand you to say that Mr Boughton's work should not be burlesqued?

BOSTOCK. I was not speaking of Mr Boughton's work: I was speaking of *Music*.

BOUGHTON [*rising*] What's that you say? Do you mean that what I compose is not music?

BOSTOCK. I have the greatest admiration for my friend Boughton. Nobody can appreciate more than I the very stimulating noise he induces our more gifted townspeople to make on these occasions.

BOUGHTON. A very stimulating WHAT?

BOSTOCK. I said a noise [*he sits down*].

AUSTIN [*soothingly*] Shakespear has used the same expression, Mr Boughton. In Romeo & Juliet he writes of the band as Sneak's Noise.

BOUGHTON. I shall leave Glastonbury tomorrow. You can send for De Souza's band. You can dance ragtimes. You can all go to the movies. Boughton's occupation's gone.

BOSTOCK. The immortal composer of Iphigenia, the great Gluck—

BOUGHTON. Who brought Gluck to Glastonbury?

Did you ever hear an opera of Gluck's until I performed it for you?

BOSTOCK. Several times.

BOUGHTON. What operas of Gluck's? Name them.

BOSTOCK. Il Trovatore, Maritana, Faust, Carmen, The Bohemian Girl—

AUSTIN. Ahem! Ahem! Mr Boughton: I think this altercation is very distressing to the audience.

BOUGHTON. Not a bit of it: they like it. Besides, who began it? Bostock did. Well, snub Bostock, not me. I wont be suppressed. No man has ever silenced me.

BOSTOCK. If you will excuse my saying so, Mr Boughton, you are now talking through your hat.

BOUGHTON. I havnt a hat. Has any man in Glastonbury ever seen me with a hat? I cant afford a hat. I cant even afford to get my hair cut. I spend all my money on music for the people of Glastonbury. And now, because Bostock wants his Maritanas and his Bohemian Girls—

BOSTOCK [*rising again indignantly*] I protest. I cannot allow this. I have never wanted a Bohemian girl. I am a respectable married man. I call on you, Mr Austin, to protect me from Mr Boughton's scandalous insinuations.

AUSTIN. I must request you, Mr Boughton, to keep order.

BOUGHTON. I am in order. I am as quiet as a lamb. If you will only listen to me for half an hour or so—

AUSTIN. Certainly not. I call on you to sit down.

BOUGHTON: When you call on me, its my place to ask you to sit down.

AUSTIN. Dont quibble, sir. Sit down.

BOUGHTON. I wont.

AUSTIN. I shall appeal to the Mayor.

BOUGHTON. Not even the Mayor of Glastonbury shall muzzle me.

AUSTIN. I shall call the police.

BOUGHTON. I defy the police. No power in heaven or earth shall prevail against Rutland Boughton.

MRS BOUGHTON [*peremptorily*] Rutland: you are making a fool of yourself. Sit down.

BOUGHTON [*collapsing abjectly*] Yes, dear [*he sits down*].

AUSTIN. Thank you, Mrs Boughton. The hand that rocks the cradle rules the world. Mr Bostock: are you satisfied?

BOSTOCK. I will just ask Mr Boughton whether he thinks it fair to burlesque Gluck's music when his own music cannot be burlesqued?

BOUGHTON. Why cant it be burlesqued?

BOSTOCK. Because its too funny already.

BOUGHTON [*explosively*] Bostock—

MRS BOUGHTON [*warningly*] Now, Rutland.

BOUGHTON. I am calm, dear, perfectly calm, Maynt I just tell them why I dont write music like Gluck's?

BOSTOCK. Because you can't, Mr Boughton.

BOUGHTON. Yes I can: its always easy to do what somebody else has done before. Why is Gluck's music the finest of its kind in the world? Because he didnt imitate foreign composers, but wrote the native music of his own country. Well, his country isnt my country, especially just at present. I am writing English music in England for English people; and before I stop, I'll cut it finer still and write Glastonbury music in Glastonbury for Glastonbury people. And I'll make fun of myself all the time if I like, and of Gluck too. So there! [*He sits down*].

AUSTIN. I think we may now bring this little episode to a close. [*The limelight man cuts off his light. Austin shouts angrily at him*] Please dont take the light off my face. Youre always doing it.

LIMELIGHT MAN. If you could see your face, youd be obliged to me.

AUSTIN [*furious*] Whats that you say? [*He jumps down into the auditorium and rushes for the limelight man. Boughton and Bostock* [*grab*] *him*].

All speak together, making a fearful row.

AUSTIN. Let me go. He insulted me. I'll let him know. I'll put a face on him. I'll teach him his place. Let go, will you.

BOSTOCK. Order, order. Remember where you are, Mr Austin. The man meant no harm. Calm yourself. This is most unseemly.

BOUGHTON. Steady, steady, Austin. Never mind him, old chap. Dont kill him: we cant get on without him. Easy, easy.

LIMELIGHT MAN. Come on. I'm ready for you. It's me that makes this show fit to be seen. I'm fed up with your complaints. Come on, the lot of you.

Crash—Lights up and Play resumed.

Skit for *The Tiptaft Revue*

[Written in August 1917 for a topical revue produced by members of the Fabian Summer School at Godalming, Surrey. The Chairman and author of the first half of the revue was Norman Tiptaft, a Birmingham industrialist. Miss Mary Hankinson was a Fabian who led the group in callisthenics and taught dancing. Reproduced here from the holograph manuscript in the Henry W. and Albert A. Berg Collection, The New York Public Library, Astor, Lenox and Tilden Foundations.]

Shaw is called upon by the Chairman.

CHAIRMAN. Ladies and gentlemen: an intellectual treat awaits you. Mr Bernard Shaw.

SHAW. I have forgotten how to rise. I am too stiff to rise. I have lost the power of movement except at the command of Miss Hankinson.

Miss Hankinson gives the jumping order. Shaw rises on his toes; bends his knees; bounds into the air; and comes down in the correct attitude.

SHAW. Thank you. Mr Chairman, ladies and gentlemen. [*As he speaks he walks to and fro*] I have learnt many things at the summer school this year; and they have left me a humbler, and I hope, a better [*he reaches the side of the stage and turns with a hop*] one, two, three, one, two, three [*practising the waltz*] a better man. What is the question before us ? Surely it is this. [*He drops his emphatic manner and communes with himself perplexedly*] Do I start with the right foot or the left ?

[*He starts waltzing with the right*] No: the left. One, two, three—[*recollecting himself*] As I was saying, Mr Chairman—Look here: what WAS I saying?

THE CHAIRMAN [*kindly*] You were saying, Mr Shaw, that hope told a flattering tale.

SHAW. Was I? That's very extraordinary; for I have hardly spoken to the man for twenty minutes, and he never got a word in edgeways.

THE CHAIRMAN. All right, Mr Shaw, all right. I only said that to draw you.

SHAW. Please dont draw me any more. Mrs Wilson does nothing but draw me; and she never misses a single one of my worst points. After all, my nose is no redder than anyone else's; and, anyhow, you cant give the exact shade with a black lead pencil.

THE CHAIRMAN [*very kindly*] You have no worst points, Mr Shaw. You are, humanly speaking, perfection.

SHAW. Will you tell me this, Mr Chairman? Why has everyone been so jolly civil to me ever since Mr Webb made that speech about our being kind to the old? They are getting kinder and kinder to me every day. Why? Is it because I am getting older and older every day? Mr Chairman, I say it is a mistaken kindness. They try to teach me to dance. They sacrifice themselves as my partners. In my agitation at an unaccustomed exercise which I do not understand, I grab them by the hair; I kick large chips out of their shins; I come down with crushing weight on their toes; but they smile and redouble their kindness. Why dont they teach Webb, instead of stealing his shoes and wearing them to show how small their feet are?

THE CHAIRMAN. Are we not wandering a little from the question, Mr Shaw?

SHAW. Well, you ought to know. What is the

question? I thought *I* was the question. I generally am the question. There is not a more modest man alive; but people dont seem able to get away from me.

SOMEBODY. Why does Mr Shaw object to our civility? It does the greatest violence to my feelings. He ought to be most thankful to us. He bores me stiff.

Indignant cries of Order! Shame! Disgraceful! &c. Shaw, beaming and effusive, goes to the somebody and shakes her hand warmly.

SHAW. Thank you, dearest lady, thank you. You may sit beside me at breakfast tomorrow.

THE CHAIRMAN. May I remind you, with the greatest respect, that the subject before us is the Reconstruction of the Empire after the War.

SHAW. True, Mr Chairman. Oh, how true! But do not be downhearted. Webb will reconstruct it; and I will take the credit. Soon, I hope, this terrible war will conclude; and all Europe will be as peaceful, as harmonious, as brotherly, as charitable, as tolerant, as patient, as ready to hear the other side, as a Summer School meeting.

A VOICE. What price Tiptaft?

SHAW. Tiptaft be blowed! [*Hear, hear!*] Tiptaft comes from Birmingham [*Shame!*] Tiptaft is a Tariff Reformer [*groans*] Tiptaft's pockets are bulging with Tory money [*Spy!*] Tiptaft thirsts for the blood of our German comrades [*Coward!*] Tiptaft puts his own wretched country before Socialism [*Traitor!*] In this school, when we speak of tolerance, of harmony, of brotherhood, we dont include Tiptaft [*Not likely! and great cheering*] As our brave Allies would say, *Conspuez* Tiptaft [*Laughter and cheers*] I turn from this disgusting subject to the end of the war which Tiptaft would prolong to the last syllable of recorded time—if he could. I call your attention to an important economic point which we have not yet discussed. It will be raised by the repatriation of our army when peace breaks out. I say that the State should pay the returning officers' expenses.

A VOICE. No politics!

SHAW. You idiot, I dont mean the returning officers' expenses.*

VOICE. Well, what do you mean?

SHAW. I mean the expenses of the returning officers.

ANOTHER VOICE [*judicially*] After all, does it matter?

SHAW [*hopelessly puzzled*] What?

THE FIRST VOICE. What do you mean?

THE OTHER VOICE. Simply, does it matter?

SHAW. Does what matter?

THE CHAIRMAN. I think we have now reached a stage at which the audience would appreciate some remarks from the next speaker.

SHAW. Saved! [*He collapses into his seat; and the meeting proceeds*].

&c &c &c.

* This somewhat obscure jest depends on the knowledge that "returning officers" is a term referring to men who, in elections, are responsible for verifying the accuracy of the votes and announcing the results. [Editor]

The War Indemnities

[Written on 21–22 March 1921 for Frank Harris, to whom Shaw wrote on the 22nd: "I am dead beat, and can scrawl only a few lines of rubbish. However, it will fill up a column." Published in *Pearson's Magazine*, New York, June 1921; reprinted in *American Mercury*, New York, August 1935.]

How it would clarify the question of the so-called indemnities if the parties would only call things by their right names! Indemnity for war is flat nonsense: you cannot shoot a man and unshoot him again by treaty afterwards. Even Mr Lloyd George sees that, and seizes the opportunity to make a magnanimous gesture of foregoing what he knows he cannot get.

War is a game in which the takes are plunder and conquest. Germany lost; and the winners now proceed to take what they can get; and that will not be indemnity or reparation or any such nonsense, but booty pure and simple. But the simpler the language, the more apparent becomes the complexity of the fact. For example, the Germans admit that they must pay something; and they accordingly propose to pay England in coal. Hereupon ensues something like the following:

LLOYD GEORGE. Coal! Good God, no. Not a sack, not a lump. What are you dreaming of? You would throw our coal miners out of employment.

THE GERMANS. Well, will you take it in steel?

LLOYD GEORGE. Worse and worse. No country in Europe shall produce steel but England if I can help it.

Steel indeed! Dont you dare to trifle with me. Your attempts to avert payment are too transparent. [*Aside to Marshal Foch*] Rattle your sabre a bit, will you, my dear Marshal? [*Foch does so*].

THE GERMANS. Well, what on earth are we to pay in? You know we cannot pay in gold.

LLOYD GEORGE [*aside to Foch*] What are they to pay in, Marshal?

FOCH [*aside to Expert*] What are they to pay in, *mon cher*?

EXPERT [*aside to Foch*] Potash.

FOCH [*aside to Lloyd George*] Potash.

LLOYD GEORGE [*aloud, menacingly, to the Germans*] You know as well as I do. You shall pay in potash.

THE GERMANS. But *Donnerwetter*, there is not five thousand millions worth of potash in the world.

LLOYD GEORGE. Come, come! No prevarication. There are other products: for example, perlmutter. So let me have no more nonsense.

DR SIMONS. *Blödsinn!*

LLOYD GEORGE [*blushing*] Oh! Nice language that! Can no German ever be a gentleman? Fie for shame, sir!

DR SIMONS. You really must propose something practicable.

LLOYD GEORGE. Must I? Pray, who won the war: you or we? "Must," as Queen Elizabeth said, is not a word that is addressed to British prime ministers. However, how would it be if you were to raise a loan to pay England?

DR SIMONS. Raise it where?

LLOYD GEORGE. In America. They have lots of money there. Or in France.

FOCH. *Comment!!!*

LLOYD GEORGE. An excellent investment for your

peasant proprietors, my dear Marshal. Think of how well they did out of the 1871 indemnity.

FOCH. But why should your own people, our brave allies, be deprived of such an opening for their little savings? After all, it doesnt matter to you where the money comes from, does it? Money is money. *Non olet.*

LLOYD GEORGE. My French is shockingly bad. What does *nong olay* mean?

FOCH. It means that all money smells alike.

LLOYD GEORGE. True; but how—?

FOCH. You see, *mon cher Loi Georges*, if this German *farceur* can arrange to make the proletariat pay, does it matter greatly which proletariat it is? Yours, or ours, or theirs, or the American *canaille*: what does it matter?

LLOYD GEORGE. *Non olet*, eh?

FOCH. Well, not exactly *non olet*. But they all smell alike.

LLOYD GEORGE [*sternly to Dr Simons*] I have consulted with my illustrious friend and ally, Marshal Foch. We are agreed that you can find the money if you choose. If a satisfactory proposal to that effect does not reach us by the middle of next week, we shall occupy every city on the Rhine.

DR SIMONS. And what then?

LLOYD GEORGE. What then! You shall see what then. None of your insolence with me, if you please. What then, indeed!

DR SIMONS. The money your troops will spend will be very useful to us.

LLOYD GEORGE. Fifty per cent on every one of your exports for that speech, young man.

DR SIMONS. Ah, well! The consumer will pay.

FOCH. What does he say? What is that word?

LLOYD GEORGE. Consumer. *Le consommateur*, you know. *Le shallong.*

FOCH [*with military pith and brevity*] *Je m'en jous!*

Curtain

This is the kind of thing that we are being landed in by diplomatists and soldiers who know nothing, pushed from behind by commercial adventurers who do not know the A.B.C. of finance, but who, having got noses for money, may be depended on to sniff their way to a solution which will mean that the workers will have to support an additional burden of idleness and waste all the world over. And it is quite likely that the victors will bear the heavier share. As to asking America or any other country to trade in German promissory notes payable 42 years after date, I will only quote what a Belgian historian and diplomatist [André Vandervelde] has just written to me: "I believe that ten years hence Germany and Russia will be masters of Europe."

The Yahoos

[First published in the *Evening Standard*, London, 20 January 1927.]

Mr Bernard Shaw, acting as extra-special correspondent of the "Evening Standard," sends us the following verbatim report of the second meeting of the Yahoos, the new club for the Suppression of Hypocrisy and Inconsistency in Public Life:—

PRESIDENT. Brother Yahoos, our first business tonight is the adjourned discussion on the Smethwick election. That hypocrite Mosley—

ALL. Yah!

PRESIDENT. Yah by all means, brothers; but since we met last, the blighter has got in. [*Shame!*] Our protest has been disregarded by the electors of Smethwick. They call themselves working men, and then go and vote for a capitalist.

ALL. Yah! Yah!

PRESIDENT. That shows what they are, doesnt it? Curs, I call them!

VICE-PRESIDENT. If you ask me, Mr President, I say that the women made them vote for him. Women voting for a man, mind you. Is that consistent?

ALL. Yah!

A YAHOO. Working men's wives voting for the husband of an earl's daughter!

ALL. Yah!

ANOTHER YAHOO. What right has a Socialist to be an earl's daughter?

A MILD YAHOO. Well, she can't help it, can she, mate?

PRESIDENT. Not help it. Why can't she help it? Hasnt this Government just made a law that anybody can adopt a child and be the same as its natural parent? Well, you can't have a thing like that both ways. If a parent can adopt a child under the Act a child can adopt a parent. What was to prevent Mosley's wife—

THE VICE [*ironically*] Lady Cynthia!

ALL. Yah!

PRESIDENT. What was to prevent her adopting old Trotsky for her father if she believed her own principles?

THE MILD YAHOO. That is a point, certainly. But she may not have thought of it.

ALL. Yah!

PRESIDENT. Order! Order! Members must not yah one another.

THE VICE. There's too much of this kind of thing. Look at Wells!

A YAHOO. Who's Wells?

ANOTHER YAHOO. Boxer. Aint you never heard of Billy Wells?

THE VICE. No: not him. H. G. Wells, the reporter.

THE MILD YAHOO. An author, sir, I think.

THE VICE. Author be blowed! He writes in the "Sunday Express": what's that but reporting? He's wrote two books to say that in future we shall all go naked. And does he live up to it? Not he. I saw him in Whitehall-terrace las' Tuesday dressed up like you or me. New trousers, too.

ALL. Yah! Yah!

A YAHOO. Just like them writing chaps. Look at Bunnard Shorr preaching that we should all have equal incomes. Well, I put him to the acid test. Has one of you ever had a penny off him?

ALL. Not a farthing. Yah!

PRESIDENT. That man calls himself a Socialist and has two cars, while we ride in the bus or tramp in the mud. Hypocrisy, I call it. What right has he to two cars?

ALL. Yah! Yah!

ANOTHER YAHOO. Yes and—would you believe it? —the stingy swine carries a gun-metal watch.

ALL. Yah! Yah!! Yah!!!

THE VICE. The Communists are worse than the Socialists. Look at Cook! Not a penny off the wage, he shouts. Not an hour on the day. Can he deny that there are miners at this moment working eight hours a day for forty-five bob a week? Why dont he raise their wages? Why dont he repeal the Eight-Hour Act?

ALL. Yah, yah!

A YAHOO. The clergy are the worst of the lot. Take Inge, the Melancholy Dean!

THE MILD YAHOO. The Melancholy Dean's name was Hamlet, sir, I think.

PRESIDENT. That's quite all right. Our brother meant to say the Gloomy Dean.

THE YAHOO. I stand corrected, since youre so particular. But mind! I never blamed him for being gloomy. What is he paid for? Is it for dancing the Charleston at night clubs? No: it's for being the dean of London's cathedral; and I say he's right to take it seriously. It's his job to be gloomy. Would you have a religious man look cheerful?

PRESIDENT. Just so, brother. But then what have you against him?

THE YAHOO. I'll tell you what I have against him, Mr President. Did he or did he not say that the inhabitants of the south and west of Ireland ought to be exterminated?

PRESIDENT. I certainly understood him so, brother.

THE YAHOO. Then why doesnt he go and exterminate them, instead of sitting by his comfortable fire in his deanery and leaving the poor lost creatures to exterminate one another?

THE VICE. That shows you what parsons are.

ALL. Yah!

A YAHOO. The women are worse than the parsons. Lady Astor—

THE LANDLORD [*looking in*] Closing time, gents, if you please. [*He withdraws*].

PRESIDENT [*setting the example of reluctant rising*] Closing time! Do you suppose that man believes in closing time?

ALL. Yah!

THE MILD YAHOO. But what can he do, after all?

PRESIDENT. Do! He can suffer for his principles, can't he? Goodnight all.

The proceedings then terminated.

The Garden of the Hesperides

[Fragment of dialogue, undated [*c.* 1930s]: British Museum Add. Mss. 50739, ff. 1–5.]

In view of the garden of the Hesperides. Summer day reddening towards sunset.

FIRST TOURIST [*entering, takes stock of distant Hesperides, and calls back down path*] Hallo! Arthur!

SECOND TOURIST (ARTHUR) [*without*] Hallo!

FIRST TOURIST. We can see it from here. Come along. I want your field glass.

ARTHUR. See what?

FIRST TOURIST. It, you duffer. The garden of the Hesperides. The castle of the Sleeping Beauty.

ARTHUR. Honor bright! Not a trick to make me get up and go on?

FIRST TOURIST. Honor bright.

Arthur gets up and hastens to join First Tourist, taking his field glass from its case as he does so.

FIRST TOURIST [*pointing*] What do you make of that? Do you see the arcaded terraces?

ARTHUR [*looking through his glass*] By Jingo! So it is. There she is.

FIRST TOURIST. Get out. Let's see. [*He snatches at the glass: Arthur evades him*].

ARTHUR [*still looking*] Half a minute. Yes: I can see her quite distinctly. The tree with the golden apples is in the middle, near the fishpond. She's in a hammock of purple cords, dressed in cloth of gold. I can't make out quite clearly what she's reading, but I think it's a volume of my poems. The dragon's asleep in the shrubbery.

FIRST TOURIST. Dont fool. Let's have a look.

ARTHUR. See for yourself.

FIRST TOURIST [*looking through the glass*] What a paradise! [*Adjusts focus & looks again*] Upon my soul, Arthur: there is something there like a hammock there to the right of that fountain looking thing.

ARTHUR [*incredulous*]. No! Let me see. [*Snatches glass and looks again*] I believe it is. [*Lowers glass, somewhat dumbfounded*] Well, I'm dashed!

FIRST TOURIST. Beginning to believe, eh?

ARTHUR. Well, seeing's believing. There's the enchanted garden—at least a very jolly garden. And that pale purple and gold thing *may* be a hammock with a woman in it. Whether she will be up to your expectations when we come close is another thing.

FIRST TOURIST. We shan't get close tonight. It will be dark by the time we get to that village in the valley.

ARTHUR. That must be Dulcigno.

FIRST TOURIST. Yes: that's Dulcigno. We shall sleep there and get on to the garden tomorrow afternoon.

[Text ends here]

The Girl with the Golden Voice

[Written as a dialogue for a telephone conversation between Shaw and Ethel Cain, a telephone operator known as "the girl with the golden voice." Broadcast from Radiolympia by the B.B.C. on 17 August 1935. Reproduced here from the typescript in the British Museum: Add. Mss. 50705, ff. 82–84.]

MISS CAIN. Hello hello! Is that Mr Bernard Shaw?
SHAW. Yes. Who are you?
MISS CAIN. Radiolympia.
SHAW. What?????
MISS CAIN. Ray Dee Oh Lympia. R for raspberries, A for apples—
SHAW. What on earth are you talking about? I dont want any raspberries or apples. Are you a greengrocer?
MISS CAIN. No, Mr Shaw. I am a telephone operator.
SHAW. That accounts for your very agreeable voice. Where did you get it?
MISS CAIN. It is my business to have an agreeable voice.
SHAW. Not at all. It is the business of the public to have agreeable voices. They have only to listen to you for a moment; but you have to listen to them all day. Dont they drive you mad with their slovenly articulation and horrible accents?
MISS CAIN. I am trained to exercise self-control, Mr Shaw. I must not complain.
SHAW. But wouldnt you like to let yourself go for once in a way and just tell the telephone subscribers what you think of them and their vulgar speech and bad manners and bad tempers and complaints?
MISS CAIN. What good would that do? Besides, they

are not so bad. I can generally soothe them with my voice when they complain.

SHAW. They dont deserve it. I should cultivate a good rasping voice for special occasions.

MISS CAIN. Perhaps I do. Dont provoke me to give you a sample of it. Remember, you have only three minutes; and you have wasted more than a minute already.

SHAW. Sorry. I'm afraid I interrupted you. You wanted me to buy some raspberries and apples.

MISS CAIN. No, no, no. Let me explain. I am at Olympia, in London.

SHAW. I see. A harvest festival, I suppose. You are keeping a fruit stall. Is that how you usually spend your holidays?

MISS CAIN. I am not having a holiday: I am working my hardest. Will you please listen to me for a moment?

SHAW. I will listen to you for a year. It is a pleasure to listen to such a voice. By the way, have you ever fallen in love with a voice?

MISS CAIN. Really, Mr Shaw, you are spoiling this interview. Another minute gone; and we have not begun yet.

SHAW. All right, all right: I apologize. What about the apples?

MISS CAIN. If you mention apples to me again I shall ring off.

SHAW. But, my dear young lady, you speak with such beautiful distinctness that I could not possibly be mistaken. You started by mentioning raspberries and apples.

MISS CAIN. I was trying to explain to you that I am at a great exhibition of radio apparatus at Olympia in London, and that there is a large audience present who wish to hear you speaking to me from Malvern, where you are staying for the Festival of your plays there.

SHAW. And so you said raspberries and apples. Quite! Quite! I did not catch on at first; but now I have got it perfectly. What do you suppose the large audience wants me to say to you?

MISS CAIN. Oh how can I possibly tell, Mr Shaw?

SHAW. But I dont know what to say.

MISS CAIN. Cant you say something about the Festival, or your new play, or the Malvern Hills, or something? Do hurry up or we shall be cut off.

SHAW. I bet you anything you like that the audience does not care tuppence about me or my plays. They dont know where the Malvern Hills are, and dont care. All they think about now is somebody called the Girl with the Golden Voice. Why dont you talk to her?

MISS CAIN. Mr Shaw: I AM the Girl with the Golden Voice. At least that is what the silly newspapers persist in calling me.

SHAW. Great Heavens, why didnt you tell me that at first instead of raving about raspberries and apples? Dont you know that I write plays, and that those plays depend on being spoken musically and distinctly and beautifully. Look here. If I promise you a leading part in my next play will you chuck this telephone business and go on the stage?

GRUFF MALE VOICE. Three minutes.

SHAW. Damn!!!!!

MISS CAIN. I feel exactly as you do, Mr Shaw. Goodnight.

Arthur and the Acetone

[Published in the *New Leader*, London, 29 November 1936; reprinted in Shaw's *Complete Plays with Prefaces*, New York, 1962, and in Fenner Brockway's *Outside the Right*, 1963.]

ACT I

1917. SCENE: *The Foreign Secretary's room at the Foreign Office. Arthur is contemplating with dismay a document which has been handed to him by an attaché.*

ARTHUR. Boy, this is awful. Are you sure your figures are correct?

ATTACHE. They have been checked three times over, sir.

ARTHUR. This is really what the war is costing us?

ATTACHE. Under the mark, if anything, sir.

ARTHUR. Young man, do you realize—but no. Only a Scot can feel as I feel about it. Look at this one item alone. £5,038 15s 9⅞d for cordite enough to kill a single German. How can any country stand such a strain?

ATTACHE. It's not the cordite, sir. It's the acetone that is so expensive. Cordite cannot be made without acetone.

ARTHUR. I don't know what acetone is; and I don't care. All I know is that if we go on like this we shall have to give an order to cease killing Germans. Dead Germans cost too much . . . Are our chemists trying how to find something cheaper?

ATTACHE. They are doing their best; but nothing has come of it so far. There's a chemist in Manchester who has a microbe that makes acetone for next to nothing.

ARTHUR. Send him here instantly. Why hasn't he been sent here before?

ATTACHE. Impossible, sir, unfortunately.

ARTHUR. Nothing is impossible when we are at war. Why is it impossible?

ATTACHE. He is a Jew, sir.

ARTHUR. Is his microbe a Jew?

ATTACHE. I suppose not, sir.

ARTHUR. Is Sir Herbert Samuel a Jew or is he not? Is he in the Cabinet or is he not?

ATTACHE. But it is a coalition Government, sir. All sorts of people are let in.

ARTHUR. Any other objection?

ATTACHE. Well, Manchester, you know, sir. Provincial. And Owens College! If it were Cambridge, now, we might stretch a point.

ARTHUR. If this Jewish gentleman is not in this room in three hours, you go to the trenches.

ATTACHE. Oh, if you make a point of it, of course. But we shall lose tone.

ARTHUR [*roaring*] Get out!

The attaché shrugs his shoulders and goes out.

ARTHUR [*clutching his temples as he again pores over the sheet of figures*] Five thousand and thirty-eight golden pounds to put one Boche out of action! And we have to exterminate the lot of them!

ACT II

As before, three hours later, but with Dr Chaim Weizmann instead of the attaché.

ARTHUR. Doctor Weizmann, we must have that microbe at your own price. Name it. We shall not hesitate at six figures.

DR WEIZMANN. I do not ask for money.

ARTHUR. There must be some misunderstanding. I was informed that you are a Jew.

WEIZMANN. You were informed correctly. I am a Jew.

ARTHUR. But—pardon me—you said you did not ask for money.

WEIZMANN. Precisely. I do not want money.

ARTHUR. A title, perhaps? Baron? Viscount? Do not hesitate.

WEIZMANN. Nothing would induce me to accept a title. I should have to pay more for everything.

ARTHUR. Then may I ask, without offence, since you want none of the things that everybody wants, what the devil do you want?

WEIZMANN. I want Jerusalem.

ARTHUR. It's yours. I only regret that we cannot throw in Madagascar as well. Unfortunately it belongs to the French Government. The Holy Land belongs naturally to the Church of England; and to it you are most welcome. And now will you be so good as to hand over the microbe.

ACT III

Mr Bernard Shaw in his sumptuously furnished study reading the announcement of the Balfour Declaration.

MR B. S. Another Ulster! As if one were not enough.

CURTAIN

Sequence for *The King's People*

[Written for John Drinkwater's Coronation film *The King's People*, 1937. Published in the *New York Times*, 9 May 1937; reprinted in Shaw's *Complete Plays with Prefaces*, New York, 1962.]

G.B.S. Hallo, John! What on earth is all this about?

J.D. Well, in fact it's about the British Empire. I am making a film of it.

G.B.S. Too late, John, too late. Haven't you heard? The British Empire is dead. It's been replaced by the British Commonwealth of Nations. You have to thank Ireland for that. We refused to belong to that ruffianly political old empire, or to any empire. But a commonwealth is another matter. Any self-respecting nation can belong to a commonwealth of nations. Every self-respecting nation ought to belong to it. Don't forget that Commonwealth is now the official title. In Ireland hatred of the British Empire is a sacred hatred. But it is quite consistent with our willingness to give the Commonwealth a trial.

J.D. Are you sure it's the official title?

G.B.S. It's in the treaty, my boy.

J.D. What treaty?

G.B.S. In Ireland there is only one treaty. The treaty that established the Irish Free State.

J.D. Oh, quite so. I forgot.

G.B.S. Ah, yes, we are forgotten now. John, would you believe it? I can remember the time when the British Parliament for forty years talked of nothing but Ireland. And after all we had to fight it out like savages. In those days I was an interesting man solely because I was an Irishman. Now that Ireland is free and forgotten, nobody knows nor cares whether I am an Irishman or a Hottentot. We gained our freedom and lost our splendid publicity. But you must mention in your film that the last act of the old oppressed Ireland, the Ireland that all the world talked about, was to give the infamous old British Empire a new name and a new birth.

J.D. Why don't you go back to Ireland and live there?

G.B.S. Man alive, they think nothing of me in Ireland: the people are forbidden to read my books there. Besides, like yourself, I belong to the highly select community that is above nationality: the realm of art and letters.

J.D. Well, talking of that, what about "Candida"? Let me show you something. Have you ever seen this?

G.B.S. What is it?

J.D. A program of the very first performance of the play. It was in South Shields in 1895. My father played the poet in it.

G.B.S. Bless me, so he did. But I wasn't there. I don't know where South Shields is.

J.D. Neither do I. But look. Here's the evidence! [*Shot. Close up of program, &c.*].

J.D. That was more than forty years ago. And it's filling a London theatre today. You were half a century ahead of your time.

G.B.S. Not a bit of it. The theatre was fifty years behind the time. You and Barry Jackson waked it up in the provinces. Ibsen waked it up in London. It is fairly up to date now. To get thoroughly behind the times now you have to go into the House of Commons.

J.D. You old anarchist! You would abolish the House of Commons if you could.

G.B.S. On the contrary, I would establish ten Houses

of Commons and keep them all busy. Why don't you read my books? I read your confounded poems.

J.D. I do, occasionally. I suppose your plays have helped as much as anything to give women their place in public life. Do you think they've stood up to it?

G.B.S. If you mean in a hostile sense, yes. They use their votes to keep women out of Parliament. Do you remember the 1918 election, when the women voted for the first time and carried everything before them? Result: One woman in Parliament: Lady Astor. One woman up against 614 men! Think of it! And she got in only because no mortal power could keep her out of anywhere she wanted to go.

A New Ending for Clemence Dane's *Cousin Muriel*

[Written on 27 March 1940 for Edith Evans after reading Desmond MacCarthy's review of Clemence Dane's play *Cousin Muriel* in the *New Statesman* on 23 March. "Here," Shaw told Miss Evans, "is how *I* should end it happily."]

[*Desmond MacCarthy had written:*
The first thing to say is that Miss Clemence Dane's play *Cousin Muriel* is excellent entertainment. Few will have difficulty in forgetting themselves in the Globe Theatre while watching her characters living before their eyes; while the youthful charm of Miss Peggy Ashcroft as "Dinah" is sure of enchanting them. I would like to go again just for the sake of the lift her performance gives to the spirits. It tempts one to a digression.

Acting implies complete awareness of the means you are using to make a particular impression on others. Yet no actor or actress is perfect in a part until this self-consciousness has been transcended. It must be recoverable—since adjustments may have to be made—but something approximating to an impersonal attitude towards your own personality is necessary. Now, in playing parts in which success depends on conveying a charming impression of youthful candour and spontaneity, it is vitally important to transcend self-consciousness, while in such parts it is peculiarly difficult to do so. The actor or actress cannot help knowing that in behaving in a particular way, he or she is delighting the audience; though in the eyes of a sensitive spectator the real charm of such a part vanishes the moment any self-awareness creeps into the acting. It requires either a personal humility, rare in the histrionic temperament, or a most impersonal interest in the art of acting to forget yourself entirely in a charming part—perhaps it needs both. When we talk of an actor or actress becoming spoilt, we are nearly always thinking of the change in their acting due to their appropriating sympathy or admiration as tributes to their own personalities. At first this change may even improve their performance by increasing self-confidence, but soon or late it stultifies. They end by selecting parts (and interpreting them too) accordingly as those parts offer opportunities for recreating this flattering relation with the audience. Or if they do not do this on their own initiative, managers tempt them to do so. Miss Peggy Ashcroft plays this part with such delightful and unselfconscious naturalness that one trembles at the idea of that gift being exploited. If I had not seen her in *The White Guard* (a more complex part) I might have thought young love was her speciality.

But that is not all there is to this play—far from it. There is "Cousin Muriel" herself, an unusual character study, complex as a living person, and interpreted with a fine sense of all its implications by Miss Edith Evans—indeed, so much so that I gather from the close of the play having been altered that many people were as bewildered by Miss Edith Evans, in the sense of not knowing how much to like Muriel or detest her, condemn her or forgive her, as they would have been had they had to deal with a real Mrs Meilhac herself. In this part that is, undoubtedly, a tribute to the art of the actress, but is it equally complimentary to that of the dramatist? Is it enough (it is certainly a great deal) to create a natural character in whom callousness or sympathy, treachery and affection, sense and childish irresponsibility are convincingly mingled? Or have we a right to make the further demand that the novelist or dramatist should also devise circumstances which will so expose that character that we shall be in no doubt how far she will go in villainy, if pushed? Of course, such a verdict must not be *thrust* upon us, but ought we not to be in possession of the data necessary to judgment? It is a point on which I think no ruling is possible; but in drama it is certainly *safer* to leave the audience knowing the worst or the best of the main character in a play. As it was we left the theatre (on the first night) in a state of mind, not unlike the disgusted bewilderment, that prompted Sir Hubert Sylvester (eminent Harley Street physician) to leave the room without a word in the middle of "Cousin Muriel's"—what shall we call them?—mocking admissions. That is a most remarkable speech and delivered with the subtlest sense of character and situation.

The situation (the plot hitherto) is this: "Cousin Muriel" has been running the widowed Sir Hubert's house for some years—and extremely well as a paid housekeeper. She has been much more than that to him, and there is no doubt that she has put a devotion into her service which was prompted by love (at first) on her side, and recognised most gratefully and trustfully by him. In fact, she has made him a success and you can see that she is the sort of woman who might well give a man confidence in his career—give him that feeling of success which leads to it. Mr Alec Guinness as Richard Meilhac puts a subtle fineness and convincing strength into one of those inarticulate parts which so often bore us. (He *looked* so happy, for instance, when his mother asked him what attracted him in Dinah and he tried vainly to express it.)

Why should Sir Hubert oppose the marriage so violently? He tells Richard that he dreads his heredity: the late Mr Meilhac was a reckless speculator who put his head in a gas-oven. Then, he adds that he cannot forgive him for having come down again and again on his mother for large sums of money which he (Sir Hubert) had of course furnished. Richard denies he ever asked his mother for money; Sir Hubert is not convinced. But it is the truth. Sir Hubert discovers that not only had "Cousin Muriel" made these requests in Richard's name, but also that she had been in the habit of adding "ty" to cheques made out for nine and six pounds. The dramatic scene of her "confession" or "defence" begins by his silently handing her one such cheque, while she is playing the piano. She remarks quietly "So you have found it out," and begins her ingenious confused explanation. Presently, she discovers that she has been talking some minutes to an empty room. That is an extremely telling moment, and I think my colleague Mr Agate was right in saying that it was upon her calm surprise or resigned indifference that the curtain ought to have fallen. In the first version this moment was succeeded by her arrest on a charge of shoplifting. That was a blunder and it has now been altered: Sir Hubert returns and pays her off with wages and £50. She will find no doubt another crow to pluck. Well, I should have preferred the silent curtain. The great merit of this play is that for the greater part of the time, suspense is centred on the young lovers. Will they marry? But that comparatively commonplace though when well presented always real interest, is skilfully used to present something more intriguing—Cousin Muriel's character.

Reprinted by permission of the New Statesman.]

He calls her unscrupulous.

SHE. Well, remember, John, there must always be some unscrupulous person in a household or how could it get on? It is very nice to have high principles; but high principled people have such a lot of scruples that they mustnt do anything. Running a house means doing something all the time. If you had to run this house you would jolly soon have to get rid of your scruples.

HE. Muriel: have you no moral sense? Do you not realize that altering a cheque is a very serious crime? That people are in prison for doing it?

SHE. John: let us understand oneanother. I hope you are not accusing me of dishonesty.

HE. No. At least—

SHE. Well, at least?

HE. You ask me for a cheque for nine pounds; and you alter it to ninety.

SHE. Never. Be just, John. You are so careful—so scrupulous, as you put it, that nine pounds would make you anxious and worried. I always ask you for six.

HE. And you changed it to sixty!

SHE. Of course I did. You could hardly have supposed that I could keep things going here on an occasional six pounds. But perhaps you did: men are like that: if they are asked for ten shillings for the house they think it too much. Sometimes it was hard enough to do with sixty; for I have to dress extravagantly to keep up your position: I have to pay thirty pounds for a dress when a thirty shilling reach-me-down would be good enough for me if I had only myself to think of.

HE. Well, you could have asked me for the thirty pounds.

SHE. Yes: I should like to have seen your face if I had. Why should I worry you, poor dear? It made you perfectly happy to get off so cheaply. So I made you happy with the six pound cheques and comfortable with the sixty. Was that dishonest?

HE. Of course, if you look at it in that way—

SHE. Well, do you want to look at it in any other way? You dont suggest, I presume, that I stole your money!

HE. No; but—

SHE. But but but but but! Do put your budget of scruples in your pocket; and listen to this nice old tune that I am going to play you.

She turns to the piano and plays Home, Sweet Home. He puts his fingers in his ears and steals out of the room. She plays on, humming the tune, and finally singing with great expression and emphasis.

There's no - o - o - o place like Home

She turns to him, expecting applause. He is not there.

SHE [*outraged*] Well!!!

He comes back, rather awkwardly.

HE. I er—er—er—

SHE. Well? You what?

HE. I—er. I apologize.

SHE. Of course, dear, I knew you would. [*She kisses him in a friendly hug*] I forgive you.

CURTAIN

Sequence for
A Pageant of Plays and Players

[A dialogue between Shaw and the English theatre manager Charles Cochran, written for St John Ervine's B.B.C. Jubilee Theatre Programme, recorded at Ayot St Lawrence on 5 November 1947 and broadcast on 7 November. Reproduced here from the revised typescript in the British Museum: Add. Mss. 50705, ff. 122–125.]

COCHRAN. Does the theatre ever change?
ANNOUNCER. Ever change! Surely—
SHAW. Silence. Do not interrupt Cochran with your revolutions in the theatre. You know nothing about it; art is not subject to revolutions. Come on, Cochran. Enlighten this youngster. You loved the theatre above all things. You even loved actors. You have thrown away handfuls of money bringing famous foreign actors here just that London might see them. You began as an actor. You could have succeeded as an actor. Why did you leave the stage?
COCHRAN. I did not leave the stage. The stage left me. I was pushed off it.
ANNOUNCER. I did not know that you had ever acted.
SHAW. No: you are too young. Tell him how you were pushed off, Cochran. We must educate him.
COCHRAN. My dear Shaw, nobody knows better than you that the theatre is never at a loss for players. Players are a race apart: they are incapable of business. They read nothing but their parts, their cues, and fairytales. Money slips through their fingers like water. I thought I was on the highroad to fame as an

actor when I got my first engagement with a famous actor-manager in New York. When he sent for me before the end of the week my heart sank. I expected nothing but the sack. But no. He invited me to sit down and gave me a cigar. Then he asked me was it true that I had worked in an office and could write business letters and add up figures and keep a bank account. I was fool enough to say yes. He then asked me whether I thought I should ever be a great actor like himself. I thought I could; but I had to say that I dared not aim so high. He then said he had a first-rate part to offer me, at a salary beyond my dreams. It was the part of his secretary and acting manager: the only sort of theatre manager who never acts. That was how I was pushed off the stage into the boss's office. That was how a beginner of no account blossomed into a famous showman. All the managers who were not born in the business wanted to act but were pushed into management as I was. Barry Jackson, Nugent Monk, Annie Horniman and Lilian Baylis of the Old Vic, who wanted to be an opera singer.

SHAW. You have left out the greatest of them all.

COCHRAN. Who was that?

SHAW. Shakespear.

COCHRAN. Shakespear?

SHAW. Yes, Shakespear. When he ran away to London he tried to get employment in the theatre because he wanted to act. But he had had a spot of business training with his father in Stratford. The theatre was not short of actors; but it was in desperate need of someone who could organize the business of looking after the horses of the rich playgoers in the boxes. There is no serious evidence that Shakespear ever held the horses. Anybody can hold a horse. Any actor can shout "My kingdom for a horse!" But only five percent of the human race can manage a department. That was how William got his foot into the theatre. They found out also that he could write blank verse like Marlowe's. So he dropped the horses and became a script writer. He remained a script writer to the end of his life; for he never invented a plot: he only touched up old plots. He could take a play about a village idiot supposed to be funny, and a ghost crying Revenge, Revenge, like an oysterwife, and make Hamlet out of it. But he had to leave the acting to Burbage.

ANNOUNCER. This is all very interesting, Mr Shaw; but let us get back to the revolution in the theatre made by yourself.

COCHRAN. Nonsense! You are mad about revolutions. Mr Shaw made no revolution. He went straight back to Shakespear and to the great acting of the palmy days, from Burbage and Betterton to Barry Sullivan.

ANNOUNCER. Mr Shaw go back! Mr Shaw old-fashioned! It is you who are mad.

SHAW. Think, man, think. I tell you the theatre has its changing fashions; but its art never changes. It is just what it was when the first strolling story teller told tales and recited verses at fairs and on the race courses, and took his hat round for pennies. I have seen this done on a Sunday morning in Ceylon. My stage technique and Molière's is that of the first circus clown jesting with the first ring master a thousand years ago. It will be the same for the next thousand years.

ANNOUNCER. But surely you made a great change.

SHAW. I did, by going back to Shakespear, to Aristophanes. When I began, the London stage was crowded with French dramatizations of police and divorce cases spoilt by the translators in deference to

British prudery. No character in them had any religion, any politics, any profession, any relation to life but the charm of the young players and the bugaboo of the middle aged heavy villains. Speeches of more than twenty words were considered impossible and too long: I knocked all that into a cocked hat by giving my characters religions, politics, professions and human nature. In my first play I made the heroine commit a violent assault: a thing thought unwomanly on the stage. But it was only a mild return to Euripides, whose heroine murdered her mother with an axe. So much for your revolutions!

ANNOUNCER. I can only quote Shakespear and say that you do me wrong, insupportable wrong.

SHAW. I have upset you. I am sorry. I am too old: I oughtnt to be here. Come, Cochran. Goodbye, everybody.

COCHRAN. Goodbye.

VOICES. Goodbye, goodbye, goodbye.

Exeunt Shaw and Cochran

Why She Would Not

A LITTLE COMEDY

[Composition begun 17 July 1950; completed 23 July 1950. St John Ervine and others have claimed that the work was intended to be in six scenes and was uncompleted at the time of Shaw's fatal accident in September 1950. The original shorthand manuscript, however, bears a note by Shaw at the foot of the final leaf: "End of Scene 5 and of the Play" (Humanities Research Center, University of Texas at Austin). Published in *London Magazine* and in *Theatre Arts*, New York, August 1956. First collected in Bernard Shaw, *Ten Short Plays*, New York, 1960.]

First presented by the Shaw Society of America at the Grolier Club, New York, on 21 January 1957.

Serafina White *Melodi Lowell*
The Man (A Robber)
Henry Bossborn
Reginald White
Jasper White
Montgomery Smith
} Men's roles shared by *Hal Hamilton*, *William Loew*, and *Robert Kimberly*
A Nurse-Housekeeper
ALSO two clerks and three or four members of the Board of White Sons & Bros. Ltd.

SCENE 1: *A Path through a Wood. A fine Summer Afternoon*
SCENE 2: *At the Gates of a Pretentious Country House, "Four Towers"*
SCENE 3: *The Boardroom of White Sons and Bros. Ltd.*

SCENE 4: *The Drawingroom of "Four Towers." Two Years Later*
SCENE 5: *The Lounge of an Ultra Modern Country House,* 1950

SCENE I

A path through a wood. A fine summer afternoon. A lady, goodlooking, well dressed, and not over thirty, is being conducted along the path by a burly and rather dangerous looking man, middle aged, ugly, dressed in a braided coat and mutton pie cap which give him the air of being a hotel porter or commissionaire of some sort.

THE LADY [*stopping*] Where are we now? I should hardly call this a short cut.

THE MAN [*truculently*] I'm damned if I know. Two miles from anywhere.

THE LADY. But you must know. You are a forest guide.

THE MAN. Guide my foot! I'm no bloody guide. How much money have you got on you?

THE LADY. Why?

THE MAN. Because I mean to have it off you, see? Hand over.

THE LADY. Do you mean to rob me? You said you were a guide; and we agreed for seven-and-sixpence. I meant to give you ten shillings if you were civil; but now I will give you your seven-and-sixpence and not a penny more. If you dare try to rob me I'll call the police.

THE MAN. Call away. There isnt a copper within five miles. Are them pearls round your neck real? Whether or no I mean to have them. You have three pounds in notes in your handbag: I saw them when you paid the taxi. Are you going to hand over quietly or shall I have to take them? It'll hurt a bit.

A YOUNG MALE VOICE [*very affable*] Is there anything amiss? Can I help?

The Man and the Lady start violently, not having noticed the newcomer until he arrives between them. He is a likeable looking juvenile in a workman's cap, but otherwise might by his clothes be an artisan off duty or a gentleman. His accent is that of a wellbred man.

THE MAN [*ferociously*] Who the hell are you?

THE NEWCOMER. Nobody but a tramp looking for a job.

THE MAN. Well, dont you come interfering with me. Get out of here, double quick.

THE NEWCOMER [*sunnily*] I'm in no hurry. The lady might like me to stay. If she wants a witness I'm on the job.

THE LADY. Oh yes: please stay. This man is trying to rob me.

THE NEWCOMER. Oh dear! That wont do, you know, matey. Thou shalt not steal.

THE MAN [*with exaggerated fierceness*] Who are you calling matey? Listen here. Are you going to get out or have I to sling you out?

THE NEWCOMER [*gaily*] You can try. I'm game for a scrap. Fists, catch as catch can, up and down wrestling, or all three together? Be quick. The mounted police patrol will pass at six. Take off your coat; and come on.

THE MAN [*he is an abject coward*] Easy, governor, easy. I dont want no fighting. All I asked of the lady was my money for guiding her.

THE NEWCOMER [*to the Lady*] Give it to him and get rid of him.

THE LADY. I never refused to give it to him. Here it is. [*She gives the Man five shillings*].

THE MAN [*humbly*] Thank you, lady. [*He hurries away, almost running*].

THE LADY. How brave of you to offer to fight that big man!

THE NEWCOMER. Bluff, dear lady, pure bluff. A bully is not always a coward; but a big coward is almost always a bully. I took his measure; that is all. Where do you want to go to?

THE LADY. To Timbertown. I live there. I am Miss White of Four Towers: a very famous old house. I can reward you handsomely for rescuing me when I get home.

THE NEWCOMER. I know the way. A mile and a half. Can you walk it?

THE LADY. Yes of course. I can walk ten miles.

THE NEWCOMER. Right O! Follow me.

They go off together.

SCENE II

At the gates of a pretentious country house surrounded by a high stone wall and overshadowed by heavy elm trees. The wall is broken by four sham towers with battlemented tops.

The Newcomer and the Lady arrive. She opens her bag and takes out a key to unlock the wicket.

THE LADY. Here we are. This is my house.

THE NEWCOMER [*looking at it*] Oh. Is it?

He is not as much impressed as she expected. She fingers the cash pocket in her bag, and is obviously embarrassed.

THE NEWCOMER. You are safe at home now. I must hurry into the town to get a night's lodging. Goodnight, lady. [*He turns to go*].

THE LADY. O please wait a moment. I hardly know—

THE NEWCOMER. How much to tip me, eh?

THE LADY. Well, I must reward you. You have done me a great service. I promised—

THE NEWCOMER. You did. But rescuing ladies from robbers is not my profession: it is only my amusement as an amateur. But you can do something for me. You said your name was White. Your people are the greatest timber merchants and woodmen in the county. Well, I'm a carpenter of sorts. Could you get me a job in the timber yard at three pound ten a week? I cant live on less.

THE LADY. Oh, I'm sure I can. My grandfather is chairman of the Board. My brother is manager. What is your name? Where do you live?

THE NEWCOMER. My name is Henry Bossborn. I live nowhere, or where I can: I have no address. I'll call on Thursday at your kitchen door: you can leave word with your maid if there is any news for me. Good night.

THE LADY [*very graciously*] Au revoir.

BOSSBORN. Not necessarily. Adieu: remember me.

He goes decisively. She unlocks the wicket and goes home.

SCENE III

The boardroom of White Sons and Bros. Ltd. In the chair old Reginald White, still keen and attentive, but mostly silent. Jasper White, domineering but not quite up to his father's mark. Montgomery Smith, counting-house chief, and two clerks who make notes but say nothing, and three or four members of the Board, silent lookers-on. Bossborn, looking quite smart in a clean white collar and well brushed suit, is before them, bareheaded.

OLD REGINALD. Well, Bossborn, you have done a plucky service to my granddaughter, Miss Serafina White, who holds many shares in this concern.

BOSSBORN. Oh, nothing, sir. I could have killed the fellow.

OLD REGINALD. The lady says he was twice your size and weight. We must find you a job. You want one, dont you?

BOSSBORN. I want three pound ten a week, sir. I must live.

OLD REGINALD. You are a white collar case, I suppose. We shall have to make room for you in the counting house.

BOSSBORN. No, sir, manual worker, carpenter on the wages list. Three pound ten and the usual bonus, same as the rest in the carpenters' shop.

OLD REGINALD. Oh well, if you prefer it: that will be easy. [*To Jasper*] Tell him his duties.

JASPER [*much more distant and peremptory*] Youll be here at six on Monday morning, and clock in sharp to the minute. We dont allow unpunctuality here. The foreman will direct you to a place on the bench, where you will be expected to work—to work, mind you, not to dawdle—until eleven, when you can knock off for five minutes for a cup of tea. Half an hour off for a meal at one. Work again at the bench until four. Overtime wages one and a half. Five day week: nothing on Saturdays. A week's notice if you are a slacker. Thats all. You can go.

BOSSBORN. I'm very grateful to you gentlemen for offering me this job. But I'm afraid it will not suit me. I must take to the road again.

JASPER. Why? It is what you ask for.

BOSSBORN. I'm not that sort of man. I cant clock in, and work at regular hours at the bench. I cant do what you call work at all. It is not in my nature. I must come when I like and go when I like and stay away when I like. I get up at eight, breakfast at nine, and read the papers until ten. I've never in my life got up at five in the morning.

JASPER. In short, you are an unemployable walking gentleman. You expect to be paid three pound ten a week for doing nothing.

BOSSBORN. Three pound ten and the bonus. Not exactly for doing nothing. I ask to have the run of the works and just loaf round to see if there is anything I can do.

SMITH. Well, of all the—! Just to snoop round and find out all our trade secrets and sell them to the next timber yard.

OLD REGINALD. We have no secrets here. All the world is welcome to learn the ways of White Ltd. Straightforward work and first quality. Let those who can copy us and welcome.

SMITH. Yes, sir, we know that. But this young fellow can make a living by going from one firm to another, taking a job and being sacked as a slacker at a fortnight's notice; then going on to the next shop and doing it again.

BOSSBORN. I can meet you on that. Take me on for a fortnight on my own terms. If at the end of the fortnight you find me worth keeping for another week you pay me for the whole three weeks; but if you find me no use I get no wages at all, nothing but the sack.

OLD REGINALD. How is that, Mr Smith?

SMITH. Well, sir, if you want a sleeping partner, this is the man for you. That is all I can say.

OLD REGINALD [*rising*] We'll try him. Come with me, Bossborn: my granddaughter is waiting in my private room to hear how you have got on.

BOSSBORN. Good morning, gentlemen. [*He follows old Reginald out*].

SMITH. The old man is going dotty. You really ought to take over, Mr Jasper.

JASPER. Let him have his way. We shall soon be rid of this rotter.

SCENE IV

The drawingroom of Four Towers, overcrowded with massive early Victorian furniture, thick curtains, small but heavy tables crowded with nicnacs, sea shells, stuffed birds in glass cases, carpets and wall paper with huge flower designs, movement obstructed and light excluded in every possible way.

Two years have elapsed since the incident in the wood.

Bossborn, now a very smart city man, matured and important looking, is being entertained by Serafina.

BOSSBORN. Twice round the world!

SERAFINA. Yes, twice. And a winter in Durban.

BOSSBORN. Why twice?

SERAFINA. Once for sightseeing. But life in a pleasure ship is so easy and comfortable and careless and social that at the end of the trip you just stick to the ship and start again for another round-the-world cruise, mostly with the same people. Quite a lot of them spend their lives going round and round. It costs only about a thousand a year; and everything is done for you.

BOSSBORN. Then why did you come back here?

SERAFINA. Homesick. For me there is no place like Four Towers. Besides, I had to come back after father's death to settle about his will and all that. I shall never leave dear Four Towers again. I was born here; and I shall die here.

BOSSBORN. Hmmm! There are better places.

SERAFINA. Not for me. Nowhere on earth. But never mind that now. What about yourself? I hear you have made terrible changes in the company, and that you and Jasper are on very bad terms. You have pensioned off poor old Smith and dismissed four clerks who had been with us for sixteen years and never had a word against them.

BOSSBORN. Their work is done by a girl with a calculating and invoicing typewriter as big as herself. Smith was twenty-five years out of date. The waste of labor all over the place was frightful.

SERAFINA. Before I went away Jasper said that either you or he would have to go when father retired. We Whites like to be masters in our own house. I like to be mistress in mine.

BOSSBORN. Oh, that is all over. Ive trained Jasper in my methods, and am now in business on my own.

SERAFINA. Have you set up in opposition to us?

BOSSBORN. Not at all. I'm still a director and shareholder. My own business is land agency, dealer in real estate, private banking, building, and so on. Anything there is money in and that I understand.

SERAFINA. How wonderful! And only two years ago you were a tramp looking for a job.

BOSSBORN. And you got one for me. What can I do for you in return?

SERAFINA. Well, there is something you could perhaps advise me on. My old nurse and housekeeper thinks there is something wrong with the drainage here; and the gardener thinks that two of the four towers are not quite safe. Would you greatly mind if I asked you to have a look round and tell me if there is really anything wrong, and if so what I ought to do about it?

BOSSBORN. I need not look round. I have had my eye on Four Towers for some time; and I know it inside and out. There is no drainage.

SERAFINA. No drainage! But there must be.

BOSSBORN. Absolutely none. The sewage has been simply soaking into the soil for heaven knows how many years. None of the towers are worth repairing. The one thing to be done is to blow them up, get rid of that prison wall, cut down those trees that shut out the sunlight, and knock down this ugly, unhealthy, troublesome, costly house. It is not fit to live in. I'll build you a modern house with a beautiful view in a better situation. This neighborhood was fashionable fifty years ago: it is now east end. I'll build six prefabricated villas lettable at moderate rents to replace your four rotten old towers and bring you in a tidy addition to your income.

SERAFINA [*rising in boiling wrath*] Mr Bossborn: leave my house.

BOSSBORN. Oh! [*rising*] Why?

SERAFINA. I can hardly speak. My house! My house, the great house of Timbertown. My beautiful house, built by my people and never lived in by anyone else. I was born here. And you dare—!! Go; or I will call my servants to shew you out. And never approach my door again: it will be shut in your face.

BOSSBORN [*quite unmoved*] Think it over! I'll call again in a month. [*He goes promptly*].

Serafina rings the bell and strides about the room, raging, then rings again violently three times. Her old nurse-housekeeper rushes in, alarmed.

NURSE. Whats the matter, dearie?

SERAFINA. If that man calls here again, shut the door

in his face. Slam it. Set the dog on him if he wont go. Tell the maids.

NURSE. Oh, we couldnt do that. Hes such a gentleman. We'll say you are not at home.

SERAFINA. Youll obey my orders. Gentleman! Do you know what he has done?

NURSE. No, dearie. It must be something dreadful to put you into a state like this. What was it?

SERAFINA. He said that my house—Four Towers!—is ugly, unhealthy, troublesome, not fit to live in. My house! The house I was born in.

NURSE [*unimpressed*] Well, you know, dearie, it is troublesome. We cant do without seven housemaids, and they are always complaining and wont stay long. There are always one or two of them sick. Theres no lift in the house with all those stairs to drag scuttles of coal up and down because there is no proper heating, only the old open grates. And the place is so dark with all those trees, and nothing to look at but a stone wall. In the kitchen they are always wondering why you live here instead of moving into a nice new house with every convenience.

SERAFINA [*astounded*] So you—you!—agree with him!

NURSE. Oh no, dearie, I could never agree with anyone against you. I know you think the world of the old house. But you can hardly blame the gentleman for saying what everybody says. He is such a nice gentleman. Think it over, dearie.

SCENE V

The lounge in an ultra modern country house dated 1950, contrasting strongly with Four Towers. As before, Serafina hostess and Bossborn visitor.

BOSSBORN. Well, what is the matter today? Why have you sent for me?

SERAFINA. I want to have it out with you about my Thursday at-homes. You have stopped coming to them. Why?

BOSSBORN. Have I? Well, you see, I am full up of business all day. I have my own business to attend to all the forenoon, and in the afternoon there are Board meetings of directors and the County Council, and appointments of all sorts. Much as I like to turn up at your at-homes for the pleasure of seeing you I simply cannot find time for society and small talk. I am, unfortunately, a very busy man.

SERAFINA. How charmingly you pay out that budget of lies! A busy man can always find time to do anything he really wants to do, and excuses for everything he doesnt.

BOSSBORN. That is true. Ive not thought about it. To be quite frank, I dislike the society of ladies and gentlemen. They bore me. I am not at home among them. You know I am only an upstart tramp.

SERAFINA. Very clever. But a much bigger lie. I dont know where you got your courtly manners and the way you speak and carry your London clothes; but I know you are a cut above me socially, and look down on us poor provincials and tradespeople.

BOSSBORN. Well, suppose it is so. Let us assume that I was brought up as a court page, and was so bored by it that I broke loose from it, threw myself on the streets penniless just as Kropotkin when he grew out of being Tsar Alexander's page, chose an infantry regiment in Siberia instead of the Imperial Guards at the top of the tree in Petersburg. Such things happen. You may pretend that it happened to me. But if so does not this prove that I am not a snob?

SERAFINA. At last you may be telling the truth. But if you are not a snob why have you stopped coming to my at-homes? Answer me that.

BOSSBORN. Whats the use of answering if you will not believe a word I say? You seem to know the truth, whatever it may be. It is for you to tell it to me.

SERAFINA. The reason you have stopped coming is that you think I want to marry you.

BOSSBORN. Oh, nonsense!

SERAFINA. It is not nonsense. Do stop lying. It would be a social promotion for me. My old nurse, with her talk about your being a very nice gentleman, selected you for my husband from the time she first saw you. Everybody thinks I ought to get married before I am too old. If you came always to my at-homes they would think you are the man. That is what you are afraid of. You need not be afraid. I have sent for you to tell you that nothing on earth could induce me to marry you. So there. You can come as often as you like. I have no designs on you.

BOSSBORN. But have I offended you in any way? Are my manners inconsiderate?

SERAFINA. No. Your manners are perfect.

BOSSBORN. You just dont like me. Simply natural antipathy, eh?

SERAFINA. Not in the least. I like you and admire you more than any man I have ever known. You are a wonder.

BOSSBORN. Then why?

SERAFINA. I am afraid of you.

BOSSBORN. Afraid of me!!! Impossible. How? Why? Are you serious?

SERAFINA. Yes: afraid of you. Everybody is afraid of you.

BOSSBORN. Is there any use in saying that you have no reason to be afraid of me?

SERAFINA. Yes I have. I like to be mistress in my own house, as I was in Four Towers.

BOSSBORN. But you would be mistress in my house if we married.

SERAFINA. No one will ever be mistress in any house that you are in. Only your slaves and your bedfellow.

BOSSBORN. This bewilders me. Have I ever forced you to do anything you did not want to do?

SERAFINA. No; for I always had to do what you wanted me to do. I was happy at Four Towers: I loved it: I was born there and mistress of it and of myself: it was sacred to me. I turned you out of it for daring to say a word against it. Where is it now? And where am I? Just where you put me: I might as well have been a piece of furniture. Here in this house of your choosing and your building I have heard my four towers being blown up, bang, bang, bang, bang, striking on my heart like an earthquake; and I never lifted my finger to stop you as I could have done if I had been my own mistress. At the works, where my grandfather always had the last word until he died, you came; and with Jasper and Smith and all the rest against you, you turned the whole place inside out: poor old Smith and his clerks had to retire; Jasper had to knuckle under; our splendid old craftsmen had to learn new machines or be sacked and replaced by American mechanics.

BOSSBORN. Yes yes yes; but they consented: they were willing. I doubled, trebled, quadrupled the product and the profit. You could not live in Four Towers now because you are so enormously more comfortable and civilized here. You can all do far more as you like with the leisure my reforms give you than you could before I came. Leisure is the only reality of freedom. I coerce nobody: I only point out the way.

SERAFINA. Yes: your way, not our way.

BOSSBORN. Neither my way nor yours. The way of the world. Some people call it God's way.

SERAFINA. Anyhow I will live my own life, not yours. If I marry, my choice will not be a Bossborn.

BOSSBORN. Is that final?

SERAFINA. Yes. Friendship only.

BOSSBORN. So be it. Good day to you.

He rises and goes out promptly, as before.

[The following sequence, preserved in typescript only, in the Humanities Research Center of the University of Texas at Austin, apparently was deleted from the play before Shaw sent it to the printer in July 1950. This may be the "missing" scene called for by St John Ervine.]

BOSSBORN. And what then becomes of the companionship, the fellowship, of marriage? Marry a nincompoop and he will bore you to death. Marry a born slave, and you will discover that in a slave state it is the slave that rules. Deny your husband any share in the ordering of his home and he will be unhappy and seek consolation in drink or gambling, or seek some free union with another woman. Refuse all offers of marriage because of these dangers and your need for fellowship will drive you to find it in a union with one of your own sex, who will be called your Sunday husband and suspected of being something more. Better become an unenclosed nun, though that will make you the slave of your God; for this, though the deepest of all slaveries, can alone save you from your original sin and wickedness.

SERAFINA. How you talk! I can bear it every second Thursday at my at-homes; but in my house day after day, never.

BOSSBORN. Married people do not talk that way at home. The surest way to stop a man talking is to marry him.

SERAFINA. You are never at a loss for an answer. What are you up to? Are you trying to make me change my mind and marry you?

BOSSBORN. No. The surest way to set a woman talking is to marry her. We should talk one another's heads off. Besides, neither women nor men want to be married. But marriage is the price of other things that they want urgently, so they pay the price; but what they want is love, money, fellowship, security, children and sympathy. The most selfish dullard needs a housekeeper, the least desirable woman a breadwinner: both of them are sex driven. All the ugly frumps and selfish brutes are married. All the old maids and old bachelors are clever and attractive people.

SERAFINA. You have a fairly good opinion of yourself.

BOSSBORN. And of you.

SERAFINA. What is all this leading up to?

BOSSBORN. I dont know. I can tell you how matters stand today, not what will happen tomorrow.

SERAFINA. Hadnt you better marry a nice obedient patient Griselda? I should feel safer.

BOSSBORN. Perhaps I will; for I too should feel safer. Many attractive men marry anybody to get rid of all the hosts of women who are setting their caps at them.

SERAFINA. There we part company. Lots of men come courting me; but I like it.

BOSSBORN. When Diana goes a-hunting the more stags the better fun for her and the worse for the stags.

SERAFINA. Diana? Who was Diana?

BOSSBORN. A Greek goddess who changed a man into a stag and set her dogs on him because he saw her bathing with her clothes off.

SERAFINA. Serve him right. A woman without clothes is only an animal.

BOSSBORN. Is a man anything more?

SERAFINA. To me, yes. I could not marry an animal; but I could marry a man, clothed or unclothed. But if you wont stop talking about sex, I shall go mad. I know no decent language for it.

BOSSBORN. And yet you are supposed to be an educated woman. It is the first thing they should have taught you. However, I agree. The subject is barred for ever between us. But the thing remains. The world must be peopled.

SERAFINA. Let it be peopled. But not by us.

BOSSBORN. Why not? You are not the only woman in the world, nor I the only man. Nature will still torment us with its demand for more children. I may come across a woman with whom I could not live for a single week. You may come across a man with whom the Life Force tells you you should mate, but with whom you could not talk for an hour without being bored beyond endurance. Yet your babies might be prodigies and mine geniuses. Nature does not care a rap for our happiness, only for our progeny. And, sex or no sex, we must leave the world better than we found it or this war-ravaged world will fall to pieces about our ears.

Bernard Shaw is 94 Today

(Extract from a written questionnaire-interview given to G. Prince-White. *Daily Mail*, London, 26 July 1950.)

"... I've written another play. I've labelled it 'a little comedy,' and called it 'The Lady She Would Not.' It is in five scenes. I wrote the whole thing in seven days.... People seem to think that I ought to go on writing big plays like 'Back to Methuselah' and 'The Doctor's Dilemma'—but why should I? I've said all I wanted to say; now I can write little things to amuse myself."

Index

to the entire Edition

Compiled by A. C. Ward

Abbreviations of play titles in Index

A & L Androcles and the Lion
A & M Arms and the Man
AB The Admirable Bashville
ABE Annajanska, the Bolshevik Empress
AC The Apple Cart
ADB Augustus Does His Bit
BB Buoyant Billions
BM Back to Methuselah
C & C Caesar and Cleopatra
Cand Candida
CBC Captain Brassbound's Conversion
CR Cymbeline Refinished
DevD The Devil's Disciple
DJH Don Juan in Hell (*M & S* Act III)
DLS The Dark Lady of the Sonnets
DocD The Doctor's Dilemma
FasF The Fascinating Foundling
FFF Farfetched Fables
FFP Fanny's First Play
GC Great Catherine
GDFB A Glimpse of the Domesticity of Franklyn Barnabas
Gen Geneva
GKC "In Good King Charles's Golden Days"
GM Getting Married
GR The Glimpse of Reality
HH Heartbreak House
HHL How He Lied to Her Husband
IP The Inca of Perusalem
JA Jitta's Atonement
JBOI John Bull's Other Island
M & S Man and Superman
MB Major Barbara
MD The Man of Destiny
Mil The Millionairess
Mis Misalliance
MWP Mrs Warren's Profession
M-C The Music-Cure
O'F O'Flaherty, V.C.
OR On the Rocks
Over Overruled
PPP Passion, Poison, and Petrifaction
PC Press Cuttings
Phil The Philanderer
Pyg Pygmalion
SBP The Shewing-up of Blanco Posnet
SC The Six of Calais
StJ Saint Joan
SUI The Simpleton of the Unexpected Isles
SvS Shakes versus Shav
TTG Too True to be Good
VW Village Wooing
WH Widowers' Houses
YNCT You Never Can Tell

Index

Page numbers in ordinary type relate to the nearest preceding volume number in black capitals

and, delighted with them as a tribute to his wife, he resents the poet's denial and plans a de luxe edition
Apocalypse: **VI** 760, 813, 844
Apollo: **IV** 476; **VI** 758
Apollodorus: in *C&C* (**II** 159, 161–292), dandified Sicilian carpet merchant; conveys Cleopatra to Caesar hidden in a carpet, and shows an escape route to the threatened Romans
Apollyon: (Greek rendering of the Hebrew Abaddon, "the angel of the bottomless pit" in the Book of Revelation; also in *The Pilgrim's Progress* by Bunyan) **VII** 390
Apostles, Acts of the: **IV** 547, 555–7, 790
Apostles' Creed: **II** 823; **IV** 70; **VI** 408; **VII** 422
Apostolic Succession: **VI** 54, 161
Appian of Alexandria: (Roman historian) **II** 306
Applause, Shaw on: **II** 1023–5; **IV** 254–5
APPLE CART, THE: *A Political Extravaganza*
Preface, **VI** 249–79
Act i; Interlude; Act ii, 281–375
Mr Shaw Replies to His Critics, 376
A Walk and a Talk with Mr Shaw, 377–84
Bernard Shaw's Denial, 385–6
Mr Shaw and Democracy, 386–90
The Apple-Cart Again, 390–94
And see separate entries under character names listed on **VI** 247
Aquinas, Thomas: *see* St Thomas
Arabian Nights, The: **II** 24; **IV** 63, 132; **VI** 757
Aramaic dialect: **IV** 478
Archdeacon Daffodil Donkin: in *IP* (**IV** 950, 953–82), father of widowed and bankrupt Ermyntrude Roosenhonkers-Pipstein; declines to support her
Archer, William: **V** 195, 196; **VII** 484; failure of collaboration with Shaw, **I** 17–18, 37–41, 483; booms Ibsen, **I** 130; opinion of *The Philanderer*, 269; of *Mrs Warren's Profession*, 270–71; and "serious" theatres, **II** 495; and *The Doctor's Dilemma*, **III** 437; and Censorship Committee, 675; retirement from *The Nation*, **IV** 444
Archimedes: **V** 29, 331; **VI** 867
Arden family: Shakespear's mother's relatives, **IV** 279, 317
Argyll, 8th Duke of: **III** 53
Arian schisms: **IV** 559
Aristocracy: **II** 512–13; **IV** 157–8, 165, 169
Aristophanes: **I** 20, 241; **II** 662; **III** 17; **V** 57; **VII** 28, 427

declines to preside; scornful of "jobbery and snobbery, incompetence and Red Tape in London" leading to defeat by the American colonists
As a historical figure: (Shaw's Note on, **II** 142–50) 1722–92; his election methods (M.P. 1768), 142–3; London oversight of dispatches responsible for Saratoga defeat, 144–5; his replies to General Gates's Articles of Capitulation, 147–9, 152–3
Burgtheater, Vienna: *Frau Gittas Sühne* at, **V** 724
Burgundy, Duke of: **VI** 65, 89, 93, 146
Burke, Edmund: **II** 513
Burke, John: *Peerage and Baronetage*, **III** 586; **VI** 451
Burne-Jones, Sir Edward: **I** 372; **IV** 720
Burns, John: **VI** 394; *and see* Boanerges
Burns, Robert: **II** 513
Burt, Peggy, actress: in *BB*, **VII** 305
Burton, Henry: (Independent Congregational minister: charged with seditious preaching and heavily sentenced by the Star Chamber; rehabilitated by parliament in 1640) **II** 766
Bushell, Anthony, actor: in *GKC*, **VII** 202
Bussé, Margaret, actress: in *Pyg*, **IV** 655
Butler, Samuel: **II** 531; **III** 38, 39, 197, 471, 524, 525, 700; **IV** 482, 530, 660; **V** 15, 20, 263, 297, 300–301, 304, 323, 326, 701; **VII** 40; influence on Shaw, **III** 32
The Way of All Flesh, **III** 32; **IV** 544
Erewhon, **VI** 59
on Natural Selection, **V** 20, 696
on *The Iliad*, **VI** 41
Butterfield, Walton, actor: in *JA*, **V** 718; in *StJ*, **VI** 11
Button moulder: *see* Ibsen (*Peer Gynt*)
Byford, Roy, actor: in *O'F*, **IV** 984
Byrne, Francis, actor: in *JA*, **V** 718
Byron, Cashel: in *AB* (**II** 432, 439–78), prizefighter; tenant of Lydia Carew, wealthy heiress at Wiltstoken Park, who falls in love with him; he is recognized as the long-lost son of Fitzalgernon de Courcy Cashel Byron, Overlord of Dorset; is proclaimed Deputy Lord Lieutenant of Dorset and marries Lydia by royal command
Byron, George Gordon Noel, 6th Baron: **II** 43, 44, 499, 746, 817, 918; **III** 462; **IV** 132, 254, 353, 354, 572, 898; **V** 42, 263; **VI** 21; **VII** 427
Byron, Henry James: (playwright) *Our Boys*, **IV** 353

mental romanticism displaces him in the affections of Nora Reilly and as potential election candidate for Rosscullen

Drains and drainage: **IV** 158–9

Drake, Sir Francis: **II** 882

Drama, the New: **I** 16–32, 371

Drayton, Michael: **IV** 292, 293

Dream of John Ball, A: *see* Morris, William

Dreyfus, Captain Alfred: (French army officer falsely accused of passing secret defence papers to Germans; a victim of anti-semitism, was exonerated after repeated efforts by eminent compatriots including Zola) **II** 155, 156, 762, 848

Drinkwater, Felix: in *CBC* (**II** 319, 321–417), London slum-bred hooligan type speaking Cockney dialect; described by Captain Brassbound, his employer, as "the greatest liar, thief, drunkard, and rapscallion"; makes hypocritical pretence of conversion by the Scottish missionary Rankin; nicknamed "Brandyfaced Jack"; his pronunciation, 422–5

Drinkwater, John: (poet and playwright) **V** 50, 195

Driscoll, Teresa: in *O'F* (**IV** 984, 988–1014), parlor maid and O'Flaherty's sweetheart, but repudiated by him as a mercenary wench; has slanging match with his mother

Droeshout, Martin: (Flemish engraver working in London in 17th century; his portrait of Shakespear appeared in the First Folio of the plays, 1623) **V** 633

Druids: **II** 241

Drury Lane Theatre, London: **II** 313; **III** 30; **VII** 225

Dryden, John: **I** 371, 474: **II** 30; *Aurengzebe*, **VII** 262–3, 264–6; *The Indian Emperor*, 261, 264–5

Dubedat, Jennifer: in *DocD* (**III** 223, 321–436), idealizing wife of the following; fails to induce Sir Colenso Ridgeon to treat him for tuberculosis; holds a retrospective exhibition of her husband's pictures and astounds Ridgeon (her would-be suitor) by remarrying. Shaw on her illusion, 444–5

Dubedat, Louis: in *DocD* (**III** 223, 321–436), artist of genius but unscrupulous and conscienceless in his dealings with men and women; his deserted "wife", Minnie Tinwell, endeavours to trace him; rejected by Ridgeon, is unsuccessfully treated by Bloomfield Bonington; on his deathbed utters his creed, "I believe in Michael Angelo, Velasquez, and Rembrandt; in the might of design, the mystery of color, the redemption of all things by Beauty everlasting, and the message of Art that has made these hands blessed"

Office; mother of a variety artist engaged to a duke; accepts General Mitchener's proposal of marriage

Farrell, Patsy: in *JBOI* (**II** 806, 893–1022), Irish peasant lad cunningly posing as half-witted

Farren, William, Jnr, actor: in *DocD*, **III** 223; in *GM*, **III** 450

Farringdon Market, London: Gattie's scheme for Central Clearing House in, **VI** 278–9

Farwaters, Sir Charles: in *SUI* (**VI** 743, 765–840), Governor of the Unexpected Isles, a British Crown Colony in the Pacific; conducts a eugenic experiment in group marriage blending flesh and spirit of West and East

Farwaters, Lady: in *SUI* (**VI** 743, 765–840), wife of Sir Charles; mother of Maya and Vashti

FASCINATING FOUNDLING, THE: *A Disgrace to the Author*, **III** 899–914

And see separate entries under character names listed on **III** 898

Fascism; Fascists: **VI** 758, 763, 829, 862, 869; moves for extermination of, **VI** 577

Fascisti, Italian: **VI** 61, 862–6

Fatalism: **IV** 554

Father and Son (Edmund Gosse): **VII** 395

Father (of Junius Smith): *see* Smith, Mr

Faust: **II** 653; **VI** 838

Fawkes, Guy: **II** 762; **VI** 717

Fear: **I** 629–30; **III** 39

Federal Theatre, U.S.A.: **VII** 169

Fellowship Hall, Glasgow: *GR* at, **III** 814

Feminism: **III** 19–20; *and see* Suffragists; Votes for Women; Women's Suffrage Society

Ferris, W., actor: in *CBC*, **II** 319

Ferrovius: in *A&L* (**IV** 453, 585–634), former armorer; unable to subdue his ferocious nature, though a Christian convert, he kills six gladiators in the arena; joins the Pretorian Guard

Ferruccio, Count: in *GR* (**III** 814, 815–35), young 15th cent. Italian aristocrat; throws off his disguise as an old friar when Giulia reveals plot to murder him for money; escapes on promising a wedding gift

Fessler, Ernest: in *JA* (**V** 718, 725–808), young doctor engaged to Edith Haldenstedt

Festubert: (battle at) **V** 34

Feudalism: **IV** 299; **VI** 39, 43, 71, 126, 137–8, 243

£1 as conscience money is refused by Major Barbara; naively believes herself qualified to teach morals and religion
Hilton, William: (two painters of that name: "the Elder" and "the Younger") **V** 333
Hindoos; Hindus: **IV** 577; **VI** 577, 636, 713
Hipney, Mr: in *OR* (**VI** 572, 629–736), silent member of Isle of Dogs unemployment deputation to Prime Minister; stays behind and, as a long-service trade unionist, gives the P.M. a disillusioned, wise, and prophetic discourse on the political and economic outlook
Hiroshima: **VII** 320, 435
His Majesty's Theatre, London: **II** 479–88; **III** 705, 715, 803; *DLS* at, **IV** 267; *Pyg* at, **IV** 655, 806–7, 809–12
His Majesty's Stationery Office: **III** 676
Hitler, Adolf: **V** 694; **VI** 717, 737, 858, 865–9; **VII** 17, 26, 28, 32–6, 173, 176, 317, 403; *Mein Kampf*, **VII** 34, 176
Hittites: **II** 296; **VI** 868
Hoar, J. M.: performer in *The Gadfly*, **VII** 559
Hobbes, Halliwell, actor: in *C&C*, **II** 159, 485
Hobbes, Thomas: *Leviathan*, **VII** 237, 407
Hodges, Horace, actor: in *MD*, **I** 606
Hodson: in *JBOI* (**II** 806, 893–1022), valet to Broadbent; adopts a well-spoken voice as valet, but lapses into his native cockney when off duty
Hogarth, William: **II** 38, 500, 519; **III** 648; **VII** 205, 206
Hogben, Lancelot: **VII** 176
Hohenzollern dynasty: **V** 57; **VI** 866, 867, 877; **VII** 32
Holinshed, Raphael: **II** 311; **IV** 478–9; **VII** 421
Holloway, Baliol, actor: in *A&L*, **IV** 453
Holloway Gaol: **III** 910; **IV** 388–91, 405, 415, 416
Hollywood: **VI** 220, 232–41; **VII** 179
Holmes, Oliver Wendell: **II** 602
Holmes, Sherlock: **V** 705
Holmes-Gore, Dorothy, actress: in *StJ*, **VI** 231; in *AC*, **VI** 247
Holy Ghost: **IV** 67–8, 126, 476, 479, 496, 556–7, 571, 639; **V** 328, 512; **VI** 31, 56, 135, 415; **VII** 151, 209, 353; a scientific fact, **V** 281; reality of, **V** 296
Holy Office: *see* Inquisition
Holy Roman Empire: **VI** 20, 43, 210, 419, 595
"Holy Willies": **III** 761–2; **IV** 556
Home, Dunglas: (spiritualist medium) **IV** 562; **VII** 308

everything he touched should be turned to gold; finding that gold could not be eaten, had the wish revoked) **VI** 967
Middle Ages: **IV** 510; **V** 14, 20, 31, 38, 43, 44, 45, 59, 62, 64, 68, 70, 73, 389
Middle classes: **IV** 165
Midlander, Sir Orpheus: in *Gen* (**VII** 11, 74–165), British Foreign Secretary
Mielziner, Jo, actor: in *StJ*, **VI** 11
Mikado of Japan: (Gilbert and Sullivan's *The Mikado* temporarily banned *c.* 1902 in political deference to) **III** 713, 890
Military service: **II** 846–52
Mill, Rev. Alexander: in *Cand* (**I** 514, 515–94), the Rev. James Mavor Morell's curate, with "Oxford refinement"; a "conceitedly well-intentioned, enthusiastic immature novice"; shows "doglike devotion" to Morell; commonly known as "Lexy"
Mill, James: (Scottish philosopher, economist, historian; father of the following) **V** 327
Mill, John Stuart: (philosopher and political reformer) **II** 47; **III** 38, 39; **IV** 87, 169, 297; **V** 327; **VII** 396, 414; *Essay on Liberty*, **I** 704; *The Subjection of Women*, **I** 704; **VI** 611, 863
Millenial colonies: **II** 25
Miller, Henry, actor: in *ABE*, **V** 230
Millet, Jean François: (French painter noted for his pictures of peasant life in the fields) **IV** 536
MILLIONAIRESS, THE: *A Comedy*
Preface on Bosses, **VI** 849–81
Acts i–iv, 882–969
Alternative ending, 967–9
And see separate entries under character names listed on **VI** 848
Millward, Dawson, actor: in *MB*, **III** 11
Milner, Alfred, 1st Viscount: **I** 872
Milo: (ancient Greek renowned for great physical strength) **II** 741
Milton, John: **II** 27; **III** 711; **IV** 277, 679, 785, 794, 795, 796; **V** 690
Minerva: (Roman goddess equated with the Greek Athene, goddess of wisdom) **VII** 389
Minimum Wage: **III** 26
Minto, Dorothy, actress: in *Phil*, **I** 134; in *MB*, **III** 11; in *FFP*, **IV** 343
Miracles: **V** 346, 694; **VI** 90, 131; **VII** 392–3

Needham, Joseph: (physician, surgeon, anatomist) **V** 269
Negativemongers: **VI** 527
Negress: in *The Thing Happens* (*BM* pt III, **V** 253, 439–90)
Neilson-Terry, Phyllis, actress: in *SC*, **VI** 972
Nelson, Horatio, Viscount: **II** 302, 815–17; **III** 245, 458, 512; **IV** 429; **V** 213, 270; **VI** 36, 880
Neo-Darwinism: **V** 257–61, 267, 268
Neo-Gaelic movement: **II** 808, 842
Nepommuck: in *Pyg* (**IV** 738–43), "a whiskered Pandour from Hungary", polyglot interpreter, ex-pupil of Henry Higgins; known as "Hairy-Faced Dick"
Nero: Roman Emperor, **III** 266, 267, 277, 283–4; **IV** 651, 809; **V** 307; **VI** 262, 852; **VII** 37, 38
Nestor: (wise old statesman in the Iliad, guyed by Shaw in a youthful frolic) **VII** 483
Nestor: oldest juryman, drunk and malignant, in *SBP* (**III** 671, 763–99)
Nestorian schisms: (in the 5th cent. the Christian Church split on the doctrine advanced by Nestorius, a monk from Antioch, that in Christ there were two separate Persons, the Divine and the Human; the orthodox doctrine held that Christ was a single Person, both God and Man) **IV** 559
Neue Rundschau, Berlin: **VI** 11; **VII** 379
Neues Theatre, Berlin: **II** 159
Neuve Chapelle, battle of: **V** 33, 34
Nevinson, Henry Woodd: **VI** 54
New Age: **IV** 1016–19
New Amsterdam Theatre, New York: *C&C* at, **II** 159
New Budget, The: **I** 595–9
Newcastle Daily Journal, **V** 182
Newcastle Program: (Fabian-inspired social reform proposals) **II** 874
Newcastle upon Tyne: **II** 159, 306
Newcastle, William Cavendish, 1st Duke of: **VII** 249
New Century Theatre, London: **II** 15
Newcomer, A: (not otherwise named) in *Gen* (**VII** 11, 44–165), locked out of Parliament, protests to International Court at The Hague
New Deal, The: (President Franklin Roosevelt's measures for dealing with financial crisis in U.S.) **VII** 425
New Man, the: **II** 590, 593, 594
Newman, John Henry, Cardinal: **II** 824

Peter Pan: *see* Barrie

Petkoff, Catherine: in *A&M* (**I** 388, 389–472), wife of Major Paul Petkoff and mother of Raïna; houseproud social snob

Petkoff, Major Paul: in *A&M* (**I** 388, 389–472), husband of the preceding and father of the following; militarily incompetent, is aided by Bluntschli, soon to be his son-in-law

Petkoff, Raïna: in *A&M* (**I** 388, 389–472), daughter of the preceding; she shelters a refugee enemy officer, Bluntschli, "her chocolate cream soldier", who displaces Saranoff in her affections later when he reveals himself as a rich Swiss hotelier and eligible husband

Petrarch, Francesco Petrarca: **II** 592

Petrie, Sir William Matthew Flinders: (archaeologist; author of *Revolutions of Civilisation* and many works on Ancient Egypt) **V** 266, 419

Phagocytes: (blood cells capable of destroying harmful bacteria) **III** 313, 331, 332, 346–9, 351, 365, 398

Pharisees: **III** 36; **IV** 481, 496, 520, 551, 1004: **V** 57

Pharos: (lighthouse at harbour entrance, Alexandria) **II** 223–4, 226

Pharos Club, London; *AB* at, **II** 432

Pharsalia: Caesar routs Pompey at, **II** 164, 223, 312

Phelps, Samuel: actor-manager, **IV** 813

Phidias: (greatest of ancient Greek sculptors) **V** 333, 681

PHILANDERER, THE: *A Topical Comedy of the Early Eighteen-Nineties*

Prefatory Note, **I** 135–6

Play in three (originally four) Acts, 137–227

And see separate entries under character names listed on **I** 134

Philip of Macedon: (king of Macedonia; father of Alexander the Great) **IV** 476

Philip II of Spain: **IV** 321; **VI** 419; **VII** 17

Philippa of Hainault, Queen: in *SC* (**VI** 972, 976–91), pregnant wife of Edward III; deflects her uxorious husband from hanging the six burghers of Calais

Philistines; Philistinism: **II** 510, 517; **III** 439, 664; **IV** 467, 470, 498, 639; **VI** 868; defence of, **IV** 171

Phillips, Kate, actress: **I** 129

Phillips, Minna, actress: in *TTG*, **VI** 397

Philosopher's Stone: (a substance believed by medieval alchemists to be capable, when discovered, of turning base metals into gold; the protracted search, though fruitless for its

Rains, Claude, actor: in *TTG*, **VI** 397
Raleigh, Cecil: (author of several Drury Lane spectacular dramas): gives evidence to Committee on Censorship, **III** 675
Raleigh, Sir Walter: **IV** 48, 280
Ramsden, Roebuck: in *M&S* (**II** 491, 533–733), appointed joint guardian with John Tanner of Ann Whitefield; considers himself an advanced thinker and outspoken reformer, yet abhors Tanner's revolutionary principles and declines to act with him; condemns Tanner's *Revolutionist's Handbook* but refuses to read it; in the Act III dream sequence (*Don Juan in Hell*) Ramsden resembles The Statue and is on "the pleasantest terms with Don Juan"; later, he abandons animosity to Tanner
Ramsden, Miss (Susan): in *M&S* (**II** 491, 533–733), Roebuck's "hard-headed old maiden" sister; inflexibly incensed against Violet Robinson on account of her supposed unmarried pregnancy
Ramsgate: German bombardment of, **V** 35
Randell, Frank, actor: in *M-C*, **IV** 877
Rankin, Leslie: in *CBC* (**II** 319, 321–417), Scottish Free Church pastor with the North African Mission
Raphael (Raffaello Sanzio): **II** 42, 43, 44; **V** 268, 275, 333–4; **VII** 41, 272, 443
Rationalism: **IV** 125–6; **V** 286; **VI** 28
Ravaillac, François: (assassin of Henry IV of France) **II** 770; **III** 54, 705; **VII** 268
Reading: amusement or education?, **IV** 169–71
Reason: **II** 653, 792
Rebirth: **IV** 15–17
Recruiting in Ireland: **IV** 985–7, 1015–16
Redbook Magazine (New York): **IV** 267
Redbrook: in *CBC* (**II** 319, 321–417), member of Brassbound's crew; son of a Dean; brought down by drink and gambling
Redeemer, the: **IV** 472–4, 475, 553, 570
Redford, George Alexander: Examiner (Censor) of Plays, **I** 598; **III** 678, 680, 891–5; **IV** 333; bans *SBP*, **III** 804, 811; bans *PC*, 884–95; attempts intimidation, **III** 893
Redistribution: (of income) **IV** 521–8
Redmond, John Edward: Irish leader, **II** 820; **IV** 999
Redpenny: in *DocD* (**III** 223, 321–436), medical student and dogsbody to Sir Colenso Ridgeon; has no known Christian name

Reed, Edward Tennyson: (cartoonist) **III** 885
Rees, Leslie: (journalist) **VI** 229
Reform Bill (1832): **II** 759
Reformation, the: **III** 459–60, 535; **IV** 559; **VI** 67, 210, 389, 420, 753; **VII** 427
Regent, Prince: (later George IV) **VI** 856
Regent's Canal, London: **IV** 282
Regent's Park: **III** 202, 203; **VI** 972
Registrar-General: **III** 267, 668; **VI** 581
Rehan, Ada, actress: **I** 27, 137
Reichstadt, Duke of: (Napoleon II, son of Bonaparte and Maria Louisa) **VI** 873
Reilly, Nora: in *JBOI* (**II** 806, 893–1022), "the heiress of Rosscullen" with a fortune of £40 a year; her long attachment to Larry Doyle is broken by his indifference after being away for eighteen years; overcoming her initial rejection of Broadbent the Englishman's instant wooing, she accepts him
Reinhardt, Max: (Austrian actor, manager, and producer; internationally celebrated for spectacular productions using crowds of performers—e.g. *The Miracle*, London 1911) **IV** 840; **VI** 389
Rejected Statement, The: (printed document submitted by Shaw to Select Committee on Stage Plays (Censorship) 1909 which they refused to consider) **III** 697–737
Religion: **II** 788; **VI** 602–5; *and see* Christianity
Religious art, 20th century: **V** 332–4
Rembrandt (Rembrandt Harmensz van Rijn): **I** 374; **II** 687; **III** 419, 438: **V** 334; **VII** 183, 278
Renaissance, the: **VI** 70
Rennison, Charles: performer in *FFF*, **VII** 379, 380
Repertory Theatre, Birmingham: *IP* at, **IV** 950; *and see* Jackson, Barry; *and* Malvern Festival
Repertory Theatre: (season at Duke of York's Theatre, London, under management of Charles Frohman, 1910) **IV** 254, 256–62; *Misalliance* at, **IV** 254–5, 258, 260, 262; *The Madras House* (Granville Barker) at, **IV** 258, 260, 263; *Justice* (Galsworthy) at, **IV** 263; *Trelawny of the "Wells"* (Pinero) at, **IV** 263
Repertory theatres: **I** 379–80; **II** 427
Reputations: "weeds in the soil of ignorance", **II** 48
Rescue Society: **III** 761

Preface on Days of Judgment, **VI** 745–64
Prologue and Acts i and ii, 765–840
The Simple Truth of the Matter, 841–6
And see separate entries under character names listed on **VI** 743
Sims, Albert, actor: in *GM*, **III** 450
Sin, conviction of: **II** 495
Sinclair, Arthur, actor: in *SBP*, **III** 671; in *O'F*, **IV** 984, 1016–1018
Sinclair, Hugh, actor: in *TTG*, **VI** 397
Sinclair, Upton: *The Jungle*, **III** 38, 52
Sinn Fein: **II** 1026; **VI** 356
Sirdir: (title of former British commander-in-chief of Egyptian army) **II** 155, 889
Sirr, Major Henry Charles: (sometime Dublin Police Chief) **VII** 385
Sirven, Pierre Paul: (18th cent. French Huguenot condemned to death on a false charge) **II** 839
Sisters of Charity: (religious sisterhood devoted to charitable service; founded in 17th cent.) **VI** 424
SIX OF CALAIS, THE: *A Medieval War Story*
Prefatory Note, **VI** 973–5
Play in One Act, 976–91
Author's Note, 992
And see separate entries under character names listed on **VI** 972
Slaves: **VI** 756–7, 758
"Sludge the Medium": (poem by Robert Browning) *see* Home, Dunglas
Slums: **I** 17, 42, 45, 373; **III** 25, 320; and see *WH*
Smith, Adam: *The Wealth of Nations*, **VII** 392, 401, 407, 415
Smith, (Sir) C. Aubrey, actor: in *AB*, **II** 432, 485
Smith, Gypsy: (public name of Rodney Smith, 1868–1947, born of gipsy parents; became a Salvation Army officer, then a travelling evangelist conducting large "revival meetings" at home and abroad) **IV** 792
Smith, Joseph: (Mormon leader) **VI** 853
Smith, Junius ("He"): in *BB* (**VII** 305, 313–75), declares his profession to be "world betterer"; later confesses "the Life Force has got me" and marries Clementina Alexandra Buoyant
Smith, Mr: in *BB* (**VII** 305, 313–75), father of Junius
Smith, Patricia: in *Mil* (**VI** 848, 882–969), Alastair Fitzfassenden's girlfriend; pet-named Polly Seedystockings